Reetika Khera is a professor of economics at the Indian Institute of Technology Delhi and works on social policy. Previously, she has edited two books, *Battle for Employment Guarantee* and *Dissent on Aadhaar* in English; and is the author of *Revdi Ya Haq: Samajik Suraksha Par Ek Nazariya* (2025).

Freebies or Rights

Understanding
SOCIAL POLICY
in India

REETIKA KHERA

SPEAKING
TIGER

SPEAKING TIGER BOOKS
125A, Ground Floor, Shahpur Jat, near Asiad Village,
New Delhi 110049

First published as *Revdi Ya Haq: Samajik Suraksha Par Ek Nazariya*
by Rajkamal Prakashan in 2025
This English translation published by Speaking Tiger Books in 2026

ISBN: 978-93-6336-263-5
eISBN: 978-93-6336-487-5

10 9 8 7 6 5 4 3 2 1

Typeset in Sabon Roman by
SÜRYA, New Delhi

Contents

1

FREEBIES OR RIGHTS?

A Sympathetic View on Social Policies

While pursuing my PhD, in 2002-03 I interviewed 400 families from eight villages in Rajasthan. The PhD was on the role of public relief works and public distribution system in protecting people from hardship during droughts. Relief works provided employment to all those willing to work and the Public Distribution System provided subsidised grain to eligible households. During the survey, in May 2002, I had the opportunity to visit a public relief work site in a village in the deserts of Barmer. At the work site, I saw a vast open, dry, sandy space; in one portion of this open space, some people were breaking earth, filling it in their 'tagari' and heaping it some distance away. I was surprised when I was told that this was a 'pond deepening' work, given that the area looked like an open, undulating ground to me.

It reminded me of disparaging reports in English newspapers on public relief works: 'digging holes and filling them up'. I wondered if they were right after all. Such public relief works are an important support for villagers in times of distress. City-based columnists often criticise such interventions because in their view, public works do not create sustainable assets; they feel that the government is squandering money.

The following year (in 2003) I revisited the eight villages I had surveyed in the previous year. That year I went back to the same village where I had seen the pond deepening work. This time, it was *after* the monsoons. The open ground I had seen the previous year, had transformed into a vast water body. Along one bank, people were filling water; further along, sheep quenched their thirst; elsewhere women were doing their laundry. It was then that I realised that when I had visited in the previous year what I had thought was an open ground, in fact had a gradient such that water from the lands surrounding it drained into this pond. The gradient of the land was not visible to my untrained urban eye. This incident taught me an important lesson about the limitation of the adage 'seeing is believing'. Merely seeing is not enough. Without an adequate contextual understanding, it is not possible to fully appreciate ground realities.

That was the time I began stepping out of my sheltered urban life, into rural areas for such field studies. Social policies were rarely discussed in my social surroundings, and when they were, the discussion was based on information from newspapers (for instance, the notion of public works as 'digging holes and filling them up' came from such sources).

The field surveys threw up a picture that was different from what the newspapers reported, and to some extent, even from what academic papers in economics discussed. Gradually it became clear that the limited focus on these issues missed an important part of the picture: the problems receive disproportionate attention, while the need for such interventions and the meaningful difference even these modest achievements can bring to people's lives is often overlooked.

Social Policy in India

Social policy is a multi-disciplinary approach to thinking about, and understanding, how societies organise themselves to meet human needs for health, education, work, wellbeing, etc. The focus is not merely on the government or society, but also family and other institutions. They are policies that 'directly address the interests, demands and rights of the unprivileged' (Drèze 2016). While it is not easy to delineate the scope of social policy, it would certainly include health, education and programmes of social support for children, women and disadvantaged groups.[1]

The purpose of this book is to introduce readers to social policies in India, hitherto a neglected field of study. For instance, the London School of Economics, a prestigious academic institution, has a dedicated Department of Social Policy with around 50 faculty members. The field of social policy was deeply influenced by the values of the Fabian Society that believes in 'greater equality of power, wealth and society, the value of collective action and public service, an accountable tolerant and active democracy, and in citizenship, liberty and human rights'. As far as I know, none of India's central universities have a social policy department. To the extent they are included in the syllabus, they are covered by demography, development economics, sociology, etc. This institutional vacuum is symbolic of the neglect of social policy in India. In fact, the neglect is so severe that for many the term itself needs explanation.

More specifically, the aim here is to help readers recognise India's existing social policy framework (such as it is) from 'cradle to grave' (see Table 1.1). The book focuses on seven government programmes of social support that constitute India's social policy framework, taking a life-cycle approach.

These seven programmes are maternity benefits, the Integrated Child Development Services (ICDS) Scheme, the Mid-Day Meal (MDM) Scheme, the Public Distribution System (PDS), the National Rural Employment Guarantee Act (NREGA), the National Social Assistance Programme (NSAP) and public canteens. The issues of basic education and public health services are discussed in the context of COVID-19 since the pandemic brought into sharp focus their neglect and the failings of our over-reliance on the private sector for these basic rights. Apart from canteens that are primarily an urban food security intervention, for the rest, the focus is on rural areas. The hope is that with the help of this book, readers will begin to recognise the shape of the welfare state in India.

The book is meant as a primer for concerned citizens, including students, so that they may appreciate the logic for such public action. What are the moral and economic principles underlying such policies, not just in India, but around the world? What is the social and political need of such policies in India? The book focuses on the implementation record of these policies, inter-state variations and lacunae in implementation. It takes a critical look at the implementation challenges, but the critical lens is imbued with a sympathetic tint: Why do such schemes need public support even if they underperform and are unable to achieve their full potential? How can they do better?

The book relies on primary data from field studies conducted since the early 2000s, secondary and administrative data. Each of these have contributed to my understanding of social policy issues in India. My perspective has also been shaped by discussions with different types of people (rural residents, government employees, public representatives, contractors, etc.). This understanding and perspective is largely absent from public discussions on social policy.

An Emerging Welfare Architecture

When the Welfare State was built after the Second World War in European countries, one conception of it was 'from the cradle to the grave'. The idea was that from the time a person is born and until their death, the state bears some responsibility to support and care for them. This understanding provided the broad template for the welfare state in several European countries, each adapting it to their own circumstances and needs (see Esping-Andersen 1992).

Developing countries have tried to build systems of social support according to their capacity. Many will be surprised to know that India too has a welfare regime that is beginning to resemble a 'cradle to the grave' architecture. It started becoming apparent over the last twenty years (Drèze and Khera 2017). Though almost all social policies in question have a much longer history, these schemes did not receive adequate attention until the 2000s, due to lack of revenues and political will. Once the rate of economic growth picked up in the eighties, and fiscal space was seen to be available, the political system had less of an excuse for ignoring social spending.

The three main pillars of the social policy framework are education, health and social security policies. This book focuses on social support in detail, with a short discussion on education and health.

Various government schemes are in place to support individuals from the cradle to the grave (see Table 1.1). In fact, life begins even before birth, in the mother's womb. Pradhan Mantri Matru Vandana Yojana (PMMVY) is meant to support women during their pregnancy and soon after the child is born. The Integrated Child Development Services (ICDS) scheme for children below six years of age, colloquially known as the Anganwadi programme, provides six essential services for young children. School-going age children are supposed to get state-funded elementary education, including Mid-Day Meals (MDM). The Public Distribution System (PDS) is a social safety net for food security to ensure—at least—that no one sleeps hungry. These four schemes—PMMVY, ICDS, MDM and PDS—are part of the National Food Security Act, 2013.

'*Har haath ko kaam do, budhaape mein araam do*' (work for all hands, rest in old age) is a slogan that has emerged from social movements in India. The right to work allows people to earn their own livelihood. In lieu of the right to work, through the Mahatma Gandhi National Rural Employment Guarantee Act (NREGA) 2005, rural adults have the right to wage work in their own village at minimum wages.

The slogan above also asks for a social security pension for the elderly. However, the demand for social security pensions goes beyond the elderly alone. When someone is unable to fend for themselves (e.g., due to age or disability) or for those whose economic circumstances are fragile for social reasons (e.g., as in the case of widowed, single or abandoned women), there should be some state support. The National Social Assistance Programme (NSAP) provides social security pensions to the elderly, single women and persons with disabilities.

The last of our seven focus schemes is primarily (but not only) for food security—public canteens in urban areas where one can get food at heavily subsidised prices, for example, for less than Rs 10 per plate. Unlike other schemes discussed here, public canteens are a state initiative; not all states have them though. It is the only scheme discussed in this book that is operational almost exclusively in urban areas.

Table 1.1 Cradle to grave: India's emerging welfare architecture for the informal sector

Scheme	Pradhan Mantri Matru Vandana Yojana	Integrated Child Development Services	Mid-Day Meal Scheme	Public Distribution System	Elementary school	National Rural Employment Guarantee	National Social Assistance Programme	Health Services
Legislation	National Food Security Act 2013				Right to Education 2009	NREGA 2005[1]	Nothing so far	
Directive Principles	**Article 42**	**Article 39a and Article 47**		**Article 47**	**Article 21A/86th Amendment to the Constitution 2002**	**Article 39 and Article 41**	**Article 41**	**Article 47**

Article 21A: "The State shall provide free and compulsory education to all children of the age of six to fourteen years"
Article 39: "men and women equally, have the right to an adequate means of livelihood"
Article 39a: "children are given opportunities and facilities to develop in a healthy manner.."
Article 41: "make effective provision for securing the right to work, to education and to public assistance in cases of unemployment, old age, sickness and disablement, and in other cases of undeserved want."
Article 42: "provision for maternity relief"
Article 47: "regard the raising of the level of nutrition and the improvement of public health as among its primary Duties"
[1] Replaced with Viksit Bharat – Guarantee Rozgar Aajeevika Mission Gramin Act (VB-GRAMGA) 2025 in December 2025

Following the amendment to Article 21A of the Constitution in 2002, the Right to Education Act 2009 operationalised the fundamental right to eight years of education for all. Despite this, achievements in the field of elementary education fall far short of expectations on several parameters—universal enrolment or literacy have not yet been achieved, mean years of schooling remain low, learning outcomes are sub-par, for children from disadvantaged communities their schooling and learning experience is not necessarily pleasant or productive. Health remains a neglected area of social policy in India. Although there are big announcements from time to time, government spending remains very low and health outcomes are poor in terms of infant mortality rates, life expectancy, etc. Education and health have been discussed in the context of COVID-19 because during the pandemic, the chronic issues in the field of health and education came into sharp focus in such a way that the failings were apparent to all, including the better-off sections of society.[2]

The Freebies Rhetoric

The book is about government interventions for improving people's wellbeing. The period it covers is broadly the past two decades (2004-2024), during which the welfare programmes outlined above gained some coherence through legal and budgetary support. In India there is a tendency of seeing—and of depicting—such policies as a 'burden' on the government. Interestingly, this is not unique to India. It echoes debates elsewhere in the world as well.

Writing about it in the context of the United Kingdom, Titmuss believed that government intervention in the area of welfare or social security plays a constructive role, and it would be wrong to view it as a burden (Titmuss 1968).

He enumerated several reasons for it: First, it should, in his view, be seen as a partial compensation to redress the direct (e.g., accidents and injuries) and indirect losses (e.g., pollution or slum rehabilitation) from a capitalist system. Further, such interventions can compensate for the disadvantage for which the individual themselves are not responsible (e.g., a child born in a deprived family), who should get a fair chance in life. Second, social security can play a protective role, sheltering people from infectious disease or mental illness. Third, we must view such government interventions (especially in the areas of education and health) as a personal and social investment. Fourth, they can be considered as contributing directly to personal wellbeing. Fifth, it can also be seen as a defense against a backlash emerging from the ills of a capitalist system (e.g. inequality). In a nutshell, such policies are best seen as human rights and as remedying existing inequalities.

Contrary to this view, in a political speech in 2024, the Indian Prime Minister Narendra Modi labelled some electoral promises and state programmes as 'revdi', a loose translation of 'freebies'. This statement fuelled the already widely held view that programmes of redistribution (broadly defined) are wasteful. Of course, the freebies rhetoric predates Modi and the current NDA government. It is so loud in India that at several points of time, individuals have approached courts to intervene in the matter. In fact, however, delineating the scope of legitimate government intervention is ultimately a political debate. Equally importantly, there are sound economic principles that can help us determine where and how much government intervention is desirable for efficiency and equity.

Rights-Based Development: The UPA Decade (2004-2014)

In the decade of the United Progressive Alliance (UPA) governments (2004-2014) and preceding it, there was robust economic growth. In the 2004 General Election, many believed that people voted against the 'India Shining' propaganda of the National Democratic Alliance (NDA). The decade was marked by small but concrete steps towards building a rights-based welfare system in India. Many laws related to basic rights of the people were enacted: the National Rural Employment Guarantee Act 2005, Recognition of Forest Rights Act in 2006, the Right of Children to Free and Compulsory Education Act in 2009, a National Food Security Act (NFSA) in 2013, etc.

The Right to Information (RTI) Act passed in 2005 has contributed to gradually creating a culture of transparency and accountability in government. The hope was that the RTI would alter the balance of power between people on the one hand, and authorities and people's representatives on the other. As a rural activist in Badwani (Madhya Pradesh) said, 'Earlier we used to chase the panchayat secretary, now he runs after us.' There has been grudging and partial acceptance of this over time.

In spite of the legal protections that the UPA governments enacted, they were unable to stand up for its vision entirely. The very government that enacted the laws ended up undermining them. For instance, the NREGA that guarantees 100 days of work in a year to adults of rural households at the minimum wage recognised an important right of people. It was credited for the UPA being voted back to power in the 2009 General Election. Yet, NREGA began to get hostile treatment during UPA-2 (2009-2014): budgets did not keep up with demand, persondays of work generated stagnated (except during COVID-19, 2020-2022), and delays in wage payments increased and wage rates stagnated in real terms. While serious issues like delays in wage payment were ignored, technocratic measures such as linking payments with Aadhaar, the use of electronic muster rolls began to be emphasised. An alternative framework of social security, including widespread use of biometric technology, of business correspondents, food fortification, etc., began to be pushed.[3]

Yet, in this decade, for a short window, there was some room for people's issues. This reflected in the Centre's budgetary allocations too (see Chart 12.1). Another indication of the emergence of this space was that the two main political parties became competitive over such initiatives. This was evident in the debate around the NFSA. The main opposition party (BJP) repeatedly used Chhattisgarh's Food Security Act (where the BJP was in power at that time) to argue that the central government's Bill was weak and entitlements were inadequate, e.g., lacking nutritious items like dal (that Chhattisgarh's law provided for).

For both parties, people's issues tended to become part of the party's agenda because of perceived electoral gains. In the UPA decade (2004-2014), laws on education, employment, food security etc., played a crucial role in advancing a people-centric agenda. In states where they were implemented in spirit, results were also visible.

By most international standards, India is a laggard in the field of social security (even compared to many poor countries), yet the privileged strongly opposed these laws. Some sections of mainstream media termed the UPA government's efforts to advance socio-economic rights as the return of a 'Mai-Baap sarkar' mindset. Mai-Baap sarkar is a situation where people rely on the goodwill of the government in power, rather than being in a position to demand these rights as their entitlements. Moreover, it was alleged that some laws (such as NREGA or even subsidised rations) would create dependency, rather than making people self-reliant.

In fact, legislations that recognise and establish people's rights are the opposite of a Mai-Baap sarkar mindset. Independent of any particular elected government's commitment to social and economic justice, such laws can help people secure their basic rights.

A Push-back, Return of 'Mai-Baap Sarkar' (2014-2024)

When the NDA government was voted to power in 2014, hints of a Mai-Baap sarkar began to emerge. This was very evident in Rajasthan, where Ms Vasundhara Raje took over as the Chief Minister of a BJP-run government in December 2013. Within a year, at least three of her initiatives revealed her hostile attitude towards socio-economic rights.

The first target was extra food supplies, through the Public Distribution System (PDS), for Sahariya families in Baran district. The Sahariyas are among the 'Particularly Vulnerable Tribal Groups' (PVTG), often in the headlines because of starvation deaths or news of bonded labour. In view of their vulnerable situation, the previous Congress government in Rajasthan introduced a special free food package for them through the PDS: 35 kg wheat, 2 kg edible oil and 1 kg each of pulses and ghee. It was discontinued as soon as Ms Raje came to power. For months, assurances were given that the programme would be relaunched soon, but when wheat distribution resumed in July 2014, Sahariyas were charged Rs 2 per kg (*Business Standard* 2014). The other nutritious items remained absent. After much criticism, in September it was announced that wheat would be distributed free and that the other commodities would be given by the Tribal Area Development Agency. The uncertainties continued because the extension was for a limited period; while oil and ghee resumed, quantities were lower (Abshar 2018).

Another example of programmes being run on the Chief Minister's whims was from the health sector. In 2011, the state government announced that public health facilities would provide free medicines in Rajasthan. Not only was this policy very popular, it was a commendable and sensible move, as it would attract patients to public health centres. During the 2013 election campaign, Ms Raje referred to the medicines provided by public health centres as 'poison'. Once she assumed office she decided to continue with the programme, only to announce in July, that the state government would restrict free medicines and diagnostics (the latter were introduced in 2013 by the previous Congress government) to persons on the list of the National Food Security Act (Vashisht 2014).

The third example pertains to the NREGA, unanimously passed in Parliament in 2005. Speaking at the India Today Conclave in 2014, Ms Raje said, 'By now everybody knows it [NREGA] has been a failure at the state level. You can't find labour to go into the fields anymore. People are being given doles, I mean it is literally a dole because they don't work anymore. So, you work for four hours, you pick up your money and you go home—so now you have taught people to be lazy.' (India Today Conclave 2014, 8.25 minutes) In stark contrast, around the same time, the World Development Report 2014 was projecting the NREGA as 'a stellar example of rural development'. In a letter to the Rural Development Minister in June 2014, Ms Raje asked why NREGA needed to be a law; Why not run it as a scheme? The statement was withdrawn on Twitter/X a few days later.

This Mai-Baap sarkar mentality is widespread. The Ministry of Rural Development in Delhi suggested that the share of material expenditure (restricted to a maximum of 40 per cent under NREGA) be increased. This would have led to the return of contractors, who were banned under NREGA, and who were the root cause of corruption in public employment programmes before the NREGA was enacted. More alarmingly, there was also an attempt to partially 'rollback' NREGA by restricting it to one-third of Indian districts. In December 2025 the NDA government finally replaced MGNREGA with a new law.

The government also dragged its feet in rolling out the NFSA 2013. The rollout required drawing up a fresh list of entitled families for inclusion into the PDS. It was the responsibility of the state governments to do so, but they needed data from the Socio-economic Caste Census (SECC) to proceed, and the Centre delayed release of the SECC data (Drèze et al 2019).[4]

The dwindling support for these programmes is visible in the NDA budgets. When entitlement programmes are treated as handouts, to be doled out at the whims of leaders, it undermines the fundamental reason for legally recognizing them as rights. The laws are meant to foster a sense of security among people, so that they can think long-term, beyond basic survival needs. When rights are weakened, people are pushed into uncertainty. Instead of being empowered, they remain dependent on others' goodwill, not knowing when political patronage will be withdrawn.

Context and Rationale

For the last two decades, every other year or so, we have conducted primary surveys with university students of government interventions to understand the implementation issues they face, their achievements and limitations. (A partial list of these field studies is in Appendix I, Table A1) These surveys, though small (generally covering less than 2000 households), were generally carefully designed with attention to sampling (e.g., sample areas and respondents were selected using random sampling). Over the years, these surveys have taken us to fourteen states: Andhra Pradesh, Bihar, Chhattisgarh, Himachal Pradesh, Jharkhand, Karnataka, Maharashtra, Madhya Pradesh, Odisha, Rajasthan, Tamil Nadu, Telangana, Uttar Pradesh and West Bengal. Apart from this, there have been some smaller informal surveys in Delhi, Gujarat, Kerala, Punjab and Haryana. Some of these surveys were in the nature of a 'social audit'—i.e., the main objective was to verify administrative data with respondents directly (see Table A1).

These field studies, conducted between 2002-2023, helped us develop an evidence-based understanding of rural realities. The field studies were broadly speaking 'quantitative', data collected was through pre-coded questionnaires, but the student-volunteers who participated in the surveys were able to go beyond the questionnaires. Their insights, shared during the field survey and at the debriefing workshops at the end of the surveys, enabled us to have a rich textured understanding of social policy realities in many parts of India.

I also rely on insights from secondary data such as the National Family Health Surveys (NFHS), the National Sample Survey (NSS) and other such sources. These are nationally representative sample surveys. Finally, I also use administrative data from government sources where it is relevant and likely to be reliable. In general, the book leans heavily on previously published journal papers, popular articles in dailies, online news portals, etc.

Rural areas are in focus in this book because most of our studies were in rural India. Of the seven schemes discussed here, all except NREGA are functional in urban areas too. One reason for the rural 'bias' in our surveys is that for decades poverty has been much higher there and a majority of the population lived in rural areas. Partly for these reasons, rural India has also been the focal point of government-supported social policies. Public canteens are an exception. It is primarily an urban intervention (possibly with some exceptions—e.g., Kerala). Though public canteens are primarily in urban areas, there is a role for them in some rural areas as well. It was one of the big misses in the National Food Security Act 2013.

The presentation in this book has been influenced by classroom discussions with students at the Indian Institute of Technology Delhi and the Indian Institute of Management Ahmedabad, the two places I have taught at. Those conversations have been an important reason for comparing India with countries like the US, United Kingdom, France at times. In the imagination of students, it is these countries that come up in classroom discussions. They tend to give examples of the achievements of these countries, without necessarily having some of the economic and social context.

This raises the question—which country would be the right one to compare India with? The comparisons here are a mix of three sets of countries: neighbouring South Asian countries, emerging economies of Brazil, Russia, India, China and South Africa (BRICS) and developed countries.[5] While each of these comparisons can be illuminating, there are caveats associated with them. The intention is not that we try to be like that country, but to shed light on the possibilities in different circumstances. For instance, it might seem unfair to pitch India against the UK or any other developed country. India is a lot poorer than them. Yet, those countries went from having unremarkable living conditions to their current levels of wellbeing in just a few decades. (For instance, think of the living conditions described in Down and Out in London and Paris, by George Orwell.) Attaining their current standard of living here (clean air, safety, healthy long life, decent work opportunities, etc.) are certainly worth aspiring to. With neighbouring South Asian countries, we have a shared economic history and culture, but most of them are geographically smaller. India is often clubbed with emerging BRICS economies though the Indian economy and society are quite different from them.

Interactions with people from different backgrounds and perspectives have helped understand other perspectives better. Over the past two decades of research on social policy in India, I have had a chance to see the struggles of the people in rural India. In class, I heard the views of engineering and management students; in varying social contexts, friends and family have pronounced their verdict on social policy that betray a misunderstanding about them. This book is broadly aimed at two kinds of readers. For those who are supportive, perhaps this book will equip them with facts and arguments that reaffirm their belief in social policies. More crucially, it is an attempt to initiate a dialogue between different groups, especially the sceptics of social policy, and allow them to view social policies from a sympathetic yet informed and critical lens.

2

Key Debates in Social Policy

There are four longstanding debates in the realm of social policy, which are critical to shaping policies. They are: distinguishing between growth, redistribution and wellbeing; the loose use of labels such as 'socialism' and 'capitalism' in public discussions; thinking about policy design through the universal vs targeted debate, the debate on cash vs in-kind transfers; and finally—briefly—a few words on what is viewed as 'merit' but is essentially a lottery.

Clarity on why growth matters and what our goals are (or should be), why public intervention is necessary to achieve those goals, and how far government intervention should go—these underlying questions matter if one has to come to an informed position on social policy issues.

Growth, Wellbeing and Redistribution

The debate on growth vs redistribution is centuries old. One aspect of it is whether we (society, government, policy makers) should prioritise Gross Domestic Product (GDP) growth or the wellbeing of the people. The debate on growth vs redistribution is closely intertwined with the debate on growth vs wellbeing. In recent times, economists such as Amartya Sen have helped us think of wellbeing as an end, and of GDP growth as the means to achieving that end (see Drèze and Sen 2015, for instance).

Economists who focus on people's wellbeing believe that income and living conditions are only one aspect of our overall wellbeing. Two economists, Mahbub-ul Haq and Amartya Sen, helped develop the Human Development Index (HDI) to measure wellbeing in a more wholesome way. They included one indicator each for three important dimensions of human life—income, health and education. The idea was to broaden the focus from income, to health and education, as, to be well, we need much more than income, including a long and healthy life, and a good education.[6]

For health, the HDI includes life expectancy at birth (a measure of longevity of life). For education, mean years of schooling and per capita income as a measure of the standard of living are included in the HDI. It is computed annually to rank countries for which data is available—in 2022, India's rank was 129 out of 184 countries (see Table 2.1).

Table 2.1 India and China's Rank Among 184 Countries

	India	*China*
GDP (current), 2022[1]	5	2
Per Capita Income (PPP), 2022[1]	121	74
Human Development Index, 2022[2]	129	73

Source: [1]World Development Indicators, World Bank; [2]Human Development Report 2023-24, UNDP.

GDP and its growth remain deeply embedded in public imagination and discussion—it remains, as Titmuss put it, the 'Goddess of Growth' (Titmuss 1968). It has been difficult to dislodge GDP as the key attention grabbing economic indicator. For instance, in recent times, when India is discussed in an international comparative perspective, what is brought up is that it is the 'fifth largest economy' in the world. Of the four countries ahead of India on this metric, the combined population of three (the US, Germany and Japan) is less than half of India's; only China has a bigger GDP and a comparable population. The moment one looks at this in terms of per capita income, India's rank crashes. As Table 2.1 shows, India's rank on per capita income (purchasing power parity) terms is 121 (among 184 countries).

In spite of the well-recognised limitations of focusing on GDP and its growth alone, it continues to be the main focus of policy as well. What are the problems of being so GDP focused? One, we fail to account for what the GDP comprises of. Construction and demolition activities both contribute to GDP. 'Bads' such as polluting activities or substance abuse are equally valued as 'goods' such as health care and education. [7]

Two, the old orthodoxy that emphasises GDP growth alone would have us believe that any growth of the GDP, automatically benefits everyone—similar to the 'trickle down' theory in economics. In fact, not everyone may benefit (e.g., think of people who get displaced without fair compensation). Even if everyone does, not everyone benefits fairly. For instance, in 2022-23, 90 per cent of adults in India earned less than the all-India per capita income of Rs 2.3 lakhs. The bottom 50 per cent on average earn only one-third of the all-India per capita income (Bharti et al. 2024). According to their estimates, inequality in India was higher in 2022-23 than at the end of the colonial period.

A third problem with aiming only at higher GDP and

its growth is that contrary to what many have been led to believe, it cannot solve all problems. Higher income or income growth does not guarantee wellbeing. For example, the US is among the richest countries in the world (in 2023, it ranked 12 with per capita income of USD 81,695), but it lags far behind on wellbeing indicators. In 2023, with a per capita income of less than half of that of USA (USD 33,834), the Japanese lived longer than Americans by seven years. Life expectancy at birth in the US was only 77 years (ranked 63) compared with 84 years in Japan. An important factor behind better outcomes in Japan is greater public intervention in healthcare.

Similarly, in India rates of under-nutrition do not decline automatically at higher standards of living. According to the National Family Health Survey (NFHS) 5 data pertaining to 2019-21, among the richest 20 per cent, roughly one-fifth of Indian children (23 per cent and 20 per cent respectively) were 'stunted' or underweight; 63 per cent were anaemic. Improving wellbeing requires more direct government action.

None of this is to suggest that income is not important or that income has no bearing on wellbeing.[8] Relying on income alone—even if it is fairly distributed—to improve wellbeing is unlikely to work.

Socialism vs Capitalism

In popular usage, labels such as 'Socialist', 'Leftist', 'Capitalism' are often thrown around as a slur. In some instances, their use is often based on a confused notion, even a misunderstanding, about their meaning. For instance, one misconception is that in so-called capitalist countries, 'everything' is privately organised, primarily based on principles of market exchange. Further, there is a belief that the government is small—i.e., the government's economic activities are a small part of the GDP. For many, the US epitomises this view of a capitalist economy, where (according to this misperception) the government does not play much of a role in public services such as education and health or even in other economic activities.[9]

Those who view the US as a stellar example of the success of capitalism have probably never examined the make-up of the US economy closely. Chart 1.1 shows government expenditure as a percentage of GDP for a few countries. For the so-called 'capitalist' USA, in 2022 the share of government spending in GDP was 36 per cent, higher than India's 29 per cent, even though India is projected as a 'big government' state.

During the period covered by Chart 2.1—1900 to 2022—the US government expenditure as a percentage of GDP increased steadily, and has been higher than India since 1931. Even during India's so-called 'Socialist' phase (post-Independence till about the eighties), government spending in GDP was only around 15 per cent. France and the United Kingdom are different from the United States because socialist principles had a considerable historical influence on their society and politics. In 2022, the government spending was high in France (58 per cent of GDP). In the UK, it was not substantially different from the US (44 per cent vs 36 per cent).

More than the size of government per se, what matters is which sector(s), to what extent, and in what form, government is or should be present in economic activities. Here it is illustrative to compare government spending on health and education, where the government's role is widely accepted. Government expenditure on health and education in France, UK and the US is much higher than in India. For

Chart 2.1: Government Expenditure as (%) of GDP

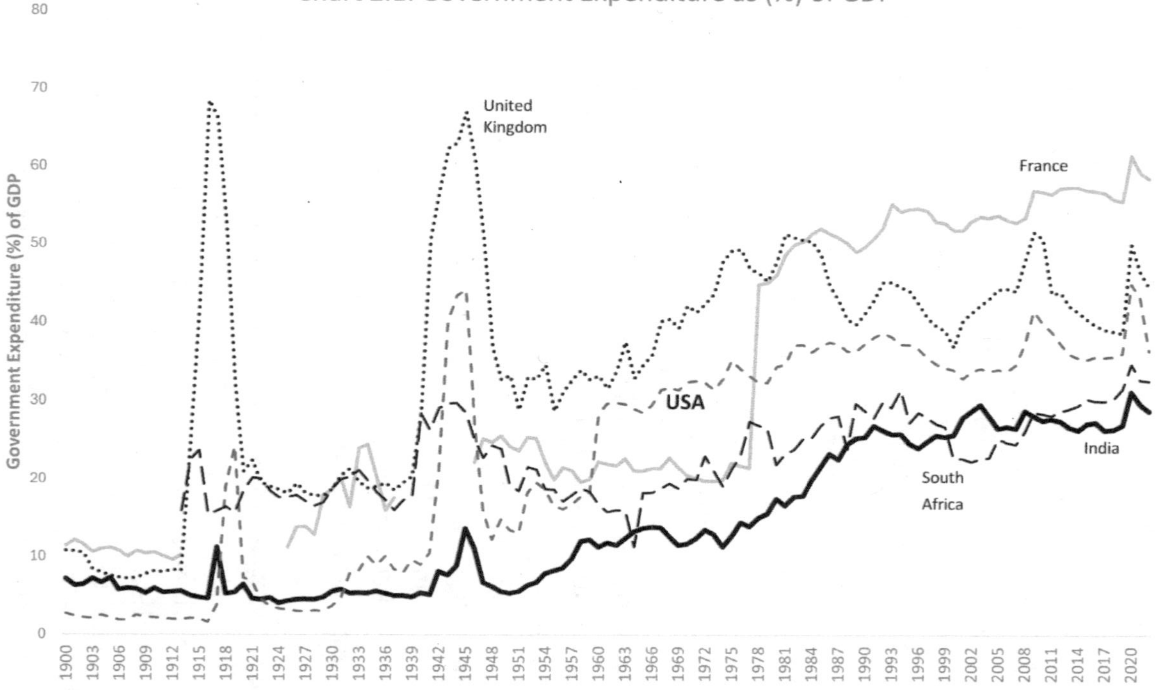

Source: Our World in Data https://ourworldindata.org/government-spending

instance, on education it was more than 5 per cent of GDP in 2020 (see Table 2.2) but barely 4 per cent in India.

The contrast is more striking when we look at government health spending: compared to 1.2 per cent of GDP in India in 2020, it was 10.7 per cent in the US, 10.2 per cent in Great Britain and 9.3 per cent in France. The neglect of health in Indian budgets is historical and persistent. In 1960, the US was spending roughly 1 per cent of GDP on healthcare (India's current government expenditure) and it was 2-3 per cent of GDP in the UK and France. Elsewhere, government spending on health has tended to increase with growth GDP. In India, it has remained around one per cent of GDP for several decades in spite of robust GDP growth.

One consequence of 'small' government presence in health and education is that people are compelled to rely heavily on private arrangements. For instance, in terms of private school enrolment at primary level, India emerges as an aberration. In 2020, 45 per cent of children in India were attending private schools, compared with merely 4 per cent in the UK, 8 per cent in the US, and 15 per cent in France. Similarly, out of pocket expenditure is very high in India (46 per cent) compared with France, US and the UK (between 9-14 per cent).

Encouraging growth and facilitating redistribution are equally important government functions. For both, the government needs to incur expenses. Many programmes of redistribution (including expenditure on health and education) contribute to GDP growth, at least as much as policies to boost growth can contribute to redistribution (e.g., by creating better employment opportunities). Think of it in an extreme situation: a country of people without basic literacy and decent health (comprising, say, of security guards and

Table 2.2 Role of Government, India vs Selected Developed Countries, 2020

	India	*United States*	*United Kingdom*	*France*
Government expenditure (per cent of GDP)[1]	31.1	44.8	49.9	61.3
Government health spending (per cent of GDP)[2]	1.2	10.7	10.2	9.3
Government education spending (per cent of GDP)[2]	4.1	5.4	5.5	5.7
Enrolment in private schools at primary level (per cent)[3]	45.1	8.3	34.1 (4.5)	15.0
Out of pocket expenditure (per cent of current health expenditure)	45.9	11.1	13.8	8.9

Source: [1]Government Spending, Our World in Data, [2]School Enrolment, Primary, Domestic General Government Health Expenditure Private and Government Expenditure on Education, Total (per cent of GDP), World Development Indicators (WDI), World Bank. [3]Author's calculation based on UK government data. The WDI records private enrolment rate of 34 per cent, but the UK government's website suggests that 4.5 per cent of children aged 5-10 years were in 'independent schools'.

brick-kiln workers) can hardly expect to experience the same GDP growth rate as a country with well-educated and healthy people (say, nurses and cooks). When GDP growth rates are robust, government revenues are likely to increase and these resources can be used for redistributive programmes. Even if health and education did nothing for redistribution or economic growth, their public provision is first and foremost a matter of people's rights.

Beyond health and education, and contrary to a widely held view in India, such social policies are not 'freebies'. Some are people's rights and others merely a part of a government's basic functions. As Table 2.2 shows, public provisioning of services such as health and education is the norm the world over.

Some believe that such provisioning should be time-bound, to be wound up as per capita GDP rises. By committing to running such programmes of social support in perpetuity, they believe India is an exception or anomaly. That is not true either. For instance, though the US is one of the richest countries in the world, it spends 17 per cent of GDP on social protection (see Table 2.3). In 1935, the US passed the Social Security Act that provides direct payments (like pensions) to older people. Its food stamp programme (Supplemental Nutrition Assistance Programme, SNAP) for food security traces its origins to The New Deal. At the time of the Great Depression, the US government enacted the The New Deal in 1932. It was the 'employment guarantee' programme of the US that provided unskilled employment by engaging labour to construct parks, bridges, libraries, etc. (see Marmor, Mashaw and Harvey 1990 on 'America's Misunderstood Welfare State'). While the US does not have universal free school meals (only some states do), in Finland and Japan, school meals were legislated upon in the '40s and '50s respectively.

Table 2.3 Social Security: Coverage and Expenditure

	Share of population covered by social security	*Government expenditure on social protection (per cent of GDP)*		*Government expenditure on health (per cent of GDP)*
	2024[1]	2014-2015[2]	2022-24[3]	2021[3]
US	78.8 (4)	19.0	16.8	9.6
Brazil	71.2 (22)	18.3	17.0	4.5
China	75.6 (15)	6.3	7.9	2.9
South Africa	63.4 (44)	10.1	5.4	5.0
India	48.8 (32)	2.7	4.0	1.1
Bangladesh	22.0 (19)	1.7	0.9	0.4
Pakistan	20.2 (16)	0.2	1.2	0.8
Nepal	21.0 (18)	3.0	2.2	1.8

Source: [1]per cent of the population who benefits or contributes to at least one social security scheme. This includes programs such as maternity benefits, unemployment allowance and pensions. Annex 5.2 World Social Protection Report, 2022-24 (2024), in brackets, tax-financed coverage. [2]Table B.17 (p. 407), World Social Protection Report, 2017-19. Table A3 around 2020 Table A4.3 (p. 278) World Social Protection Report, 2020-22. [3]Annex 6 World Social Protection Report 2022-24. Latest available year for government expenditure on social protection.

Table 2.3 reports the coverage of, and expenditure on social security programmes in BRICS and neighbouring countries as compiled by the World Social Protection Report. According to these data, in China and Brazil, more than 70 per cent of the population is covered but just about half of the Indian population was covered in the latest year for which data were available. Between 2022 and 2024, the proportion of Indian population covered jumped from 24.4 per cent to 48.8 per cent, because in 2022 only contributory benefits were included whereas in 2024 tax-financed benefits (reported in brackets) are also included. In the US, Brazil and China, the bulk of social security comes from contributory benefits. In the other countries, tax-financed beneficiaries comprise the major share (e.g., 32 per cent are tax-financed in India, and only 16.8 per cent enjoy contributory benefits). Though guaranteed spending on social security increased in the last decade in India, China and Pakistan, it remains small as a percentage of GDP.

Thus, even in countries that are 'capitalist', governments participate in economic activities, especially in those related to providing social protection. The case of the US is illustrative. In response to the Great Depression, the New Deal included an 'employment guarantee' (discontinued after a decade or so). Other components of the New Deal, such as the food stamps programme and pensions (through the Social Security Act 1935) continue to date. This book is about similar interventions in India.

Universal or Targeted

Should social protection measures be targeted to the poor or should they be universal? A targeted system seeks to identify those in need, and focus efforts on them alone, whereas in a universal system everyone is covered.

Wouldn't the use of scarce resources in providing to those who do not need them be wasteful, ask those who favour targeting. For them, targeting is a 'deceptively simple and romantically appealing' solution—'concentrate on those whose needs are greatest' (Titmuss 1968).

Targeting raises several problems. For example, if we have to restrict a service only to the poor, then we need an acceptable definition of poverty. Should we check bank balances to segregate them or on the basis of their living conditions? Even if we are able to find an acceptable definition of poverty, operationalizing identification and categorisation of the population into eligible and ineligible is not a trivial task. Can we conduct a survey that is complete, accurate and free from bias or manipulation? Another challenge is that even if we find credible eligibility criteria and implement them well, people's situation does not remain static. All may be fine for someone until the day of the survey, but if the main breadwinner meets with a fatal accident the following day, their economic situation can change drastically (Khera 2008).

There are several arguments in favour of universal programmes. When a government service is for everyone, then the indignity often associated with social benefits will not arise.[10] Secondly, universal services help in the prevention of poverty, disease, illiteracy, thereby increasing people's capabilities. If we view social policy interventions as rights or entitlements, as humanitarian and egalitarian interventions, it is difficult to make a case for targeting for a range of social policies.

Universality raises some questions as well. The first is the question of costs. Universal benefits are expensive, so fiscal concerns need to be addressed. Secondly, how can we simultaneously advocate the same treatment for all under universalism, and preferential treatment of the most disadvantaged through redistributive programmes whose very purpose is to first serve those who do not have at all and/or give more to the most disadvantaged? One response to this important concern is that universal does not mean uniform. Everyone is entitled to a minimum, but those whose circumstances are more difficult have the right to get more. Richard Titmuss argued strongly in favour of universal programmes and paraphrasing Titmuss, Amartya Sen later wrote, 'Benefits for the poor end up being poor benefits'.

India's attempt to target the Public Distribution System was an abysmal failure. In 2005, 47 per cent of the poorest quintile (based on monthly per capita expenditure reported in the National Sample Survey 2004-5) and 61 per cent (based on the wealth index of the National Family Health Survey 2005-6) did not have Below Poverty Line (BPL) cards (Drèze and Khera 2010). With the passage of the National Food Security Act 2013, the BPL targeting approach was junked, moving instead to a combination of 'automatic inclusion' and 'automatic exclusion' of broad categories (such as Scheduled Castes and Scheduled Tribes for automatic inclusion or income tax-payers for automatic exclusion). After the rollout of the NFSA's automatic inclusion/exclusion approach, exclusion errors declined drastically. For instance, a survey in six states in 2016 found that exclusion errors (eligible households were excluded) had fallen to roughly 10 per cent (Drèze et al. 2019).

Cash Transfers vs In-kind Transfers

The debate about whether transfers should be in cash or in-kind is another old debate. In the Indian case, it was discussed in detail in the context of replacing PDS grain with cash. Other cash transfers have been introduced, e.g., cash in lieu of subsidised cooking gas (through the Ujjwala Yojana).

The debate on cash transfers instead of subsidised PDS grain occurred when a National Food Security Act (NFSA) began to be debated around 2009. That debate coincided with discussion about a Universal Basic Income (UBI). UBI was presented by some as a better alternative to PDS grain through the NFSA. Eventually, the NFSA retained PDS grain though a clause in the Act keeps the cash transfer option open for the future.

Meanwhile, the UBI proposals have transformed themselves into cash transfers for women. As cash transfers are becoming an increasing part of the social policy framework, the challenges associated with them—inflation-indexing, banking infrastructure, etc.—need closer attention.

One of the main attractions of in-kind transfers is that they protect recipients from inflationary pressures (see Gadenne et. al 2024, for instance). This is pertinent in India because there is no established principle for periodic price indexation in most welfare programmes: once the amount is fixed, it tends to be forgotten for years. Table 2.4 shows that for the cash transfer schemes listed there (social security pensions and maternity benefits), the amount is revised too infrequently (12-18 years in the examples listed) and often the revision is wholly inadequate (last column). The most shocking case is that of the pension scheme where the last increase took place 18 years ago (in 2006-7)—from Rs 125 per month to Rs 200 per month. Since then, the Centre's contribution has remained Rs 200 per month. The notable—recent—exception is Rajasthan's Minimum Income Guarantee Act, which provides for an annual 15 per cent increase in pensions. Over time, without indexation, the value of the cash support provided through these transfers diminishes.

Table 2.4 Stagnation in Selected Cash Transfer Schemes

Name of scheme	*Years since increase (Year of last increase)*	*Central Government's contribution, 2024 (Rs)*	*Amount of last increment (Rs)*
IGNOAPS, 60-80 years[1]	18 (2006-7)	200/ month	125/ month
IGNDPS and IGNWPS[1]	12 (2012)	300/ month	100/ month
IGNOAPS, 80+ years[1]	12 (2011)	500/ month	300/ month
PMMVY maternity benefits	12 (2013)	6000/ child	n/a

Source: [1]Government of India (2024a).

Notes: IGNOAPS Indira Gandhi National Old Age Pension Scheme, IGNDPS Indira Gandhi National Disability Pension Scheme, IGNWPS Indira Gandhi National Widow Pension Scheme, PMMVY Pradhan Mantri Matru Vandana Yojana

Instead of pitching cash transfers against in-kind transfers, as tends to be the case in India, the sensible way to view them is to recognise that there is a place for both kinds of transfers. Whether the benefits are delivered in-kind or as cash, depends a lot on the context. The social policy interventions discussed in this book are also a mix of both—benefits delivered through the ICDS, MDM and PDS are in-kind transfers whereas PMMVY, NSAP and NREGA entitlements are cash benefits. In fact, in some of them the two are integrated within the scheme: e.g., in some states, the sanction of a social security pension comes with 10 kg of free PDS grain. Each of these are complementary and together, they can provide a well-integrated welfare package.

A Lottery or Merit?

Often people living in poverty, remain poor for reasons over which they have little or no control (e.g., lack of well-paid work opportunities, poor access to education and so on). This is contrary to the belief—held quite widely—that the poor are themselves responsible for their poverty (e.g., that they are lazy and unwilling to work). Birth is a lottery. A person with a motor disability, or one born in a rural area or in a Dalit family cannot be blamed for requiring a more accommodative environment. In such a situation, without social interventions, birth alone may determine life's trajectory. Apart from birth, other contingencies such as illness also make corrective public action necessary. Social policies are the norm around the world to account for such circumstances.

In the Indian context, the caste system is an example of extreme disadvantage ascribed at birth, over which the person has no control. Caste affects where we might be able to live, how much we will be able to study, what job we will get, who we will befriend or marry, and so on. Though caste-based discrimination has been formally abolished, it is still very much a part of the lived experience for today's generation.[11] This seemingly abstract idea was succinctly explained by a Dalit student at IIT a few years ago. He said, 'First you cut off our legs, then you ask us to run the same race as others.'

Other than caste, region and class are traits that we do not choose, but they significantly impact our capabilities. A person born into a rural family is more likely to trail behind an urban person; on average, outcomes for girls in India are worse than those for boys. Similarly, some of the literature on disability suggest that the disability is created by social arrangements, and can be remedied by them as well (e.g., if buildings have ramps those with motor disabilities can regain a lot of mobility). They affect every aspect of our life, be it health, education, employment, etc. Active social interventions can help a person overcome the adverse circumstances related to the lottery of birth and other contingencies in life.

Indian elites are far more likely to be sympathetic to gender justice than to caste justice—for instance, affirmative action ('reservations') for Scheduled Castes and Scheduled Tribes remains a contentious issue. Yet, as mentioned earlier, there is an important parallel between the two (i.e., they are both an accident of birth). Along with reservations, robust social policies can help disadvantaged groups: a good public education and health system, support for employment and food security are short- and long-term means of creating a more level playing field.

The philosopher John Rawls suggested a thought experiment to encourage empathetic policy decisions (Rawls 1971). Before making a new policy, the policy maker should remain behind a 'veil of ignorance'. For example, in making public transport policies, they could end up as a pedestrian, a cyclist, a bus rider, or a motorist. Not knowing what they might end up as, there is greater likelihood of taking into account the needs of each concerned group. More generally, if decisions are made behind the veil of ignorance, the hope is that policy makers will pay serious attention to the needs of the most disadvantaged. This thought experiment may not help counter the harsh social realities in India, but perhaps it helps to see the lottery that birth is, as opposed to a question of merit, as many believe.

3

MATERNITY BENEFITS

Some Women Are More Equal

Some years ago, I came across an infographic on X that plotted the duration of paid maternity leave for select countries. The infographic was attributed to UNICEF. It sought to embarrass the United States, because women there are not legally entitled to paid maternity leave. According to that infographic, India (with twenty-six weeks of paid maternity leave) ranked second after the UK.

It is true that according to the Maternity Benefits (Amendment) Act 2017, some Indian women are entitled to twenty-six weeks of paid maternity leave. Indeed, it is a matter of pride that India is in the same league as the UK and better than the US. Yet, it was exasperating to see this infographic. Why? Because, the 1961 Maternity Benefit Act (amended in 2017) is applicable only to women employed in the organised sector. Employment in the sectors to which the law is applicable is barely 20 per cent of total employment; women's share is lower still. Most Indian women work in the unorganised sector and the generous benefits under the 2017 law do not apply to them. In fact, until 2013 when the National Food Security Act was passed, women in the unorganised sector did not have a legal entitlement to maternity benefits (see Table 3.1).

The National Food Security Act (NFSA) 2013 envisaged maternity benefits as a universal right of women, providing Rs 6,000 per child.[12] Note that for women in the organised sector, there is job protection and full wage compensation for almost six months. In the unorganised sector, however, where the most disadvantaged women work, a flat-rate compensation of merely Rs 6000 is provided.

Table 3.1 Disparity in Maternity Benefits

Four aspects of maternity benefits	*Organised sector*	*Unorganised sector*
Is it a legal right?	Yes. Since 1961.	Yes. Since 2013.
Job protection	Yes	No
Wage compensation	Yes. 100 per cent of salary	Partial. Flat-rate, Rs 6000-18,000[1]
Full-rate salary compensation	26 weeks	2-6.5[2] weeks

Note: [1]Rs 6000 under National Food Security Act and Rs 18,000 under Tamil Nadu's Dr Muthulakshmi Reddy Maternity Benefit Scheme. [2]At Rs 400 per day, the wages for 15 days (2 weeks) will be Rs 6000.

Maternity benefits consist of cash support, job protection and health services. As paid maternity leave is supposed to be a wage compensation, at the very least women in the unorganised sector should have been compensated for twenty-six weeks at the wage rate applicable to them. (Even this would be less than what women in formal employment get as women's wages in the unorganised sector are typically substantially lower than salaries in formal employment.)

To get a sense of the unfair treatment inherent here, we can set Rs 400 as a benchmark daily wage. This would amount to roughly Rs 72,000 for twenty-six weeks. By contrast, the provision in the NFSA 2013 (Rs 6000) is not even 10 per cent of this very modest benchmark wage.[13] Moreover, there is no provision for inflation-indexing the flat-rate cash support. Consequently, there has been no increase since the law was passed in 2013, more than ten years ago.

The injustice to women in the unorganised sector does not end here. Their rights as per the law passed in 2013 remained on paper for more than three years. After demonetisation in November 2016, when the government was scrambling for some remedial measures to counter the damage from it, it fell back on the provisions of the NFSA 2013. On 31 December 2016, the Prime Minister announced maternity benefits of Rs 6000. Another six months passed before the Pradhan Mantri Matru Vandana Yojana (PMMVY) was implemented to operationalise the provisions of the NFSA.

Surprisingly, the PMMVY reduced women's legally mandated entitlement (and the PM's announcement) of Rs 6000 to Rs 5000. Instead of giving it for all births, it was limited to the first 'live birth' only.[14] Both were violations of the National Food Security Act, yet few people objected.

The contrast in the public reception to the amendment of the Maternity Benefits (Amendment) Act, 2017 and to PMMVY was revealing. When the PMMVY was announced, some expressed their displeasure. They believed that giving Rs 6000 as maternity benefits would act as an incentive to have more children. There is little empirical basis in India for the assertion that cash support (even of the generous kind) increased fertility. The likelihood of this happening when the cash support is merely Rs 5000-6000 is even lower.

Oddly, some of these critics were themselves beneficiaries or supporters of twenty-six weeks of paid maternity leave. Such objections were not made when the Maternity Benefit Act 1961 was amended in 2017, to increase leave from twelve weeks to twenty-six weeks. In fact, that move was widely welcomed. It would seem that when privileged women are the target, there is little difficulty in recognizing maternity benefits as women's rights, but when it comes to disadvantaged women, they are readily called freebies.

Table 3.1 shows the status of maternity benefits in India on four dimensions. The maternity benefits law passed in 1961 was limited to those in organised sector employment. With the passage of the National Food Security Act (NFSA) 2013 that changed. Maternity benefits became a legal right of women in the unorganised sector as well. This is not a small achievement.

Yet, on at least three counts, women covered by maternity benefits under NFSA 2013 are at a disadvantage compared to those covered by the Maternity Benefits (Amendment) Act 2017. One, only the jobs of women in the formal/organised sector remain secure. Two, as mentioned earlier, there is a big difference in compensation given to women in the two sectors. Converting the flat-rate compensation of Rs 6000 into daily wages at Rs 400 per day, would imply that women covered by NFSA 2013 are wage compensated for fifteen days. In Tamil Nadu, the flat-rate maternity benefit is Rs 18,000, implying a compensation for forty-five days (6.5 weeks). Both are much lower (2-6.5 weeks) than the twenty-six weeks of full compensation for women covered by the Maternity Benefits Act and the International Labour organisation (ILO) benchmark of eighteen weeks. Three, the ILO's 1919 proposal included free health services, which in theory are universal in India, but the reach and quality of government health services is quite poor for many.

Returning to international comparisons with which the chapter opened, paid maternity leave is now common among almost all developed countries. The US is an exception, where there is no federal law that ensures maternity benefits for women. Some American states have state laws. Besides this, some private companies may voluntarily offer maternity benefits.

Chart 3.1 depicts countries with the lowest (the US) and highest (Romania) number of weeks for which full wage compensation is provided to pregnant women, with the ILO's benchmark (18 weeks) in the middle. Between the two extremes lie the 'two Indias'—the organised sector (26 weeks) and unorganised (2-6.5 weeks). Thus, maternity benefits for women in the unorganised sector in India are among the lowest in the world and much lower than the ILO recommendation (18 weeks). On the other hand, the organised sector is almost twice the ILO benchmark and compares favourably with other developed countries. These double standards are evident in other dimensions of social policy too (e.g., pensions).

Why Maternity Benefits?

The history of maternity benefits goes back to the First World War. In November 1919, as a result of women's struggle, the ILO passed a resolution that had three main demands: one, twelve weeks paid leave (increased to eighteen weeks in 2000), two, free health facilities during pregnancy and immediately after delivery, and three, job security while on maternity leave (see Siegl 2019 and Jarvis 2010).

In India too, the debate on maternity benefits has a

long history. It began before Independence, with Dr B. R. Ambedkar raising this issue in the Bombay Presidency (Tillin 2025 and Drèze et al. 2021).

Maternity benefits are recognised as a legal right for several reasons. First, child-bearing and child rearing need to be recognised as work. Women should be entitled to some social support for such work.

Second, female labour force participation rates in India are low, so fewer Indian women are economically independent, limiting their ability to support themselves. Those who are employed are often compelled to choose between family and career in the absence of maternity benefits. Without the benefits during their pregnancy, they end up quitting their jobs. By the time they are able to work again, i.e., their children are older, they encounter problems in re-entering the job market. Maternity benefits can facilitate women's participation in the labour market and simultaneously enjoy safe motherhood.[15]

Third, women have special nutritional and health needs during pregnancy. Data from India show that under-nutrition and vulnerability are high among Indian women. According to the fifth National Family Health Survey (NFHS), 57 per cent of women aged 15-49 years were anaemic in 2019-21, showing no improvement over the previous round of the NFHS conducted in 2015-16, when 53 per cent of women in the same age group were anaemic. According to the NFHS, one in every five women is stunted. Research has shown that health and nutrition have inter-generational effects, i.e., the mother's health affects that of the child. The chances of a child being under-nourished are higher when the mother is poorly nourished. It is therefore not surprising that children's nutrition outcomes in India are also poor.

For instance, according to NFHS-5 (2019-21), two-thirds of Indian children aged 6-59 months were anaemic. Given this, and the lack of economic independence, cash support to pregnant women becomes critical for accessing better nutrition and health services for themselves and the child.

Fourth, the economic independence that maternity benefits offer allows women to enjoy both rest and access to better nutrition. Without such benefits, women would have to choose between rest and work so that they can meet their nutritional and health needs.

Fifth, maternity leave allows women to follow the recommended practice of exclusive breastfeeding for six months. This is necessary for the healthy growth of the baby. As infants have to be fed at short intervals, women need to be close to their child. This is only possible if either crèches are available at the workplace (by and large non-existent in India, even in the formal sector where it is a legal requirement) or if women get leave from work.

Child-bearing and child rearing *is* work. Indian women struggle for economic independence on account of poor participation in paid work. During pregnancy and soon after, they have special nutritional and health needs; rest and a supportive environment that allows exclusive breastfeeding for the first six months of the child's life are necessary. Maternity entitlements exist as a recognition of women's rights during this challenging phase of their life.

Research on maternity benefits can be classified into two broad groups: its impact in, one, developed countries and, two, in developing countries. Studies of maternity benefits in developed countries focus on three major outcomes: fertility rates, child mortality, and women's work participation rates. In addition, in developing countries, maternity benefits can

Chart 3.1 Duration of maternity leave with full wage compensation (in weeks), 2023

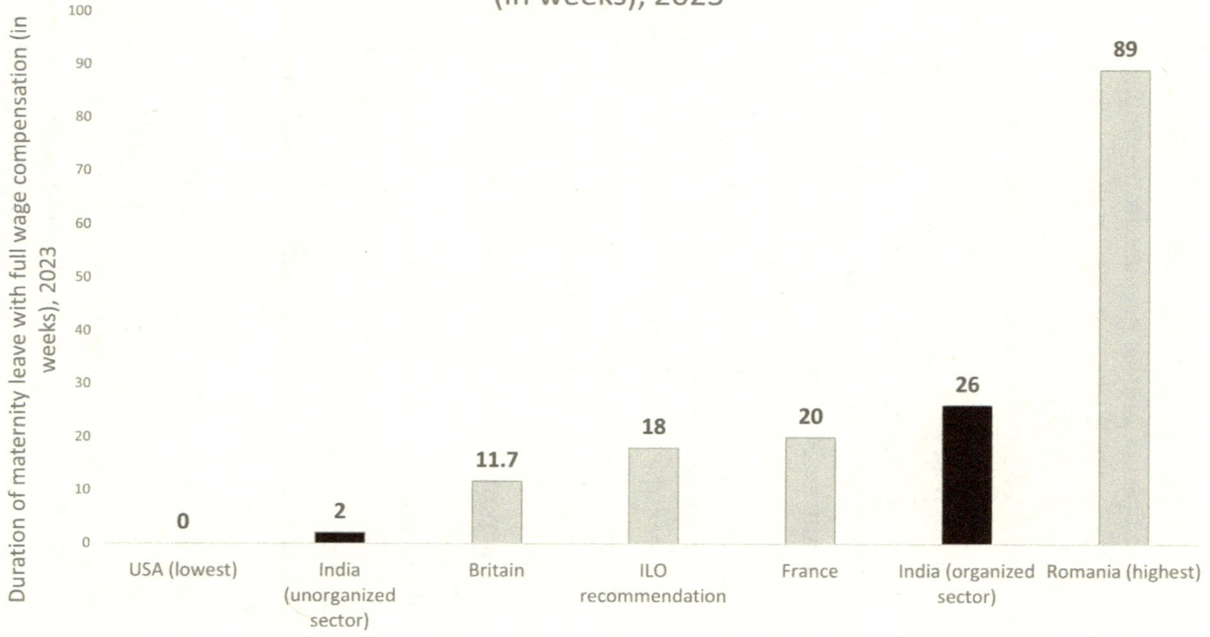

Source: OECD (2024), OECD - Family Database, Parental Leave System also affect outcomes such as duration of breastfeeding, and birth weight of the child. Most studies of maternity benefits are from developed countries because in developing countries (where the unorganised sector is larger) maternity benefits are not very widespread (Fallon et al 2017).

Amin and Islam assessed firm-level data from 111 developing countries to understand the impact of these benefits on women's work participation and found that having maternity benefits increases their participation (Amin and Islam 2022). Similar results have also been seen in developed countries, although there, the length of leave also determines the extent to which women's participation will be affected. As mentioned earlier, maternity leave can also affect the duration of breastfeeding (by staying at home the mother can feed the baby from time to time). A review found that twenty-one studies suggest that maternity benefits can increase the duration of breastfeeding (Navarro-Rosenblatt and Garmendia 2018). Recently, a paper on PMMVY finds that it has a positive effect on post-natal care and wasting (Taneja and Roy Chowdhury 2025).

For these reasons, the PMMVY, launched as part of the National Food Security Act 2013, measly though it is, is an important initiative. Further, there are few countries in the world that have universal non-contributory maternity benefits (Drèze et al. 2021, 47).

The Jachha Baccha (JABS) Survey 2019[16]

In June-July 2019, we conducted the Jachha Baccha (JABS) Survey across six North Indian states. The survey states were Chhattisgarh, Jharkhand, Uttar Pradesh, Madhya Pradesh, Himachal Pradesh and Odisha. The JABS Survey 2019 aimed to understand the status of pregnant and lactating women and the implementation of PMMVY. Across the six survey states, we interviewed 706 pregnant and lactating women about their experience of pregnancy and childbirth.

Pregnancy in Rural India

During the survey, at an Anganwadi in a village of Chhattisgarh, we met a woman who had come to register her pregnancy in what we were told was her seventh month (she did not look it). The norm is for pregnancies to be registered in the first trimester. When scolded by others for the delay in registration, the Accredited Social Health Activist (ASHA) worker (a frontline health worker) accompanying her said that the woman did not realise that she was pregnant. When her periods stopped, she did not feel comfortable talking to anyone in her marital home. Recently, she happened to visit her natal village (where we met her) and her pregnancy was discovered. This incident is revealing in a couple of ways at least: the lack of awareness of very basic information for some women (e.g., that she did not suspect she was pregnant when her periods stopped) and the extent of helplessness or alienation a young woman might feel in her marital home (she did not talk about her condition to anyone until she was visiting her natal home).

This vulnerability is combined with a lack of awareness of women's needs during a pregnancy. A major takeaway from the JABS Survey 2019 was that pregnant and lactating women remain in the dark about their special needs during this crucial phase of their lives. For example, according to international standards, women with a low BMI should gain 13-18 kg during their pregnancy. In contrast, the average weight gain among the women in our sample ranged between 4 kg (in Uttar Pradesh) to 11 kg (in Himachal Pradesh). To some this might seem 'okay'; so it is worth mentioning that many women in the sample weighed only 40 kg *after* gaining weight during their pregnancy.

What was even more alarming is that 40 per cent of lactating women in Uttar Pradesh could not even tell whether they gained or lost weight! Often, the women looked so frail that it was difficult to believe that they were in the last trimester of their pregnancy.

During pregnancy, expecting mothers need to pay special attention to their nutrition. We asked the women if they were eating more or less than usual during their pregnancy. Only one in five women said they ate more than usual. Similarly, we asked if they were consuming a more *nutritious* diet. More than half of the women said that they never or rarely had more nutritious food during their pregnancy. Himachal Pradesh was an exception—80 per cent of women reported eating more nutritious food. The National Food Security Act 2013 has a provision for a meal to pregnant and lactating women at the Anganwadi, but at the time of the JABS Survey, most survey states had not implemented it.[17]

Apart from weakness and inadequate food, women in our sample were also overburdened with domestic work. When asked if they were working during their pregnancy, most of them said no. When asked specifically who fetched the water and firewood, or who did the housework (cooking, cleaning), etc., they admitted that they were doing it themselves. Their perception or definition of work seemed to preclude fetching heavy pots of water or collecting firewood from the forest—these were 'merely' domestic chores. In fact, 85 per cent of the respondents reported doing household work regularly during their pregnancy. These tasks ranged from cooking and cleaning, to heavy tasks such as fetching firewood from the forest, and washing. Only a few women said that they were not doing any 'heavy work'.

Nearly two-thirds (63 per cent) of the respondents worked until the very end of their pregnancy. Around the time of the delivery, they managed to get a short break from all the work. After delivery, although most women (95 per cent) said they took 'complete rest', on average they reported taking only one month of rest. Soon after the delivery, they would find themselves back on the treadmill, taking care of themselves as well as the newborn.

When young women become pregnant, they find themselves in a 'heads you win, tails I lose' situation. If they live in a joint family, where other members could support and help them, their domestic responsibilities are far more substantial. On account of being a young daughter-in-law, they carry a disproportionate burden of such domestic responsibilities. For instance, a respondent in Odisha said that 'living in a big family, it does not feel good if one is ignored'. On the other hand, if they live in a nuclear family, where domestic responsibilities are manageable, there are no members (from the extended family) to help them. In Sonbhadra (Uttar Pradesh), Anita said there was no one to even help with fetching a bucket of water (Sharma 2024). In the JABS Survey 2019, there were two exceptions to this predicament of women. For Adivasi and Himachali women things were somewhat different, as they got more help and comfort from others.

One significant improvement over the past fifteen years is that institutional deliveries have become the norm and are almost universal. According to NFHS data, in 2005-6, 39 per cent deliveries took place in institutions and this proportion had risen to 89 per cent in 2019-21. However, when women arrive at health facilities, there is little guarantee that they will get quality government health services. In the JABS Survey, many women reported that they were treated rudely by the nurse, some were advised to go to private hospitals after labour began, in some places the nurses were expecting bribes, etc. Some of the mistreatment is the result of them being perceived (by hospital staff) as people who can be treated poorly, on account of being poor.

Apart from being in a socially vulnerable position, the respondents were also economically weak. Free and adequate health services are an important part of maternity benefits (it was part of the ILO's 1919 resolution). Yet, they are actually not available uniformly to all women across India. For instance, respondents in the JABS Survey reported spending an average of Rs 6,400 per delivery. If we consider Rs 400 as the daily wage, their delivery expenses are equivalent to roughly half a month's earnings. For women who ended up in private hospitals (7 per cent of women in our sample), their average expenses were even higher—Rs 45,000. (The corresponding costs reported in NFHS-5 are Rs 10,035 on average, going up to Rs 24,663 for those who delivered in a private facility.) Not surprisingly, one-third of the respondents reported having to borrow or sell something at the time of delivery.

Women who got adequate rest and nutrition gained more weight during pregnancy. Both are essential for a healthy pregnancy and child birth, and both can be influenced through policy interventions. For poor rural women overburdened with domestic responsibilities, maternity benefits can go a long way—buying nutritious food, putting her in a position to be able to offer a small token reward to a family member for helping out at home, or accessing necessary health services.

Differences Across States

Among the six JABS states, the social situation and economic status of women varied, as did the implementation of PMMVY. The implementation of PMMVY in Himachal and Odisha was better than other states.

Odisha has had its own maternity benefit scheme named Mamata Yojana since 2011. Women were getting Rs 5000 until 2024; in 2024, in the thirteenth year of the scheme (on the eve of state elections), the amount was increased to Rs 10,000. Odisha's Mamata Yojana is more inclusive than the central government's PMMVY: benefits are available for the second child, and for Particularly Vulnerable Tribal Groups (PVTGs), women get benefits for all births (not just the first two). In Odisha, in the JABS Survey, we found that 90 per cent of pregnant women were eligible, but in the other survey states, only half were eligible for PMMVY.

Since Odisha was running its own scheme, it has been compared to other JABS Survey states below. On the one hand are the JABS Survey states (Jharkhand, Chhattisgarh, Madhya Pradesh, Uttar Pradesh and Himachal Pradesh) where the Centre's PMMVY had been around since 2017 and on the other is Odisha, with the state's Mamata Yojana since 2011. Compared to other survey states, respondents in Odisha had greater awareness about the benefits. One of the reasons being that when the JABS Survey was conducted in 2019, Odisha's maternity benefit scheme had already been running for eight years; in other states, it was only two years old. Moreover, in Odisha, Mamata benefits are universal and that had a direct impact on awareness.

Due to higher levels of awareness, almost all eligible women in Odisha had applied for maternity benefits. On the other hand, only two-thirds of pregnant respondents in other survey states knew that they were entitled to Rs 5000 under the PMMVY scheme, so only two-thirds had applied.

Eligibility and awareness raise the proportion of women who apply; that in turn has a positive effect on the proportion of women who receive benefits. While two-thirds of respondents in Odisha had received at least one instalment of Mamata Yojana, only 15 per cent reported getting PMMVY benefits in the other JABS states. The entitlement under the *law* is universal, but according to the eligibility criterion of PMMVY (taking into account the restriction to the first live birth), a very small proportion (30 per cent) of eligible women received PMMVY benefits.

When eligibility is universal, but an adequate budget is not provided (more on this later), the government is compelled to ration eligible women. One rationing mechanism is to increase the administrative burden. The JABS Survey suggests that paperwork compounded by daunting digital procedures for PMMVY benefits play the role of rationing pregnant women. For instance, at the time of the survey, PMMVY benefits (Rs 5000) were being given in three instalments (the number of instalments was reduced to two later). For each instalment eligible women had to fill out a separate form. In the initial years (even in 2019) the application form was twenty-three pages. The form had to be submitted with many supporting documents—the 'Mother and Child' card, the woman's Aadhaar card/number, her husband's Aadhaar card/ number, bank passbook and so on. Besides this, some women were told that the address on their Aadhaar card should be that of her marital home (not her natal home). If it still had the mother's natal address (18 per cent of the respondents had encountered this problem), they end up making rounds of Aadhaar correction centres to get their

Aadhaar details corrected or updated. It appeared as if the system was designed to tire eligible women (ironically, for a benefit that was introduced to help her rest), so that she gave up (see Paikra 2020 also).

Some pregnant respondents (13 per cent) complained that while applying, they were asked for money by an Anganwadi worker; other issues were lack of information (15 per cent), that they filled the form but there was no further response (19 per cent). A total of 40 per cent of all respondents faced at least one of these issues at the time of application.

While pregnant and lactating women were entangled in paperwork, Anganwadi workers (who were also interviewed as part of the JABS Survey) tasked with completing their application, were themselves feeling burdened by the paperwork. The biggest hindrance was the (de facto) compulsory use of Aadhaar. Anganwadi workers said that at the time of application, more than half of the women faced some problem related to Aadhaar. In almost half (44 per cent) of the cases, they themselves struggled with some confusion related to the applicant's Aadhaar. In Odisha's Mamata Yojana, Aadhaar was not mandatory—this was probably one of the reasons that the proportion of women who received maternity benefits was higher there.

Before the Pradhan Mantri Matru Vandana Yojana

Until 2010, maternity benefits were a part of the umbrella 'National Social Assistance Programme'. The Indira Gandhi Matritva Sahyog Yojana was introduced in 2010 on a pilot basis in fifty-three districts. It provided Rs 4000 as maternity benefits. Its implementation, however, was unimpressive: for instance, in 2014-15 the scheme achieved only 23 per cent of its target (Sinha et al. 2016).

In some other states, maternity benefit schemes were running before the NFSA introduced them. Apart from Odisha (discussed above), Tamil Nadu has had the Dr Muthulakshmi Reddy Maternity Benefit Scheme (MRMBS) since 1987 (Balasubramanian and Sundari Ravindran 2012). The state has had a long history for pioneering social policy initiatives. MRMBS began with Rs 200 and since 2017, pregnant women receive Rs 18,000.[18] Since 2015, maternity benefits come with a 'baby care kit' that includes items such as towels, soap, massage oil, mosquito nets, etc. for the newborn and the mother.

Telangana had a 'KCR Kits' (or MCH kits) scheme since 2017. The scheme entitled pregnant and lactating women to a baby kit and cash benefits—Rs 12,000 if it is a boy and Rs 13,000 if it is a girl. Like Odisha, benefits were for two children; for 'Particularly Vulnerable Tribal Group' mothers, the two-child limit did not apply (*Telangana Today* 2022 and Janayala 2020). There appears to be no study about the implementation of this scheme and reports suggest that the scheme was discontinued when the Congress came to power (Gopal 2024).

States that have their own maternity benefit schemes have a decent track record on implementation. In Tamil Nadu, where such a scheme was first implemented, in 2007-08, 60 per cent of all deliveries received maternity benefits (Balasubramanian and Sundari Ravindran 2012). In 2022-23, when the Central government's budget was Rs 2145 crore, the budget for the MRBMS was Rs 816 crore, covering an estimated 78 per cent of all births.

Returning to Odisha, a survey in 2014 covered 233 women beneficiaries across four districts of the state (Khera 2015). In addition, there were around 300 women with children ranging from seven months to less than three years of age. Two-thirds of the respondents' names were on the Mamata Yojana list and 72 per cent of the women had received the full amount. On average, respondents got Rs 4722, i.e., 94 per cent of their entitlement of Rs 5000. This is commendable because there is a widely held belief that government benefits do not reach people. There was scope for improvement in the scheme—10 per cent of respondents reported receiving nothing and 18 per cent did not receive the full amount. Along with delays, there were other problems too. For instance, those who did not get anything said that it was either due to corruption or there were problems related to bank accounts. In the JABS Survey 2019, the state maintained its good track record on implementation of Mamata Yojana. Of all eligible women, 88 per cent applied for maternity benefits and 75 per cent had received the first instalment.

PMMVY in the Union Budget

Although women working in the unorganised sector are entitled to Rs 6000 as maternity benefit under the NFSA since 2013, the central government has not adequately budgeted for it. For universal coverage at Rs 6000 for each child, the Central budget needs to be approximately Rs 14,000 crores annually. Contrast this with the actual budget: since the PMMVY began, its annual budget has not exceeded Rs 2500 crore. Thus, the actual budget is one-fifth of the requirement for universal coverage at Rs 6000. According to data received under the Right to Information Act, the expenditure on PMMVY was only Rs 870 crore in 2023-2024. Chart 3.2 shows the gap between the budget required as per the provisions of the law (horizontal line above) and

Chart 3.2 Gap in funding for maternity benefits

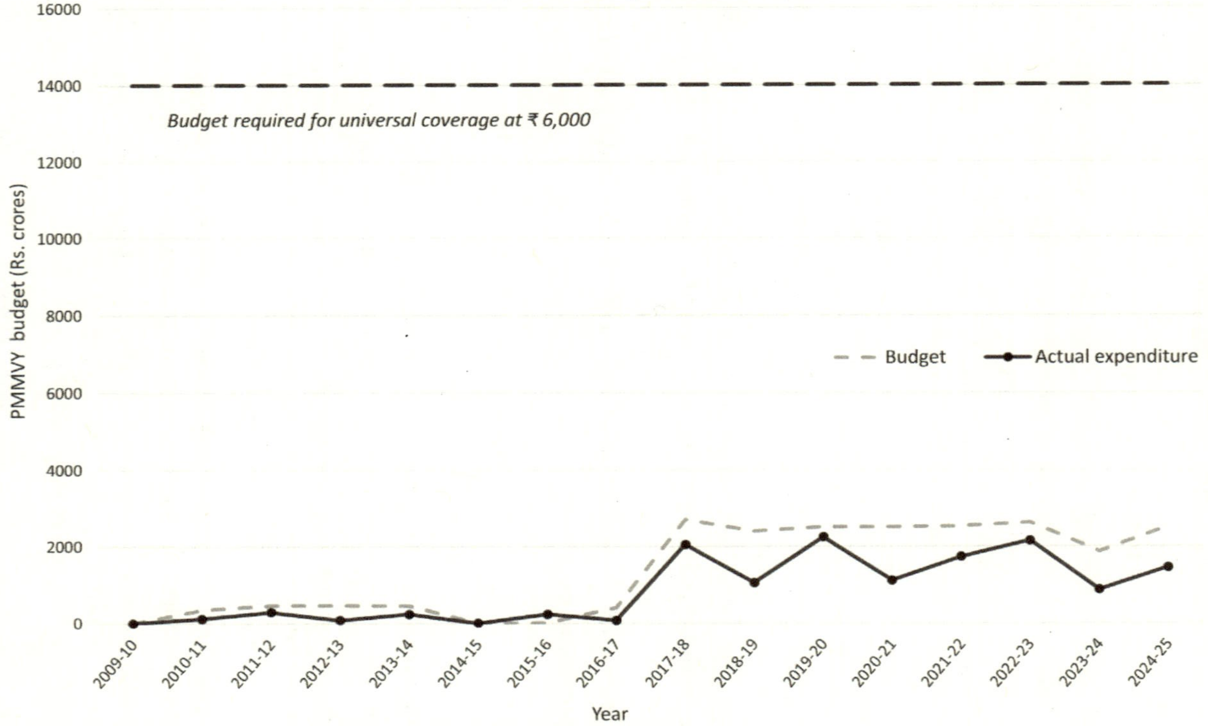

Source: Drèze, Khera and Somanchi (2021) and budget documents

Chart 3.3 Estimated beneficiaries of PMMVY, All India
(% of pregnant women who received at least one instalment)

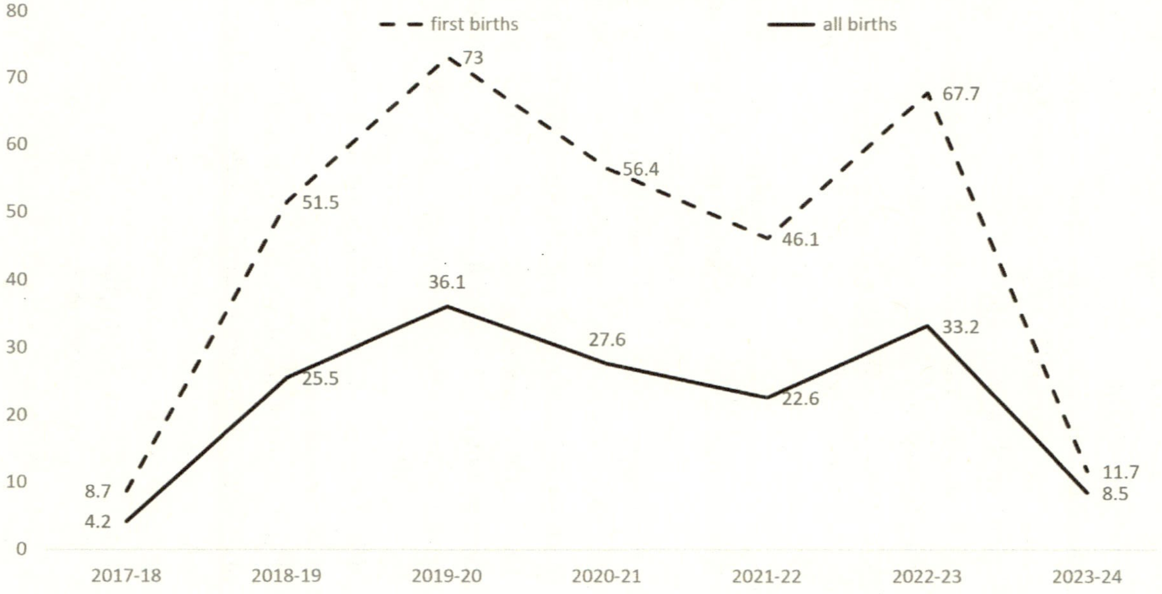

Source: Official PMMVY data obtained under RTI; birth numbers were estimated from birth rates and projected population.

the actual budget (creeping along the x-axis) for the years since its implementation.

Combining administrative data on the number of beneficiaries of PMMVY (obtained through a Right to Information application) and of state schemes with total estimated births, we can estimate the approximate coverage of PMMVY. Map 3.1 plots state-wise proportion of births for which women received 'any' instalments and Map 3.2 plots the proportion who received 'all' instalments in 2022-23.[19]

When we look at state-wise coverage, a familiar pattern emerges—coverage rates are better in southern states and in states with their own scheme. Among the states where maternity benefits were implemented only after PMMVY was rolled out, Karnataka and Kerala in the south along with Himachal Pradesh and Jammu and Kashmir performed better than other states. Three states that had launched their schemes before the PMMVY (Telangana, Odisha and Tamil Nadu) were ahead in implementing maternity benefits, especially Tamil Nadu (78 per cent) and, Telengana and Odisha (64 per cent). Coverage is poor in the northern states.

Poor implementation of PMMVY is also reflected in the fact that the proportion of women receiving 'all' instalments is less than women receiving 'any' instalment. The two worst performing states were Gujarat and Jharkhand where less than one-tenth of women got 'all instalments' (Map 3.2).

The data in Chart 3.2 explains in large part why only 23 per cent of pregnant women across the country (excluding Odisha, Tamil Nadu and Telangana) received all instalments of maternity benefits in 2022-23 (see Map 3.2). Any new scheme takes time to gain a foothold. Unfortunately, within three years of PMMVY coming into force in 2017, the

COVID-19 pandemic hit in 2020. This severely impacted the performance of the scheme at a time when women needed it the most. In the second year of COVID (2021-22), the proportion of women receiving all three instalments fell to 15.7 per cent (Appendix I, Table A2). The pandemic threw everything into disarray; there was some improvement in 2022-23, yet less than a quarter (23 per cent) of women received all three instalments. As Chart 3.3 shows, the estimated percentage of women who received any instalment remains dismally low—despite the improvement in 2022-23, only one-third of women received any instalment. In 2023-24, coverage dropped again—only 12 per cent first births and 9 per cent of all births got any instalment of PMMVY.

***

In many ways, the most commendable achievement of the National Food Security Act 2013 was the inclusion of universal maternity entitlements. Recognition of women's maternity benefits in the unorganised sector as a legal right was a pioneering move, especially outside the developed world.

But this provision has several weaknesses. The benefits are meagre and unchanged since its inception in 2013. The law does not provide employment security and the flat-rate wage compensation under PMMVY leaves women working in the unorganised sector far worse off than their counterparts in the organised sector, who are in any case more privileged.

Women in India rarely find paid employment outside the home, and when they do, it is more likely to be in the unorganised sector. Yet, the implementation of the Pradhan Mantri Matru Vandana Yojana was delayed by four years.

Map 3.1 Maternity entitlements for women in the unorganised sector, 2022-23

Proportion (%) of all births that received any instalment of PMMVY

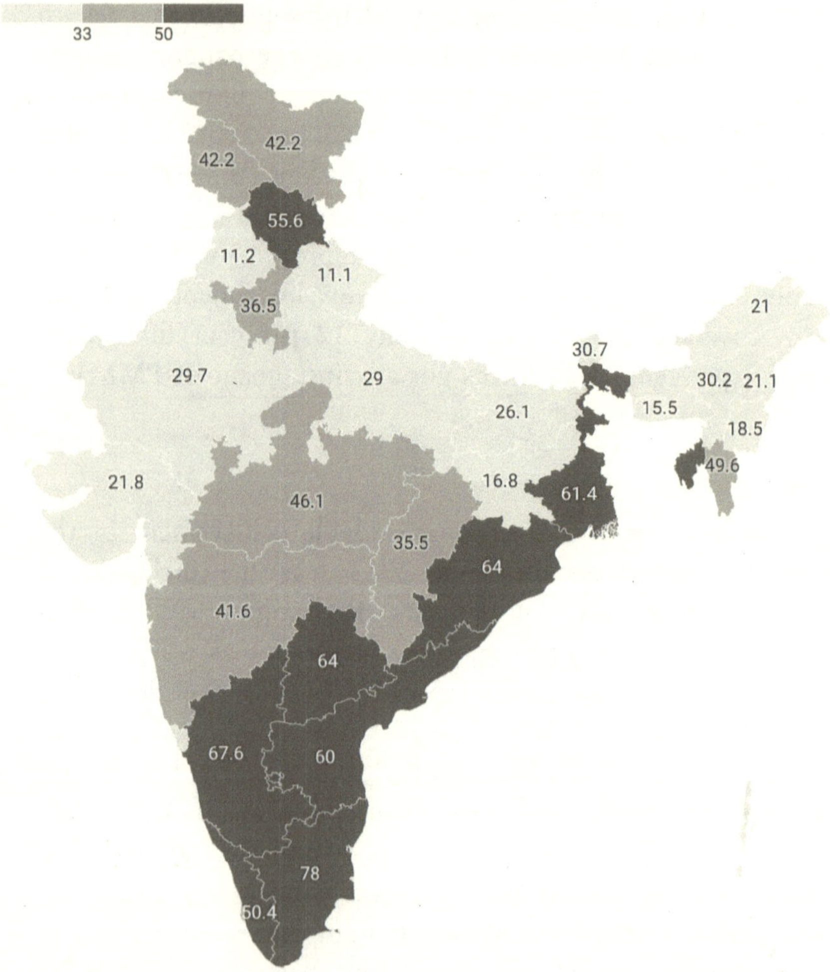

In India, 33% of women in the unorganised sector received maternity benefits through the Pradhan Mantri Matru Vandana Yojana (PMMVY); states with coverage below the national average are highlighted in the lightest shade. Maternity benefits in most states are provided under the PMMVY. Three states have their own schemes: Mamata Yojana (Odisha), Dr. Muthulakshmi Reddy Maternity Benefit Scheme (Tamil Nadu) and the KCR/MCH Kit (Telangana). The total number of births are estimated using birth rates and projected population data.

Map data: © OSM • Created with Datawrapper

Map 3.2 Maternity benefit for women in the unorganised sector, 2022-23

Proportion (%) of total estimated births that received all instalments of PMMVY

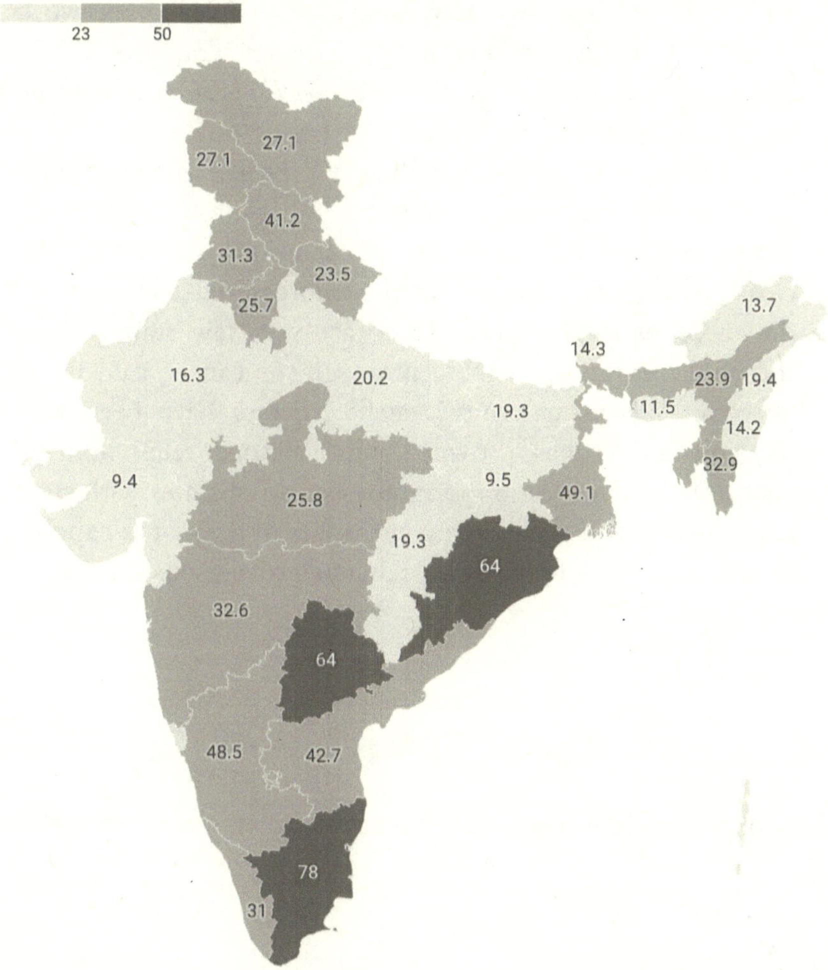

In India, 23% of women in the unorganised sector received maternity benefits through Pradhan Mantri Matru Vandana Yojana (PMMVY); states below this average are highlighted in the lightest shade. In most states, maternity benefits are provided under the PMMVY. Three states have their own schemes: Mamata Yojana (Odisha), Dr. Muthulakshmi Reddy Maternity Benefit Scheme (Tamil Nadu) and KCR/MCH Kit (Telangana). The number of total births is estimated using birth rates and projected population.

Map data: © OSM • Created with Datawrapper

Moreover, budget allocations have fallen far short of what is required for universal coverage. Thus, a universal entitlement with inadequate budgetary provision ends up being rationed. Awareness levels are also low, entangling people in paperwork and digital processes related to Direct Benefit Transfers (DBT). The digital- and paper- work for PMMVY is so cumbersome that many women have failed to get their due.

Since its rollout, the full PMMVY benefits have at their peak reached less than a quarter of all births. Research on young mothers and on the implementation of the PMMVY clearly shows that women in the unorganised sector are in dire need of this support. There are very few states where the implementation of the central scheme can be said to be effective. Where maternity benefit schemes have been well implemented, it has provided much needed relief in their very difficult lives. An important lesson from states with state schemes is that if the government wants to do it, it is capable of doing it—it is fiscally and administratively possible.

4

ANGANWADIS

The Foundations of a Child's Future

Under-nutrition in India

Why should we be so concerned about under-nutrition? Good nutrition is essential for the wellbeing of a person. An under-nourished person is vulnerable to various health issues and ailments that have a direct impact on their wellbeing. Child under-nutrition is of particular importance because research shows that under-nourished children may not able to achieve their full mental and physical potential. More importantly, early interventions are more effective than later in life (Heckman 2006). Good nutrition improves a person's wellbeing as well as that of their family and society and allows them to contribute to their fullest potential.

Discoloured/brown hair, distended belly, etc. are all signs of poor nutrition. However, the most widely used indicators of under-nutrition are anaemia (low haemoglobin), stunting (i.e., height-for-age), wasting (weight-for-height) and underweight (weight-for-age). The National Family Health Survey (NFHS) is a source of valuable information on these and other indicators of people's health and nutrition. It provides data on a wide range of related issues, including information on the mother's health and nutrition, access to essential public services, socio-economic circumstances and so on. It is considered the most reliable source for nutrition statistics.

The NFHS data shows that key indicators of child nutrition (proportion of underweight and stunted children) did not improve significantly between NFHS-2 (1998-9) and NHFS-3 (2005-06). According to the data in Table 4.1, only anaemia (74 per cent to 70 per cent) and stunting (51 per cent to 48 per cent) improved and that too marginally. Facing criticism for the lack of progress, one response of the then United Progressive Alliance-2 (or UPA-2) government was to postpone the next round of the survey. Following sustained pressure, NFHS-4 was finally held in 2015-16 after a gap of ten years (instead of being conducted every few years). In the intervening period, there was no credible and nationally representative survey in India on key indicators related to people's wellbeing.

Another—more positive response—was a gradual increase in the budget for the Integrated Child Development Services (ICDS) scheme, partly in response to public pressure. The ICDS scheme provides services to children under the age of six, their mothers (and to a lesser extent adolescent girls). Its services are delivered through Anganwadis. Between 2008-9 and 2012-13, the ICDS budget almost tripled. Central government expenditure on ICDS, as a percentage of GDP, rose from 0.05 per cent in 2004-5 to 0.16 per cent in 2014-15. The NFHS-4, conducted in 2015-16, results showed an appreciable improvement over NFHS-3 (see Table 4.1). Anaemia and stunting came down by roughly ten percentage points. This was (at least partly) the result of increased commitment to programmes for women and children.

The NFHS was in the news again when the NFHS-5 results for 2019-21 were made public (see Table 4.1). And the news wasn't good. The results from NFHS-5 suggest that the rate of improvements seen in the previous decade could not be sustained (Drèze 2020). As before, the standard of living appears to improve, but the results on key indicators of child nutrition are sobering—for example, roughly one-third of children remain either stunted or underweight and two-thirds were anaemic.[20]

Table 4.1 Changes in Children's Nutrition, India

	NFHS-2 1998-99	*NFHS-3 2005-6*	*NFHS-4 2015-16*	*NFHS-5 2019-21*
Anaemia of any kind (6-59 months)[1,2]	74	70	58	67
Stunting (per cent below 2SD)[a,3]	51	48	38	36
Underweight (per cent below 2SD)[a,3]	43	43	36	32

Note: [a]For stunting and underweight, NFHS-2 statistics are for children under three years of age while NFHS-3, NFHS-4 and NFHS-5 results are for children under five years of age.

Sources: National Family Health Survey (NFHS) [1]Table 7.19 and Table 7.15 NFHS-2; [2]Table 10.13 NFHS-3, NFHS-4 and NFHS-5; [3]Table 10.3, NFHS-3, NFHS-4 and NFHS-5.

Beyond national averages, as always, the inter-state contrasts remain (see Map 4.1). Take for instance, proportion of stunted children (among children aged 0-59 months)—six states have more stunted children than the all-India average of 36 per cent. These are Gujarat, Madhya Pradesh, Uttar

Pradesh, Bihar, Jharkhand and Meghalaya. The lowest proportions are reported in Manipur and Kerala (23 per cent), Sikkim (22 per cent), and Puducherry (20 per cent). A similar pattern emerges for other key indicators of poor nutrition.

A key reason for poor nutritional outcomes is that children do not get adequate nutritious food. Map 4.2 provides a glimpse of this. Eggs are easily available, affordable and nutrient-dense foods, a kind of superfood for children. Map 4.2 plots the proportion of children (aged 6-30 months) whose mothers reported giving their child an egg in the 24 hours before the survey. In most states, less than one-fifth of children in this age group had had an egg.

Unlike some other problems (say polio where four doses of polio drops provide life-long protection), there are no quick fixes for under-nutrition. Nutrition outcomes are not determined by food intake alone. Along with adequate and nutritious food, appropriate health interventions (e.g., safe childbirth, vaccinations), clean drinking water, public sanitation and hygiene, etc., are equally important. Under-nutrition is an inter-generational issue. An under-nourished mother is more likely to give birth to an underweight, anaemic, stunted child. Some of these inter-related indicators are presented in Table 4.2.

Consider three states—one where poverty has been high yet the state government machinery is sluggish in terms of social policy action for women and children (first column, Table 4.2); second, a state with good GDP growth and sluggish social policy (second column) and third where poverty has been high but the government machinery has been working actively for women and children for two decades (column three). Based on these broad characteristics, and the indicators in Table 4.2, can you identify the states?

Table 4.2 A Quiz: Identify the State

Indicator, NFHS-5 (2019-21)	*State 1*	*State 2*	*State 3*
Public Services			
Households with an improved source of drinking water[1] (per cent)	99	98	91
Institutional delivery (per cent)[2]	76	94	92
Children's Health			
Stunted children, height-for-age (per cent)[3]	43	39	31
Anaemic children aged 6-59 months (<11.0 g/dl) (per cent)[4]	69	80	64
Status of Women			
Low Body Mass Index (BMI) (<18.5 kg/m2) (per cent)[5]	26	25	21
Owner of the house (alone or with someone)[6]	54	42	43
Answer key to the quiz	Bihar	Gujarat	Odisha

Source: NFHS-5 [1]Table 2.7, [2]Table 8.31, [3]Table 10.2, [4]Table 10.13, [5]Table 10.20.1 and [6]Table 14.23

Map 4.1 Proportion (%) of children who are stunted, 2019-21

Children aged 0-59 months

< 31   31–36   ≥ 36

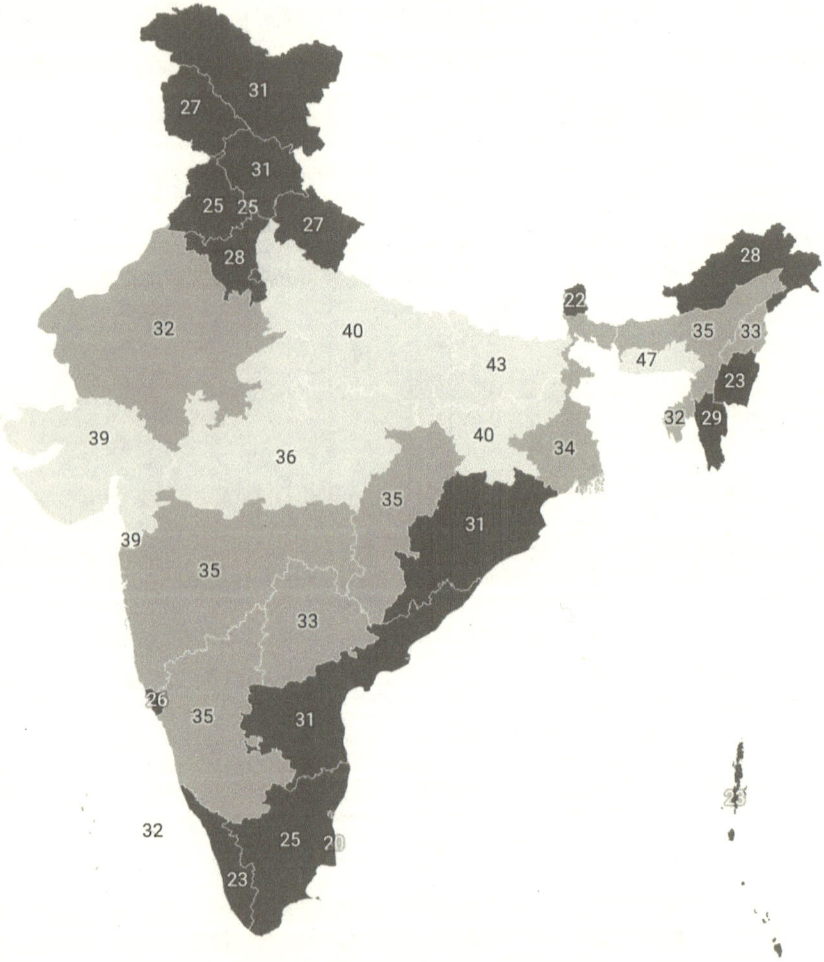

Children are considered stunted if their height for age is two standard deviations from the child growth norms of the WHO. At the all India level, 36% children are stunted. The states in the lightest shade of grey have stunting levels equal to or higher than the India average.

Source: National Family Health Survey, 2019-21 • Map data: © OSM • Created with Datawrapper

Map 4.2 Proportion of children (%) who were given eggs on the previous day or night, 2019–21

Children aged 6-30 months

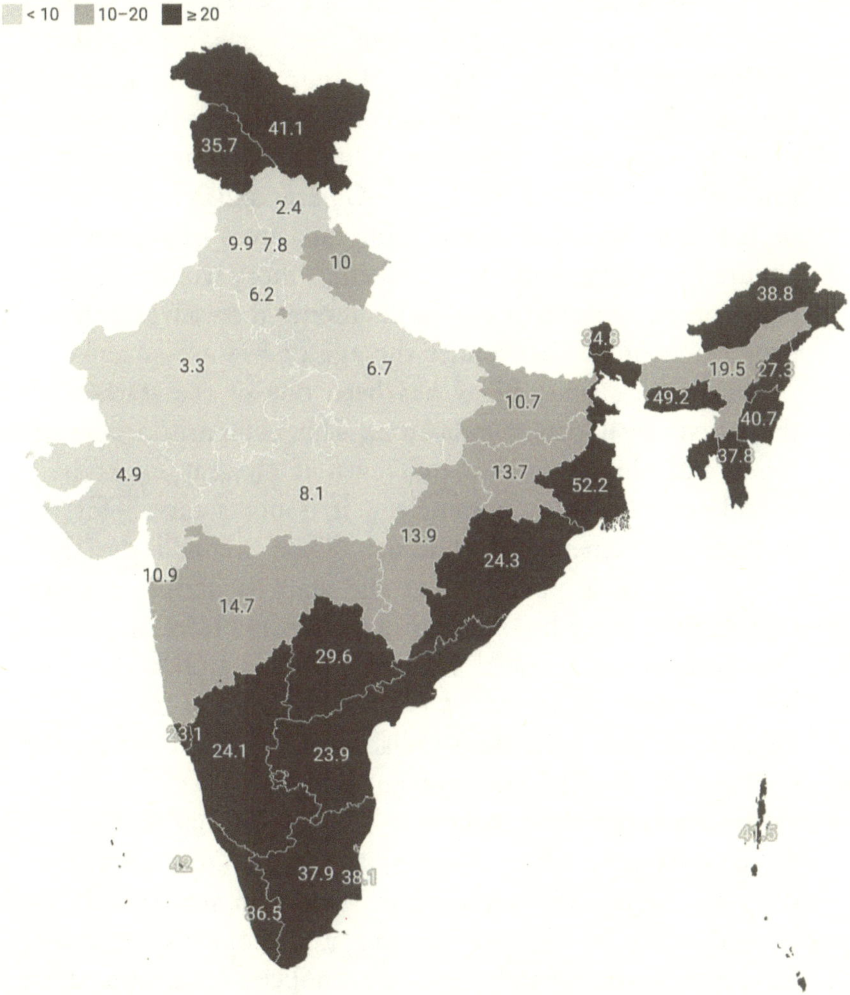

Source: Calculated from the National Family Health Survey (NFHS 5), 2019-21 • Map data: © OSM • Created with Datawrapper

The three states are Bihar, Gujarat and Odisha (see last row). Out of 127 indicators in the NFHS, Gujarat outperformed Bihar on eighty-one indicators. Public health services in Gujarat, for example, are better: three out of four women received four antenatal check-ups, near-universal institutional deliveries and child mortality was lower in Gujarat. But on other key outcome indicators—proportion of under-nourished or anaemic children, full immunisation rate, women with low BMI, etc.—Gujarat and Bihar are more or less indistinguishable. On some indicators of women and children's wellbeing, Bihar does better: more women in Bihar enjoy property rights, use mobile phones themselves, a lower proportion of children under the age of five are anaemic.

For a long time, Bihar has been one of the states with the worst development indicators. This comparison between Bihar and Gujarat shows that even if Gujarat might be a model state on other parameters, it is not a model for the welfare of women and children. When we add the third 'model' (there is poverty, but the state is active in social policies), the story becomes more interesting. Here, it appears that proactive state social policy for women and children can help overcome the obstacles posed by poverty. Compared to Gujarat, in the third state Odisha (in the last column) the situation of children and women is better.

Under-nutrition in India is a serious issue, one that affects the coming generation; and despite rapid GDP growth over the past twenty years, the improvement in this sphere has been dismal. To improve children and women's outcomes, special focus on strengthening social policies targeted to them is necessary. Gujarat's outcomes reported in Table 4.2 show that relying on GDP growth is unlikely to yield results. Other states, including Odisha, Tamil Nadu, Kerala and Himachal Pradesh, appear to have understood this.

The Role of ICDS

The services delivered through the Integrated Child Development Services (ICDS) scheme are designed keeping in mind the factors that matter for better nutrition, especially the intergenerational aspect of under-nutrition and the need to think more broadly. The National Food Security Act 2013 includes two programmes for children—ICDS scheme for children up to six years of age and their mothers, and the Mid-Day Meal (MDM) Scheme for school-going children; and one for pregnant and lactating mothers (Pradhan Mantri Matru Vandana Yojana).

The ICDS scheme was launched in 1975, but its performance in most states was indifferent for many years (see Maps 4.3-4.5). Its implementation was fuelled by two Supreme Court directives in 2001 and 2006, which paved the way for more Anganwadis to be opened, and established ICDS services as entitlements for women and children.

According to government norms, for every 1000 people, there should be one Anganwadi.[21] Generally, each village has one or two Anganwadis. Six important services are provided for children by the ICDS scheme. These include supplementary nutrition for children, nutrition and health education for women and adolescent girls, pre-school education, immunisation, growth monitoring (i.e. weight and height monitoring) and health referrals (e.g., if a child is not growing well, referring them to a doctor).

Anganwadis are for children below six years of age. Children aged three to six years (pre-school children) are expected to go to the Anganwadi daily. Every Anganwadi across the country is supposed to have an Anganwadi worker and a helper, but finding vacancies is not uncommon. The Anganwadi helper helps the Anganwadi worker bring the children daily, cook food and care for them. The Anganwadi worker has the primary responsibility for pre-school education, coordinating with the Auxilliary Nurse and Midwife (ANM) for basic immunisation and other services.

Pre-school children are to be given cooked food as supplementary nutrition at the Anganwadi. Initially, there was a provision to give food to children once during their 4-6 hour stay. Recently, many states (Odisha, Gujarat, Himachal Pradesh, Telangana, etc., to name a few) have introduced breakfast when they arrive, along with hot cooked food around lunch time. Providing breakfast on arrival attracts children to the Anganwadi and lunch after a few hours, helps to keep them there. This helps the Anganwadi worker to conduct pre-school education activities.

Pre-schoolers stay at the Anganwadi for 4-6 hours (the duration varies from state to state, and can be considerably less in the states where the scheme is not implemented well) during which they are taught how to count, read letters, hand-eye coordination games and so on. For example, in one Anganwadi in Chhattisgarh, the Anganwadi worker had drawn the outline of a flower on the ground, in the soil, and gave small pebbles or tamarind seeds to the children. The children were tasked with arranging the pebbles/seeds along the outline of the flower. Children are also given the task of colouring letters and other drawings. Thus, children are taught through play and drawings. The syllabus includes songs and poems also. A less appreciated aspect of this is that the children who come to the Anganwadi learn to be without their mothers, to do their own odd chores (eating, drinking, sleeping), socialise with other children and interact with strangers, etc. These social skills prepare them for schooling.

Take-home rations (THR) are distributed on a weekly or

monthly basis for children aged six months to three years ('toddlers') and to pregnant and lactating women. THR is supposed to comprise of calorie dense dry rations that can be prepared at home. In many states, they may also get vaccinated at the Anganwadi.

The ICDS scheme is well-rounded, designed keeping in mind the inseparable needs of both mother and child in that phase of life. Medical and nutritional research shows that the first 1000 days (from the period from the womb) are very important for a child's nutrition. If the child is not protected from under-nutrition in the first few years, the chances of subsequent efforts being successful are lower. This explains why the ICDS is important—it is the only major programme that is aimed at children in that critical age group.

Ground Reality of Anganwadis

Between 2004 to 2019-21, the ICDS scheme has seen many improvements—access to Anganwadis has increased (in 2004, the nearest Anganwadi for a quarter of habitations was more than 1 km away; that went down to 14 per cent in 2014) and a daily routine is visible in many states. Just as one is used to seeing school-going children from 7-9 a.m., one can see these pre-schoolers heading towards the Anganwadi. Many states have started giving uniforms to Anganwadi children to impart seriousness to the pre-school education component of the ICDS; it is increasingly viewed as more than a 'child-minding' or supplementary food facility.

In 2014, we visited the Anganwadi in Tasarda village in Odisha's Mayurbhanj district for a survey. The government-appointed Auxilliary Nurse and Midwife (ANM) was there that day for 'Mamata Diwas', the day to provide Ante-Natal Care (ANC) services to pregnant and post-natal care to lactating mothers. ANC services include a general check-up, with some blood tests, measuring their blood pressure (BP), weight, etc. As soon as the ANM started checking one woman's BP with her instrument, the young children of the Anganwadi started playing nurse. One child made a small fist with their hand, and started pumping an imaginary BP instrument, as the ANMs do. After a few seconds, the child made a '*phisss*' sound (the sound a BP instrument makes when pressure is released) and then they all started giggling. We learned an important lesson that day—that Mamata Diwas was a regular activity at the Anganwadi and that the ANM has a fixed vaccination schedule for every village, so much so that the children had learned to imitate the government nurse (ANM).

Broadly speaking, the first decade in the period (2004-2014) saw improvement in infrastructure and there was some focus on quality, i.e., 'Universalisation with Quality' (Drèze 2006). The next decade (2014-2024) has been marked by a perceptible decrease in the Central government's commitment to the programme and possibly greater ownership by many state governments.

In 2004, the 'Focus on Children Under Six' (FOCUS) survey was conducted in six states. During the Survey, two types of states were evident in the country: where Anganwadis were 'active' (Tamil Nadu, Maharashtra and Himachal Pradesh), and where they were 'dormant' (Rajasthan, Uttar Pradesh and Chhattisgarh) and where the programme was running in minimalist mode. The potential of Anganwadis was clearly visible in active states—provision of nutrition, some learning activities, Anganwadi workers and helpers to look after them, regular monitoring of their health and growth. In the dormant states too mothers reported that they valued them and wanted steps to be taken to make Anganwadis active.

In 2014, the Anganwadis covered in the 2004 FOCUS Survey were revisited. During the revisit, many signs of improvement were evident: in 2004, only one-third of Anganwadis had their own buildings; that proportion increased to 87 per cent in 2014. Where earlier only 60 per cent of children were going to Anganwadis regularly, in 2014, this figure was 81 per cent (Centre for Equity Studies 2016).

While conducting the PEEP Survey in 2013 (Drèze and Khera 2017), the Odisha Survey in 2014, and then the JABS Survey in 2019, we also surveyed Anganwadis. Our own surveys also show signs of Anganwadis becoming vibrant spaces.

Table 4.3 shows the improvement in service delivery at Anganwadis between 2005-06 and 2019-21, using data from the NFHS. In 2005-6, only 17 per cent of breastfeeding mothers were getting 'any' services from Anganwadis; by 2019-21, their number increased to 66 per cent. (Note that the 2019-21 round of the NFHS coincided with COVID-19, when Anganwadis were closed for a long time, so the NFHS-5 figure might be the lower-bound.) Between NFHS-4 and NFHS-5, there have been further improvements: supplementary nutrition for children (i.e., cooked meals or take-home rations) rose from 48 per cent to 62 per cent. Pre-school education increased from 38 per cent to 51 per cent. On all parameters, the ICDS looks more active than before.

There is still a lot of variation at the state level, even as the overall functionality has improved: Maps 4.3-4.5 (see Page 82-84) depict the proportion of women who reported that their child (aged 0-71 months) was getting 'any service' for the last three rounds of the NFHS. The states where less than

Table 4.3 Anganwadi Services Received by Mothers and Children

	NFHS-3 2005-6	*NFHS-4 2015-16*	*NFHS-5 2019-21*
Mothers who said that they get any ICDS service during[1]			
Breastfeeding	17	49	66
Pregnancy	23	54	70
Fully vaccinated 12-23 months old children[2]	44	62	77
Among children under the age of six years[3]			
Received Supplementary Nutrition	26	48	62
Received pre-school education	23	38	51
Received any service	33	54	68
Received all services	7	26	41

Source: [1]National Family Health Survey (NFHS), Table 9.25 NFHS-3, Table 9.20 NFHS-4 and NFHS-5; [2]Table 9.4 NFHS-3, NFHS-4 and NFHS-5; and [3]Table 9.24 NFHS-3, Table 9.18 NFHS-4 and NFHS-5.

40 per cent women reported getting any service are shown in the lightest shade of grey, and that area has now shrunk to just one state in the north-east. By 2019-21, in most states more than 60 per cent mothers reported getting some service.

What was the impact of these ICDS services? Jain (2015) used data from NFHS-3 (2005-6)—when the ICDS was still in sleep mode in many states—to ask whether the cooked food provided in the Anganwadi and nutrition received from take-home ration affected children's heights. If Anganwadis were working effectively, children should be taller. She finds that girls who received support from Anganwadis were taller than those who did not (the difference was 1cm and was statistically significant). Nandi et al. (2020) find that adults who were exposed to ICDS services in the first three years of their life attained higher levels of schooling. As Table 4.3 suggests, overall functionality of ICDS has improved considerably over the past decade, so now is a good time for such research.

Where Does the Problem Lie?

The ICDS scheme has provided us with the 'infrastructure' to reach women and children and yet their nutrition indicators remain poor. There can be three possible answers for this: the low political priority accorded to women (and children); budgetary squeeze; and neglect of frontline workers' issues.

Political Neglect: Bangladesh vs India

One clue to the answer can be gleaned by comparing India with its neighbour, Bangladesh. The slow progress in India on child nutrition is even starker when we do so. The main reason for comparing with Bangladesh is that over the last twenty years, there has been an impressive improvement in

Map 4.3 Proportion of children (%) who received any service from ICDS, 2005-06

As reported by mothers with children aged under six years

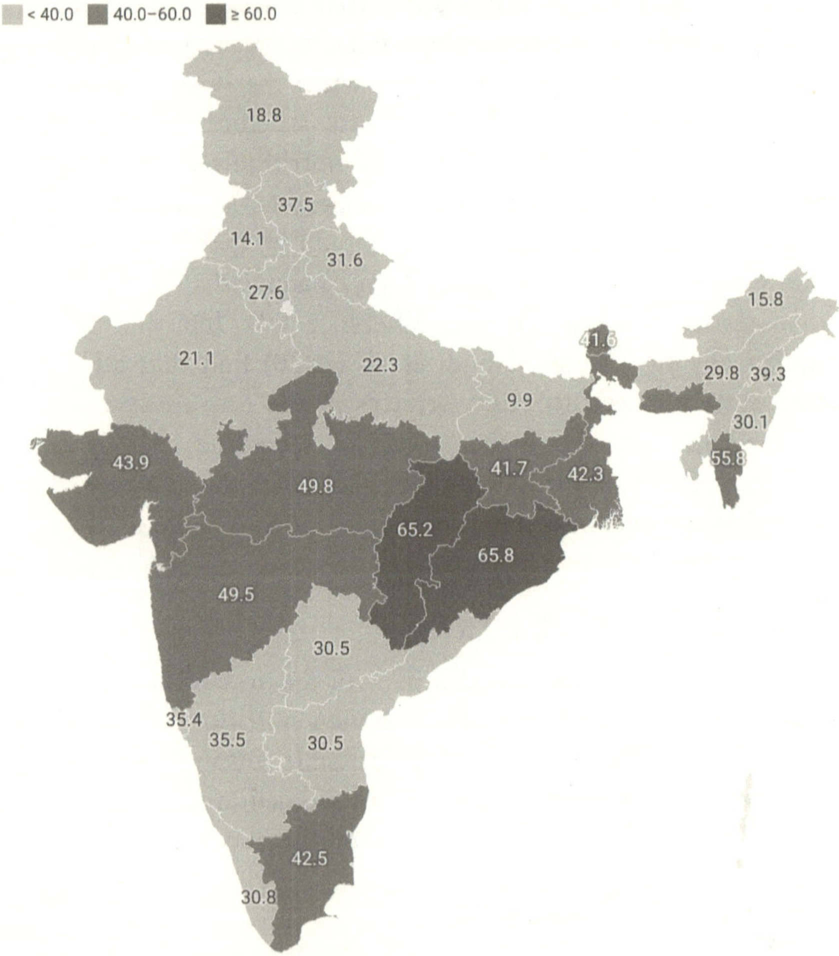

Source: Table 9.24, p. 261, NFHS-3 National Report • Created with Datawrapper

Map 4.4 Proportion of children (%) who received any service from ICDS, 2015-16

As reported by mothers with children aged under six years

< 40.0 | 40.0–60.0 | ≥ 60.0

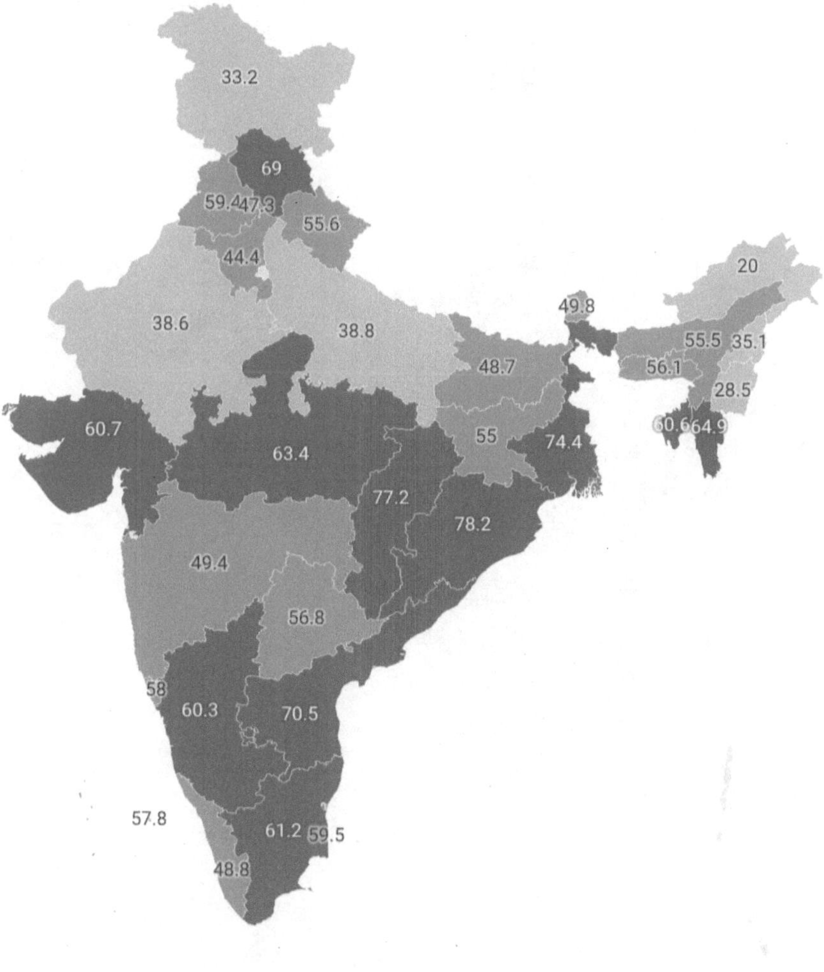

Source: Table 9.19, p. 288, NFHS-4 National Report • Created with Datawrapper

Map 4.5 Proportion of children (%) who received any service from ICDS, 2019-21

As reported by mothers with children aged under six years

< 40.0 40.0–60.0 ≥ 60.0

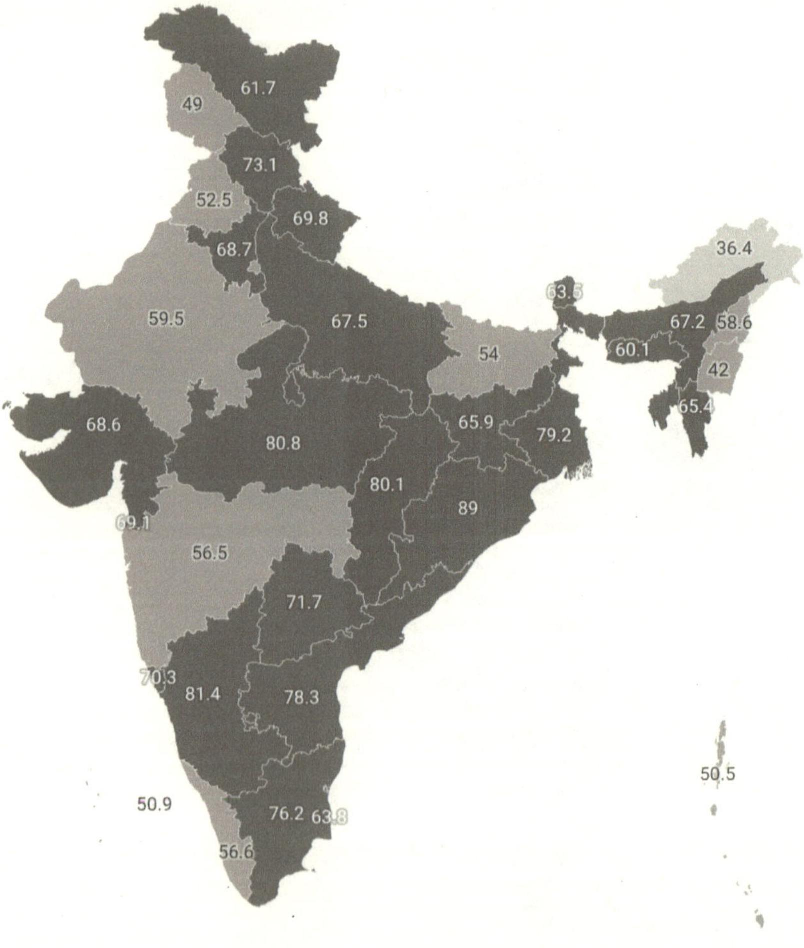

Source: Table 9.19, p. 368, NFHS-5 National Report • Map data: © OSM • Created with Datawrapper child-related indicators in Bangladesh (Drèze and Sen 2015). Glimpses of this improvement are shown in Table 4.4 below. Over the past decade, Bangladesh has been doing better than India. For example, on stunting and vaccination the situation in India in 2019-21 was similar to Bangladesh's achievements in 2015: 77 per cent of children in India were fully vaccinated in 2019-21, something Bangladesh achieved in 2015 itself. Today, 88 per cent of children in Bangladesh are fully vaccinated. These improvements in Bangladesh are especially noteworthy because they have managed to do this in spite of having, until 2018, a lower per capita GDP than India and apparent Islamic orthodoxy. In Bangladesh, the role of women's agency has been emphasised by several scholars (Kabeer 2024 and Hossain 2017).

In India, children are not a political priority. Here again the contrast with Bangladesh is illustrative. Chart 4.1 plots the count of three words ('child', 'children' and 'childhood'), in the budget speeches of the Finance Ministers of India and Bangladesh from 2004-5 to 2024-2025. In the first few years, there was no difference between India and Bangladesh, but after 2008-9, children began to get more attention in Bangladesh's budget speeches. Far from 'putting your money where your mouth is', in India we don't even talk about children.

Those in India who are concerned about the neglect of hunger and nutrition-related issues, are often compelled to rely on media 'pegs' such as the release of the Global Hunger Index (GHI) to draw media attention to issues of children's wellbeing. Sadly, only one-two such 'pegs' are available each year. Even without relying on a questionable GHI, the problem of under-nutrition is more than apparent (Khera 2021).

Table 4.4 India and Bangladesh

	Bangladesh		*India*	
	2015	*2022*	*2015-16*	*2019-21*
Any type of anaemia (children 6-59 months old)	44[1]	43[1]	58[4]	67[4]
Stunting (less than 2SD)	33[1]	24[1]	38[4]	36[4]
Fully immunised children 12-23 months	78[2]	88[3]	62[5]	77[5]
Exclusive breastfeeding for first six months	55[1]	63[1]	55[5]	64[5]

Source: [1]World Bank (World Development Indicators); [2]Government of Bangladesh 2016, 139; [3]Khanam and Jahan 2024; [4]See Table 3.1; [5]Table 9.4 NFHS-4 and NFHS-5; NFHS-5, 377.

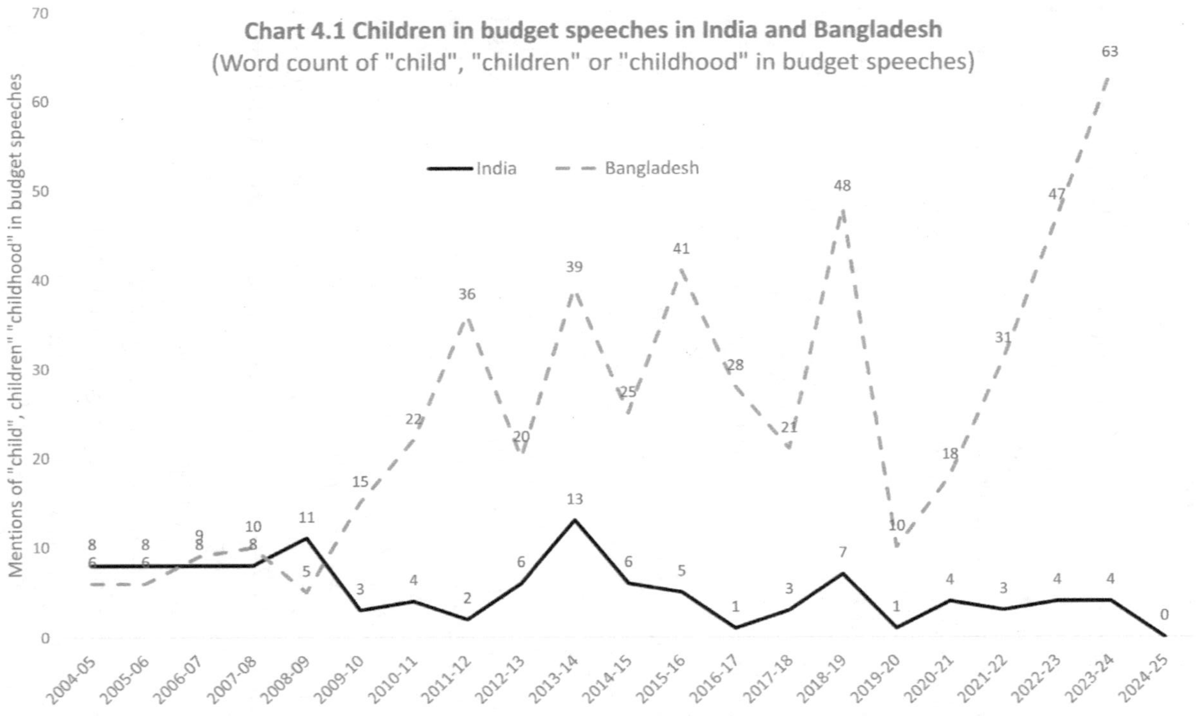

Chart 4.1 Children in budget speeches in India and Bangladesh
(Word count of "child", "children" or "childhood" in budget speeches)

Source: Budget speeches, various years. **Note**: For both countries, mentions in the description of personal life experiences (e.g., in some budget speeches referring to PM Sheikh Hasina), annexures, sub-headings in boxes, table of contents, ministry names are not included in the word counts.

Consequences of Low Budgets in India

In a world where children matter, the logical consequence would have been for the government to allocate more for the ICDS in the budget that was presented two months after the sobering NFHS-5 results were declared. Instead, in the Union Budget for 2021-22, the budget for the ICDS which provides essential and time-bound services for mothers and children was cut further.

One could argue that the low budgets for children are a consequence of the low political priority accorded to them. Take three important Central schemes for women and children together: the Pradhan Mantri Matru Vandana Yojana, the ICDS scheme, and the Mid-Day Meal (MDM) scheme. They are part of the National Food Security Act 2013 but are under-funded. Chart 3.2 in the previous chapter shows the extent to which PMMVY is under-funded. In recent rejigging, other schemes were merged with the ICDS budget head, so comparing directly with previous budgets is not straightforward. In real terms, the Central budgets for the MDM scheme for school-going children and the ICDS fell by about 40 per cent in 2023-24, compared to 2014-15, according to estimates by economist Jean Drèze. As a percentage of GDP, it declined in this period (from 0.15 per cent to 0.07 per cent), although one expects that as a country's GDP grows, such spending will increase.

The retreat of the Union government can only partially be explained by the changes resulting from the implementation of the 14th Finance Commission that changed the Centre-State funding pattern, and increased the state's contribution to programmes such as the ICDS. Indeed, the total expenditure (Centre and state combined) does make up to some extent for the lower Central budgets. Even so, states are dependent on the Centre for devolution of funds. They might be deprived of their legitimate share of resources by the Centre, either due to the delayed release of their share in GST collections or due to the increased use of cess by the Centre (revenues generated through a cess are not shared with states). Thus, while the obligations of states have increased after the 14th Finance Commission, their sources of raising revenues directly have shrunk. The dependency on the Centre, and resulting uncertainty, has squeezed the spending capacity of states.

Moreover, there are issues related to the flow of funds and paperwork in accessing budgets. The flow of funds from the Centre to the states, and from there to the Anganwadis is not smooth and this causes serious delays and disruptions in these essential services. The problem of low budgets is exacerbated by misplaced spending priorities (e.g., excessive focus on digitalisation) of the meagre resources.

Frontline Workers' Issues

Take Anganwadi Workers (AWW) and Helpers (AWH). This team of two helps young children get accustomed to sitting and eating on their own, being without their mother for a few hours. Gradually, the number of states where they engage children in playful learning activities such as rhymes, arts and crafts, counting, etc., has increased (HardWork NoPay 2019).

Chart 4.2 plots the monthly salary of MDM cooks, Anganwadi workers (AWW) and Anganwadi helpers (AWH) in 2023 on the x-axis. On the y-axis, female wages for one category of agricultural work (sowing) are plotted. Agricultural wages, such as wages for sowing, are often treated as the 'reservation wage' (i.e., the wage below which people would refuse to accept work). Each triangle is a combination of AWW salaries (x-axis) and female wages for sowing (y-axis) for any one state. Similarly, each dot (dash) is a combination of AWH (MDM cooks') salary and the agricultural wage. When a triangle, dot or dash falls on the 45-degree line, it means that AWWs/AWHs/MDM cooks in that state are getting the equivalent of the agricultural wage rate. Most triangles (AWW salaries vs sowing wages) are below the 45-degree line, i.e., they earn more than the agricultural wage in most states. Conversely, if a triangle/dot/dash is above the 45-degree line, the salary for those frontline workers is less than the agricultural wage. This is true for AWHs (and MDM cooks) in all states. The only two states where the salary of an AWH is comparable to the agricultural wage are Telangana and Madhya Pradesh.[22]

The problem of low salaries is compounded by stagnating salaries. The last increase in the Central contribution to the AWW/AWH's salaries was in 2018, i.e., seven years ago and the increment was between Rs 750-1500 over the Central contribution that ranged between Rs 2250-4500 (Government of India 2024).[23] Interestingly, the government does have a system for formal government employees. The 'Dearness Allowance' (DA) compensates for potential loss of purchasing power due to inflation. Besides this, salaries of government employees increase (in real terms) every few years through the recommendation of Pay Commissions. Neither of these principles are applicable to most frontline workers.[24] One example of wage indexation in the informal sector is that of NREGA wages. Wages are increased each year and though they lead to very small gains (e.g., in 2024, the increase was between Rs 7-34 per day), it shows that it is possible to index salaries of informal sector workers.

When wage compensation is not fair, it hurts everyone: if the workers are not happy, they are likely to shirk, not work diligently and protest. For years, every few months, AWWs, AWHs and ASHA workers have been forced to stage sit-ins and demonstrations for their entitlements in one state or another. Protests to demand better wages disrupt the smooth functioning of Anganwadis, school meals, etc. Some workers find ways to 'compensate' themselves, e.g. by indulging in corrupt practices. There are some exceptions—in Tamil Nadu, for example, Anganwadi workers and helpers are treated as regular government employees and, like other workers, have provisions for pension and maternity leave.

Disruption in the flow of funds also means that cash may be unavailable to buy food supplies (such as pulses, oil, eggs, etc.). Reports of Anganwadi workers spending money from their own pockets to ensure regular meals to children appear intermittently. Both the Centre and the states are responsible for these issues. The bottom line is that a low and irregularly paid workforce cannot be expected to function effectively (Sinha et al. 2021).

The political neglect of women and children, partly reflected in low allocations in the Central budget, pose a serious challenge to realising the potential of the ICDS.

New Challenges

Another worrying development is that meagre social spending may be funnelled back to corporates and philanthropic-capitalists. This is perhaps best illustrated by the central government's flagship nutrition programme called 'Prime Minister's Overarching Scheme for Holistic Nutrition' (POSHAN Abhiyaan), launched in March 2018 (Government of India 2022).

In theory, POSHAN Abhiyaan includes some useful interventions, such as mass awareness, education and

Chart 4.2 Frontline workers are poorly paid

Frontline workers salaries compared with female wages in sowing

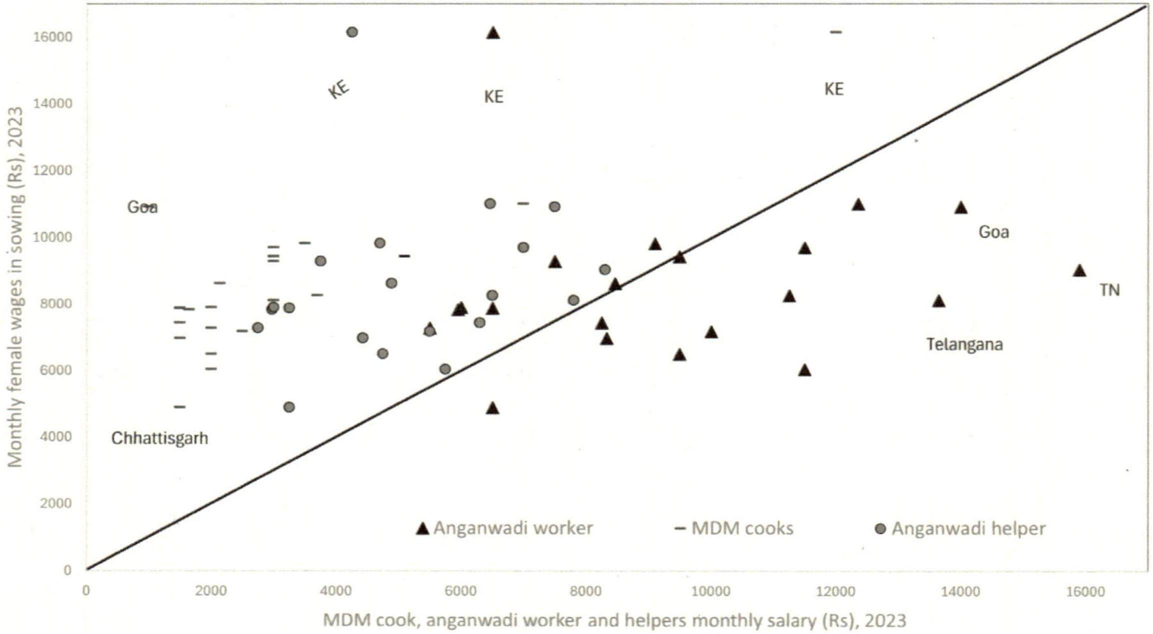

Sources: Labour bureau for sowing wages (https://labourbureau.gov.in/rural-wages); Salaries of anganwadi workers and helpers, Rajya Sabha Question No. 1152 (13.12.2023) and No. 633 (7.2.24). The salaries of AWWs, AWHs and MDM cooks include state top-ups to the Central contibution.

behaviour change. There is no doubt that we need to do much more about nutrition education in India and in principle, POSHAN Abhiyaan can help achieve this. For instance, six months of exclusive breastfeeding is strongly recommended for optimal growth, development and health of a child. To achieve this, the best strategy is to improve awareness of its importance, and encourage behavioural change. Yet, between 2015-16 and 2019-21, the proportion of women breastfeeding exclusively for the first six months improved only marginally (from 55 per cent to 64 per cent).

In fact, on the ground, POSHAN Abhiyaan was primarily about giving smartphones to Anganwadi workers with ICDS-CAS (Common Application Software developed in collaboration with BMGF) installed on them. Have these smartphones helped or hindered their work? Did it facilitate more reliable surveillance? For example, at its launch in Gujarat, a Gujarati newspaper gave ICDS-CAS front-page space: the chief minister tried calling a handful of numbers, but none of them responded in the first attempt. The news item projected Anganwadi workers as negligent towards their duties. No one bothered to find out why they didn't answer the phone. Were they busy with their duties, or due to a phone malfunction, or if they were indeed snoozing, as implied?

Some ground reports suggest that phones and tablets were not used for record keeping for several months in 2020 due to server and internet problems. Software design was centralised—the result is that it does not meet the needs of all states. For example, every state has different opening hours, menus, vaccination procedures, etc., but such state-wise features were not possible to capture with a centralised software. The Annual Reports of the Ministry of Women and Child Development do not mention the ICDS-CAS after 2019-20; instead, 'Rapid Reporting System', 'POSHAN tracker' and 'Real Time Monitoring' take its place. We do not know much about the usefulness of this intervention.

The nutrition agenda seems to be increasingly driven by BMGF, UNICEF, IFPRI and other international agencies. UNICEF now raises funding from corporates and philanthropist-capitalists. In India, according to its website, it partners with Johnson & Johnson, Unilever, Louis Vuitton, CII and NASSCOM, among others. While corporates and philanthropist-capitalists can increase the availability of funds, they also use it to advance their own agendas. In fact, UNICEF's 'Impact4Nutrition' platform openly invites private sector participation in the nutrition campaign as 'Good Nutrition is Good for Business'. Among the 'Direct Gains for companies' listed there are recognition as 'nutrition champion', 'enhanced relations with government' and 'economic growth'. One way to understand this is that such collaborative initiatives open the backdoor for these companies to influence government policies in their favour.

What was earlier shunned on account of a 'conflict of interest' is today reinventing itself in the form of a 'win-win' formula (i.e., both sides will benefit). This is also evident in the POSHAN Abhiyaan. More than 70 per cent of its budget was spent on community events and Information and Communication Technology (ICT)-enabled real time monitoring through the ICDS-CAS software (Accountability Initiative 2021). That is, some of the expenditure made in the name of children ended up in the pockets of these companies as well.

In December 2017, Rs 9000 crore was allocated for ICDS-CAS, half from the Government of India and the other half as

World Bank loan. This could have been spent on interventions whose health and nutrition benefits are well established: e.g., giving nutritious food to children, hiring more ICDS staff (vacancies in Anganwadis ranged from 6-8 per cent to 25 per cent among Child Development Programme Officers, CDPOs), better salaries, and so on. Instead, it was spent on interventions whose benefits are unclear: smartphones, software, and holding gatherings during 'nutrition month' for 'behaviour change.' This Rs 9000 crore budget could have bought 150 eggs a year for the roughly 10 crore children enrolled in Anganwadis.

Window of Opportunity for Children's Policies

There is one clear message from a vast literature on children—that investments in the early years of a child have lifelong effects on a person's wellbeing. Later life interventions can also help, but may not be as effective as investments in the earlier years. If we ignore today, we will repent at leisure.

The ICDS scheme—in its design—does exactly what the research suggests—provide well-rounded nutrition, health and educational support to young children. In India, contrary to the policy message that the research conveys and the ICDS attempts to put into practice, children below six years of age are not on the radar of policymakers. The lack of any vision at the Centre for children manifests itself in many ways: budget cuts, intermittent suggestions of replacing THR with pre-packed food or cash, frequent policy changes without much substance to give the impression that the ICDS is being taken seriously, a data collection overdrive for real-time data ostensibly for monitoring but in fact either not using the data or accumulating junk, inaction on corruption. Some of these threaten to jeopardise the existing system. Meanwhile, creative thinking in a handful of states shows that there are low-hanging fruit (e.g., more nutritious food such as eggs, uniforms) that can make a difference to the functionality of the ICDS. The Central government has stubbornly refused to engage with these lessons from the states.

5

MID-DAY MEALS

Much More Than Food

Everyone should visit a government school at mealtime. My own experience of mid-day meals in rural areas goes back to 2002 when government schools in Rajasthan began serving cooked meals for the first time. The Supreme Court had issued an order in the 'Right to Food' case directing all states to provide *cooked* mid-day meals in government and government-aided schools. In Rajasthan, that order had been taken seriously, and when term opened in 2002, schools began providing cooked food.

Before the November 2001 interim order of the Supreme Court, cooked meals were served only in a handful of states, including Tamil Nadu and Gujarat. Cooked food was also provided in the tribal/scheduled areas of Odisha and Madhya Pradesh. In most states, especially in the north, the norm was to distribute dry rations only (3 kg of rice or wheat per month, if the child's attendance was more than 80 per cent) in lieu of mid-day meals.

The times were such that the Rajasthan state government felt compelled to follow the Court's order (Bihar took a few years to comply with it), but the administration had not prepared much for it. When schools reopened, most schools did not have kitchen sheds, cooks and helpers had not been appointed in the schools, no arrangements for fuel wood and water had been made, there were no utensils to cook and serve food in most places.

Despite the chaos, in July 2002, primary school children in Rajasthan started getting mid-day meals. By way of providing children a cooked meal, they began by serving 'ghooghri', a preparation of boiled wheat, sometimes sweet, sometimes salty. The shortage of kitchens, utensils, water, wood was made up by the teachers and the children themselves. In spite of the chaos and the makeshift arrangements, a memorable image lodged itself in my mind: of children licking their fingers with their shining eyes. The joy evident on their faces made it clear that this was a much-needed intervention.

Many years later, I had a similar experience in Surguja district (Chhattisgarh) in June 2019. I asked children at a government school, 'Who will eat eggs if they are provided?' Again the same big shining eyes, heads nodding excitedly in agreement greeted me.

A lot has changed in those intervening seventeen years (2002-2019) in the Mid-Day Meal (MDM) scheme. More or less everywhere cooking arrangements are in place: cooking sheds or kitchens, utensils for cooking and serving, other basic infrastructure (drinking water, gas cylinders in some states) and cooks and helpers have been appointed. Now, if the school does not serve food for a few days, or if there is a shortage of cooking utensils or plates to eat from, or if a cook has not been appointed, it is treated as an aberration and is likely to be in the news.

Where in 2002 'ghooghri' was fed to children in Rajasthan as their mid-day meal, today most states have tasty and

Map 5.1 States providing eggs in the mid-day meal scheme, 2023-24

No provision for eggs · Partial/Announced only/Disputed · 1-5 eggs provided per week*

**The total number of eggs provided per week varies by region: Andhra Pradesh, Tamil Nadu, and Lakshadweep provide five eggs per week; Telangana and Goa provide three eggs; and Jharkhand, Odisha, and parts of Assam provide two eggs. In some areas of Assam, eggs are provided inconsistently, and provision is disputed in parts of Goa. In all other states, one egg per week is given wherever it is provided. This map was adapted from an earlier version by Swati Narayan and updated based on information from the MDM Poshan Minutes, 2023-24.*

Source: Information obtained from the government website, https://pmposhan.education.gov.in/ see statistical appendix • Map data: © OSM • Created with Datawrapper nutritious items on their menus. In the southern states like Tamil Nadu, Andhra Pradesh, Kerala, and even poorer eastern states of Odisha, Jharkhand and West Bengal, eggs are on the menu (Map 5.1). In spite of many improvements, more than twenty years after the Supreme Court's orders, the battle for children's right to food and right to education remains a challenge.

Mid-Day Meals and Education

Mid-day meals are closely linked to children's right to education. Meals help three aspects of schooling: enrolment, attendance and learning and socialisation. More than anyone else, perhaps poor parents understand the value of school education for their children. The promise of one meal can make school an even more attractive option and help ensure enrolment of the child.

If children are not treated kindly in school, then persuading them to go to school can be a task in itself. For many children, school is a place of joy, freedom and learning, while there are others who may not have a pleasant schooling experience—they are made to sit in the back, or asked to clean up, or subjected to caste abuse in other ways. In such an adverse environment, a hot, tasty, nutritious meal at school can help children see a more appealing side of the school and encourage them to attend regularly.

Children studying in government schools tend to be from poorer families. Many used to be sent off hungry in the morning, and in the absence of the MDM they only ate after they went home after school. It is quite evident that very little learning is possible on an empty stomach. If children are fed at school, they are likely to be able to concentrate better. From this perspective, the mid-day meal scheme is an integral part of education.

Several studies have documented these three effects of MDM on school education. Jayaraman and Simroth (2015) documented significant effects on enrolment between 2002-2004, the early years of the transition to cooked meals. Afridi (2011) found that as a result of the transition from dry rations to cooked meals, daily participation of children was positively affected and the effects were larger for girls. Enrolment too was higher, though the effects were not statistically significant. Chakraborty and Jayaraman (2019) document its positive effect on reading and math scores; Afridi et al. (2013) find that learning efforts were higher among those children who had eaten the school meal in Delhi's schools.

If nutritious meals are served, the MDM programme can also address under-nutrition. Many states have been providing nutrient-dense food items such as eggs, peanuts, black gram, soya bean, etc. Afridi (2010) found that among primary school participants, daily protein deficiency decreased by 100 per cent, calorie deficiency by almost 30 per cent and iron deficiency went down by 10 per cent. Singh et al. (2014) find that in Andhra Pradesh, the MDM protected children's nutrition outcomes (captured by anthropometric indicators) from the adverse effects of a severe drought.

A few years ago, a colleague mentioned how in their decision on which (private) school to send their child to, whether the school served a mid-day meal was a crucial factor. Not only for their own convenience (both parents work) but also because when children carry lunch from home, they compare with others, and that can have an adverse effect on children. For example, if a child takes an egg sandwich, and another has instant noodles (say, Maggi), then children will be attracted to instant noodles, even though it is less nutritious. Moreover, the MDM scheme can be used to impart nutrition education.

When it's time to eat, children first wash their hands, their plates, sit in row (or line up) to be served, sit together and eat. Each of these is important: handwashing before eating is a simple yet essential health and hygiene lesson. The importance of the habit of forming a queue cannot be over-emphasised in India. If children belonging to different social groups sit and eat together, it helps to break down social (especially caste) barriers. That, in turn, is an important step towards the creation of a democratic society. The MDM scheme can, thus, contribute significantly to enhancing social cohesion.

The Mid-Day Meal scheme has an important gender dimension. Sending a young child to school in the morning can be an event in some homes. It is not easy for parents (mothers tend to have this responsibility) to get their child ready for school first thing in the morning. Waking the child up, bathing and grooming them, either feeding or packing some food—each can be a task in itself. For working mothers, mid-day meals at school can lighten the burden of their daily morning chores and can support them.

Further, almost all cooks and helpers employed by the mid-day meal scheme are women. Administrative data presented in Table A4 (Appendix I) suggests that in all states barring Bihar (63 per cent) and Gujarat (69 per cent), the share of female cooks and helpers is more than 80 per cent. Contrary to international trends, the participation of women in the workforce in India had been declining rather than increasing over time; it remains low even today. In such a situation, the fact that the MDM scheme provides employment to roughly 20 lakh women across the country is noteworthy.

In many developed and developing countries of the world (e.g., Finland, Brazil) mid-day meals are provided free of cost to all school children. In addition, a mid-day meal is provided in many countries, but to be paid for according to the financial condition of parents. This includes countries like the USA, UK and France. The National Food Security Act (NFSA) passed in India in 2013 included the MDM scheme. India is not the only country where such meals are a legal right. For example, in Japan, a School Meal Law was introduced in 1954 and is included in the 1948 Education Act in Finland (*The Economist* 2022, World Population Review 2024). In spite of this, in India, even today questions about the usefulness of this scheme remain and it is sometimes referred to disparagingly.

Part of the reason is that much needs to be done to improve its implementation. The scheme caught international media attention in 2013 when children died in Bihar (edible oil was packed in pesticide bins due to lack of a kitchen and cooking utensils in school). There is a steady trickle of media reports of bad menus, children falling sick after consuming the MDM at school and so on. These incidents tend to overshadow the fact that 10-12 crore children eat at school every day. It goes largely unnoticed and unappreciated by people and journalists.

A Short History

Tamil Nadu pioneered the scheme by serving cooked food in all schools. The first and short-lived attempt, on a much smaller scale, was made in the 1920s by the Justice Party. In the 1950s, Kamaraj resurrected the scheme. In 1982, the then chief minister, MG Ramachandran, stood firm despite widespread opposition and vociferous condemnation. The state remained focused on remedying the implementation issues that cropped up (Chawla 2014). Some other states followed suit: school meals began being served in Gujarat in 1984 and in the tribal areas of others (Madhya Pradesh, Odisha, etc.).

Based on these experiences, the Centre's Mid-day Meal Scheme, initiated in 1995, was intended to ensure that children get cooked food. Instead, for several years many states were giving 'dry rations' (uncooked grain) to children. If the child's attendance was 80 per cent, they were to be given 3 kg of food grains per month. Dry rations defeated the purpose of mid-day meals and in any case, fell prey to corruption in its distribution.

Table 5.1 Milestones in the Mid-day Meal (MDM) Scheme

Year	*Milestone*
1982	Mid-Meal Scheme in Tamil Nadu called 'Noon Meal' initiated
1984	MDM scheme begins in Gujarat
15 August 1995	Central government launches 'National Programme of Nutritional Support to Primary Education' for children of classes 1-5
28 November 2001	Supreme Court directs all states to serve cooked food
2009	MDMs extended to upper-primary children (classes 6-8), scheme renamed 'National Programme of Mid-Day Meals in Schools'
September 2013	National Food Security Act 2013 includes MDM scheme; provision of 450-700 calories and 12-20 grams of proteins
2021	Scheme renamed 'Pradhan Mantri Poshan Shakti Nirman' (PM Poshan)

Source: Government of India (2022)

After the Supreme Court's Interim Order in November 2001, there was some panic in most states. The Supreme Court ordered that cooked food would have to be given to all primary school children, by the time schools reopened the following year. It was a time when the administration was seemingly afraid of violating the Supreme Court's order.[25] The Right to Food Campaign played an important role in creating that kind of environment. In several parts of the country, organisations associated with the Campaign took on the responsibility of monitoring the implementation of the order, and where it was not being followed, they organised public protests. To comply with the Supreme Court order, many states started giving mid-day meals in a hurry. As noted in the opening paragraphs of this chapter, this often meant that even without basic infrastructure (kitchens, utensils, cooks, etc.), children began to be given something to eat.

At that time (in 2002), I undertook a small informal survey in Barmer (Rajasthan). The state government was not at all prepared—the school-teacher and children got together to prepare 'ghooghri'. Bad press about lack of facilities created pressure on the state government, and gradually systems began to be put in place—appointment of cooks and helpers, purchase of utensils, and later construction of kitchen, drinking water arrangements with the help of the Central government, etc. In some states like Bihar, it was not until 2007 that the order was implemented.

Among the 'first generation' implementation issues, regularity in serving meals was a big one. Between 2002-2012, a lot of progress was made in putting the basics in place so that meals become a part of the daily routine at school. Proper cooking arrangements, including basic facilities like firewood, water, utensils, cooking sheds gradually became the norm across all government schools. For example, according to administrative data, 29 per cent of schools in the country were using cooking gas in 2013; this increased to 80 per cent in 2021-22 (though administrative data needs to be taken with a pinch of salt). Public scrutiny increased—e.g., irregularity in serving MDMs tended to become 'news', creating enough local pressure to ensure compliance.

Initially, the mid-day meal scheme was limited to primary school children only (see Table 5.1). In the Union Budget 2008-09, it was extended to upper primary school children as well, i.e., upto Class 8. Since then, daily dietary and nutritional norms have been set according to the child's schooling level. For primary (upper primary) school children it is 100 (150) grams of cereals, 20 (30) grams of pulses, 50 (75) grams of vegetables and 5 (7.5) grams of oil daily. The NFSA 2013 provides for 450-700 kilo calories and 12-20 grams of protein per child. In some states, it has been extended to Class 10 from state resources and/or a breakfast/ snack is provided along with the main meal.

Apart from nutrition, serious caste issues were highlighted in the decade after the Supreme Court's 2001 order. There were two important aspects of caste issues: caste discrimination among children while eating and in the appointment of cooks and helpers. Many reports of discrimination against children emerged, including reports of children being made to sit according to caste, having separate plates, asking Dalit children to bring plates from home, having a separate pitcher for water, etc. (Thorat and Lee 2005) At some places, parents who consider themselves 'upper caste' also objected to their child sitting and eating with Dalit children.

Overt incidents of caste discrimination have surfaced in the appointment of cooks and helpers for the MDM scheme as well. People sometimes question the appointment of Dalit cooks (at times, the appointment of Muslims was also opposed on similar grounds). In 2004, the Supreme Court ruled that Dalits and Adivasis should get priority in the appointment of cooks and helpers.[26] Partly as a result of this order, administrative data suggests that 43 per cent of cooks and helpers are Dalits, Adivasis or from other minorities, a similar proportion are OBCs (42 per cent) and the rest (15 per cent) are from the general category. In 2023-24, the proportion of Dalits and Adivasis among cooks and helpers was less than their share in the population in only three Indian states. The three states are Himachal Pradesh, Uttarakhand and Rajasthan. Between 2013-14 and 2023-24, their share has increased in many states (Table A4).

It is not easy to determine how widespread such discrimination is. But since such issues have been in the news, it also suggests that people are raising their voice against it. In some places, after the incident came to light, the district collector intervened, went to the village, ate food prepared by Dalit cooks themselves to convince those who objected. If they did not agree, then it was also said that there should be no compulsion, their children should not eat in school, if they object to eating with children of other castes. Nevertheless, the fight against caste discrimination in the scheme is an on-going battle.

Issues of the Second Decade

A major issue in the second decade (since 2013) has been the nutritional value of the meal. In the first decade, neither the state governments nor the central governments were willing to spend much money on mid-day meals. Over time, in states that had initiated the mid-day meal scheme after the Supreme Court's direction, support increased.

In this context, it is important to note that the situation is not the same across the country. Some states were already ahead—e.g., apart from Tamil Nadu, the scheme had been doing well in undivided Andhra Pradesh and Kerala. The introduction of eggs in Bihar, Jharkhand and Odisha was partly a result of public pressure and the popularity of the scheme. For example, despite being among poorer states, the Odisha state government has been providing eggs twice a week. On 15 August 2014, Jitan Ram Manjhi, the then-Chief Minister of Bihar, announced that eggs would be served to children in Bihar.

On the other hand, the introduction of eggs has been opposed vehemently by a tiny segment of society in states like Madhya Pradesh, Chhattisgarh and Karnataka. Some oppose eggs because they are vegetarians—in Madhya Pradesh, for example, the opposition has come from members of the Jain community. It is worth remembering that Gandhiji had said that those who drink milk should not have an objection to unfertilised/sterile eggs. The result of the opposition is that eggs are no longer on the agenda in Madhya Pradesh.

Similarly, in Karnataka, intermittent efforts to introduce eggs were aborted due to vociferous opposition by an organisation named Akshaya Patra that supplied MDMs to government schools. Irrespective of which political party was in power, they were unwilling to stand up to the opposition. After years of the stalemate, in 2021, eggs were introduced on pilot basis in seven districts of North Karnataka (a dry and relatively poorer part of the state). Based on the success in those districts, the state government extended it to all districts in 2022.

In Chhattisgarh, there was an opening in 2019 when the Congress party came to power. When the state issued an order, there was opposition from Kabirpanthis. To circumvent those who opposed the policy, the state ordered that each Gram Panchayat pass a resolution on the introduction of eggs, and on the basis of that District Collectors were instructed to make funds available from their 'District Mineral Foundation Fund'. Thus, there was no provision for inclusion of eggs in the state budget and this has led to patchy implementation.

Many states of North India still lag in the provision of nutritious items such as eggs in the MDM scheme (see Map 5.1). For example, while eggs are included in the menu of mid-day meals in most states of the south and east, in Uttar Pradesh, Madhya Pradesh and Rajasthan, not only are eggs off the menu, they have also not been able to provide other affordable nutritious alternatives like 'chikki' (made with protein-rich peanuts and gur) or fruits such as guava, bananas, dates, etc. regularly.

Why the emphasis on eggs? Eggs can be considered a 'super food' from a nutritional point of view. Eggs have all the nutrients besides vitamin C. It is an especially rich source of protein which is very important for a child's growth, but is lacking in the Indian diet (see Map 4.2, Page 72). Milk, soybean nuggets, pulses are also protein-rich, but they pale in comparison to eggs.

Another advantage of eggs is that they have a long shelf life, especially compared to other protein-rich options like milk, where there is a fear of spoilage, especially in summer. In states where milk is provided, it is either as milk powder (e.g., Karnataka) or in tetrapacks (e.g., Gujarat). Eggs can survive longer without refrigeration. Milk and pulses etc. are also more prone to being diluted (by adding water to it). Eggs cannot be diluted. Bulk cooking eggs is easier too. Thus, eggs provide a practical option for good nutrition in rural areas.

Some oppose eggs for any child because not all children consider them a vegetarian item. Such a stand tends to ignore that no one is forcing a child to have eggs, and just as a policy of *force-feeding* eggs would be wrong, *forcefully* denying those who do eat them is wrong too.

Some years ago, in an Anganwadi in rural Bengaluru, I was told by the Anganwadi worker that Lingayat mothers from vegetarian families would request her (the Anganwadi worker) to ensure that their child gets an egg because it is something the mothers cannot feed their child at home. This gives hope that with better nutrition education, better sense will prevail. The breakthrough in its egg policy in 2021 in Karnataka may have had something to do with such wider acknowledgement of eggs as a good source of nutrition.

Losing the Plot

In the last ten years, India's MDM scheme could have been similar to that of a developed country like Japan, if it had political and administrative support. Unfortunately, the Central government's commitment has dipped perceptibly in the past decade. There were sharp cuts in the Union Budget in 2015-16: from Rs 13,215 crores to Rs 9145 crores, i.e., a 30 per cent reduction in the budget compared to 2014-15 in nominal terms.[27] Ordinarily, the budget increases every year to account for inflation. Besides, as the GDP increases, it is expected that more resources will be made available for such schemes. The highest expenditure (as a percentage of GDP) on the MDM scheme by the central government was in 2007-8 and 2008-9 when it was 0.15 per cent of GDP. In 2023-24, it had come down to just 0.03 per cent of GDP.

Instead of increasing funds for the MDM scheme, the government is tightening its purse strings. For example, on

7 August 2015, the central government issued a notification ending the LPG subsidy given to schools for mid-day meals. Could there have been a better beneficiary of LPG subsidy than children studying in government schools?

To some extent the decline is related to the stagnation of child enrolment in government schools. That in turn is partly due to a slowdown in the rate of population growth and partly due to higher private school enrolment. Between 2022 and 2024, the daily per child allocation remained stuck at Rs 5.45 for primary school children and Rs 8.17 for upper primary children. Of this, the Central government contributed Rs 3.27 and Rs 4.90 for primary and upper primary respectively. Food grains are provided free of cost by the Union government. A much-delayed revision of the per child daily norms only led to rates being revised to Rs 6.19 and Rs 9.29 in December 2024 (with the Centre's contribution rising to Rs 3.71 and 5.57 per day respectively for primary and upper primary children.) Several states like Kerala, Tamil Nadu and Telangana contribute more than the mandated 60-40 sharing ratio, yet the meagre allocations affect the quality of the meals.

The salaries of women who cook in school are also very low, in some states less than the government minimum wage (Chart 4.2). Leaving aside all these issues, the focus of policymakers has been diverted to imposing inappropriate technology and centralised kitchens.

Role of Aadhaar in Mid-day Meals

On 28 February 2017, the Ministry of Human Resource Development issued a notification invoking Section 7 of the Aadhaar Act (Government of India 2017). According to the notification, in case a child was not enrolled for Aadhaar, they would have to submit two other documents besides their Aadhaar enrolment slip to be eligible for mid-day meals.[28]

The move to link Aadhaar with mid-day meals was questionable for two reasons. First, forcing children to enrol could mean that they can be tracked for life (without their consent, since when they enrolled, they would still be minors) without any real chance of being able to opt out in the future. Several parents tweeted about how they were forced to enrol their child for Aadhaar.[29]

Secondly, Aadhaar has no role in the mid-day meal scheme. Even the government notification stated that the government merely wanted children to enroll for Aadhaar. Children who ate mid-day meals in government schools were already enrolled there and entitled to a school meal without any additional requirement. By mandating 'voluntary' Aadhaar for school-children, contrary to the rhetoric that Aadhaar is a tool to make access to benefits barrier-free, it was creating barriers.

The consequences of pushing for compulsory registration could prove extremely disruptive—it could derail the mid-day meal programme and harm education-related activities in schools. Teachers and school authorities, already burdened with a lot of paperwork, had to divert teaching time to make arrangements for Aadhaar registration of children. After registration, the entire system might have to be rejigged to make it Aadhaar-compliant (e.g., matching dates of birth, spellings of names, biometric authentication, etc.), which is wasteful.[30]

Biometric technology is unreliable. If the government's plan was to move towards biometric verification of all children after enrolling for Aadhaar before serving the meal, it would have disrupted the smooth functioning of the mid-day meal programme. In 2017-18, government residential schools in Jharkhand began real time biometric attendance. The idea was that school children authenticate their presence in these residential schools every day, and schools were required to upload attendance online. At that time, we visited eight schools where this was happening. Surprisingly, at one school, there were 100-130 children according to online attendance. At meal time we did a head count of children present and found that there were about 230 children present! School teachers said that there were 238 sanctioned seats and enrolment, but about 40 children could not register for Aadhaar, so they cannot mark their attendance biometrically. Of the remaining 190 children (who have Aadhaar), the biometric machine was only able to verify thumb impressions of 130-132. At another school, only around 100 of the 187 students were successful in biometric authentication. In short: paper attendance matched the 'ground reality', and was higher than the 'online reality' of only 100-130 children being present. As per the Aadhaar 'playbook' (used across schemes), a few months after the notification a news report suggested that registering children for Aadhaar had led to the discovery of lakhs of 'fake' enrolments when in fact, it was just that lakhs of children had not been able to enrol successfully for Aadhaar.

The first question that arises is what problem in the functioning of the MDM scheme was the government trying to solve through Aadhaar enrolment and/or biometric verification? The only possible argument could have been inflation of daily attendance: that is, recording some children's attendance even when they are absent from school.

There tend to be two reasons for inflating school attendance. One, the official daily allocation is insufficient to provide food based on the menu. For instance, the daily allocation per student was around Rs 5 and on days when the mid-day meal is supposed to include an egg with rice and dal, the allocation was inadequate (market prices of eggs were closer to Rs 7 per egg). Teachers manage this shortfall by inflating attendance, where possible. Teachers also report bargaining to procure items at lower prices, and in some cases, communities also chip in. The second is fund manipulation. In such cases, records are inflated by administrators (teachers, organisers, cooks and assistants) with the intention of siphoning off funds allocated, but not utilised due to poor attendance. The introduction of Aadhaar and biometric authentication will result in punishing students for no fault of theirs. Meanwhile, those guilty of corruption get a free pass.

This is not to deny that attendance records may be inflated with the intention of siphoning off resources from the MDM. According to IHDS 2011-12 data, 82 per cent of children receive mid-day meals and 64 per cent study in government schools. According to the Census, the number of children aged 6-14 years in 2011 was 19 crore: i.e., 12 crore (64 per cent of 19 crore) children study in government schools, and 82 per cent of them (i.e., 10 crore) receive their mid-day meal. According to administrative data, 10.5 crore children eat mid-day meals. This suggests a close correspondence between meals served as per administrative records (10.5 crores) and actual meals consumed (10 crores).

If we take the number of children enrolled in classes 1-8 instead of the number of children aged 6-14 years, the corresponding numbers are: 12.3 crore children enrolled in government schools, of whom 10.7 (87 per cent) crore reported getting mid-day meals. This is slightly higher than the government figure of 10.5 crores, not less (Yadav 2017).

As far as stopping theft in mid-day meals is concerned, there are other, simpler, ways of stopping it. For example, each school could be asked to report its attendance to the Block Education Officer (BEO) every day. The BEO could inspect a small number of schools, randomly selected, to verify the reported attendance. Such a surprise inspection through lottery, followed by exemplary action against those found inflating attendance is likely to be effective in curbing the practice and more practical than aiming for 100 per cent biometric attendance.

The benefits of the mid-day meal are very substantial, especially in terms of school attendance, improved nutrition, greater learning, etc. The most pressing problems related to mid-day meals—a better menu, providing safe storage, proper cooking space, timely release of funds, etc.—cannot be solved by Aadhaar-linkage.

Centralised Kitchens

The mid-day meal scheme reaches 10-12 crore children in the country. While there is still room for improvement (there are intermittent complaints of diluted milk or dal being served and other forms of corruption), it remains among India's most successful social policies.

Across the country, the main mode of providing mid-day meals is on-site cooking arrangements on school campuses. This includes the physical infrastructure (kitchen sheds, stoves, utensils, etc.) and staff (cooks and helpers). In this decentralised model, in each school a team of one to three people are responsible for preparing and serving the mid-day meal. Some states have also appointed an 'organiser' along with cooks and helpers. The MDM scheme employs over 20 lakh women as cooks and helpers.

Over the years, the practice of centralised kitchens has grown along with on-site kitchens. Food is prepared at the centralised kitchen and transported to schools. Initially it was seen in urban areas where the density of schools is high, so it is possible to supply food to schools using vehicles. In some urban schools, it may not even have been possible to build a kitchen afresh. Thus, in densely populated cities, centralised kitchens emerged as an alternative. In states like Delhi, almost all schools were supplied by centralised kitchens as early as 2013-14.

Who runs these centralised kitchens? State governments have started contracting out the responsibility of cooking meals to private institutions. For instance, in 2021-22, of the nearly 45 lakh beneficiary children of the mid-day meal scheme in Karnataka, roughly 8 lakh (17 per cent) were provided meals by organisations such as the Akshaya Patra Foundation (APF). According to their Annual Report, 2024-25, APF feeds 22.5 lakh children in India (including children at Anganwadis (Akshaya Patra Foundation 2024-25). This institution is known to many because it is associated with the ISKCON temple and many people have eaten food at these temples at some time or the other.

For the mid-day meal scheme, APF gets free food grains from the government as well as the daily cooking costs, as per the norms for government schools. According to the APF Annual Report 2024-25, it received Rs 420 crores, half of their income, from state governments. Yet, the popular perception is that APF itself feeds the children. Its expenditure on advertising probably explains the perpetuation of such a perception: 4 per cent of their expenditure, roughly Rs 34 crores, was spent on "fund raising". For instance, if you search for 'mid-day meal' on the Internet, there are many links about this organisation which suggests it spends heavily on advertising.

Realistically speaking, the state government does not need APF. More than 80 per cent of children in government school are served their MDM cooked on-site by cooks and helpers. It is quite likely that APF needs the MDM scheme as a brand-building exercise. On the basis of this work, it receives substantial private donations that were possibly used to augment the budgetary support from the government.

The Performance Audit Report of the CAG raised questions about ISKCON (Government of India 2015). At that time no one paid much attention and no action was taken. In 2020, the group was in the news again. Some questions were raised in its private audit due to which an independent trustee of the institution resigned. The questions were serious. One allegation was that accounts of money and grains were rigged in half of their kitchens. The cost per child is very high—it was recording double the cost compared to government schools. Additionally, the kitchens that prepared school meals were also used to provide for meal at ISKCON temples. This meant that accounts of the MDM scheme and temple meals were mixed up. All this pointed to the possibility that (some part of) the government grain and monetary allocations that were being given to Akshaya Patra for school children, was also used to run ISKCON temples. Instead of conducting an independent inquiry, the trustees of the ISKCON temple who were working at Akshaya Patra, were blocking the investigation. Thus, the inclusion of institutions like APF in a government scheme hinders accountability.

When any private institution receives government funds, it should be subject to both CAG audits and the provisions of the Right to Information Act. Such safeguards assume greater importance given the growing prevalence of 'public private partnerships' (PPPs) in the domain of social policy, even as the programmes where such PPPs are allowed needs to be debated.

Moreover, for years Akshaya Patra was able to block the inclusion of nutritious foods like eggs in Karnataka in the menu of the MDM scheme. That affected not only children in schools served by Akshaya Patra, but all 40 lakh children studying in government schools in the state. More recently, Akshaya Patra was also trying to push for meals without onion and garlic, as per their faith. If Akshaya Patra were running a charity with private funds, it might have made sense for it to decide the menu and ingredients. But in the case of the MDM, a large part of the budget is public money, so it should be run according to the government menu and public interest.

From 2021 onwards, when the state finally stood up for the inclusion of eggs, Akshaya Patra refused to give eggs. The state decided that it will make arrangements to deliver eggs separately to those schools where food is provided by APF.

Interestingly, in Karnataka, no matter which party was in power till 2021, they were unable to stand up to Akshaya Patra's bullying. Why? Trustees at Akshaya Patra were either wealthy people or religious gurus of the ISKCON temple. It appeared that child nutrition was being held hostage to religious beliefs and the wealthy.

Gradually, the practice of using centralised kitchens has spread to rural areas as well. In rural areas of Jharkhand, Rajasthan and Odisha, private organisations are now engaged in mid-day meals. A survey in Jharkhand's Chaibasa area in 2024 found that children did not enjoy food supplied by centralised kitchens. Many were seen throwing it away.

An earlier 2015 study in Rajasthan found that there were implementation issues where Akshaya Patra had been contracted to provide meals (Whittaker 2015). It was not following the government-prescribed menu (fruits were given to children once a week in schools with on-site kitchens, but not in schools supplied by Akshaya Patra), by the time roti reached the children, it was inedible. Moreover, Akshaya Patra's centralised kitchens were not using garlic and onion which affected the taste.

In an older 2006 MDM study in Delhi, researchers found that women are less likely to be employed in centralised kitchens, whereas they are employed in large numbers in on-site kitchens (Samson et al. 2007). Teachers also said that with centralised deliveries, if an issue arises then even they are at a loss as to who to complain to. With on-site kitchens, their presence on the school campus can have a disciplining effect.

Despite these problems, the number of children receiving mid-day meals from centralised kitchens increased marginally from 4 per cent in 2013-14 to 5.6 per cent in 2023-24. In states like Gujarat the numbers have doubled from 7 per cent to 14 per cent in this period. In some others (e.g., Haryana and Karnataka), almost one-fifth of schools are served by centralised kitchens (see Table A4 for all states).

Compared to ten years ago, more states rely on centralised kitchens. In 2023-24, at least fifteen large states were using them, whereas in 2013-14 it was only in ten major states. Worryingly, some of this increase is driven by its expansion in rural areas where they are not at all well suited.

'Mid-day meals have reduced the school to dal-bhaat (feeding) centres'; 'Will teachers teach or feed children?'—misinformed statements such as these are not uncommon, although as suggested here, the reality of—and challenges faced by—the mid-day meal scheme are quite different. Of course, school-teachers still oversee some aspects of the MDM schemes, especially during lunch hour. A far more serious and wasteful source of diversion of teaching time is the burden of record keeping duties. Any diversion of teaching time is definitely a matter of concern, and remedies are readily available (e.g., appointment of non-teaching staff at schools can help with all record keeping as well as overseeing the MDM). The MDM scheme's contribution to boosting enrolment, attendance, learning, education and nutrition in India is by now well-documented. School meals are—and can be—much more: it plays a role in fostering one-ness among school children and breaking caste barriers, provides meaningful employment opportunities and some relief from domestic work for mothers of young children.

6

PUBLIC DISTRIBUTION SYSTEM

Beyond Foodgrains

Roots of Public Distribution System

Of the seven welfare schemes discussed in this book, the Public Distribution System is the oldest, going back to the Second World War. At that time, due to the food shortages caused by the war a system of 'rationing' was established. The British Indian government intervened in some cities, by controlling the distribution (rationing) of some essential food items that were in short supply. Interestingly, the history of the Public Distribution System (PDS) begins in the cities, although today it has greater reach and importance in rural areas.

After Independence, the Green Revolution brought major changes in the PDS. It breathed new life into it. As productivity of wheat and rice increased substantially after the Green Revolution, and total production of these crops rose significantly, it became necessary to set up a procurement system so that farmers who had invested in the Green Revolution technologies (new seeds, fertilizers, pesticides, etc.) could get remunerative prices. Government intervention was necessary because if left to the market, the increased production could have led to a fall in market prices and farmers, instead of benefiting from the Green Revolution, would have suffered from a glut.

Thus, in the sixties, the Food Corporation of India (FCI) began procuring wheat and rice at Minimum Support Prices (MSP). The FCI maintains food stocks to fulfill three main functions—price stabilisation (if there is inflation, the government tries to ease the situation by selling grains from their stocks through open market sales), buffer stock (for use in disasters, like famines, natural calamities, war, etc.) and food security (for subsidised distribution through the PDS).

Over time, FCI's operations, though still heavily concentrated on wheat and rice, grew in scale and scope. In the 1980s, concerns about an 'urban bias' in the PDS arose. The network of PDS outlets was more widespread in urban areas whereas hunger and poverty were especially high in rural areas (Jha and Howes 1992).

In the 1990s, however, ideas of economic liberalisation gained traction. Economic liberalisation not only affected industry, but the extent of social support provided by the government began to be questioned. As a result, steps were taken to make what was theoretically (but not in fact) a universal PDS, 'targeted'. A first serious attempt was made in 1992 to target poor areas (Revamped Public Distribution System). After this, in 1997 and 2002, two 'BPL surveys' were conducted to identify 'Below Poverty Line' (BPL) households, based on which people were given BPL and APL (Above Poverty Line) ration cards. Those who had BPL cards would continue to get cheap/subsidised PDS grains and the subsidy for APL households ended (see Swaminthan 2000 for more).

Reforms in Public Distribution System (2002-2013)

Corruption was the big issue in the PDS through the nineties. Chart 6.1 depicts 'leakage' of PDS grain from 1999-2000 to 2022-23. 'Leakage' here refers to the difference between what the states lift from the FCI ('offtake') and the quantity of grain people actually get from their local PDS outlet ('purchase'). The Monthly Food Grain Bulletin of the Food Ministry publishes state-wise offtake data for wheat and rice separately. This offtake data provides information about the supply of FCI grain to the states. The National Sample Survey (NSS) provides data on the purchase of food grains from PDS per person per month. Combining these two, one can estimate how much grain has 'leaked' from the supply pipe.[31] The difference between offtake and purchase could be due to other factors (for example, spoilage in godowns, transportation losses, etc.), so the leakage estimates are likely to be upper bounds. Most importantly, they are just that—estimates (Drèze and Khera 2010 and Khera 2011).

Chart 6.1 plots the estimates of leakages for India and Bihar from the late 2000s to the latest year for which estimates are available (2022-23). The trend is clear: leakages have come down in the last 20-odd years. The improvement in Bihar is most impressive (from nearly 90 per cent leakage to about a quarter). Years ago, during a survey in Bihar, when a respondent was asked if they got PDS grains, they replied emphatically, 'Of course—every Diwali and Holi!' Awareness levels were so poor that they did not realise that they ought to get PDS grain each month, not merely on Holi and Diwali. The situation—though still far from ideal—is much better today. In many states, small cuts (instead of giving 5 kilograms per person each month, dealers give only 4.5 or even 4 kilograms per person) remain the norm. But where more than half of the food grains were estimated to be leaking at the All-India level, it was down to 22 per cent in 2022-23.

In 2010, we had the opportunity to see the reforms firsthand in Surguja district of Chhattisgarh (Drèze and Khera 2010 and Drèze 2017). Ration card holders we interviewed reported that they were getting their full quota of 35 kilograms of grain every month, regularly, and that too at the right price—Re 1 or 2 per kilo depending on the type of ration card. The grain reached the village on time—on the seventh of every month—and was distributed immediately. There were no complaints of fraud. Surguja used to be an area of high PDS leakages not that long ago (see Appendix I, Table A5).

How did this happen? One of the early PDS reforms in Chhattisgarh was the reversal of the privatisation of ration shops. Since 2001, private dealers in Chhattisgarh were allowed to obtain licenses for PDS shops. Before that, PDS shops were run by a network of state cooperative societies. Granting private licenses helped widen the network of ration shops, but also created a new nexus of corrupt players. Dealers indulged politicians to get licenses, to avoid action against them when they engaged in corrupt practices. In 2004, despite fierce protests from dealers, the state government reversed an earlier order that allowed private individuals to be given PDS licenses. Instead of private dealers, gram panchayats, self-help groups, and other community institutions were put in charge of ration shops. Apart from bringing ration shops closer to people, this also enhanced accountability in the PDS. When PDS ration shops are run by the panchayat or self-help group, the scope for theft of food grains decreases. Community institutions like gram panchayats may not be

Chart 6.1: Revival of the PDS predates Aadhaar integration

Estimated "leakage" of PDS grain, 1999-2000 to 2022-23

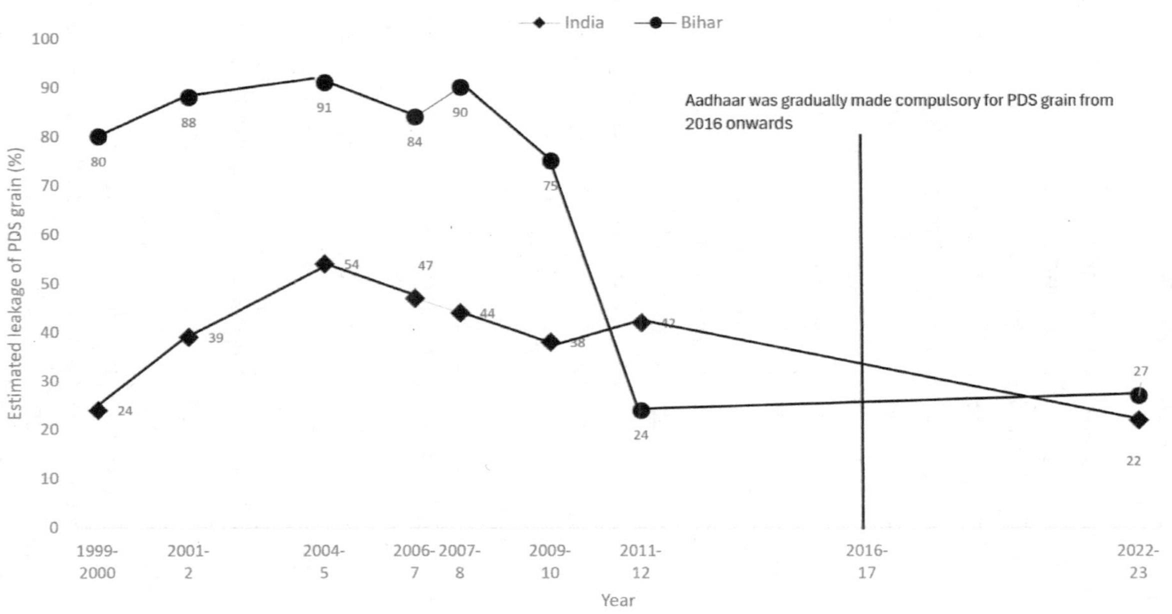

Source: Khera (2011a), Drèze and Khera (2015b) and Khera (2024)

people's institutions in spirit, yet, they are better than corrupt dealers.

It is well known that corrupt dealers make 'cuts' while selling to cardholders (dealers often refer to this as 'bachat' or savings) and sell the grain thus saved at market prices in the open (or 'black') market. Diverting PDS grain can help them make big profits because the difference between PDS price (it has gone down since the NFSA was enacted) and market prices (that have been rising steadily) has grown over time.

What was less known is that when the dealers themselves transport grain from the FCI godown to their PDS outlet, PDS grain was often diverted en route, *before* reaching the village. The dealers could then innocently claim to be helpless in the face of corruption at the FCI godowns.

To circumvent this, Chhattisgarh initiated 'doorstep delivery' of PDS grains. Doorstep delivery meant that PDS grains were delivered to the village PDS outlet every month by state agencies, instead of the dealers having to lift their quota from the nearest FCI godown. The separation of transport and distribution of grain, made it harder to divert grain—it would require that the PDS dealer to collude with the transporter. Moreover, once PDS grain is delivered to the village PDS outlet, it became harder for dealers to cheat; people were more likely to protest.

Another creative reform was to paint PDS delivery trucks yellow with a toll-free number on the truck itself. Anyone who saw a transporter offloading grain from a yellow truck in the open market could alert the authorities by calling the toll-free number provided on the truck. There were other smart, light-touch uses of technology. For example, a system of informing interested citizens about the movement of PDS grains through SMS alerts was introduced. All records related to supplies, sales, etc. were computerised.

There were some mis-hits too: for instance, to prevent cheating in the weighing process, the state government experimented with pre-packed 35 kg bags, but the practice had to be discontinued as it was found that the bags were being tampered with. Later, they shifted to electronic weighing machines.

Perhaps the most important step was to improve grievance redressal mechanisms. For example, active helplines were introduced. The helpline was often used by cardholders, and people got a timely response if a complaint was lodged; the complaint was unlikely to remain buried somewhere in the government system. Government action was not limited to investigation; in many cases, FIRs were filed against corrupt dealers and some even ended up in jail. Grain was recovered from trucks that were caught unloading their stocks at private shops.

Transparency is an important anti-corruption tool. Simple transparency measures were taken to eliminate fake ration cards in Chhattisgarh. For example, information walls were used to bring transparency.[32] Each house had a large round sign by the door, displaying the family's ration card type and the corresponding entitlements (price and quantity). It served the dual purpose of creating awareness about rights and 'naming and shaming' those who had ration cards (such as Antyodaya cards) for which they were not eligible.

'Demand side' PDS reforms in Chhattisgarh also played an important role. Here, the most important step was a major expansion of PDS coverage. Dr Raman Singh (the then BJP chief minister of Chhattisgarh) expanded the coverage of the PDS before the 2007 state elections. Nearly 80 per cent of the rural population, including all SC/ST families, became entitled to PDS grain at one or two rupees per kg. This led to the majority of rural households having a strong stake in the PDS, creating huge pressure for distribution (especially at PDS outlets).

Expanded coverage and lower prices—both steps contributed to amplifying the voices of otherwise poor and powerless rural cardholders. Rajiv Jaiswal (the then Joint Director, Food and Civil Supplies) put it succinctly: 'Today we are using only 80 per cent of the rural community's voice. When PDS becomes universal, the entire community, including the better educated and vocal sections, will start putting pressure on the system.'

The PDS in Chhattisgarh was reformed for political gain. Raman Singh began to be called 'Chawal-Wale Baba'. The reforms also contributed, in part, to the BJP's repeated electoral victories in the state from 2000 to 2019. Given these successes, adjoining states—including Odisha, Jharkhand, Bihar—began to take an interest in PDS reforms. Chhattisgarh had provided them a template of reforms to choose from.

In the decade 2000-10, several states began taking an active interest in reforming the PDS. These reforms helped to reduce the estimated leakage in Chhattisgarh from 50 per cent (in 2004-5) to just 9 per cent (in 2011-12). In Bihar, it went down from 90 per cent to 24 per cent and from 76 per cent to 25 per cent in Odisha. In Himachal (around 27 per cent) and southern states (around 10 per cent in Tamil Nadu, for example) the PDS was already functional.

Role of National Food Security Act 2013

The growing political interest in the PDS also contributed to the inclusion of a food security law in the manifesto of the Congress party before the 2009 General Election. After winning the election, the draft Bill that was prepared to fulfill that electoral promise revealed a lack of vision within the Congress. For instance, the first draft promised *only* grain, *only* for BPL families, neglecting the needs of young children, pregnant and lactating mothers, etc., entirely.

At the same time, a new debate around food security arose: what is the most effective way to ensure food security for the people—the distribution of subsidised grains through the PDS or transferring cash.

After four years of a fraught debate, the National Food Security Act (NFSA) was passed in 2013. The Act includes four major entitlements—maternity benefits through Pradhan Mantri Matru Vandana Yojana, health, nutrition and pre-school services for children under six through the Integrated Child Development Services scheme, school meals through the Mid-Day Meal and subsidised grain through the Public Distribution System. Together, all this costs roughly two per cent of India's GDP.

The NFSA brought about three major changes in the PDS—first, the proportion of ration card holders in the country increased. Under the NFSA, 75 per cent of the rural population and 50 per cent of the population in urban areas (about two-thirds of the entire population at the time) were included in the PDS and entitled to cheap food grains. After the implementation of the NFSA, roughly 80 crore people are covered by the PDS. At the same time, there was a partially successful attempt to eliminate the unreliable BPL category. The NFSA recognises 'Priority' and 'Antyodaya' households, formally ending the BPL category (although even today Priority is often referred to as BPL in many states, and the BPL category still exists in some states).

The second major change was the reduction in 'issue prices', the price at which wheat and rice were sold by the

FCI to the states. Before the NFSA came into force, the issue price of wheat was Rs 4.65 per kg for BPL families. Under the Food Security Act, for Antyodaya and Priority cards, states began to get it at Re 1 per kg (ragi, bajra, etc.), Rs 2 per kg (wheat), or Rs 3 per kg (rice).

The third reform was that entitlements were specified per person for priority households, rather than per family. Members of priority category would get 5 kg of grains per person per month. Earlier, entitlements were specified per family for all categories of ration cards. Entitlements varied by state (20-35 kg of grains, per eligible family). Antyodaya households are the poorest of the poor, and often widows or elderly people, i.e. smaller households. They were protected by retaining entitlements per household (35 kg grains per month).

Some readers will immediately recognise the earlier PDS reforms in the states from 2000-2010 reflected in the National Food Security Act: an expansion of the PDS, a reduction in prices was directly influenced by those earlier reforms. Other reforms such as transparency in the list of ration cards, computerisation of records, a pre-specified schedule for distribution of grain, etc., were also incorporated as enabling provisions in the NFSA on the basis of earlier state reforms.

After the implementation of NFSA, the list of eligible families became more credible, rational and inclusive than the earlier BPL list. Interestingly, Bihar was among the first states to implement NFSA. Bihar still has a long way to go in terms of running the PDS smoothly, yet, the progress that Bihar made in this direction would have been considered impossible till a decade ago.

The experience of Madhya Pradesh is worth dwelling on. Like Bihar, the PDS in Madhya Pradesh was more or less dysfunctional (Drèze and Khera 2015a). List of eligible families were unreliable, with too many exclusion errors, distribution was irregular and diversion/black-marketing was very high. The Public Evaluation of Entitlement Programme (PEEP) Survey in 2013 revealed that BPL families in Madhya Pradesh were getting only 37 per cent of their entitled food grains. Though the sample was small (around 200 households in eight villages of Mandla and Shivpuri districts), the findings were in line with the findings using National Sample Survey data (see Appendix I, Table A5).

Two years after the PEEP Survey 2013, in July 2015, we revisited the sample households from 2013 in Mandla and Shivpuri to see if the situation had changed. In the intervening period, Madhya Pradesh had initiated the PDS reforms mandated by the NFSA. A fresh list of eligible households had been drawn up. The state government had made serious efforts to streamline the PDS.

Like other states that did so, Madhya Pradesh witnessed a drastic reduction in exclusion errors with the expansion of PDS under NFSA. In the PEEP Survey 2013, about 50 per cent of the households were excluded from the PDS. These families either had APL category ration cards or no ration cards of any kind. Many poor families were deprived of BPL cards because the earlier BPL survey was messy and unreliable. By 2015, most of the households surveyed, including almost all SC and ST families, had new ration cards under the NFSA. With PDS coverage reaching 80 per cent of the population and the use of more reliable data prepared by the state's Social Security Mission, very few households were left out of the PDS system.

Secondly, the regularity and reliability of PDS grain distribution improved substantially. Days for distribution of

PDS grains were fixed and even if it was not strictly followed, timely distribution of grains each month had become the norm. The lack of a fixed schedule for distribution used to create inconvenience and uncertainty for PDS card holders, and it opened the door to corrupt practices, as it made it difficult for people to keep track of their entitlements.

Third, people's ability to get their entitlement and avoid fraud improved dramatically. The sample households were clearly aware of the quantity of food grains they were entitled to as this information was printed on their ration card. With the PDS price being only Re 1 per kg, people were determined to ensure that they get their full quota of PDS grain. Madhya Pradesh is not the only state that realised that if PDS coverage is high, entitlements are clear and the PDS price is kept low, then these simple measures (as well as comprehensive reforms in PDS) can help reduce PDS leakages. The phasing out of APL quota also helped in correcting the shortcomings. The APL quota had major transparency flaws that encouraged widespread black-marketing (see Drèze and Khera 2015).

None of this implies that people's grievances and concerns had been resolved. Many complained that they had to pay a bribe (between Rs 100 and Rs 2000) for a new ration card. The system was set up in such a way that to get the name of a family member added or deleted (in the event of a birth or death) on the ration cards, the Social Security Mission database would have to be updated. This gave local officials an opportunity to ask for a bribe. About one-third of the respondents complained that the rice received from the PDS the last time was of poor quality, while about 20 per cent of the respondents said the same about wheat and maize received from PDS. Despite these and other complaints, most respondents said they were getting more PDS food grains in 2015 than they did two years ago in 2013.

The experience of Bihar and Madhya Pradesh suggested that even states with poor/indifferent administration are capable of overhauling the PDS and that the rollout of the NFSA played a positive role.

Along with these positive changes, there was scope for further expansion of the law—for example, there has been a long-standing demand that pulses and edible oil should also be included in the PDS. States such as Tamil Nadu, Himachal Pradesh, Andhra Pradesh, etc., have been supplying these commodities at subsidised prices for many years using state resources. Indian diets are protein deficient, often because people cannot afford them. Subsidised pulses can help remedy this. Similarly, consumption of edible oil (an important source of fat) is low in the diet of poor families. These suggestions were ignored, but 12.2 (f) of the NFSA clearly states that over time more food items should be added to the items supplied by the PDS.

While wheat and rice are the main grains supplied through the PDS, instead of these, millets (such as bajra, ragi) or maize supplies could be increased. Millets have better nutrition than wheat and rice and they are better suited for cultivation in dry/arid monsoon-fed areas (the crops are sturdier and less water intensive). The NFSA has a provision for millets, and a handful of states have begun to operationalise it, at least on a small scale (for example, Odisha and Karnataka).

Grain or Cash Transfers?

Governments across the world combine cash transfers with in-kind transfers in their welfare basket (see Khera 2014). The PDS in India is an important example of in-kind transfers, as it provides grain (and pulses and oil in some states) at a subsidised price. When the discussion on the National

Food Security Act began, many asked whether food security was best ensured by supplying subsidised foodgrain or by transferring cash into people's accounts.

In its 2015 report, the Shanta Kumar Committee made suggestions on this issue as well. The committee had ostensibly been constituted to deliberate on 'reorienting the role and restructuring of Food Corporation of India'. The committee suggested cash transfers instead of grains through the PDS (p. vii, 23, Government of India, 2015). The basis of this suggestion, as it turned out, were incorrect estimates of PDS leakages. About 25 per cent of PDS grains were diverted in Bihar, but the committee's faulty estimate put it at 68 per cent. Their estimates suggested that there had been no change in the leakage from the PDS. In doing so, it ignored the improvements in the PDS (discussed earlier; see Appendix I, Table A5 also). Blissfully unaware of the success of PDS reforms in several states, ignoring the ground realities of rural areas, unaware of the needs of people, it presented cash transfers as a magic wand that would tackle corruption and food insecurity.

To understand the pros and cons of cash transfers versus in-kind food transfers, we interviewed 1500 rural ration cardholders across nine states in the PDS Survey 2011 (Khera 2011 and 2015). We asked respondents what they prefer, between PDS grains and cash, and—more importantly—why. More specifically, the question was that if the government were to close the PDS outlet in their village, and instead put enough cash in a bank account for the goods they bought from the PDS outlet to be bought in the private market instead, which of these two options would they choose? Two-thirds of the respondents preferred to get grain.

Why did they care about PDS grains even though they

would have enough money to buy the same commodities in the open market at market prices? Markets in rural areas are poorly developed. Protecting people from market uncertainties was an important function of the PDS. In many rural areas of the country, markets do not work in the way that proponents of the free market imagine. People regularly fall prey to exploitative traders, who do not hesitate to adopt any tactics to increase their profits. The supply of rice, wheat, and pulses through PDS serves other useful purposes. For example, in some remote areas, year round availability of grains was not guaranteed, whereas the PDS had become a reliable source of food grains.

Even if markets work properly, ration cardholders were not convinced. A second concern of the respondents was related to inflation. Prices are bound to increase, they said. With food inflation, will the government increase amount of cash transferred? they asked. They drew on their own experience with existing government cash transfer schemes. Notably, the example of social security pensions for the elderly, widows and the disabled, that at the time of the 2011 PDS Survey were stuck at Rs 200 since 2006. (Even in 2025 the Central government's contribution remained meagre; see Table 2.4) Since the monthly pension was not inflation-indexed, people believed that it would be naive to expect that money given for grains would be inflation-indexed. One respondent said, 'We know the government will increase the amount only when elections are due.'

There were other questions related to inflation: Will the government have adequate information about prices? Will the amount increase immediately in line with inflation? If local shopkeepers, with an eye on profits, deliberately create shortages to charge more, will the government do something, or will it be *able* to do anything?

Cash transfers would involve additional transaction costs for consumers. One respondent in Chhattisgarh said that with the PDS, the procurement of grains, its storage, transport, etc.—everything is the responsibility of the government. If they get cash, the responsibility for these tasks and associated expenses will shift to the poor. They feared that it will create further uncertainty in their insecure lives. If the cash is not credited to their accounts, banks will simply shrug their shoulders and pass the blame to higher authorities. (Some said that when PDS grain supplies are delayed, they at least knew where to agitate; with cash, it was harder to lay the blame on the bank staff.)

PDS outlets tend to be closer to people's homes than banks and markets. Even if they had a bank account, the distance to markets and banks and post offices (this problem persists even today) made cash a less attractive option. There were few means of commuting, when they exist, they involve additional expenses and are time-consuming. Banks tend to be crowded, and rural respondents said they sometimes have to deal with the unfriendly and/or rude behaviour of bank staff. Access to 'banks' has been sought to be improved with the setting up of 'Common Service Centres' (CSCs), but CSCs come with their own problems (see below). These arguments were advanced by invoking their experience with social security pensions or other cash transfer programmes. These were not hypothetical scenarios.

Respondents said that giving cash instead of PDS grain could cause another problem. Within the same family, different members may have a different opinion on spending the cash, and this could cause intra-household conflicts.

Some economists maintain that these arguments in favour of in-kind transfers reflect the respondents' aversion to change. In their view, the resistance to change cannot be a valid reason to shoot down a new proposal. Yet, it is also true that change creates inconvenience for everyone, even for the urban-educated. Moreover, the poor may not have the capacity to deal with the teething problems that come with the introduction of a new system. For instance, the change in the LPG subsidy regime in 2013 led to widespread problems such as delays or non-receipt of the subsidy. If a particular month's LPG subsidy did not get credited on time, not everyone could buy gas cylinders from their own pocket. Similarly for many ration card holders, if the cash for food does not come on time, it could become a question of life and death.

Experience with Cash Transfer Pilots

In public debates around the cash vs food question, the comparison was often between two disparate situations. The on-the-ground ugly realities of the PDS, with all its warts that have been researched over the years would be compared with a textbook idealised and hypothetical implementation of cash transfers. When such a comparison is made, the PDS was a clear loser.

For instance, George and Subramanian (2015) paint an optimistic and somewhat simplistic picture of cash transfers when they term it a 'quiet revolution' in the form of a JAM trinity (JAM stands for Jan Dhan Aadhaar and Mobile). JAM was projected as a surefire solution for corruption, though the ground realities were different. Key failures stemming from the current system of cash transfers involving the 'Jan Dhan, Aadhaar, Mobile' (JAM) trinity were quietly ignored. For instance, cases from Jharkhand have made it clear that corruption can thrive even with Aadhaar-enabled payment systems (Drèze and Paikra 2021).

Though the number of bank accounts has shot up, the 'banking system' that has evolved around the Jan Dhan accounts (e.g., the expansion of CSCs) can only be termed a 'second class' banking system. For instance, a survey of CSCs in Jharkhand found overcharging, queuing, etc. were common (Parathasarathy 2019). Scaled-up access to bank accounts alone is not enough to claim that the banking system is ready to deal with mass cash transfers. Bank branches tend to be over-crowded because there aren't enough branches. Without improving the reach and functioning of the banking system, it would be foolhardy to advocate mass cash transfers.

When advocating cash transfers, there is little discussion of the transition issues faced by other cash transfer schemes. The experience of the transition to bank payments of National Rural Employment Guarantee Act (NREGA) wages serves as a useful lesson. The transition in NREGA began in 2008-09. Between 2009 and 2014, 10 crore bank and post office accounts were opened. The switch to bank payment resulted in a decline in embezzlement of NREGA wages (at least initially). In 2009-10, around 20 per cent of NREGA work recorded in the names of NREGA workers was not confirmed by the workers, compared to roughly 40 per cent in 2007-08. But as field staff with NREGA responsibilities were tasked with the work of opening accounts and later of linking accounts with Aadhaar numbers, regular NREGA work suffered and delays in wage payments increased. Fifteen years after payment of NREGA wages into bank accounts was initiated, the problems have not gone away; in fact, in some ways, they have worsened (see LibTech 2020).

The transition issues were evident in other cash transfers as well. For a Rs 200 pension, elderly people, who could not even walk properly, were forced to run around to open new bank accounts. Dalit and Adivasi children, who were getting scholarships in their bank accounts, had no choice but to enrol for Aadhaar and link their accounts to Aadhaar. The LPG 'direct benefit transfer' (DBT) also did not function smoothly. Complaints of delays and irregularities in transfers were routine. People did not know where to register their complaints when such a situation arose. Gas agencies would send them to the banks and the banks would point to the gas agency.[33]

A DBT experiment for kerosene by the UPA-2 government in Kotkasim Block (Alwar, Rajasthan) revealed that either people's accounts could not be opened or when opened, many did not receive the cash transfers. Without the cash transfer, people could no longer afford to buy kerosene. Kerosene sales fell by 80 per cent. The government projected this drop in sales resulting from exclusion as a reduction in kerosene theft. Incidentally, this—projecting exclusions due to Aadhaar, as 'savings' from reduced corruption—became a widespread tool to evade problems arising from DBT/JAM.

In 2017-18, in Jharkhand, the state government experimented with cash in exchange for PDS rations in Nagri Block (Ranchi). Some ration card holders didn't have accounts, others did not know which account the money was being credited to. People had to go from one bank to another to find out where the money had gone. They ended up wasting time: on average, respondents said that it would take them 13 hours to withdraw money. The experiment created so many problems that it was withdrawn after ten months (Ranjan 2018).

Section 12 (2) h of the National Food Security Act 2013 kept the door open for a switch to cash transfers under the guise of PDS 'reforms'. Invoking this, a cash transfer experiment was conducted in Chandigarh, Dadra and Nagar

Haveli and Puducherry in 2015. An interim report found that 20 per cent in Chandigarh did not receive the money. In Puducherry, between the first phase and the second phase, the situation worsened—the proportion of those who did not receive money increased from 25 per cent to 37 per cent (Khera 2017).

Gimmicky Food Policy Experiments

Aadhaar in the PDS

Aadhaar numbers began to be issued in 2010. Soon after, Aadhaar integration with the PDS began, though it was 'voluntary' at the time. In spite of that, expansion of Aadhaar and exclusions from the PDS went hand in hand (e.g., an early pilot in Andhra Pradesh led to the deactivation of many PDS cards). From 2016 onwards, the 'Aadhaar is voluntary' mask was off. Returning to Chart 6.1, one can see that all the improvements in PDS leakage occurred before 2011-12, and predate the introduction of Aadhaar (see Khera 2024).

Table 6.1 lists the different fraudulent practices in the PDS. For most kinds of fraud, Aadhaar can—in principle—play no role. The form of fraud that Aadhaar can help with—the existence of duplicate or ghost PDS cards—has been found to be negligible. In the Muralidharan et al (2024) study, only 3 per cent of ration cardholders could not be traced. Of the fraudulent practices listed in the table, the biggest source of leakage was quantity fraud—something Aadhaar cannot stop (see Khera 2017). For instance, before Aadhaar-based Biometric Authentication (ABBA) PDS dealers forced PDS ration cardholders to sign for more than they were being given. With ABBA, the signature has been replaced by fingerprint authentication, without preventing the dealer's corrupt practices.

Table 6.1 Types of Fraud in the PDS

Type of fraud	*Example*	*Can Aadhaar help?*
Identity fraud	Duplicates and Ghosts	Yes, by linking Aadhaar-PDS databases, but only if PDS is universal and there are no duplicate Aadhaar IDs.
Eligibility fraud	Ineligible people get PDS ration cards	No
Quantity fraud	Under-selling, skipping months	No
Overcharging	Charging more than the official price, not returning small change	No
Quality	Adulteration, providing poorer quality	No

Note: Based on Khera 2017.

The haphazard and 'ultimatum method' based integration of Aadhaar-Based Biometric Authentication (ABBA) in welfare programmes, especially the PDS has been shown to be disruptive. In a study in Jharkhand, Drèze, Khalid, Khera and Somanchi (2017) find that ABBA was a case of 'pain without gain'—no gains in terms of reduced corruption and considerable pain in terms of exclusion and increased transaction costs for PDS card holders as well as PDS dealers. Another larger study in Jharkhand confirmed these findings (Muralidharan et al 2024). Several others document exclusion from the PDS connected with Aadhaar. For instance, a Lokniti survey found that 28 per cent of respondents were deprived of rations because of Aadhaar.

Other technologically more appropriate options for

portability and last mile authentication were not even considered. A 'Smart PDS' experiment in Chhattisgarh around 2013 demonstrated that portability is possible without biometrics and real time connectivity (Gupta, Haider and Jain 2014). Other states were also using smart cards for last mile authentication of PDS transactions. Yet the Union government insisted on Aadhaar and its related acrobatics (linking, biometric authentication, server connectivity, etc.).

One Nation, One Ration

During the COVID lockdowns, many urban workers found themselves stranded without work. Initially, the Central government doubled the quantity of PDS grain to be given to priority cardholders, but no relief was announced for those without ration cards. With pressure to do something for them, the central government announced 'One Nation, One Ration' (ONOR).

What is One Nation, One Ration (ONOR)? Each family with a ration card is linked to a PDS outlet in their village or neighborhood. The family's PDS quota is supplied to that outlet (Khera 2020a). ONOR is supposed to make PDS benefits portable, by giving PDS ration cardholders the choice to purchase from any PDS outlet in the country. Whether they are from Bihar or Tamil Nadu, they can get their PDS ration in any city across the country.

Portability in the PDS is expected to help migrant workers, but it can only help those who have PDS ration cards. Around 40 per cent of Indians did not have access to the PDS in 2020 (Khera and Somanchi 2020). The NFSA 2013 provides that two-thirds of the country's population be included in the PDS. When the law came into force, using the 2011 census population figures, 80 crore people were given PDS ration cards. Since then, the population has increased, but PDS coverage has remained frozen. According to our estimates, applying the coverage ratio mandated by the NFSA to the projected population in 2020, 10 crore more people would be included in the PDS.

Nevertheless ONOR/portability is appealing. However, once one gets into the nitty-gritty, several complications become evident. First, ration card holders in states like Tamil Nadu, Himachal Pradesh, Andhra Pradesh, get pulses and edible oil along with PDS grain. These commodities are supplied by the state governments. When a migrant from Jharkhand goes to Tamil Nadu, would they be entitled to them when they use ONOR? Who will foot the bill? Similar issues arise when a Tamil worker goes to, say, Mumbai: PDS outlets in Maharashtra do not even stock pulses and oil. Even if we consider only NFSA grains there might be similar issues. If the Centre reverts to NFSA prices (Rs 1-2-3 per kg) in 2026, will Bihari ration card holders in Chennai be given it free (i.e., at Tamil Nadu prices) or at the PDS price applicable in Bihar?[34] If a Bihari gets it free of cost in Tamil Nadu, who bears the additional cost—the Union government (because ONOR is a central policy) or the state government? If so which one—Tamil Nadu or Bihar.

Second, how will supply logistics be managed? In the current system, every ration shop gets a fixed amount of ration, determined by the number of ration cards/individuals served by that PDS outlet. With ONOR portability, if a card holder from Rajasthan gets their PDS entitlement at a PDS outlet in Delhi, the dealer will have that much less grain for his own PDS card holders. A larger number of PDS card holders may show up than the PDS dealer can cater to, leaving the fate of those who come later in the balance. When more people than can be served by its fixed quota, come to any PDS outlet, a system of dynamic PDS grain supplies will be needed. For inter-state portability, a Centre-State and inter-State coordination mechanism will have to be put in place. An intra-state portability pilot in Chhattisgarh had demonstrated that it is possible with simpler technology (biometric-free offline smart cards) and that intra-state portability could enhance accountability of PDS dealers (Gupta et al 2014).[35]

Studies of ONOR suggest that inter-state portability is hardly used. Intra-state portability is used more but is still around one-tenth of all PDS transaction (Agarwal and Agnihotri 2022 and Tumbe and Jha 2024). The low uptake rates could be due to lack of awareness, lack of demand for portability, operational issues mentioned above, or technological failures.[36]

Doorstep Delivery in Delhi

Another gimmicky initiative that was in the news was Delhi's 'Doorstep delivery' initiative. The Delhi government's version of doorstep delivery was that people's PDS grain should be delivered in their homes (Khera 2020b). On the face of it, it is an appealing idea, but several complexities arise when one gets into the details. If PDS ration is delivered to people's homes, its delivery can be authenticated either by using ABBA or smart cards.

With ABBA, the authentication problems that arose during the 2016 pilot are likely to come up again. In 2016, the Delhi government piloted point-of-sale (POS) machines and Aadhaar-Based Biometric Authentication (ABBA) at forty-two out of roughly 2500 PDS outlets. A small survey at one PDS outlet near the Supreme Court found that one-third of ration card holders could not get their PDS rations in August that year (Priya and Shagun 2016). Under-selling and over-charging continued. Despite these issues, possibly due to pressure from the Central government, the Delhi government extended ABBA to all state PDS outlets in January 2018. In the first month, a report suggested that thousands of families had stopped getting PDS grain, mainly due to ABBA failures. Based on this, the Delhi government immediately (and sensibly) discontinued ABBA; later the Central government forced states to implement it.

Smart cards without biometrics (like Chhattisgarh and Tamil Nadu did before ABBA was made compulsory) could also authenticate transactions at the last mile. Smart cards allow us to reap the advantages of digital technology (a digital trail of each transaction) and without the failings of biometric technology (authentication failures). This option—that allows us to keep the baby and throw out the bathwater—was not discussed at the time, because it was implicitly understood that ABBA will be deployed.

When PDS sales are made at PDS outlets, grain theft is harder—if the dealer tries to cheat on quantity (e.g., authenticating a sale of 20 kg but giving only 15 kg), others present are likely to speak up. With doorstep delivery of PDS grains, it is likely to be harder for individuals to prevent or resist corrupt practices. What is the guarantee that the delivery agent will not indulge in corrupt practices?

The Delhi government's proposal was to give flour at Rs 4 per kg instead of wheat but it was not clear whether this was based on feedback from Delhi's PDS cardholders. NFSA PDS wheat is sold at Rs 2 per kg. The proposed price of wheat flour suggested that the government wanted to charge people retail milling costs, even as it paid *wholesale* milling prices.

Relative to wheat flour, it is easier for people to judge the quality of wheat. West Bengal's experience with wheat flour suggested that there were quality issues. Finally, the resale of jute sacks in which PDS grain is supplied is an important source of income for PDS dealers. Wheat flour supplied in plastic bags could affect the financial viability of PDS outlets and encourage PDS dealers to make good the loss of that revenue stream by cheating people of grain.

***

The PDS has had a chequered history. Plagued by high rates of corruption and exclusion errors through the '90s, it made a laboured comeback through the 2000s. Exclusion errors as well as diversion of grain went down due to state-led reforms. Using 2009-10, we estimated that the implicit transfers from the PDS reduced the head-count ratio by 10-16 per cent and wiped out 18-22 per cent of the poverty gap (see Drèze and Khera 2013). Just as things were beginning to improve the PDS came under attack. Ironically, this attack came in the backdrop of the discussions around the National Food Security Act. Cash transfers became the pet proposal for most. Recognizing that the time had not yet come for cash transfers, the NFSA 2013, retained the PDS as the default option, even as it provided an opening for a switch to cash transfers in the future.

In the following decade, instead of building on the gains of the 2000s, for technocrats in Delhi, welfare programmes became fair game to test new technologies. Aadhaar became the answer to everything. Policies such as Aadhaar Based Biometric Authentication (ABBA) end up diverting attention from the real issues and demands of PDS card holders—

diversification of commodities supplied, continuing corruption, sporadic complaints related to quality, lack of grievance redressal mechanisms, etc. Meanwhile the technocratic policies threaten to derail the gains in reducing corruption in the PDS which has become a lifeline for millions of people. The redeeming moment in the history of the PDS came during COVID-19, when its fiercest critics were compelled to acknowledge its importance and the NDA government leaned heavily on it to help tide over the humanitarian crisis.

7

NREGA

Challenges to Realising its Vision

The Mahatma Gandhi National Rural Employment Guarantee Act (technically MGNREGA, but simply NREGA here) was passed in 2005 and came into force on 2 February 2006. That day, along with social activists, we visited a few Gram Panchayats in Dungarpur district (Rajasthan). We wanted to see if the enactment of the law would remain a remote event or whether it would translate into action on the ground. In the handful of Gram Panchayats we visited, it felt like a mela (a village fair). Camps had been set up to initiate the process of making NREGA 'job cards' for people in every village; we spotted colourful marquees, loudspeakers and mobile jeeps for publicity here and there.

To ensure that the momentum of 2 February 2006 would continue, two months later in April 2006 we returned to Dungarpur for a padyatra. Hundreds of people participated in it, crisscrossing the length and breadth of Dungarpur's panchayats. A large number of NREGA works were open. We met local residents working at NREGA worksites, with a view to creating awareness about the law. We explained that under the NREGA, they could demand work, and if they did not get it within fifteen days, they would be entitled to an unemployment allowance. In a sense, we were telling them that the key to unlocking work opportunities in the village was now in their hands. They looked at us disbelievingly—could such a thing be possible?

Between then and now (2026), 20 years have passed. Did these years of NREGA live up to their promise? Did, for instance, the law succeed in unlocking opportunities for local employment and development? In 2009 the World Bank, an NREGA skeptic, believed that by offering place-based employment it created 'barriers' to development. Five years later, in 2014, the same World Bank called it 'a stellar example of rural development'. What led the World Bank to change its tune? The new tune suggested that the perception battle had been won. Soon after, however, Prime Minister Modi called it a 'living monument' to the failures of the UPA government in a Parliament speech in 2015. Yet, his government was compelled to fallback on NREGA during two major crises: demonetisation and the COVID-19 pandemic. There was a sense that the government felt saddled with NREGA—neither could they own it, nor could they ignore it.

In December 2025, the NDA government found a solution to its predicament with respect to NREGA: it brought a new law to Parliament—completely out of the blue to replace NREGA—the Viksit Bharat–Guarantee for Rozgar and Aajeevika Mission (Gramin) Act (VB-GRAMGA) 2025. The government claims that the new law goes further than NREGA: it promises 125 days of work, more than NREGA's promise of 100 days. The VB-GRAMGA, however, has not been notified at the time of this book going to press. For these reasons, NREGA is reviewed in the present tense in this chapter.

Vision

Before answering the questions posed above, we should examine the vision behind the NREGA. Lack of employment opportunities has been a major challenge in India's development. Millions are willing to work, but fail to get it. On the other hand, rural areas are in dire need of 'development' works—be it roads, footpaths, wells, ponds, irrigation canals, soil conservation, plantation, etc. One underlying principle of NREGA was that the government could intervene to employ rural labour to undertake such development projects. The 'shelf of works' would be decided by Gram Panchayats and as per the provision of the Act, at least 50 per cent of the NREGA funds were to be spent by Gram Panchayats (see Khera 2011 and Narayanan 2020). Thus, NREGA could also breathe life into Panchayati Raj Institutions.

By providing work at minimum wages, the government was de facto stepping in as an 'employer of the last resort'. It was expected that if employment was made available in rural areas, the creation of new employment opportunities would drive up rural wages. When work is available locally, migration to cities is likely to decrease. If rural-urban migration goes down, it will reduce the 'reserve army' of labour in urban areas, possibly putting an upward pressure on wages in urban areas as well. Thus, the creation of new work opportunities through NREGA was expected to impact both rural and urban wages, by making the labour market a bit tighter. If these spillover effects materialised, the resulting upward pressure on rural wages could provide economic support to the lowest paid workers, even those who do not work on NREGA worksites (see Muralidharan et al 2023).

It was also expected that NREGA would play an important role in empowering women. Female labour force participation rates have been low in India, and in rural areas, women have few opportunities to earn a cash income. NREGA provided employment in the village itself (within a 5km radius). It would thus make available work that would allow them to fulfil their domestic responsibilities along with having an opportunity to earn independently.

When the passage of NREGA was being discussed in 2004-05, many expressed a range of reservations: 'Why a law?', said some; after all, an employment scheme can also achieve these objectives. 'What about corruption?' NREGA works will be useless ('digging holes and then filling them') or at best will create poor quality assets ('roads that get washed away'). 'Private farmers will not get workers'. Many people believe(d) that people have become lazy due to NREGA. In the face of such scaremongering, and despite its own wavering commitment to NREGA, the UPA government of the time was compelled to bring the law to Parliament because of public pressure from social movements. Though the Opposition parties were resisting it outside Parliament, ultimately the law was passed unanimously.

Workers' Rights under NREGA

The NREGA promises 100 days of work to every rural household at the minimum wage or at NREGA wages. Rural adults can demand work and under the law, they have to be given employment within fifteen days. If the government fails to provide work, the applicants are entitled to an unemployment allowance. This 'work on demand' right created the hope that the key to work now lay in the hands of workers.

Basic worksite facilities including drinking water, shade for rest are provided under the law. The Act has specific provisions for women—one-third of work opportunities are for them, with care for children below five years at the workplace. The law allows for an NREGA worker to be employed at the workplace to look after children if need be.

Under NREGA, there are two alternative provisions for the wage rate: either the statutory minimum wage for agricultural labourers in the relevant state or central notification of NREGA wages. (In 2009, the Union government switched from statutory minimum wage for agricultural workers to centrally notified state-wise NREGA wages.) Furthermore, NREGA wages are not paid on a daily wage basis; instead, it is de facto a piece-rate system, where the NREGA wage is the maximum they can get for a day, if they complete the required task (as specified in the schedule of rates, based on time and motion studies). If workers come to the worksite to mark attendance, but do not work, their output at the end of the day or week will not meet the pre-specified task, and thus they will be paid commensurately lower wages than the NREGA wage. Workers are also entitled to be paid within fifteen days of working. In case of delays in payment, they are entitled to a compensation.

The law has other labour-favouring provisions—not more than 40 per cent of the NREGA budget can be spent on material in order to maximise employment generation, the use of machinery and of contractors was also banned.

Coming close on the heels of the Right to Information Act 2005, the NREGA established a new benchmark for transparency in government programmes to check corruption.

For example, the government's NREGA website has NREGA related information for every family in every village of the country, so that people can monitor what is being spent in their name.

Workfare vs Welfare

While the need for social protection in poor countries is universally acknowledged, there are several challenges to providing European-style 'unemployment benefits'. One challenge is that measuring employment in the Indian case is not straightforward (e.g., people combine various economic activities over the year or even within a day). Further, it is a widely held view among economists that most developing countries cannot afford to have unemployment benefits for all.

Workfare has served as a substitute for welfare in such resource constrained economies. The biggest advantage of programmes like NREGA is that the non-poor are automatically excluded. How does this happen? Anyone who is able to get work at a wage rate that is higher than NREGA wages, will not ask for work at an NREGA worksite. For instance, if an agricultural worker can get Rs 500 per day for sowing, and the NREGA wage is Rs 300, it is unlikely that she will demand work under NREGA. Only when no work is available or the wage rate offered is less than the NREGA wage, will they resort to NREGA. Thus, the government emerges as an employer of the last resort. 'Self-selection' (or 'self-targeting') into workfare does away with the need for an administrative mechanism to identify the poor to whom government transfers should be directed. This is important because the track record of governments on such identification mechanisms tends to be poor (such as

Chart 7.1: Expenditure on NREGA (as % of GDP)
2006-07 to 2023-24

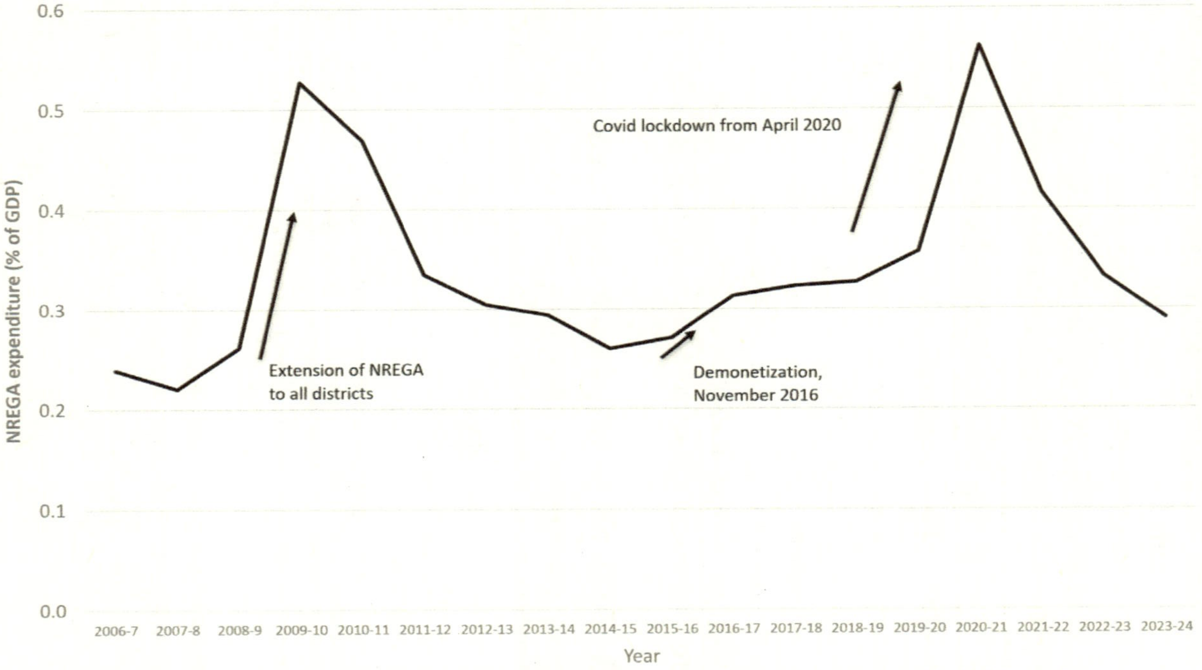

Source: Government of India (various years), Expenditure Budget, Ministry of Finance, https://www.indiabudget.gov.in/doc/eb/allsbe.pdf

the 'BPL Surveys' used for the PDS). Self-targeting also saves administrative resources (time and money) that would have been spent on selecting programme recipients.

The self-targeting design of NREGA increased its appeal among economists of different hues. Even *The Economist* (a magazine usually in favour of restricting government spending on the poor) supported an intervention such as NREGA.

Implementation

There can be several parameters on which to evaluate NREGA implementation. Some of these are: what is the scale of employment generated, did self-targeting work (i.e., were those who got NREGA work among the disadvantaged), did it have any impact on wage rates in the private labour market, did it have an impact on poverty, distress migration, etc., were rural assets created and so on.

Starting with the scale of NREGA employment, according to government data, roughly one-third of all rural households received NREGA work in 2022-23. Though the Act makes a provision of 100 days of work per year, till date, the average per job card has hovered around twenty-five days, even during COVID-19 (2020-21). In 2020-21, 5 per cent of job cards got full 100 days of work. There can be two reasons for this—first, all job cards holding households may not need 100 days of employment per year and second, the demand for 100 days per year exists but remains unmet due to inadequate budgetary provisions or increasingly unreliable wage payments.[37] Though estimating demand for NREGA work is not straightforward, there is evidence that there is unmet demand. For example, in a 2008 NREGA survey of six states, 98 per cent of respondents said they wanted 100 days of work, but only 14 per cent of them actually got

100 days of work. In the PEEP Survey 2013, 83 per cent were interested in 100 days while only 8 per cent had got it in the previous year. Most recently, in March 2025, in a small survey in one Block each of Ajmer and Rajsamand (Rajasthan), while 10-20 per cent of respondents got 100 days of work, 96 per cent reported wanting 100 days or more. Unmet demand is the main cause for the low average days of work (twenty-five days per job card) and a small minority of job card holders getting 100 days of work.

The cost of running NREGA had always been a cause for concern. For instance, to make good on only *half* (fifty days) of the legal guarantee of 100 days of work for 14 crore job card holding families, at a daily market wage of Rs 400, one would require Rs 2.8 lakh crores. If one compares this estimate above with actual NREGA expenditure, it is roughly twice as much as the highest allocated during one of the COVID-19 years, and more than thrice as much as the 2025-26 budget.

In terms of share of GDP, actual NREGA expenditure peaked in 2008-9 and 2009-10 at around 0.5 per cent of GDP (see Chart 7.1).[38] During the first full budget of the NDA government in 2015-16, Prime Minister Modi launched an unprecedented attack on NREGA in Parliament, calling it a 'monument' to the failures of the previous government. Thereafter, other than for the three COVID years (2019-20 to 2021-22), the NREGA budget did not exceed 0.3 per cent of GDP (see Charts 7.1 and 7.2).

Self-targeting

There are several dimensions of self-targeting: across individuals and social groups, within (seasonal) and across years, and regional.

Chart 7.2 Personsdays of employment (crores) and Nominal expenditure on NREGA (Rs. crores)

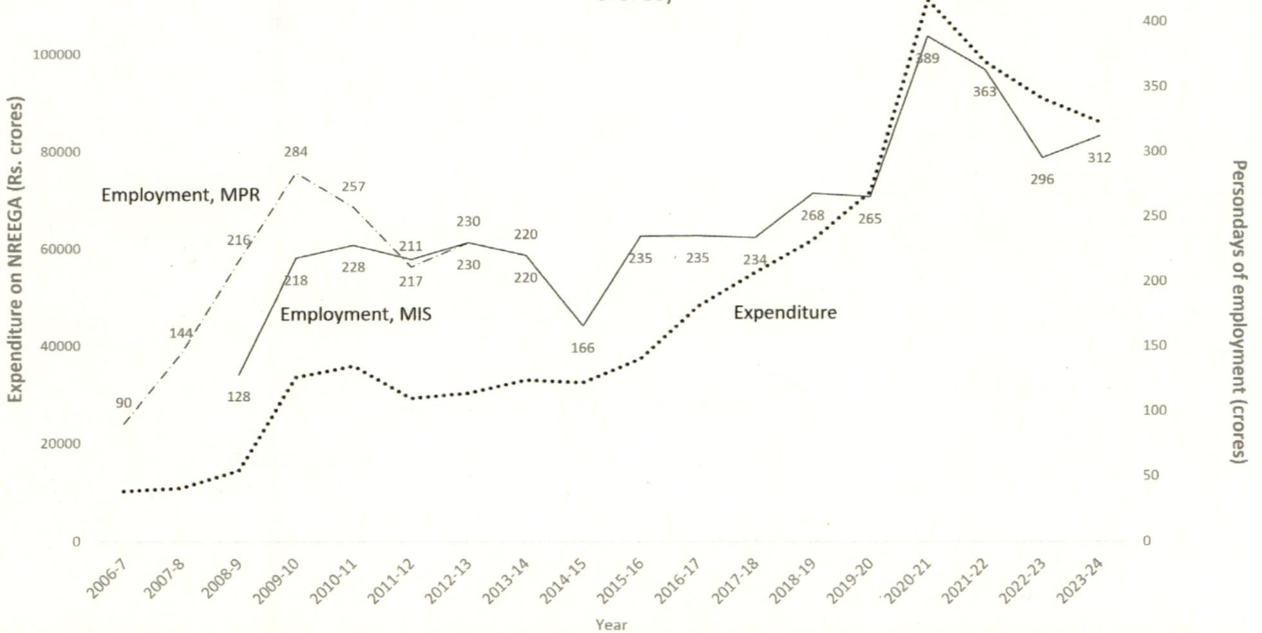

Source: Before 2014-15, Khera (2014). For the early years, as the Ministry put its data management systems in place, the Monthly Progress Report (MPR) and Management Information System (MIS) provide the upper and lower bounds for employment generated. From 2014-15 onwards, Report 5.1.1 on nrega.nic.in (downloaded on 29 July 2025). For expenditure, see Chart 7.1.

Chart 7.3: Participation of disadvantaged groups in NREGA 2006-07 to 2023-24

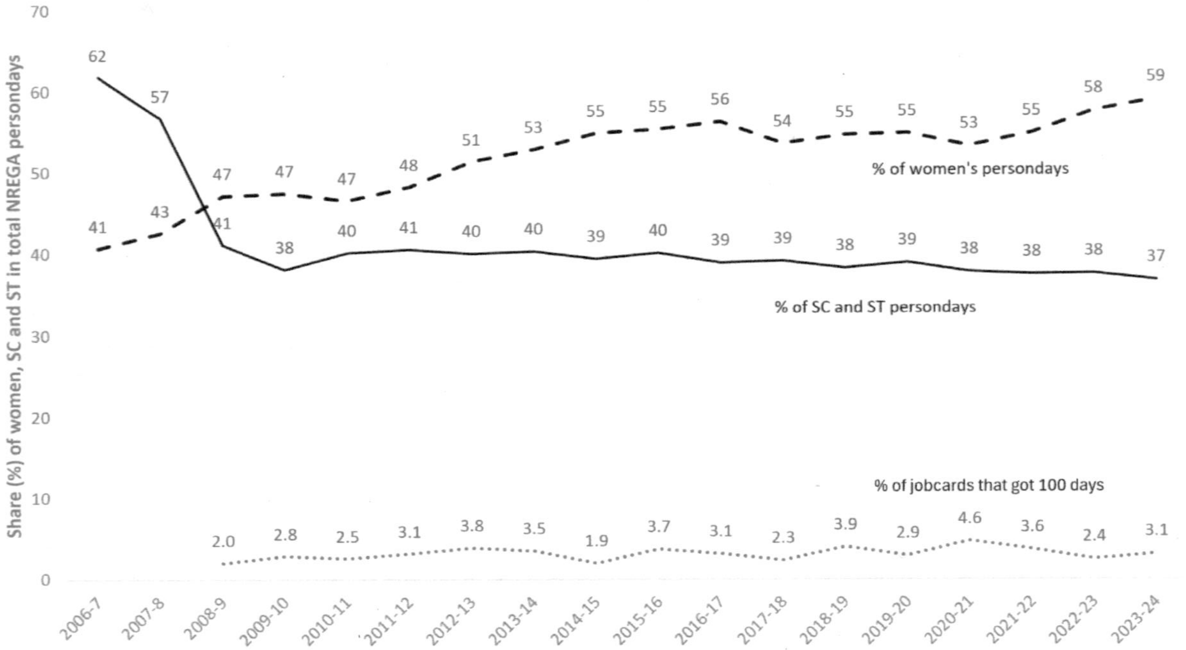

Source: Government of India (various years), report number R.5.1.5, Social category wise employment generated, Ministry of Rural Development. For 2006-7 and 2007-8, data is from Monthly Progress reports; number of jobcards getting 100 days was not reported for those two years.

NREGA has been largely successful on self-selection in terms of favouring workers from vulnerable social groups. Participation of the most disadvantaged groups has been high. Women's share in total NREGA employment has been over 50 per cent (see Chart 7.3), much higher than the legal requirement (one-third, by law). Dalits and Adivasi communities have also received significant employment under NREGA—around 40 per cent of the total persondays generated every year (Chart 7.3). Maps 7.2 and 7.3 show the inter-state variations in the participation of SC and STs and of women respectively for 2023-24.

Besides this, in the early years of implementation, there were several efforts to involve people with disabilities (e.g. employing them to serve water at the NREGA worksite, looking after children, etc.).

Although the law envisaged that funds would be provided according to the demand for work, that never actually happened. As the demand for NREGA work exceeds what can be provided with the budgetary allocations, NREGA work has—de facto—always had to be 'rationed' (e.g, creating a roster for NREGA work). Administrative involvement for rationing, means that someone decides who gets work and who doesn't and this dilutes the 'self-selection' feature of NREGA. Barrett and Liu (2013) find that while self-selection works in terms of demand for work, when there is rationing, those who get rationed out tend to be the poorest; rationing brings a middle-class bias.

What about targeting across states? Interestingly, from a regional perspective, NREGA has provided more work in the better off states. Map 7.1 plots average days of NREGA work per job card in 2023-24 for each state. States such as Kerala, Andhra Pradesh and Tamil Nadu reported more

Map 7.1 NREGA personsdays per job card, 2023-24

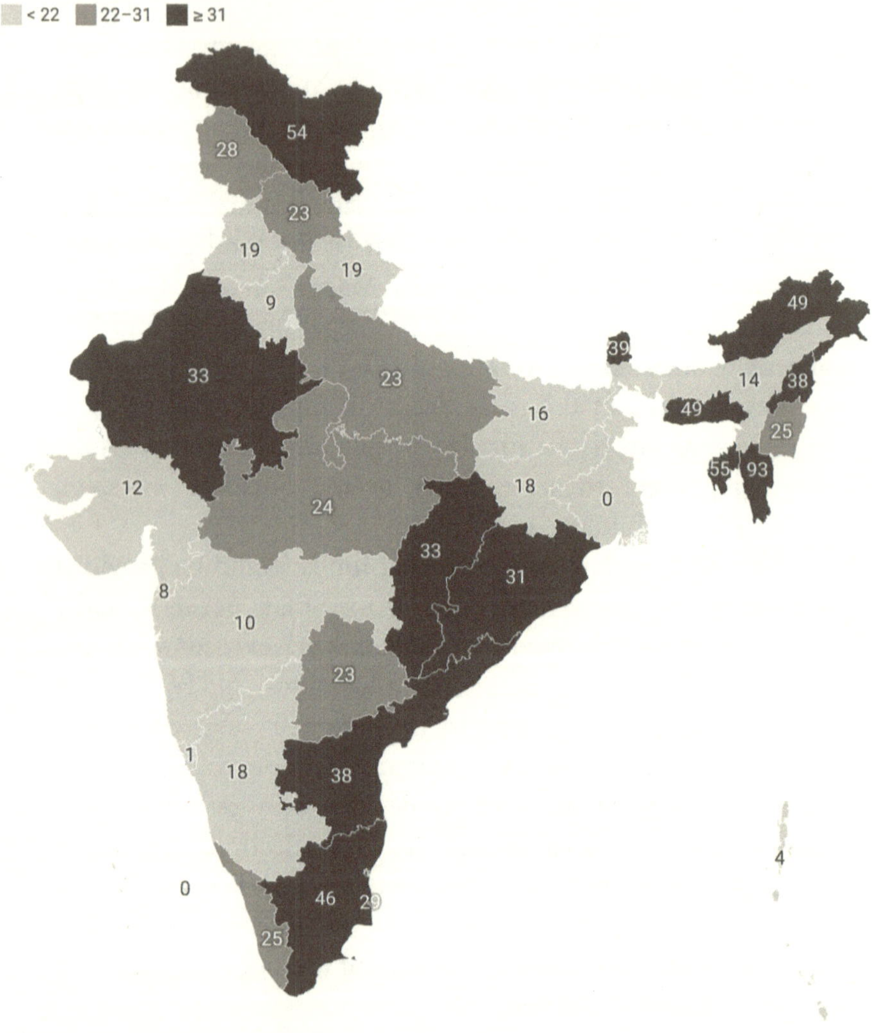

The all-India average of NREGA persondays per job card in 2023-24 was 22 days. States with less than India's person-days average are shown in the lightest shade.

Source: Information obtained from the government website, https://nrega.nic.in/MGNREGA_new/Nrega_home.aspx • Map data: © OSM • Created with Datawrapper

Map 7.2 Participation of Dalits and Adivasis in NREGA, 2023-24

The proportion of Dalit and Adivasi persondays (%) in total persondays

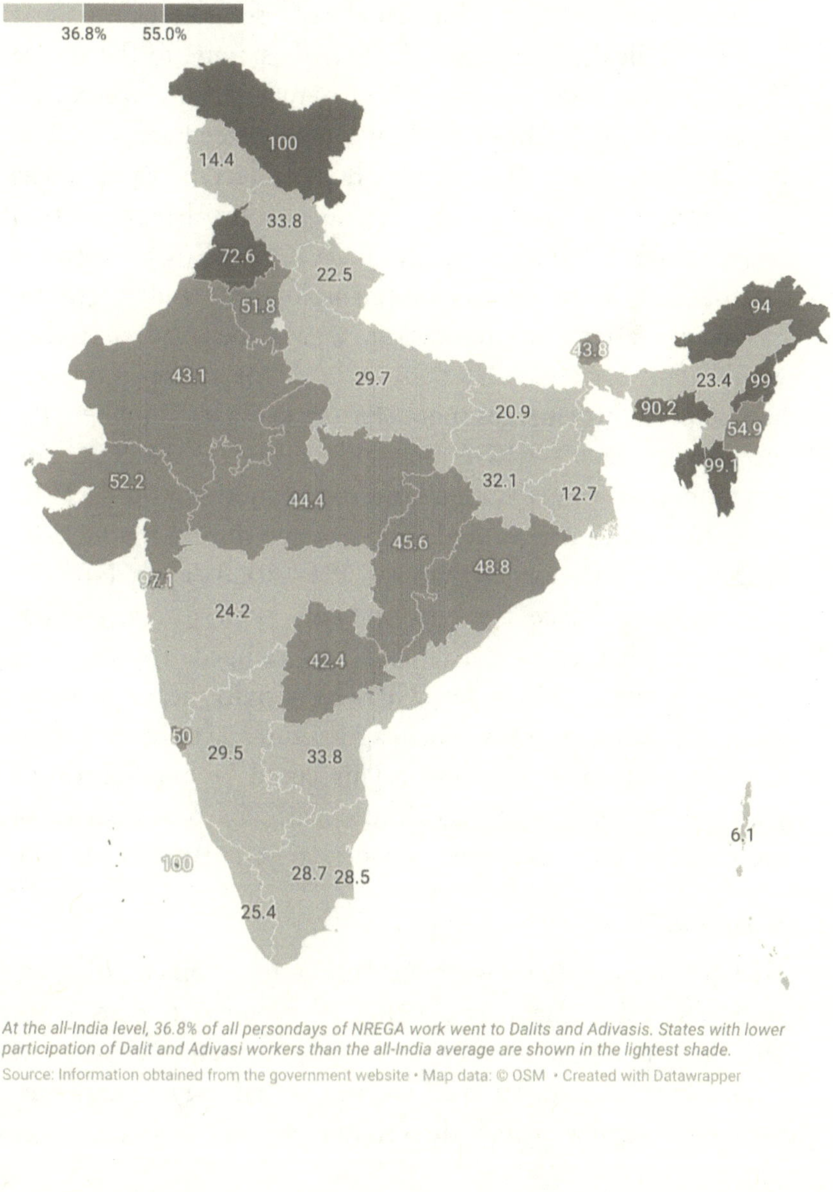

At the all-India level, 36.8% of all persondays of NREGA work went to Dalits and Adivasis. States with lower participation of Dalit and Adivasi workers than the all-India average are shown in the lightest shade.

Source: Information obtained from the government website • Map data: © OSM • Created with Datawrapper persondays of work than poorer states like Uttar Pradesh or Bihar.[39] The other two states where substantial work was available were Rajasthan and Chhattisgarh.

There is another dimension of self-selection—as a counter-cyclical programme. NREGA has come to the rescue in economic crises. Chart 7.1 also reflects this where the expenditure on NREGA is shown as a percentage of GDP. Barring 2008-9, whenever the NREGA budget increased it was in response to an economic crisis (e.g., after demonetisation in November 2016, during the COVID lockdowns between 2020-2022). With reports of unemployment and migration to villages after demonetisation, it was believed that they would fall back on NREGA to tide over the economic hardship.[40] This emerges more sharply in Chart 7.4 where the monthly average NREGA persondays from 2014-2020 and the monthly average NREGA persondays during the COVID years (2020-22) are plotted. The average during the COVID years is distinctly higher than for 2014-2020. Thus, NREGA has provided successive governments with a ready-to-use safety net that can be activated and ramped up whenever a crisis emerges. Moreover, NREGA activity peaks in May-June, the driest months when agricultural activity is lowest in most parts of the country. This could be a reflection of seasonal targeting which coincides with the first quarter of the financial year (after fresh budgets are allocated in March).

Women at Work

NREGA is an economic intervention for women. In most states of India, the participation of women in paid work outside the home is very low. One consequence of low labour force participation of women is that they do not earn their own income, which directly undermines their economic

Chart 7.4 Average persondays of employment, by month

Pre-Covid and Covid-19 years (in crores)

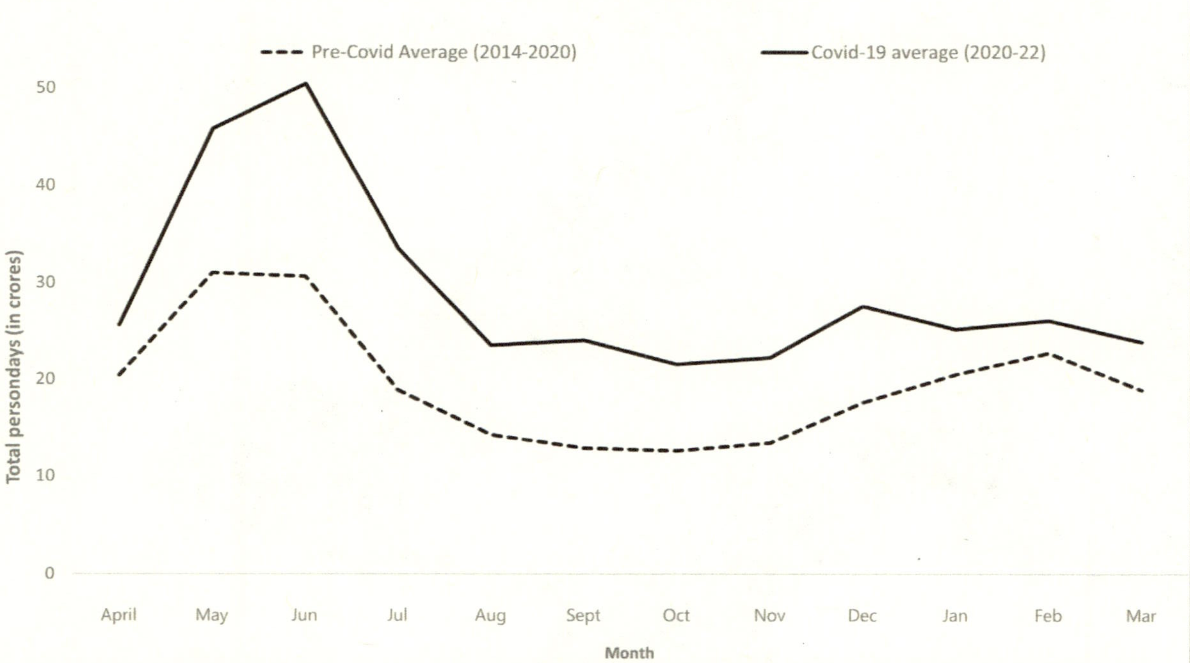

Sources: Government of India (various years, Report R 2.2.2, Projected persondays and persondays generated, Ministry of Rural Development

Map 7.3 Women's participation in NREGA, 2023-24

Share of women's persondays in total persondays

< 45 45–59 ≥ 59

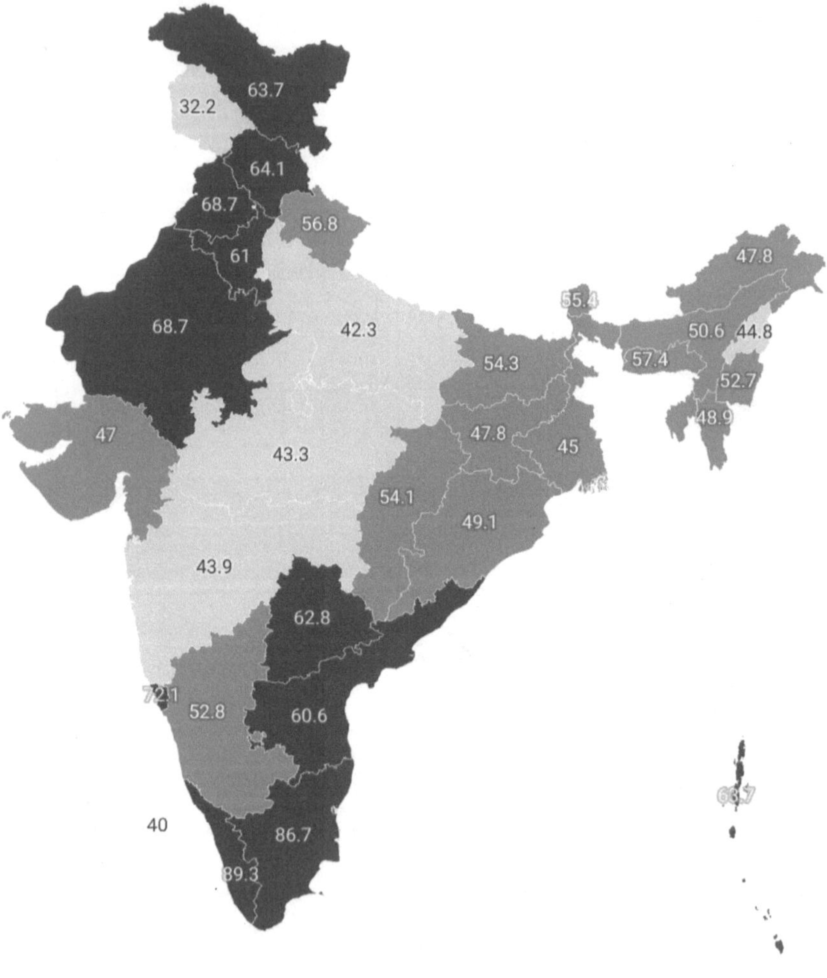

The average share of female persondays at the all-India level is 58.9%. States with higher female participation than the all-India average are indicated in the darkest shade.

Source: Information obtained from the government website • Map data: © OSM • Created with Datawrapper independence. For rural women, NREGA provides earning opportunities in the village itself and that facilitates their participation. NREGA has specific provisions for women—they are supposed to get one-third of NREGA work, equal wages, work within five kilometres of the household and (in principle at least) child care facilities at the worksite for children below five years.

Chart 7.3 shows that women have always participated in large numbers in NREGA work. They received roughly half of the total NREGA persondays generated. In Map 7.3 inter-state differences in women's participation clearly stand out. In states like Tamil Nadu, Kerala and Rajasthan, women have embraced NREGA. In Kerala and Tamil Nadu, women's participation was more than 85 per cent in 2023-24.

One of the reasons that NREGA is an attractive option for women is that in the private labour market, women's wages tend to be lower than those of men (see Chart 7.5, Page 184), whereas NREGA promises equal wages for equal work (it is a promise it delivers on too). Further, research suggests that NREGA led to higher wage rates in the private labour market, and the effect was significant for women (Imbert and Papp 2015 and Berg et al. 2018).

In a survey of six states of NREGA in 2008, women working on NREGA works said that they liked NREGA work because it was near their homes, their work hours were fixed and because they were less likely to be exploited. Interestingly they said that NREGA work was seen as 'government' work by household members. Thus, even in families where women are otherwise debarred from working outside the home, participation in NREGA was considered acceptable. Female respondents also hinted that there is dignity associated with government/NREGA work, in ways that other work outside the house is not (Khera and Nayak 2009).

NREGA is especially important for single women, whose economic condition tends to be very weak. They are vulnerable to economic and other forms of exploitation, if and when they engage in private work. When a family has only one breadwinner (the single woman), they are compelled to take up whatever work comes their way, even if it is risky or physically demanding and pays little money. For such women, the benefits of NREGA are greater—availability of work in the village provides protection against migration, there is a possibility of getting better wages than before (compared to work in the private labour market), and economic independence. In the case of single women, the inter-connectedness of these factors were clearly visible.

Creation of Assets

Asset creation through public works is not uncommon in history—it was one of the major thrusts of the 'New Deal' in the US. In India too, 'famine' or 'relief' works pre-date Indian independence and were later used for creating rural assets. Asset creation is an important objective of the NREGA. Rural areas are in dire need of basic infrastructure such as roads, water conservation, protection against soil erosion, etc.

Because of the cap on material expenditure (upto 40 per cent of the NREGA budget), many (especially urban) believe that all NREGA works are 'mud works'. Besides, they cannot conceive that useful assets can be created without use of cement, bricks and steel. A common perception about NREGA assets is that they are either useless or of poor quality: as mentioned earlier, 'digging holes and filing them up' or 'roads that get washed away'.

In fact, many useful works are possible without any material (think of the pond in the opening paragraph of the book). Moreover, though asset creation did not get much attention in the early years of its implementation, there were some successful projects in spite of the neglect. For example, drainage channels along roads, digging and deepening of ponds, footpaths, fair-weather roads, etc. In West Bengal's Nadia district, a drain was dug in the middle of someone's fields. The owner explained why: the field used to get submerged in the monsoon waters, but now the channel built under NREGA drains the excess water, so he is able to cultivate vegetables there. In Bundi (Rajasthan), existing irrigation canals were never cleaned, resulting in growth of bushes that obstructed the flow of water especially to fields downstream. Every year, the villages in that area witnessed fights over water between upstream and downstream villages. The district administration would have to send the police. These canals were cleaned using NREGA funds resulting in an increase in agricultural production, fewer conflicts and relief for the administration.

Since urban people are accustomed to four- or six-lane roads and highways, the importance of 'kachcha' (fair-weather) roads is not evident to them. But for rural residents, sometimes even footpaths can be transformative. In Latehar, residents of a village told us that it used to be difficult for them to bring the body of a deceased person to the cremation ground or graveyard for their last rites, whereas because of a narrow road made through NREGA, they could now wheel a sick person to the hospital on a bicycle or motorcycle. The construction of public roads can bring relief to Dalit communities, as the right of way is often denied to them. These fair-weather roads lay the foundations for converting them into all-weather road in due course.

In the Sundarbans, earth embankments prevent flood

and tidal waters from entering settlements that would otherwise get inundated during the monsoon. Along with embankments, NREGA has facilitated mangrove plantation that are expected to prevent soil erosion in the longer term. The two together save lives as well as the environment. In Chhattisgarh and Jharkhand, fruit-bearing trees have been planted along roads, on private, forest and panchayat land and on government premises. Back-of-the-envelope estimates suggest good economic rates of return to such plantations.

The NREGA was amended early on to allow work on private lands. In Chhattisgarh, farmers have used this opportunity for land levelling and bunding, allowing for higher yields or cultivation of crops like paddy (that require the bunds to hold water). In Jharkhand, wells have been constructed on private land on a large scale. In some cases, once NREGA wells are functional, orchards have been developed—also under NREGA—after a few years.

Fish ponds are NREGA works that do involve material expenditure. Among successful fish ponds we visited (on behalf of the Ministry of Rural Development), net of expenditure on eggs, fish food, water and electricity, fish farmers reported their annual profits ranged from Rs 1.08 to 3.2 lakh; the cost of the NREGA project ranged from Rs 70,000 to Rs 2.76 lakhs.

On the other hand, many NREGA works have failed—for example, in a village in Sonebhadra (Uttar Pradesh), a pond was built—illogically—at the top of a slope (rather than at the bottom of it). This resulted in all the water flowing away, rather than accumulating in the pond. Similarly, not all wells or fish ponds are complete or profitable.

Beyond the anecdotal evidence above, in a study of 4,100 NREGA sites in Maharashtra, Kulkarni et al (2015) found that 60 per cent of the works supported the agriculture sector; such works were a major share of NREGA works—75 per cent of the works were directly or indirectly related to agriculture (Kulkarni et al. 2015). According to one estimate, investment in NREGA mango plantations in Jharkhand have an economic rate of return of 20 per cent or so (Drèze and Nair, 2023). The estimated return on wells has been 2-6 per cent (Bhaskar, Gupta and Yadav 2016 and Gupta, Kumar and Aggarwal 2012).

The examples and studies above suggest that useful public works and productive private and public assets can be created with and without material costs, when adequate technical support is available. Contrary to the widespread belief that NREGA has been a failure in terms of asset creation, the studies so far present a more hopeful picture.

Corruption

Corruption in government programmes, including public works has been a long-standing issue. Naturally, discussion on the enactment of NREGA put the spotlight on these concerns and was one of the major reasons that NREGA was being opposed. In the pre-NREGA era of famine/relief works (as they were referred to then), corruption took the form of 'ghost works' (i.e. works that existed only on paper, not on the ground) and 'ghost workers' (i.e., people who either did not work or did not exist were recorded as workers on muster rolls). Wage and material corruption were both big issues.

A widespread mechanism for siphoning off wages was to manipulate the muster roll that recorded workers attendance. Manipulation often took the form of inflating attendance (e.g., if a worker worked for a day, a '0' after the '1' was added in the muster roll to make it '10' days). In most parts of the country, muster rolls were rarely made public, so people could not see who was supposed to have worked or how many days they had worked. Inflated muster rolls would be sent forward for getting wage payments sanctioned. Once sanctioned, the worker would get what was due to them (e.g., a days' wage as per the hypothetical example above) and the rest would be divided among government functionaries according to a 'PC system'. The PC system refers to 'percentage system' whereby the percentage share of each functionary is pre-decided (e.g., 1 per cent to the mate who inflates attendance, 5 per cent to the junior engineer who inflates work measurement and so on).

In the NREGA, there was an emphasis on people's participation. Several transparency provisions in the Act were implemented, including constructive use of technology. Availability of muster rolls at the worksite is one example of transparency measures in NREGA. This allows workers to keep an eye on their attendance and demand their rights. The creation of the NREGA MIS portal (nrega.nic.in) also helped enhance transparency.

In 2008-9, the smoothly functioning 'PC system' received a jolt because the Ministry of Rural Development initiated a move from cash payment of wages at the worksite to payment of wages into worker's bank accounts. (From 2012-13 onwards, as bank accounts began to be linked with Aadhaar numbers, the same process, i.e., wage payments into bank accounts, began to be called 'Direct Benefit Transfers', or DBT.) The separation of the implementation agency (i.e., the person who records attendance) and the payment agency (those responsible for paying the worker), made corruption harder. With this, if someone inflated attendance (e.g., from one to 10 days), it was no longer easy for that person to keep the extra nine days of wages, because wages would be credited directly to the worker's account. This helped reduce wage corruption. According to one estimate, while 42-56 per cent of days of NREGA work was confirmed by people in 2007-8, by 2009-10—within two years of the transition to bank payments—70 per cent of work recorded on the MIS was confirmed by respondents. This improved further to 68-78 per cent by 2011-12 (Drèze 2017).

Then new ways of siphoning off wages emerged. For instance, NREGA functionaries began colluding with NREGA workers (they may not need to work a single day, so long as they allow their job cards to record work). Some instances of collusion between the implementation functionaries and post offices and banks also came to light: here, workers did not realise that their account is being used to withdraw NREGA wages. A third route was coercion—attendance would be inflated and when workers went to withdraw their inflated wages, they would be forced to hand over some part of it to corrupt functionaries. To the extent that workers have now been co-opted into NREGA's 'web of corruption', traditional social audits—whereby administrative records are cross-checked against either worker's testimonies or independent surveys—can no longer help uncover the scale of wage corruption. Thus, though initially payment of wages into worker's accounts helped curb corruption, it also made corruption harder to expose and this took a toll in due course. In more recent times, the plot has thickened—newer forms of corruption have come to light.

This section provides a bird's eye view of NREGA's record on the ground on a handful of parameters—scale of work, self-targeting, asset creation and corruption. The literature on NREGA is very rich and would be hard to summarise here. Absent a comprehensive literature review, an important collection of the NREGA literature has been compiled by Emilia Cooper, Jean Drèze and Pavlina Tcherneva (2024).

The Battle for Employment Guarantee: 2006-2014

In 2002-03, as a PhD student, I conducted a field study of 400 families to assess the state's role in helping rural households cope with drought in Rajasthan. The scale of drought relief works in the eight sample villages (across Barmer, Bikaner, Jaipur and Udaipur) was impressive. Being a drought-prone state, Rajasthan—like Gujarat and Maharashtra—had a long history of initiating such public relief works.

At that time, whenever a public work commenced in a village anyone who wanted to work, could simply turn up at the worksite and request to be added to the muster roll. At the end of each fortnight, some (often only notional) work measurement would be done and the muster roll would be sent to the block office for processing wage payments.

Once the payment was sanctioned, the mate (a worksite supervisor) or panchayat secretary would collect cash from the block office and distribute wages at the worksite. Names of workers would be called out, they came forward to sign for its receipt and take the cash. For relief works, payment was partly in cash and the rest in-kind (for which they would be given a grain coupon to be redeemed at the local PDS outlet). These simple transparency measures helped Rajasthan keep tabs on corruption in public relief works programmes.

Rajasthan's success in implementing drought relief works was a major factor in social movements demanding a state Act in 2002-2003, along the lines of Maharashtra's state law, the Employment Guarantee Scheme (EGS) formulated in the seventies. However, Chief Minister Gehlot faltered and passed the buck to the Centre. In November 2003, he lost the state election. Social movements did not give up, and succeeded in lobbying for its inclusion in the Congress manifesto for the General Elections in 2004. Maharashtra's EGS and the experience of state governments with public relief works set a precedent that bolstered the campaign for a national law.

In 2005, NREGA was passed. Important lessons from the grassroots in Rajasthan (e.g., muster rolls and payment of wages at the workplace) were incorporated into NREGA. These increased transparency and helped curb corruption. Attempts to replicate these lessons in other states yielded mixed results. States like Tamil Nadu and Chhattisgarh were able to implement NREGA reasonably well, while corruption (the 'PC system') was a major problem in others (e.g. Odisha).

The first few years (2006-2012) of NREGA were full of promise. Work was generated on a massive scale, that led to some increase in wages in the private rural labour market over the years, especially for women (Khera 2011). There was discussion on what works could be undertaken through NREGA. Fair weather roads, water conservation works such as ponds and check-dams, wells on private lands, etc. were built in those years.

As mentioned earlier, in 2008, wage payments began being credited to bank and post office payments with the aim of reducing corruption. It did make a significant dent on corrupt practices, initially at least. Labourers, however, suffered in the early years. For a while, they were denied NREGA work if they had not opened accounts, delays in wage payments crept into the system, and workers struggled to navigate banks in rural areas (Adhikari and Bhatia 2010).

NREGA, however, began running into trouble during the second term of the UPA. Although political gurus had projected NREGA as a major factor for the return of the Manmohan Singh government for a second term, political support seemed to wane. Sensible uses of technology were replaced with technocratic implementation during UPA-II's term. What was puzzling was that this was being done by a regime (of politicians, bureaucrats and technocrats) who were ostensibly supporters of NREGA.

The first signs of trouble emerged in 2012 when the UPA-II government felt that 'time has come for second generation reforms' and formulated an NREGA 2.0. Instead of strengthening the basic objectives of NREGA (providing work, timely payment of wages, etc.), a variety of other goals like sanitation, self-help groups, financial inclusion, etc. were thrust upon it. The original purpose of the law, 'securing livelihood' of people, began to get lost.

Dark Clouds over NREGA: 2014-2024

Flagging Political Support

NREGA received a hostile reception from the BJP-led NDA government that came to power in 2014. There were open political attacks on it. In 2014, the then Rajasthan chief minister (Ms Vasundhara Raje) questioned the necessity of a law ('why is a law needed, why not just a scheme?'). The Rural Development Minister in Delhi wanted to propose that NREGA should be amended and made applicable in the poorest 200 districts (out of roughly 600 districts in all). The government's proposal to limit NREGA to 200 districts was not sound. It would require coming up with reasonable selection criteria for which districts and/or blocks would remain under NREGA. It would significantly undermine the 'self-selection' design of the law. The reasoning behind the government proposal was that there is no demand for NREGA in better-off districts. However, ground realities suggested otherwise: better-off states like Tamil Nadu and Andhra Pradesh had already seen robust implementation of NREGA.

The proposed amendment would also undermine people's rights. Rights-based programmes such as NREGA are meant to empower people; being a law, gives people the opportunity to learn about their rights and demand them. If such rights can be unilaterally withdrawn, the very purpose of such laws is defeated. The importance of NREGA being a law, rather than merely an employment scheme became evident when both proposals died a quiet death in a few weeks because at that time the government could not muster up the courage to bring those amendments to Parliament. Ultimately, the NDA government did not amend NREGA. As we saw in December 2025, that did not, however, imply its troubles were over.

Prime Minister Modi's speech in Parliament in February 2015, revealed the BJP's hostility and double standards since the law was passed unanimously in 2005. These served as a cue to later political assaults on it, including its replacement with VB-GRAMGA in 2025.

Technocracy and Centrazliation: Aadhaar-related Problems

Though 'NREGA 2.0' was announced in 2011-12 by the UPA-2 government, its main feature that emerged gradually, and was ramped up dramatically around 2013-14, was its takeover by technocrats.

The Ministry of Rural Development (MoRD) became a den of (often well-meaning) technocrats. They believed that issues plaguing NREGA could be solved by real-time monitoring, electronic (e)-everything: e-Muster Rolls (e-MRs), e-Fund Management Systems (e-FMS), GPS-enabled biometric attendance and a National Mobile Monitoring System (NMMS) that requires geo-tagged photographs from NREGA worksites as proof of attendance. In the name of curbing corruption, attendance and wage payments have been subjected to repeated techno-manic experiments.

Instead of deploying technology to make NREGA processes simpler for workers, technocrats began using it to make their own tasks easier. For instance, the NREGA MIS began as a tool for empowering workers because it brought greater transparency to the system. Over time, the same worker-centred MIS began to be deployed as a tool for administrators to monitor NREGA from their offices: all they needed to do was gaze at NREGA's portal where many processes were supposedly being reported in real-time from NREGA worksites. Every once in a while, a bureaucrat would direct us to the MIS as proof of how well NREGA was being implementation in their area. However, the realities were somewhat different—just as corrupt functionaries had managed to overcome the barrier created by bank payments in their smoothly functioning PC system through collusion and coercion, they also found ways of escaping scrutiny of real-time systems.

An important illustration of this was the replacement of paper muster rolls with e-Muster Rolls (e-MR). The idea was that instead of bringing a fresh muster roll to a worksite and adding workers names, the names of those who demand work would be submitted to the Block office, where an e-MR would be generated. What distinguishes an e-MR from a paper MR is that names of workers and other worksite details are auto-populated through the MIS and printed, rather than being written by hand. In this process, a work demand receipt would be generated that would allow workers to claim unemployment allowance, in case they did not get work on time. It was also claimed that e-MR would prevent corruption, but it did not solve either of these problems. In practice, in some places, e-MRs were generated after the work had been done by a group of workers. Thus, 'real-time' monitoring systems were actually reflecting workers of the past week or fortnight as currently employed (see Khera 2025). e-MR increased paperwork and led to the return of middlemen in some places. As it became compulsory to demand work formally, middlemen carved out a role for themselves in helping workers navigate the application process.

When e-MRs failed to curb the incidence of 'ghost workers', the Ministry added another layer of technology: daily on-site attendance on the National Mobile Monitoring System (NMMS) was made mandatory in 2021-22 even though many flaws were found during a pilot. The NMMS requires worksite attendance be recorded photographically twice a day within scheduled time windows; photographs are geo-tagged, they could only be uploaded from the NREGA worksite. Mates reported problems in uploading photos in rural areas, due to which wages were cut or remain unpaid (Buddha and Tamang 2024). Only those NREGA workers whose mates could successfully do this got paid. In mid-2025, the Ministry of Rural Development acknowledged that even NMMS had failed. Ghost workers continue to be recorded, and anecdotally, JCB machines were used to do the work that was booked as wage expenditure. Instead of discontinuing it, the MoRD ordered verification of the thousands of photos that were uploaded on the NMMS.

The integration of Aadhaar is the most important example of mindless technocracy. Workers were given the impression that if they did not have Aadhaar, they would no longer get NREGA work. The same tactic was used to force them to link their Aadhaars to their NREGA job card and their accounts. If workers failed to do so, their payments would be held up (*The Hindu* 2021). The MoRD surreptitiously made Aadhaar-linking mandatory for NREGA (in spite of orders from the Supreme Court stating that it should remain voluntary). For instance, for a while, only those workers who had successfully linked their Aadhaar could demand work through the NREGA portal. In some cases, the pressure on state governments to link Aadhaar with NREGA led to disastrous outcomes for NREGA workers. In Chitradurga district (Karnataka), wages worth Rs 10-15 crore were delayed. Inquiries revealed that those workers who did not have Aadhaar numbers, were deleted by the data entry operator from the NREGA database. Under pressure from the administration to show 100 per cent Aadhaar-linking, the data entry person's response was to delete workers without Aadhaar from the database. After Aadhaar-seeding, the Aadhaar Based Payment System (ABPS) was introduced. Between 2019-20 and 2022-23, 10.4 crore workers were deleted from the NREGA database, and the surge in deletions coincided with circulars stating that ABPS was compulsory (Narayanan and Buddha 2024).

Though these measures were justified as counter-corruption measures, linking accounts with Aadhaar (by now labelled 'DBT') added no additional safeguards to the existing mechanism of paying wages into worker's accounts.[41] Despite reduction in wage corruption due to bank payments, the Unique Identification Authority of India (UIDAI) narrative was that Aadhaar is necessary to prevent NREGA corruption. According to them, Aadhaar was necessary to open bank accounts for NREGA workers, which in turn is necessary in the fight against corruption. While the latter is true (corruption did come down once wages began to be paid into bank accounts), the fact is that payment of NREGA wages through bank accounts had been initiated in 2008, before Aadhaar was conceived.

Why was Aadhaar made compulsory then? The most likely explanation for this is that the UIDAI needed a readymade database to ramp up Aadhaar enrolment in its early years. Aadhaar offered no additional benefits, so it was unlikely that people would queue up for it. Vulnerable workers who worried about losing access to their rights (to work and to food), queued up for enrolment (see Khera 2018).

Tamil Nadu was perhaps an exception where labourers continued to be prioritised in NREGA implementation. In 2014-15, every job card holding household got thirty-two days of work. Women got 85 per cent of the employment. This was better than states considered successful for its implementation: e.g., in Andhra Pradesh and Rajasthan, on average, households with a job card received seventeen days of work and women's participation was 59 per cent and 68 per cent, respectively. Moreover, there were some creative experiments in broadening the shelf of works in Tamil Nadu. For instance, solid waste segregation and disposal in 2000 Gram Panchayats. Tamil Nadu managed to evade the diktat on e-Muster Rolls for a while, and remained successful in making wage payments in seven days (Khera 2016). Over time, with increasing centralisation, the space available to states to design and implement their own systems has shrunk, and even states like Tamil Nadu have been compelled to follow Central diktats.

The problem of centralisation existed since the inception of NREGA. In the initial days, a Rural Development minister wanted that construction of Rajiv Gandhi Bharat Nirman Seva Kendras be allowed under NREGA.[42] Sometimes, the length, breadth and depth of the work was being specified by the Ministry in Delhi. Then, there was fierce opposition to centralisation of the list of works, because under the NREGA this list should be prepared by the Gram Panchayat and attempts to generate such target-based assets were counter-productive on the ground.

However, increasing technocratisation since 2014 has centralised the programme exponentially. When delays in wage payments arose around 2008, of the various reasons for the delays, technocrats zeroed in on the delays by lower-level functionaries in crediting workers' accounts. Their solution was to take away control from local administration. A centralised mechanism, the Electronic Fund Management System (e-FMS) was introduced. In West Bengal, a Block Development Officer (BDO) despairingly told us it took him eight hours to process one payment through e-FMS. The system could crash at any step along the way. (The feeling was similar to queuing at ATMs after demonetisation, where cash could run out just when it was your turn.) Funds, stored in the 'cloud', began to be disbursed on a first-come-first-served basis. As soon as NREGA functionaries knew that funds were available, they would rush to clear pending payments. Those with better internet connectivity (and luck!) managed successfully, delaying payments to those in more remote areas.

Worse, before one change could take root, another change would be brought about. Before addressing issues related to e-FMS, the Public Fund Management System (PFMS) was introduced.[43] Before NREGA officials could learn what PMFS stands for, a discussion on 'NE-FMS' began: one official remarked, 'Before we can read one government circular, another comes along.' This was a repeat of continuously rejigging wage payments—from cash-in-hand to account-based payments to Aadhaar-based Payment Systems (ABPS) or in the case of attendance, from paper muster rolls to e-MRs to NMMS.

Centralisation has meant that job card deletions, wage payments, compliance by states with Central directives and other important aspects of NREGA can be controlled by the central or state governments. Centralisation and technocratisation have also meant that administrative bandwidth has been diverted from their core tasks (opening, measuring and paying for NREGA work) to complying with the demands of databasing the NREGA population (generating Aadhaar, Aadhaar-seeding, etc.). 'Digital red tape'—a combination of old-fashioned paperwork and digitalisation demands—has become a nightmare.

Budgetary Woes

Though the law was meant to be 'demand driven' so that money would have to be made available as per the demand for NREGA work, it never functioned like that. As mentioned earlier, several surveys find evidence of unfulfilled demand for NREGA employment.

Another indicator of unmet NREGA demand comes from the budgets. For several years, a pernicious pattern has been repeating itself. The funds allocated in the budget in March get exhausted by October; those who work after that remain unpaid until the government supplements the allocation in the revised budget (around December) or until the following years' budget is announced. Thus, a substantial part of the following year's budget is used to clear the previous year's arrears. This cycle repeats itself the following year.

How this undermines the programme is easy to understand. If people's wages/salary remain due for months, anyone would start looking for other options. NREGA workers tend to be the most vulnerable economically (often landless workers, or small and marginal farmers), who cannot afford to wait for months to be paid. When wages are not paid in a timely manner, they begin to lose interest in NREGA.

The government has made no attempt to fix this problem. Far from correcting it, sometimes the NREGA budget has been lowered from one year to the next. Contrary to a common (mis)perception that the NREGA budget is huge, Chart 7.1 shows that over the past decade it has been 0.2-0.5 per cent of GDP.

When the government is questioned about the low budget, its responses are unconvincing. For instance, on one occasion it was said that though the NREGA budget has decreased, the budget of the Prime Minister's Awas Yojana (PM-Awas) has increased. This argument is difficult to accept because a large part of the PM-Awas budget is for material and in any case, the labour component is already paid for through NREGA. Thus, it does not generate much additional employment. Another response is that if more funds are required, they will be made available. When they have been required, in fact, funds have not been made available. Some have even gone as far as to say that the lower expenditure is an indication that the demand for NREGA work is declining because better opportunities are available to NREGA workers.

Another worrying phenomenon related to budgetary allocations has to do with the government's 'double engine' mindset. The most egregious example of this is what has happened in West Bengal since 2019. Under the guise of stopping corruption, the Centre not only stopped releasing funds to the state, but it did not transfer funds required to clear the wage arrears of thousands of NREGA workers who had already worked. Moreover, no action was taken against those who indulged in corrupt practices (if any), yet it was the workers who were punished even though it is unlikely that they were responsible for it.

NREGA Wages: Stagnation and Delays

Stagnation in wage rates and delayed payments are two serious issues that need urgent attention. Each year, there is a notional increase in the NREGA wage rate to account for inflation. Yet, the increase is so small that on several occasions workers have protested. For instance, on May Day in 2016, NREGA workers in Jharkhand decided to return the increment to the Prime Minister. That year the NREGA wage for Jharkhand increased by Rs 5 per day. Moreover, at best the government only accounts for inflation while determining the increase in the wage. In real terms, NREGA wages have stagnated for years.

Chart 7.5 clearly shows the stagnation in NREGA wages in real terms (the black bold line is more or less flat). The chart also plots wages for sowing, agricultural and non-agricultural work, known to be among the lowest in the private labour market. The chart shows that NREGA wages are now lower than private market wages for all categories. In the initial years of implementation, NREGA wages were higher than those for female agricultural workers but that is no longer true. As mentioned earlier, research suggests that NREGA put an upward pressure on private market wages for women in the early years. For male workers, wages in the private labour market are now almost twice as

Chart 7.5 NREGA and private labour market wages are stagnating in real terms, (Rs per day, 2014-15=100)

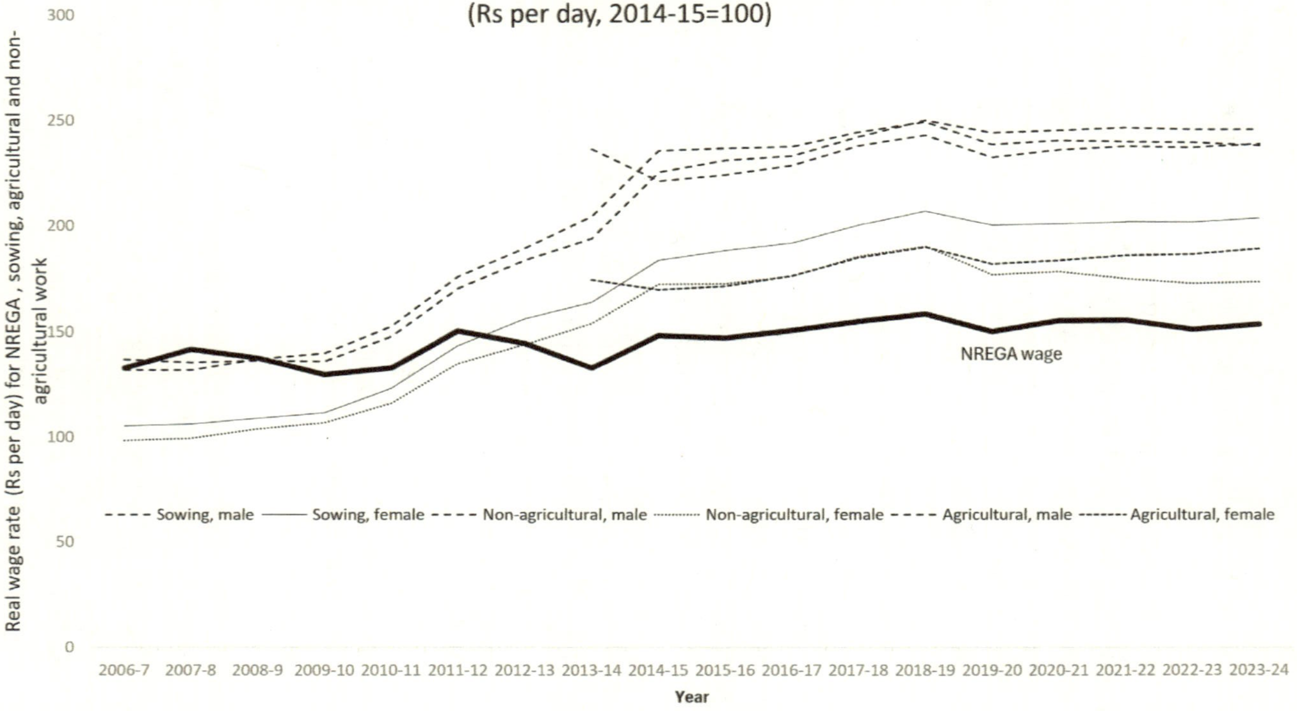

Source: NREGA wages, nrega.nic.in; Consumer Price Index, Reserve Bank of India; sowing, agricultural and non-agricultural wages, compiled by Arindam Das from https:labourbureau.gov.in/rural-wages much as NREGA, making the latter an unattractive option. Since 2014-15, even the private wage growth rate itself has flattened out.

The problem of low wages is compounded by delays in payment. Barring a handful of states, payments are not made within the stipulated period of fifteen days. Delays are chronic: budgetary allocation patterns, the introduction of Aadhaar-based payments and its attendant problems (e.g. Aadhaar-seeding), etc. lie behind these delays. Constant tinkering with the payment systems, justified in the name of making payments more secure (or faster even) made matters worse. For instance, after workers linked their bank accounts to Aadhaar, they were asked to onboard the Aadhaar Payment Bridge System (APBS). Bank accounts and Aadhaar numbers got cross-wired, e-KYC failed for many, leading to 'diverted' or 'rejected' payments. (These problems were not limited to NREGA wages (see Dhorajiwala, Wagner and Drèze 2019)). Increasing technocratisation and the centralisation it has facilitated have worsened delays in wage payments. For instance, in Karnataka and Jharkhand, the names of some NREGA workers who had worked but were yet to be paid were deleted from the NREGA MIS so that the data entry operator could show 100 per cent Aadhaar-seeding. Even after wages are credited by the concerned government authorities, people struggle to withdraw their wages either because they cannot trace their wages, or due to biometric failures, and so on (LibTech 2020).

Of the many problems facing NREGA, those related to wages are perhaps the most worrisome. NREGA wage rate being much lower than private labour market wage rates, delays in payments and a cumbersome payment process have contributed to many workers losing interest.

VB-GRAMGA: Throwing Out the Baby

In the garb of increasing entitlements (from 100 to 125 days) and reducing corruption through even greater—and admittedly failed—technocratisation, in December 2025 the government replaced NREGA with VB-GRAMGA. For many, this tectonic change in worker's rights has registered merely as a name change and an increase in the promised days of work. However, there are many ways in which the new law allows the government to render the right to work entirely hollow. For instance, the law allows the government to notify the new law selectively (within and across states); the law increases the financial obligation of the state governments from 10 per cent to 40 per cent; it fixes a "notional allocation" (to which the 60-40 cost sharing ratio applies) for each state; for expenditure beyond the notional allocation, state governments must bear 100 per cent of costs; it centralises the planning of works through convergence with Centrally notified schemes. None of the problems of NREGA—stagnating wages, payment issues, technocratisation—are dealt with in the new law (Drèze and Khera 2026). Going by its track record, there is little hope that VB-GRAMGA will help to realise the right to work.

8

SOCIAL SECURITY PENSIONS

Contingency Care

During the PEEP survey in 2013, I met Antar Kunwar in Sirohi, Rajasthan. She was old and widowed. At that time, the coverage of social security pensions in Rajasthan was very limited. As a result, Antar Kunwar was neither getting an old-age nor a widow pension. As we interviewed her, she explained how she got by: she sometimes sold cow dung, at other times, she collected grains of wheat scattered on the ground during the harvest; sometimes her brother secretly (behind his wife's back) gave her money and at yet others, her caste neighbours gave her some food. It was a moving account of how difficult life can be for elderly widows.

It was the plight of millions of others like Antar Kunwar that led to the emergence of the slogan *'Kaam ka pura daam do, budhape mein araam do'* (fair wages for work, a pension when the elderly cannot work). After a lifetime of working in the unorganised sector at low and often exploitative wages, when the labouring class grows old, they have little by way of savings. On the one hand, like children their dependence on others for basic physical needs increases, and they need assistance for routine daily tasks; on the other they lose financial independence because they can no longer earn. According to Rajan and Mishra (2024), 20 per cent of the elderly face these four challenges—lack of income, poverty, multiple ailments, and difficulties in managing daily activities. To some extent, families are able to meet these needs, but as many struggle to manage their own (nuclear family's) affairs, it is easy or convenient to forget the elders in the house.

For over a decade, public discussion has been focused on reaping the potential of a 'demographic dividend' in India. The demographic dividend refers to the advantages likely to accrue to the economy due to a large share of population in the working age group. It is worth recalling that in India, the share of people over sixty years of age in 2011 was 9 per cent, and it is estimated that in 2036 it will rise to 18 per cent (Drèze and Duflo 2022). People aged 15-59 years comprise more than 60 per cent of the total population in the 2021-2036 period, whereas the share of children aged under 15 years is projected to fall from 26 per cent to 20 per cent in the same period. Thus, as fertility rates fall, the population pyramid is likely to become 'top heavy' as the share of older people rises. Combined with rising life expectancy, the elderly will require support for a longer duration. Therefore, issues related to meeting the needs of an ageing population, including pensions and healthcare, need greater attention.

Pension provisions in India vary by sector. Table 8.1 lists four types—according to the sector of employment and whether pension provisions are contributory or not. Among those in government service, there are two types of pension arrangements—a non-contributory Old Pension Scheme (OPS) for those recruited up to December 2004 (cell 1B in Table 8.1), and a contributory New Pension Scheme (NPS) for those employed after 2004 (1A). These apply to those with regular jobs. Similarly, in the unorganised sector, there are two types of pensions—contributory, where employees or the self-employed make a monthly contribution towards their pension (2A), and non-contributory, such as social security pensions (2B). Each of these are discussed in this chapter but our main interest is in the National Social Assistance Programme (NSAP), given to cover various contingencies including (but not limited to) old age.

Table 8.1 Types of Pension

(Figures in brackets indicate estimated coverage)

	(1) Organised Sector	*(2) Unorganised Sector*
(a) Contributory	New Pension Scheme, 2004 onwards (1.7 crore)[1] Employee Provident Funds Act, 1952 (68-82 lakhs)[2]	Atal Pension Yojana (4.8 crore)[1], PM Mandhan Pension Yojana (0.7 crore)[3]
(b) Non-Contributory	Old Pension Scheme	National Social Assistance Programme (~7 crore)[4]

Source: [1]Government of India (2023), Chapter 5, pages 256–257. [2]Lower limit from Press Information Bureau (2025) and upper limit from Employees' Provident Fund Organisation (n.d.). [3]https://maandhan.in/maandhan/summary [4]Author's estimates, based on government data (see Appendix I, Table A7).

The OPS vs NPS Debate

Since 2022 the debate on the New Pension Scheme (NPS) and the Old Pension Scheme (OPS) has resurfaced. In Rajasthan, the Congress government promised to revert to OPS. Since then, political parties in other states too (Punjab, Himachal Pradesh, Jharkhand, Chhattisgarh, etc.) incorporated this promise in their manifestos and policies.

Remember, these pensions apply to formal sector government employees only, whose share in total employment is small (less than 10 per cent) and whose salaries put most of them among the top 5-10 per cent in the country. It includes government employees with permanent jobs (for example, university professors, IAS officers, judges, etc.). At the other end of the spectrum in this sector, the minimum government salary recommended by the Seventh Pay Commission was Rs 18,000 per month. According to the World Inequality Database, this is the median income in the country, i.e. 50 per cent of the people earn less than this. Thus, those who are entitled to either OPS or NPS tend to be, relatively speaking, well off.

Difference between NPS and OPS

The NPS has 'defined contributions'. This means that every month employees and their employers contribute a part (10-15 per cent) of their salary to a pension fund.[44] The amount deposited in this pension fund is invested in mutual funds, bonds, etc. by the Pension Fund Regulatory and Development Authority (PFRDA). When the employee retires, they get what is earned from these investments, according to how the stock market is doing.

There are problems in NPS and possibly the biggest is risk. For instance, the US has a similar pension system, and when the financial crisis of 2007-8 occurred, thousands of teachers and other pensioners' savings were wiped out due to poor decisions taken by their pension fund managers. One possible solution is to protect the investments from risk. This requires monitoring and controlling pension fund managers, bringing transparency in investment decisions. Making regulatory bodies transparent and controlling them is easier said than done; moreover, the US experience also shows that it is very difficult to do it.

The OPS had 'defined benefits', i.e., when an employee retires, they are entitled to 50 per cent of their salary at the time of retirement and no contributions. There are measures to protect against inflation. These pensions are tax-funded: the liabilities are to be met from the current revenue streams of government (and if they fall short, from borrowings).

OPS is expensive—at the Central level, pension expenditure was almost 6 per cent of total government expenditure in 2024-25 and has been just over 3 per cent of GDP (Wani 2024). According to one estimate, the expenditure on pensioners at the state level is one-fourth of the revenue received from taxes.

Questions about OPS

Is it a fair system? Pensions of employees, who earn anything between a few thousand to lakhs per month, are paid out of direct and indirect tax revenues of the government. Some of these revenue streams (e.g., indirect taxes) include contributions of the poor too. In the extreme, from this perspective, the OPS is regressive: to the extent that everyone contributes tax revenues through indirect taxes, the pensions of the richest are part funded by the poor also. The unfairness of the OPS is evident when one sees that the other group getting non-contributory pensions through the National Social Assistance Programme (discussed later) receive Rs 200-4000 per month as old age, widow and disability pensions. These are the very citizens who contribute (through their indirect taxes) to the pension of the best salaried OPS pensioners.

Another question is that if we revert to OPS, then today the government will save money because its contribution to NPS pension, as employers, will no longer be required. But when today's employees retire, the government will have to pay a pension. Thus, today's economic burden (pension contributions) gets passed on to future governments (pension payouts).

In the long run, since the burden of OPS on the government is higher than that under NPS, the financial burden per government employee will increase. This will compel the government to think twice before making additional appointments. India already has a lower government employee to population ratio (i.e., doctors, nurses, teachers, police, etc. per thousand people) compared to international norms. For instance, in 2019, India had 1.7 nurses per thousand people compared to 7.4 in Brazil. The spectre of the rising economic burden arising from more appointments and pension obligations, will hamper government employment, which will harm common people by restricting public services to them.

The country already spends too little on disadvantaged groups. The share of social security schemes in government expenditure is also very low. Had governments not been fiscally burdened with OPS, perhaps there would have been greater fiscal space for health, education, social security, etc.

Way Forward

Can there be a combination of OPS and NPS, a middle ground between the two? For instance, a combination of 'defined contribution' like the NPS with 'defined benefits' like the OPS? There seemed to be few takers for such an option. The reluctance to move towards this option was probably because it would be difficult to convince those on the OPS to start contributing. No government seems to have the political will to convince them, and certainly would not dare to impose such a policy on them. Yet, this is a common model in developed countries.

Andhra Pradesh is one state with a proposal resembling this: with fixed returns guaranteed to those on the NPS and the state government as a guarantor. In the short run this can derisk NPS. Recently, the Central government announced the Unified Pension Scheme (UPS) modelled on this—defined contributions and defined benefits—but it has yet to be operationalised fully.

For the long term, those on the OPS should also be moved to a contributory plan. There was a time when the salaries of the highest paid government employees were not very high, but after the Fifth Pay Commission the situation changed. There is no economic rationale for continuation of non-contributory, tax-funded pensions to government employees.

Chart 8.1 shows the shares of the total expenditure by the Central government on various types of pensions. Total expenditure on pensions is divided into three parts—expenditure on 1(a) and 1(b) vs expenditure on 2(a) (contributory pension for the unorganised sector) and 2(b) (the NSAP). Throughout the twenty-year period plotted on Chart 8.1, more than 90 per cent of pension expenditure was on government pensioners (1A and 1B). As far as 2(b) is concerned, it ranged between 5.6 per cent to 12.0 per cent in the first ten years (i.e. during the two UPA governments) but has steadily declined to 3.9 per cent since 2014. The NDA government has prioritised pension schemes in category 2(a), but the current expenditure levels on them are negligible (in Chart 8.1 that series is indistinguishable from the x-axis) as the pension payouts will begin some years down the line.

Chart 8.1 Government expenditure on various types of pensions

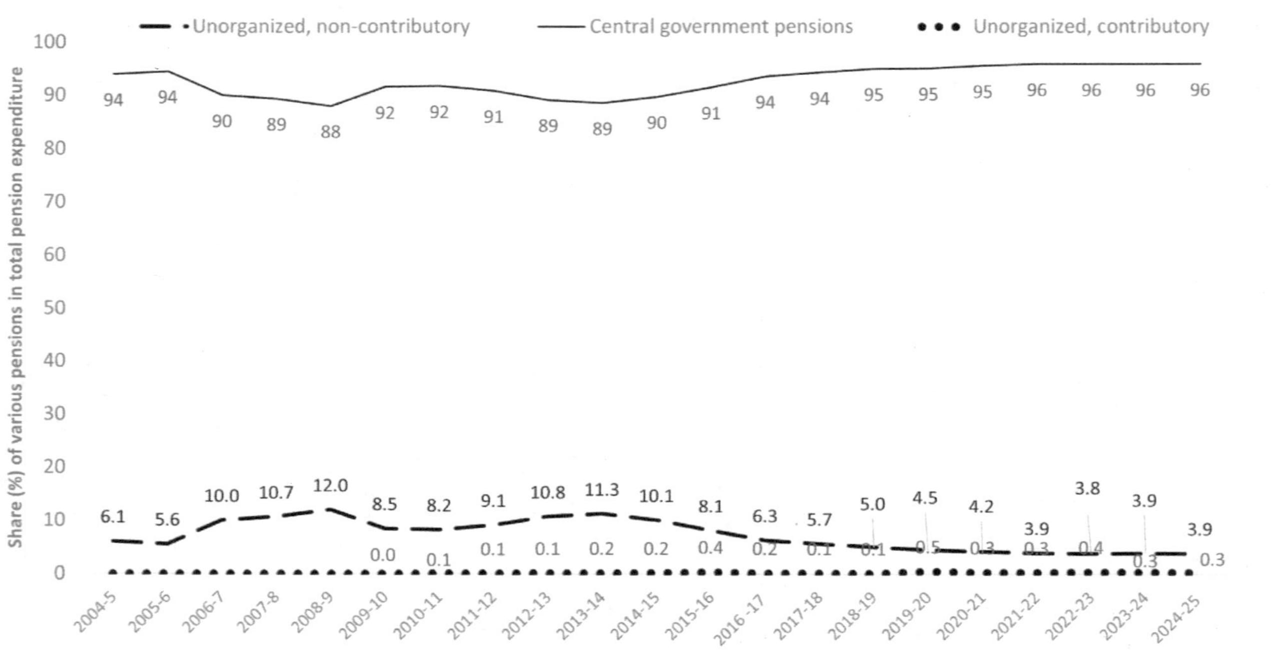

Note: Unorganized, non-contributory (National Social Assistance Programe); Unorganized, contributory (Swavalamban scheme, Atal Pension Yojana, PM Shram Yogi / Kisan Maandhan/NPS (Traders and self-employed); Central government pensions. Source: Government of India (various years); Budget division. https://www.indiabudget.gov.in/budget2021-22/doc/Budget_at_Glance/bag7.pdf and https://www.indiabudget.gov.in/budget2021-22/doc/eb/allsbe.pdf

Social Security Pensions

The discussion, thus far, has been on pensions for the formal sector (1(a) and 1(b) in Table 8.1). We now turn to non-contributory pensions for the unorganised sector (i.e., 2(b)) provided through National Social Assistance Programme (NSAP) and paid for from the budget.

The NSAP provides three types of social security pensions—old age, single women (including widows, abandoned) and disability pensions.[45] Those aged sixty years and above are entitled to old age pensions with those aged eighty years and above getting a higher pension than those aged 60-79 years. In 2009, a pension for widowed women and persons with disabilities was introduced. Based on the recommendations of a Task Force, in 2014 the government expanded the widow pension scheme to single, separated, divorced and abandoned women (Government of India 2013). Disability pensions are given to those with 80 per cent disability.

Central Apathy towards NSAP

The NSAP began in 1995 but from 2002-3 to 2014, it was transferred to the state governments. In 2016, the NSAP was listed as a 'Core of the Core' programme of the Centrally Sponsored Schemes (CSS) (Government of India 2016). The Core of the Core CSS are supposed to get 100 per cent financial support from the Centre. An audit report of the Comptroller and Auditor General (CAG) cited four reports of the Parliamentary Standing Committee where the committees expressed their concern over the stagnating budget for NSAP. The government responded by saying that it was unable to increase the amount 'in the wake of decision taken at the highest levels in Government to continue with the existing system' (Comptroller and Auditor General 2023).

According to the CAG report, the Centre restricted the number of old age pensioners to 3 crore as per 2001 census. Given the centrally imposed cap, states have added roughly 3.5 crore more people using their own resources. According to population projections, the total population over sixty years is around 14 crores. Thus, even with the states stepping in, less than half (approximately 40 per cent) of the elderly get an old age pension through NSAP.

There is significant state-wise variation in commitment to these pensions: in some states, the number of pensioners supported by the state is much higher than the number of central pensioners. For example, in Odisha, 53 per cent of pensioners are wholly supported by the state; in Rajasthan, 85 per cent are state supported.

State governments have risen to the challenge not only by expanding coverage, but also by increasing pension amounts. The monthly pension contribution from the Central government is Rs 200 (for the elderly below 80 years of age), Rs 300 (for widows, single women and people living with disability) and Rs 500 (for the elderly above 80 years). Since 2012, the Central government has not revised this despite repeated demands to do so.[46] In fact, for pensioners below eighty years of age, there has been no upward revision since 2007; the Central government has been giving only Rs 200.

Realizing that it is not possible to survive on Rs 200-500, almost all states increased the pension (a 'top up') using state resources. In 2024, only Goa, Manipur and Nagaland were not topping up pensions with their own resources. Other state government top-ups range from Rs 50-150 (in Assam, Chhattisgarh and Madhya Pradesh) to Rs 2500-3500 (in Haryana and Andhra Pradesh), so that pensioners get a total of Rs 250-4000 per month (see Appendix I, Table A7).

With the expansion at the state level, the NSAP is a 'Central' scheme in name only. For instance, the CAG's audit 2023 NSAP report states that in the 2017-21 period, the Central government spent Rs 34,432 crore and all the state governments put together amounted to Rs 109,044 crore—that is, only 24 per cent of the total expenditure came from the Centre. My own preliminary estimates suggest that the Centre contributes less than 10 per cent of the total expenditure.

Expansion at the State Level

Map 8.1 shows the monthly pension (central and state contributions combined) provided in different states to those aged eighty years and above, who are given the highest pension. The pension amounts in most states are in the Rs 1000-2000 per month range (see Map 8.1, Page 200, and Table A7). The highest amount is in Andhra Pradesh (Rs 4000), followed by Haryana (Rs 3000).

Map 8.2 depicts the estimated proportion of elderly (aged 60 years and above) who get a pension in each state.[47] Only a few states have achieved coverage that is close to universal, with some interesting surprises (such as Bihar, Jharkhand and Rajasthan). Also somewhat surprisingly, pension coverage in Tamil Nadu—otherwise among the best performing states—is less than one-fifth of the elderly (15 per cent), and similar to Gujarat (11 per cent).

Map 8.3 plots the proportion of pensioners who are exclusively supported by the state government—their entire pension is paid for by the state government. This map also throws up some surprises—the northern and north-western states (e.g., Punjab, Rajasthan and Haryana) have done well, whereas Tamil Nadu, usually a pioneer in social policy, has among the lowest share of state-supported pensioners.[48]

Several states have undertaken laudable social security pension reforms. In Rajasthan, in the first phase of reforms the government focused on the number of pensioners and the pension amount. In the second phase, the state government implemented a 'Rajasthan Guaranteed Minimum Income Act 2023'. The law has two parts—one, employment guarantee in rural and urban areas and second, social security pension for the elderly, disabled persons, widows and single women. The law made social security pensions universal in Rajasthan. As per latest available data, 85 per cent of all elderly pensioners in Rajasthan were getting it from the state government; the Central share had shrunk to merely 15 per cent. The estimated elderly population in Rajasthan is 68-82 lakh (2021 and 2026 census projections). According to Rajasthan state statistics, 56.5 lakh elderly were being given a pension—i.e. 69-83 per cent of the elderly in Rajasthan were getting a pension. Thus, in spite of the law, Rajasthan has not achieved universal pension coverage, though coverage improved substantially. In the PEEP Survey in 2013 we had found that among households where there were any elderly people above sixty years of age, only 31 per cent of households in Rajasthan had a pension for the elderly.

One problem with social security schemes has been that financial allocations are not linked to inflation. Many years pass without the pensions being increased. As mentioned earlier, since 2007, the Central government's contribution to pensions has been stuck at Rs 200 per month. In a pioneering move, the Rajasthan Minimum Guaranteed Income Act provides that the amount of pension be increased by 15 per cent every year to protect pensioners from inflation.

Similarly, there is a lot to learn from Odisha, also a poor state, in the matter of social security pensions. It has a longer history of expanding coverage: in 2008, it merged older state pension schemes to launch the Madhu Babu Pension Yojana. The estimated population of older persons in Odisha is 52-62 lakh, and in 2023-24, 29.9 lakh were getting pension in Odisha, i.e. 48-58 per cent of the elderly were under the pension net. In the PEEP survey 2013, 79 per cent of older households were receiving pensions. In Odisha, 53 per cent of elderly pensioners are on the state scheme. The pension amount used to be Rs 500 (with Rs 300 being contributed by the state government), and in the 2024 budget, it was increased to Rs 1000 per month (i.e., the state contribution increased to Rs 800 per month). Apart from this, Odisha improved its pension payment mechanism to make it convenient *and* transparent. One of the problems in cash payment of pension used to be that the functionary in charge (whether postman or panchayat secretary) would not deliver the full amount. Odisha came up with a solution to stop this corruption—the state government ordered cash payments to be made in front of everyone in the panchayat building on a fixed date each month. With payments being made in front of everyone, it became difficult for the panchayat secretary to siphon off any money.

Ground Realities[49]

The PEEP Suvey in 2013 was conducted across ten states. It included interviews with old age pensioners such as Antar Kunwar to understand the situation of the elderly, along with other social security schemes.

As mentioned earlier, the NSAP has been running for several decades, yet its scope has remained quite limited. After fixing the number of pensioners on the basis of the 2001 census and the number of people living below the poverty

Map 8.1 Old age monthly pension (Rs/month)

For elderly citizens aged 80 and above, including state contributions, 2017–24

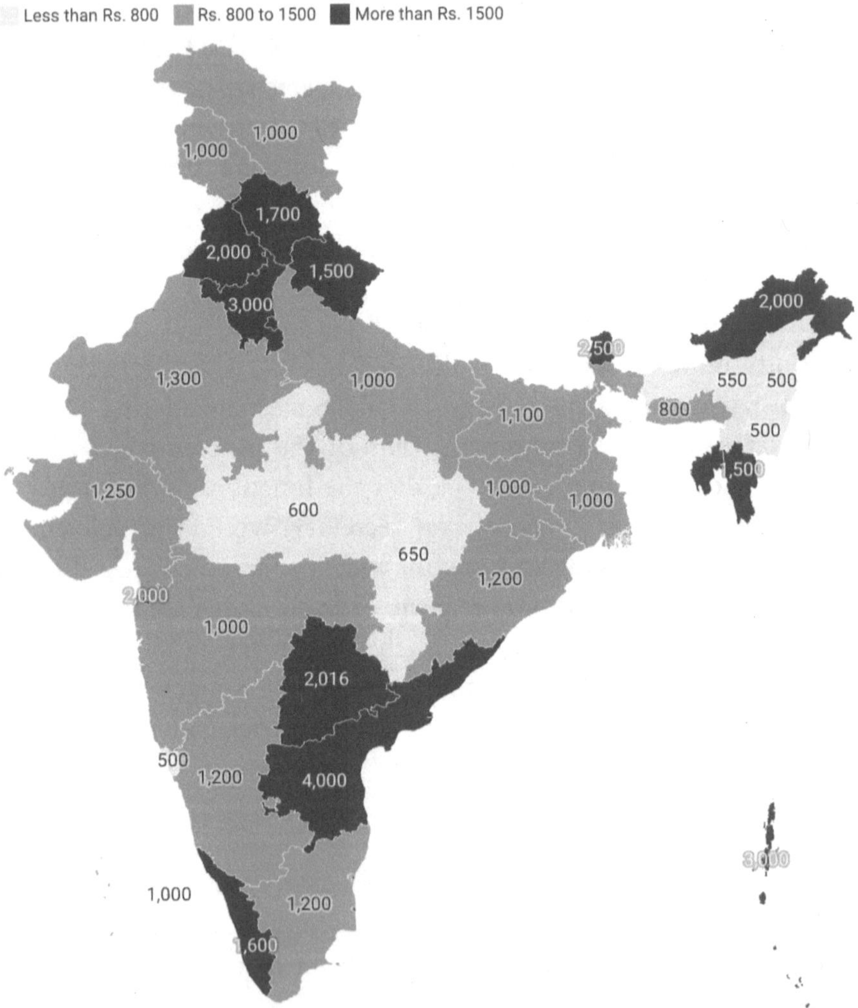

Latest year between 2017-24 for which data is available. The central government provides pensions of Rs 200/month to individuals aged 60-80 years, Rs 300/month to widows, single women, and persons with disabilities, and Rs 500/month to those above 80 years. State governments "top-up" the pensions using their own budgets. This map shows the latest information taken from Rajya Sabha Question No. 1475 answered on 9.12.25 for pensioners aged 80 years and above. For Rajasthan and Odisha it is taken from state sources (see Appendix II).

Map data: © OSM • Created with Datawrapper

Map 8.2 Proportion of elderly receiving old-age pension (%), 2024

Central and state pensioners as a proportion (%) of all aged 60 years and above

< 41 41–60 ≥ 60

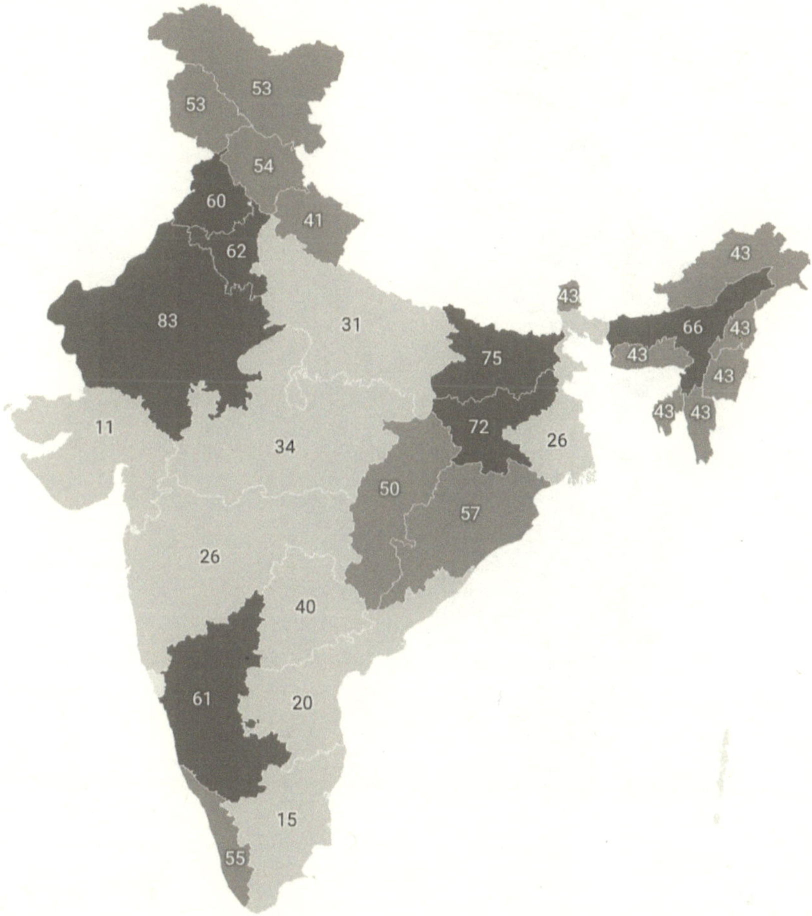

At the national level, 41% of the elderly receive pensions. States in the lightest shade are those where pension coverage is below the national average. The number of pensioners includes central and state schemes; that is divided by the projected population aged 60+ years in 2021. For the northeastern states (excluding Assam), as state-level projections are unavailable, regional average is reported. For Ladakh, the Jammu and Kashmir average is reported. Data from Rajya Sabha question numbers 2222 and 2212 answered on 9.8.24 (see Appendix II).

Source: Central coverage data is sourced from central government websites, while state coverage data is obtained from state government websites and state reports. • Map data: © OSM • Created with Datawrapper

Map 8.3 Old-age pensioners supported by states, 2024

Proportion (%) of all old-age pensioners supported by state schemes

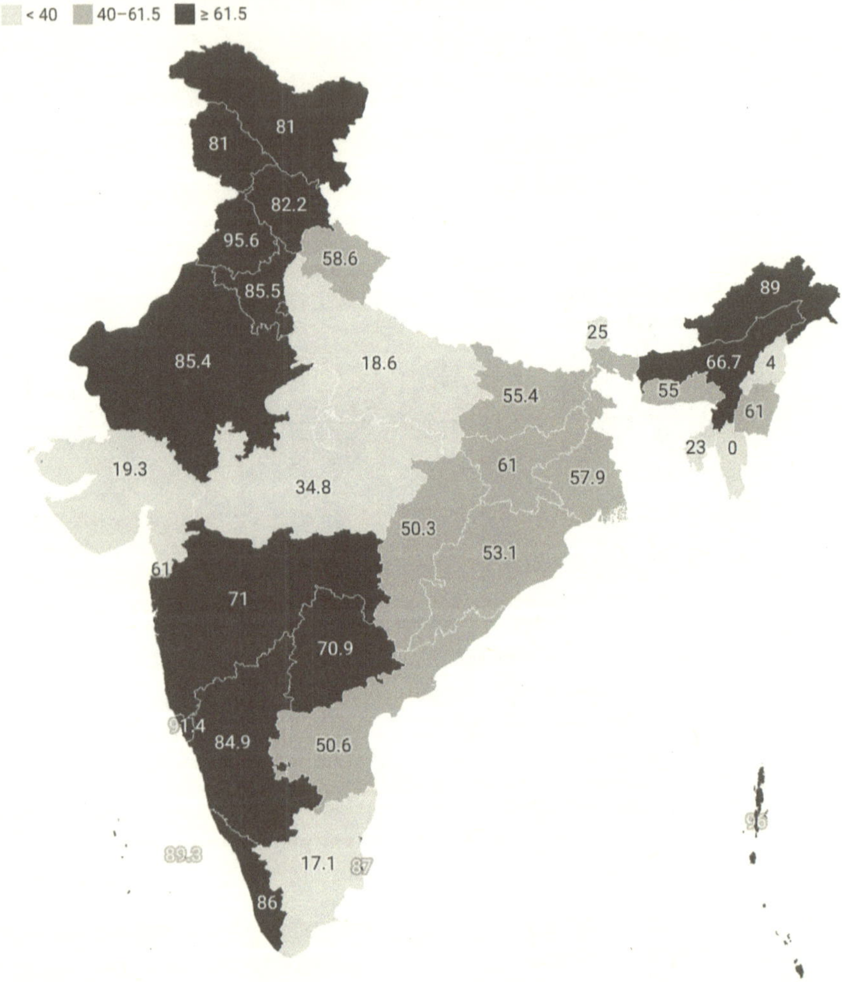

Most states provide pensions to elderly persons through state pension schemes. This map shows the share of state-supported pensioners among all elderly pensioners. Overall, 61.5% of elderly pensioners get state government pensions. The states in the darkest shade cover more pensioners than the national average, through state pension schemes. Data from Rajya Sabha Questions No 2222 and 2212 on 9.8.24.

Map data: © OSM • Created with Datawrapper

line, the Central government froze the numbers. The CAG audit report found that even the meagre cap (3.19 crore pensioners from the Centre) was not fully realised. Besides this, the pension amount has remained very low as discussed earlier.

Despite these weaknesses, interviews with almost 900 elderly and widow pensioners in 2013 clearly showed the importance of the scheme. Nearly half of the respondents were either living alone, or only with their spouses, or only with unmarried children. Most of the pensioners were unable to work. The lack of family support and their inability to support themselves through work meant that the pension played a key role in their lives.

Encouragingly, our study corroborated earlier findings by Dutta et al (2010) that corruption was lower in this programme compared to other social policies such as NREGA and PDS. Only 3 per cent of pensioners in the sample were not getting pension despite their names being on the pension list. Some of them were pensioners whose names had been approved, but had not started getting the pension yet. Most respondents said they were getting the full pension amount. One-fifth were not getting the full amount, and most of them (especially in Rajasthan and Tamil Nadu) had to pay something or the other as a bribe to the postmaster or other middlemen (such as the person at the 'e-Mitra' centre) while withdrawing the pension.

Another positive finding was that pensioners generally had the basic information about their pensions—for example, how much they should receive. High awareness helped in ensuring that people get their full entitlement.

Pensioners reported spending their pension on food, medicines, health, and other needs. In the PEEP Survey, one-third of the respondents said that pension money was used occasionally to help others.

Some believe that pensions can weaken the tradition of family support. On the contrary, pensioners in the PEEP Survey said that they felt that if they did not get the pension, their position in the family would be further weakened. With access to their (measly) pensions, as they have some money at their disposal, they were able to contribute in small ways to household expenses; this made space for them within the family. In a nutshell, pensions impart a modicum of dignity and sense of empowerment despite their vulnerable position.

Scope for Improvement

While the pension scheme appears to make a real difference on the ground, it remains in dire need of improvement. Three main areas where urgent reforms are needed: the pension payment mechanisms, delays in payments and streamlining the application process.

Payment Problems

The payment mechanism is a big issue. During the PEEP Survey 2013, there was a range of modes of payment across the ten survey states. In some states, payments were made through bank accounts, in others through the post office, in yet others, the postman delivered a money order at their doorstep and finally, as cash in hand, in some states.

While crediting bank and post office accounts with pensions has the advantage that it is less vulnerable to corruption, the problem with relying on banks is their poor penetration in rural areas especially. For many of the elderly who get a pension, mobility is compromised. Yet, for over a decade, the Central government has been exerting pressure (possibly even resorting to blackmail, e.g., by threatening non-release of funds) on states to move towards payments into Aadhaar-linked bank accounts ('Direct Benefit Transfers' or DBT). Barring Odisha, most other states, under this pressure from the Centre, moved to Aadhaar-linked bank payments. This move created a new problem for the elderly, widows, single women and persons with disability who had to run from pillar to post to open bank accounts.

Around the time that the transition to DBT began (in 2012), we were in a village of Ratu block (Ranchi district). A small group of pensioners had gathered in the community hall of the Panchayat to open their accounts for pensions to comply with the government's orders. Due to lack of some papers, one of them could not open his account, so he returned disappointed. When we left the community hall after discussing the account opening process with the banking correspondent, the same old man was squatting by the road 100-200 meters away—he was tired, so he was resting for a while. It was shocking to see how the elderly were being given the runaround for a meagre pension.

The transition was not a one-off headache (i.e., that once their accounts are opened, everything goes smoothly). Going to the bank or banking correspondent every month is a struggle for many NSAP beneficiaries. When this new system began in Alwar, while in conversation with some women, they said they end up spending a fair amount on reaching the bank. Tempo rides are expensive. Climbing onto to a bus isn't easy. Some were riding on their family members' motorcycles, who expect some reward for the favour. In remoter areas, given the high transportation costs, the elderly resort to withdrawing their pension once in 2-3 months rather than each month to save on fare. Pensioners also mentioned the hassles they faced due to crowding at the bank.

Like the NREGA, opening accounts for pensions were only the first step. Transitioning to DBT was easier said than done. Once people managed to open accounts, they were asked to link these accounts with Aadhaar, then to onboard these accounts to the Aadhaar Based Payment Systems required another round of paperwork and e-KYC. While the problem of poor access was partly reduced through a system of banking correspondents, in some pockets banking correspondents became middlemen of the DBT regime, taking cuts for every transaction (opening an account, Aadhaar-linking, withdrawals, and so on) and cheating in other ways.

Many pensioners in many states were not informed about the need to link Aadhaar to their bank and pension profile, so they missed the deadline. Such people were declared 'duplicates' or 'dead' by the state governments and their names were deleted or their pensions were discontinued without informing them why. In Rajasthan, people declared 'dead' were actually alive and did not understand why their pension had stopped. (In 2024, hundreds of such cases were highlighted again in Rajasthan, possibly due to KYC requirements.)

Aadhaar-linking was ostensibly to weed out duplicates, but a 2017 survey in Jharkhand's Khunti district found that only 20 per cent of those (16 per cent of respondents) who were declared 'duplicates' could not be found; more than one-third were those who could not produce Aadhaar-related paperwork and hence their names were deleted (Malhotra and Somanchi 2018). In the PEEP Survey in 2013, we found that 98 per cent of NSAP beneficiaries were alive and receiving their pensions.

Aadhaar-linked pensioners have faced other problems as well—if the date of birth on the Aadhaar card is incorrect, they have to rectify Aadhaar. Otherwise, they risk losing their pension. Correcting information on Aadhaar is not always easy—it costs money, the hassle of going to an Aadhaar center plus there is no guarantee that the problem will be resolved. Remember, many pensioners may not have proof of date of birth. There were some cases where the pension application was rejected because the applicant was deemed ineligible on the basis of a (wrong) date of birth on the Aadhaar card. In states where Aadhaar-Based Biometric Authentication (ABBA) is required at the time of withdrawing pensions, the elderly face another problem—the machines often fail to verify them because the fingerprints of the elderly may fade.

The integration of Aadhaar in welfare schemes has been disruptive all round. More than any other scheme, it is in the pension schemes that its cruelty is most evident. Persons with disabilities and elderly who have mobility issues have been callously declared dead and struck off the rolls without any warning, in the name of efficiency. These experiences raise the question: whose life is the DBT process making easier—the pensioners' or that of government functionaries?

There are other payment problems in the pension scheme as well—chief among them is delays in payment of pensions. In 2001, the Supreme Court had ordered that pensions should be paid by the seventh of every month. The 2023 CAG report also raised the issue of delays. According to it only eleven states make pension payments on a monthly basis. Four states give pension after every three months. Even in the states where payment is being made every month, there are many where they are unable to pay by the stipulated time. If the payment schedule is not fixed, it is an issue for pensioners because they may end up making unnecessary trips to the bank. This wastes their time, and in far-flung areas increases their expenses.

Application Process

In the NSAP, pensions do not start automatically when a woman is widowed, or upon attaining the age of eligibility for old-age pension. They are expected to apply for it, but the application process is not simple, transparent or time-bound. Middlemen also take advantage of this. In the 2013 PEEP Survey, many pensioners said that they had to pay money to get the pension sanctioned. Less than 10 per cent complained in Himachal Pradesh, but half of the respondents in Tamil Nadu and Uttar Pradesh had this complaint.

Contributory Pensions for the Unorganised Sector

We finally turn to contributory pensions for the unorganised sector. There are several Central contributory pensions schemes for people in the unorganised sector (e.g., Atal Pension Yojana, Pradhan Mantri Shram Yogi Mandhan Yojana, Pradhan Mantri Kisan Maandhan Yojana and National Pension Scheme for Traders and Self Employed). All schemes were introduced by the NDA government, and they have very nominal budgets (the series that is crawling along the x-axis in Chart 8.1), and provide a very modest amount as pension.

Take the Atal Pension Yojana (APY) announced by the NDA government in 2015-16. Under this, a person has to contribute Rs 100 per month, and on attaining the age of sixty years, they get a pension of Rs 1000-5000 per month (Arora and Kundu 2018). By 2019, the Centre seemed to give up on the Atal Pension Yojana, and brought in the Pradhan Mantri Shram Yogi Mandhan Yojana, similar to the APY, giving people Rs 1000 per month. Contributions range from Rs 50-100, and on attaining sixty years, the pension is upto Rs 3000 per month (Lalwani 2019).

Apart from low uptake, these pension schemes have faced other problems. Due to pressure on banks to enroll people into the scheme, bank employees added people to them without consent, and the bank began deducting a contribution every month (Gairola 2022).

The total expenditure on APY since its inception till 2024 has been Rs 3113 crore and the maximum in any one year has been Rs 725 crore (in 2022-23). Thus, it is not that the budget squeeze on the old (NSAP) pension scheme is compensated for by increased spending on newer pension schemes. Therefore the stagnation in NSAP expenditure and the shrinking role of the Centre cannot be justified on the grounds that only the budgetary head has changed, not the commitment to providing pensions.

Even in the 2024 General Elections, there was very little discussion of the elderly, widows, disabled. The Congress manifesto promised to increase the Central contribution from Rs 200 to Rs 1000 but was silent on increasing the coverage and indexation. There was no mention of this scheme in the BJP manifesto.

Social security pensions can provide a modicum of dignity to people like Antar Kunwar, who are eligible for pensions under National Social Assistance Programme and whose life is very difficult: they are physically fragile, economically vulnerable, even resorting to begging at times to survive. Two impediments to NSAP's potential being realised are low coverage and low central contribution to the pension. The interest taken by state governments has managed to overcome these two challenges substantially. The Central government's constant tinkering with the payment process further dampens its positive effects. In spite of evidence that suggests that corruption is relatively low, the payment process is becoming more cumbersome, thereby increasing the transaction costs of withdrawing pensions.

Of all the schemes discussed so far, this is the only one that is not protected by law, even though it was included in some of the earlier drafts of the Food Security Act. The fact that the NSAP got kicked between the Centre and states between 2002-3 and 2014 is an illustration of the importance of enacting laws for such social security provisions.

9

PUBLIC CANTEENS

An Idea Whose Time Has Come[50]

In November 2023, while preparing for a survey of public canteens, I had dinner on a 'luxury' train, Vande Bharat. The next day, as I had lunch at a public canteen on the Rajasthan University campus, it occurred to me that the rotis there were much better than the rotis on Vande Bharat!

Public canteens like Indira Rasois (now called Annapurna rasois) in Rajasthan, Amma Unavagam in Tamil Nadu provide subsidised, cooked hot food. For example, at Annapurna Rasois 5-6 rotis, one vegetable and dal is sold for Rs 8 only.

In 2013, when the then Chief Minister of Tamil Nadu, Ms Jayalalithaa started Amma Unavagam, it created news all over the country, not all of it positive. Over the years, as its value has become apparent many state governments have emulated the scheme.

Across the world there are variants of what are termed 'public canteens' here: community kitchens, soup kitchens, food banks, etc. All of these are aimed at ensuring food security for those who are struggling to survive or are food insecure. Canteens may be government-run, or run by local communities, NGOs and religious bodies. For example, churches are known to run soup kitchens and Gurudwaras have langars.

Internationally, canteens have come into the spotlight during periods of crisis such as the financial crisis of 2008, COVID-19, wars, etc. One interesting example is the large-scale community kitchen programme in Brazil known as 'Popular Restaurant'. These government-run subsidised canteens seek to guarantee food security where 'a large number of people eat their meals outside their home' (Finco, Finco and Coelho 2012). Public canteens have not got much attention as an instrument of urban food security even though the problem is well recognised.

Public Canteens in India

Before the COVID-19 pandemic, most canteen schemes were opened in response to episodes of high food inflation that adversely affected food security. During the pandemic, the sudden lockdown announced by the Central government resulted in a humanitarian crisis. Some states governments resorted to public canteens to provide relief to affected workers in urban areas. For instance, in August 2020, the Rajasthan government started with 200 canteens and by 2023 there were around 1200 canteens in the state. Kerala expanded its network of 'Janakeeya Hotels' run by Kudumbashree, an initiative for women's empowerment. In a 2019 Public Interest Litigation (PIL), the Supreme Court of India issued orders in 2020 directing that community kitchens be set up (*Indian Express* 2021).

Map 9.1 shows the availability of canteens across the country and is based on publicly available information. Even as someone who keeps tracks of this scheme, it was a surprise

Map 9.1 Status of canteens

Availability of canteens per 10 lakh population

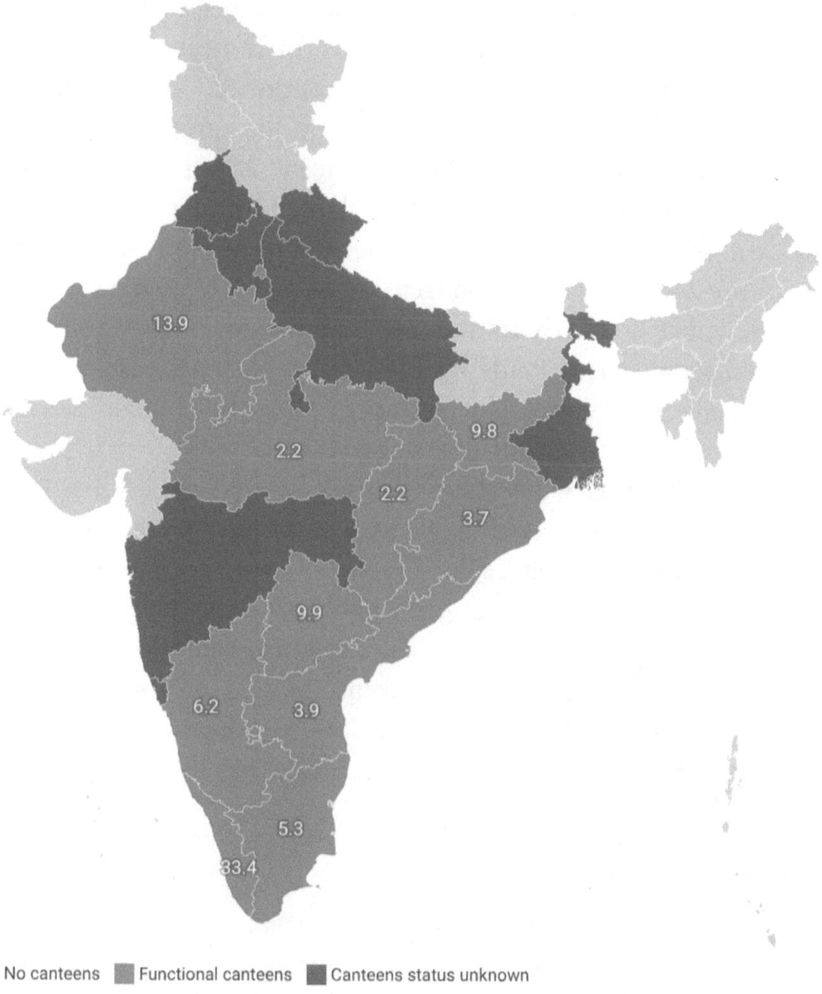

"No canteens" refers to no information being available for canteens in that state. "Functional canteens" refers to states where we can say with confidence that canteens are operational, but the number of canteens is based on the best available source. "Canteens status unknown" refers to states where online information suggests that canteens are operational, but we have not been able to verify the information.

Map: Reetika Khera • Map data: © OSM • Created with Datawrapper to see how widespread canteens were. Barring Gujarat and Bihar and the hilly states in the north and eastern regions, all other states run a scheme on some scale.[51] States where internet sources report the existence of canteens, but whose operational status could not be confirmed, are shown in black. In West Bengal, information on the current status and scale (if functional) of 'Maa Canteen' is not available. In Punjab according to publicly available information only one canteen is operational in the state. Canteens were announced in the 2025 Delhi state budget, and some were inaugurated in December 2025. Getting an accurate picture of the spread of public canteens is made harder because they are easy victims of petty politicking. For instance, after the Telugu Desam Party (TDP) government lost power in Andhra Pradesh, its Anna Canteens were almost entirely wound up by the next state government. With TDP back in power, Anna Canteens have made a comeback.[52]

For the states in dark grey, public canteens are functional and some information on the scale of operations is also available. The density of canteens (plotted on the map per million population) is quite varied—e.g., Kerala has thirty-three canteens per million and Odisha has the lowest (3.7 per million).

Canteen Survey 2023

Canteens are under-researched not only in India, but elsewhere too (however, see Rajendran 2013 and Gummadi and Jyotishi 2025). Therefore, in November-December 2023, we conducted The Canteen Survey 2023 in three states—Karnataka, Rajasthan and Tamil Nadu. The purpose was to understand the role of canteens and how well or poorly they are implemented.

One persistent problem with canteen schemes is that they have fallen prey to petty politicking at the state level. This can take different forms: in Andhra Pradesh, Anna Canteens were closed en masse. In Karnataka, the Congress government introduced Indira Canteens in 2017. When the BJP government came to power in the state, there were budget cuts, layoffs and in some canteens, opening hours were curtailed. Tamil Nadu's Amma Canteens, which started in 2013, benefited from the fact that the party that introduced the scheme (the AIADMK) remained in power until 2021. When the government changed, there was a widespread perception that Amma Canteens were being neglected.

Rajasthan's Indira Rasois were just three years old, when elections became due (in November 2023). This created the possibility that a change in government could lead to the neglect or closure of canteens. The Canteen Survey 2023 was conducted before this could happen in Rajasthan, and to study the implementation of older canteen schemes in Karnataka and Tamil Nadu.

In Rajasthan, we picked six cities—Jaipur, Bikaner, Udaipur, Ajmer, Chittorgarh and Churu. According to the government's 'Jan Soochna Portal', at the time of the survey, only 107 out of a total of 1209 canteens in Rajasthan were in Jaipur. Thus, canteens were quite widely dispersed across the Urban Local Bodies (ULB) of the state. Contrary to this, most of the canteens in Karnataka and Tamil Nadu are in their respective state capitals. Chennai had more than 400 canteens while the next largest cities had roughly ten canteens. Similarly, Bengaluru had around 250 canteens, while others had around ten. In Karnataka and Tamil Nadu, we surveyed two ULBs, Mysore and Bellary and Coimbatore and Vellore respectively, along with state capitals (Bengaluru

Table 9.1 Timings, Menu and Prices at Canteens

State (cost price of meal)	*Open at the time of arrival*[1]	*Breakfast*	*Lunch*	*Dinner*
***Karnataka* (Rs 62[2])**	92 (97)	7.30-10.30 am Rs 5/plate (weekly menu)	12-3 pm	7-9.30 pm
			Rs 5/plate of rice, two options everyday	
***Rajasthan* (Rs 25)**	92 (97)	*9 am to 2 pm*		*5-9 pm*
		Rs 8 per plate (5-6 rotis, dal or kadhi and one vegetable)		
***Tamil Nadu* (n/a)**	93 (96)	7-10 am Sambar with Re. 1/idli and Rs 3/Pongal plate	12-3 pm Curd rice: Rs 3/plate, Variety rice (lemon, curry leaf powder) or White rice and sambar: Rs 5/plate	6-9 pm Rs 2 for two chapathis with dal

Notes: [1]In brackets, proportion that were open or opened within 5 minutes of survey team's arrival [2]Shared by state government and ULB (Thadhagath 2023) and Chennai). Canteen staff at each canteen and a total of 704 guests were interviewed; of this 384 guests were from Rajasthan.

Role of Canteens

One common query about the need for canteens is whether and why they are required when 80 crore people have access to free or cheap grains through the Public Distribution System (PDS). If coverage is not adequate, why not just expand PDS coverage instead of having yet another scheme for food security. Another response is that we should focus on the 'One Nation, One Ration' that would make PDS entitlements portable so that migrant workers' needs can be fulfilled.

In fact, canteens and the PDS should be seen as complements rather than substitutes. PDS rations can provide food security for those who have access to cooking facilities. However, this is not always the case in urban areas, especially among migrant workers. Indeed, between 11 per cent to 47 per cent of survey respondents did not have cooking facilities. For them, dry rations from the PDS can do little to guarantee food security, even if the PDS allows portability.

By being open to all, canteens can ensure that people do not go hungry. Canteens tend to be imagined as a food security measure for destitute, homeless, vagabonds and those relying on alms. Indeed, such individuals benefit immensely from canteens. In our survey, roughly one tenth of our respondents were from these groups (see Table 9.2). A similar proportion of respondents admitted to being worried about having to sleep hungry the week before the survey and nearly one-fifth (18 per cent) reported sleeping hungry sometimes before canteens became an option (Table 9.2). Apart from chronic hunger, canteens also serve those who are suffering from an economic/health shock and are at the risk of going hungry (e.g., for instance, in Churu, Haroon who said he had to go hungry when he met with an accident and couldn't work).

Moreover, subsidised meals also contribute to food security. The provision of cooked food at the canteens at heavily subsidised prices (usually Rs 5-10 per plate, see Table 9.1) helps those who cannot afford enough food or for whom survival is a struggle. For example, the sale price of a plate in Rajasthan's Indira Rasois was Rs 8, whereas the cost price was Rs 25 and a comparable meal in the market would cost even more.

Guests were asked how much they save (minimum and maximum) for each meal consumed at the canteen. The average of 'minimum saving' per meal ranged from Rs 40 in Karnataka to Rs 45 in Rajasthan and Tamil Nadu. For those eating at hospitals, the saving per meal amounted to around one-tenth of their daily earnings (see Table 9.3).

Yet, it would be wrong to view canteens as a food security and food subsidy intervention alone. There are at least four other roles that canteens play: correcting market failures, supporting women, fostering democratic public spaces and creating meaningful jobs.

In the market for street food, the scheme can remedy several market failures. These include protection from inflation, providing an option that offers nutritious and hygienically prepared food, and a clean place to eat. First, when food inflation is high, canteens provide an assured supply of food at fixed and controlled prices. Second, street food tends to be de facto unregulated; it may not be prepared hygienically. If public canteens can ensure safe and hygienic conditions in their kitchens, they can set a standard in the eating out market. This could spillover to private street food outlets. If people have two options, public canteens or private street food outlets, and if hygiene is guaranteed in the public canteen, then private vendors will have to up their game to remain an attractive option. Third, if governments pay more attention to nutrition, canteens can address the lack of nutritious food options among private vendors. For instance, Kerala's Janakeeya hotels regularly serve fish and meat for a modest price with the Rs 20 meal. The limited availability of nutritious food is not just a question of cost (for example, pulses, meat, dairy products are protein-rich, but expensive). It is also due to lack of nutrition education (many people may not know the importance of a protein-rich diet or that eggs are a cheap source of animal protein).

For women there are two further benefits from canteens. First, they create employment opportunities, many of which go to women. In at least three states (Odisha, Tamil Nadu and Kerala), employment in canteens, in a way, is reserved for women because the responsibility of running the canteens has been given to self-help groups. In Kerala they are run by Kudumabashree groups and some of Odisha's Aahar Kendras are run by self-help groups of Mission Shakti in Odisha (*Orisa Post* 2021 and Government of Odisha 2021).

At Tamil Nadu's Amma Canteens the entire team comprised of women, and was heartening to observe. In the other two survey states (Rajasthan and Karnataka), women work alongside men at canteens.

In patriarchal societies, women tend to be responsible for cooking family meals. When family members consume meals at canteens, women end up getting a break from the drudgery of having to cook all meals for all family members. This is especially true for women who juggle a 'double burden',

Table 9.2 Canteens were Diverse Spaces

	Karnataka	*Rajasthan*	*Tamil Nadu*	*All states*
Elderly (aged 55 years and above, per cent of respondents)	18	15	34	20
Students (per cent of respondents)	12	13	6	11
Graduates and above (per cent of respondents)	31	24	23	25
Scheduled Castes and Scheduled Tribes (per cent)				
Guests	22	37	30	33
Canteen Workers	25	44	28	38
Residence (per cent of respondents)				
Slums or no dwelling	12	28	20	23
Other areas of the city	67	40	53	48
Out of town and other	21	33	27	29
Proportion (per cent) of respondents getting PDS ration	69	58	85	67
Proportion (per cent) who reported worrying about skipping meals last week	3	14	12	11

being responsible for running the household and working outside the home.

In India, canteens have contributed to creating democratic spaces in urban areas. Guests and canteen workers belong to different castes, classes, and religions. Dalits, Adivasis and Muslims made up 16 per cent of the guests in Karnataka, one-fourth in Tamil Nadu and one-third in Rajasthan. Similarly, most canteens had workers from these disadvantaged communities. Only ten per cent of canteens in Rajasthan had no members from marginalised groups but this was higher in Tamil Nadu (about 30 per cent). Workers from minority groups were involved in all roles: cooks, helpers, cleaning staff and for billing. There was considerable flexibility in rotating tasks among themselves. There were no overt signs of discrimination based on caste or gender.

It would be difficult to find public spaces in India where slum dwellers, homeless people or those living in shelters, bus stands, etc. (12-28 per cent guests) share space with those who live in pukka houses (more than half of the respondents in our sample), where motorcyclists, pedestrians, or commuters by bus eat together. Many guests during The Canteen Survey proudly remarked—'From government employees to daily wage labourers, everyone eats here together'; in Bellary, one guest said, 'Everyone comes—those who have money and those who don't'.

Canteens have created a fair number of employment opportunities, relatively egalitarian workspaces for meaningful and satisfying work. The egalitarian nature of canteens was reflected in two ways: one, workers did not hesitate in rotating tasks (cooking, billing, serving, and cleaning). Two, the payment structure was quite flat within and across states. Salaries ranged from Rs 7250 to Rs 10,000 for canteen

Table 9.3 Savings for Regular Canteen Guests

	Karnataka	*Rajasthan*	*Tamil Nadu*	*All states*
Number of guests the day before the survey (hospitals only)	241 (284)	259 (397)	224 (530)	247 (382)
Proportion (per cent) of 'regular guests'[1]	41	52	57	51
Among regular guests, proportion (per cent) who eat both meals at the canteen[2]	36	67	24	49
For regular guests eating both meals				
Saving per meal (Rs), Minimum-Maximum	39-48	47-61	55-68	47-60
Earnings, Rs/month				
Mean	21,163	10,282	10,847	12,090
Median	16,500	9,000	12,500	10,000
Savings as per cent of monthly earnings[3]	14	33	49	32
Proportion (per cent) worried about skipping meals				
before they started using canteens	5	24	52	26
in the week before the survey	0	18	22	17

Notes: [1]Regular guests are those who use the canteen every day or almost every day. [2]'Both meals' (if the guest reported eating both/all meals at the canteen). [3]Capping the 'minimum savings' reported by respondents at Rs 100 and assuming 60 meals per month.

staff in Rajasthan and Karnataka. In Tamil Nadu, everyone was paid Rs 300 per day (i.e., Rs 9000 monthly), including those who were designated as 'Thalaivi' (the main point person who liaised with higher authorities). In Tamil Nadu, there was a palpable sense of pride in their work. Workers highlighted their role during the devastating floods in Chennai ('we never closed') and during the lockdowns in Chennai and Karnataka.

Of course, workers had several legitimate complaints. In Tamil Nadu, wages had barely increased since 2013-2015. They did not enjoy employment benefits such as weekly or other leave, insurance, medical benefits, etc.

Who Eats at the Canteen?

On average, each canteen served 247 guests on the day before the survey, according to information provided by canteen staff during the survey. There was little inter-state variation in this average: Tamil Nadu had the lowest, 224. Canteens had 'regular' guests who ate 'every day or almost every day' (just over half the guests were regulars), 'occasional' guests who ate 'sometimes' and 'first timers'. First-time and occasional guests tended to be attendants of patients at hospitals, visitors to the city, passengers at train stations and bus stands, etc. Among the regulars, there were five broad groups.

Migrants and Working Men

Working men were the largest group among our respondents. Within this group, there was a lot of diversity. Interstate and intra-state migrant workers—for instance, a Swiggy delivery worker, originally from Assam, said that whenever he is hungry, he uses Google Maps to locate the nearest Indira Canteen. Locals whose jobs require them to move around all day (autorickshaw drivers, couriers) find canteens very convenient. Ahmed had a permanent job as a driver in Bruhat Bengaluru Mahanagara Palike (BBMP). Since his wife had gone to her natal village for delivery three months ago, he had been eating at the Indira Canteen.

Other guests were those who did not have cooking facilities at their residence or were dependent on canteens as there was no time to cook for themselves. For example, in Bangalore, Subramanya (from Kolar) was a school bus driver, but the bus also served as his dwelling in the city. He ate two out of three meals every day at Indira Canteen. Several guests said they were eating at canteens as they had run out of cooking gas at home. Another had been eating regularly at the canteen since his mother's death. One of the reasons for being a regular is that he liked the staff members at the canteen.

Women

It was disappointing that very few women used the canteen as guests. Among respondents, they were 9-13 per cent only. For women who do use them, canteens provide relief in at least two ways. Each meal consumed at the canteen saves them cooking time at home, as cooking tends to be their responsibility. This matters a lot for working women, who tend to carry a 'double burden' (earning outside the home along with household responsibilities).

For example, on Sunday morning in Chennai, several male respondents were having breakfast in the canteen. When asked why they were eating at the canteen, they explained that it was their working wives' weekly day off, and they didn't want to trouble their wives for breakfast. They intended to take home a parcel for their wife and others.

In Bangalore, Vanitha, a domestic worker, was the only earning member in her family. Her husband was unable to earn since he had an accident, and had also become an alcoholic. She had gone to her children's school during lunch break at work and had stopped at an Indira Canteen for a quick meal.

Elderly

In all survey states, the teams met very vulnerable elders. In Tamil Nadu, one-fifth of the guests were aged sixty years and above, much higher than Karnataka (6 per cent) and Rajasthan (8 per cent). For them, canteens are important as they get meals that are like home-made food (non-spicy and easily digestible) at an affordable price. Many respondents said that the canteen was a safe and friendly space where elderly people like them, feel a sense of belonging. Canteen staff recognised them and would set aside food for them in case they were late.

Individuals with Difficult Personal Circumstances

Investigators met people who openly admitted to their own mental health issues or hinted at it, respondents whose relationships with their family (especially between husband and wife) were strained. They were few in number, but worth mentioning as canteens play an important role in their lives. The canteen made it possible for them to access food that was like home-made food, with dignity. For those who were staying with a relative due to tensions in their own homes, thanks to the canteen, they were able to be less of a burden on their hosts.

Kuppu in Chennai, was a seventy-year-old widow. Although she lived with her family, their relationship was strained with regular fights at home. She had moved to Chennai as she lost her land to a creditor. She had to stop working after a paralytic attack. She said that she eats at the canteen if she does not get food at home, and if there is no food at the canteen, she skips a meal.

In Chennai, seventy-two-year-old Seliah made a living by selling sweets. He had stopped working, did not live with his family, though his son gave him Rs 1500 each month for expenses. He was a regular at the canteen. As he described his situation, he almost broke down.

A relatively well-off sandstone supplier who had a strained relationship with his wife, was living with his sister. He ate regularly at the canteen to be less of a burden on his sister. Sudhakar went to the canteen when there were fights at home. He said that for him Indira Canteen is like 'a temple' and the food there 'prasad'.

Students

In most survey cities, we found some canteens that were located near colleges or universities. More than 10 per cent of the respondents were students. For students staying in hostels or paying guest accommodation, canteens were a God send. Apart from being cheap, students appreciated that the food at the canteens was like home-made food. In fact, most guests highlighted this aspect of canteen food.

Churu attracts youth from far and wide to train as sportspersons at the government Churu Sports Stadium. We met two such men who told us that when they came to Churu from Gwalior and Nagaur, they surveyed various food options (including some Indira Rasois). They settled on the canteen where we were interviewing them because its protein-rich dal (lentils) was good (he emphasised that proteins are essential for athletes) and was served with a mother's love (*'maa ka pyaar'*, in his words).

In all three states, the variety of guests using the canteens was an eye-opening experience. For some, the wide range of guests (from the very destitute to reasonably well-off people) may be a concern. Some guests mentioned that not everyone should be allowed to eat at the canteen because it is, in their view, for those who cannot eat elsewhere. However, the wide spectrum of guests is an important marker of their success: the poor feel welcome, and the canteen is good enough for the better off suggesting that the quality of food and hygiene practices at the canteens are of acceptable levels.

Other Issues at Canteens

Menu and Cooking Arrangements

Canteens in all three survey states were—by and large—following prescribed menus. Rajasthan and Tamil Nadu had some decentralised control over menus. In Rajasthan, each meal was supposed to have either *dal* or *kadhi*, the vegetable to be provided on a particular day was not prescribed. In Tamil Nadu, the canteen staff decided which vegetable(s) to put in the *sambar*. In Karnataka, food is supplied from centralised kitchens but we were not able to find out who sets the menu at the centralised kitchen. There was some variation between what the two major suppliers provided. For example, one menu included idli and kesari bhaat for breakfast, while other did not (see Table 9.1).

From the nutrition point of view, the menu at Indira Canteens was the most disappointing, though in the other two states menus were not particularly impressive either. Guests in Karnataka were most likely to complain about monotonous menus, followed by Tamil Nadu. In Karnataka, the state government had announced that it would revamp the menu (there was mention of adding ragi *mudde*, sandwiches, etc.), but this change had not been implemented. In Tamil Nadu, the menu had not been revised since the scheme began in 2013. It was also disappointing to see that though eggs are on the menu for Anganwadi and school children, they are not served at Amma Canteens.

When canteens rely on centralised kitchens for food supplies (e.g., in Karnataka), it created some issues. Food was supplied around 12 noon, so guests who came later were likely to get cold food as the canteens did not have reheating facilities. At a few canteens (15) in Rajasthan, food and/or rotis were supplied by a nearby canteen. Guests often complained about this, especially rotis made by a roti-maker.

Moreover, Indira Canteens received a fixed number of meals per meal-time, and the number was set arbitrarily. As a result, food often ran out. Canteen workers (42 per cent) in Tamil Nadu reported that food ran out 'sometimes' or 'often' more than in Karnataka. But investigators saw this happening more often in Karnataka than in other states. In Karnataka, it was the only reason that anyone was turned away. In Rajasthan and Tamil Nadu, the survey teams noticed canteen staff cooking afresh in a few cases, when food ran out. In Tamil Nadu, about half of the canteen staff reported that they had to turn people away because of lack of food; it was the most common reason for anyone being refused a meal at the canteen.

For public canteens to be successful, it is essential that they always have food available; they must remain a reliable source for a meal. If guests are turned away because food has run out, they are less likely to give canteens a chance, the next time they need it.

Cleanliness and Hygiene

As mentioned earlier, canteens can set a standard in hygienic cooking and eating practices in the market for street food. If they do so, it is likely to have a spillover effect on private eateries, as they compete for guests. Survey teams were asked to rate canteens and 88 per cent of canteens were rated as pleasant places to eat.

However, there were concerns regarding cleanliness, especially in Rajasthan. Only 38 per cent kitchens and 24 per cent washing areas in Indira Rasois were rated clean by the team. Overall, in Tamil Nadu, 58 per cent of the canteens were rated clean. Sometimes, the approach road to the canteen was not pleasant—only 7 per cent (Tamil Nadu) to 10 per cent (Rajasthan) of canteens were reported as having a clean approach. One of the reasons for this is that in Tamil Nadu and Rajasthan, spaces for canteens were carved out within existing spaces, unlike Karnataka where all Indira Canteens were newly built structures. The municipal corporation managed to find space to build a uniformly designed attractive canteen, which included a billing counter, serving food, standing tables inside and outside the building. There is a dedicated space for washing hands and dishes. Most canteens had an open space with trees around them.

In Karnataka and Tamil Nadu, standing and eating is common. Seating was limited. In Tamil Nadu, guests often sat on the floor to eat (most were clean enough for them to do so). In Rajasthan, guests appreciated that canteens had benches for them to sit and a table to place their plates on. Most canteens (64 per cent) had seating for 11-25 people.

Location Matters

The location of canteens played a role in how well it was used. The most popular and well-used canteens were those at hospitals, railway and bus stations. On average, there were four guests at the canteen at the time of arrival of the survey team and 247 guests had been served food the day before the survey. The average number of guests the day before the survey at the popular locations (hospitals, railway and bus stations) was 290, higher than the overall average (see Table 9.2).

The average was even higher at hospitals alone (382). Government hospitals attract patients suffering from serious illness from among the poorest sections (as treatment is more or less free). Therefore, having canteens near them makes a lot of sense. Though the patient is taken care of, the patient's attendant has to fend for themselves. Caregivers end up spending a lot on food especially. Respondents at canteens in the hospital premises reported that if the public canteen was not available, they would have spent Rs 64-83, i.e. they were saving Rs 56-75 per meal (see Table 9.3).

Workers and Remuneration

When Indira Canteens opened in Karnataka in 2017, there used to be around five employees at the canteen. By the time of our survey in December 2023, the number of employees had decreased (on average, each canteen had three staff members). Canteen staff said that (presumably) during the BJP government, some workers were laid off. Another reason for the smaller teams in Karnataka was that they were supplied by centralised kitchens. In Rajasthan and Tamil Nadu, where cooking happened on-site, the teams were larger (up to 16 in Tamil Nadu, an average of 9).

The salary structure for canteen staff was quite flat (between Rs 7250-10,000), with one exception. The highest paid canteen staff were the marshals in Bangalore, who got Rs 25,000 per month over and above an army pension.

(In Karnataka, provident fund deductions are made). In Bangalore, in single-worker canteens, the injustice of marshals' appointment was particularly poignant. While the marshals had very light duties (for which they were paid Rs 25,000), the lone worker had to do the accounts, serve food, wash utensils and clean the premises for a measly salary of Rs 7250.

Workers had many grievances. In Tamil Nadu, a majority of workers were recruited either in 2013 (when the canteen was set up) or in 2015 (during the scheme's expansion). Since then, for the workers in Chennai, the only wage increase (of Rs 25/day) happened after The Canteen Survey.[53] Workers do not enjoy any other benefits (leave, insurance, medical benefits, provident fund, etc.). If they take a day off, they lose a day's wage.[54] There were complaints of delayed payments, but workers were able to cope because their job allows them to eat in the canteen.

When staff included men and women (in Rajasthan and Karnataka), it is likely that women were getting paid less than men. For example, in Rajasthan, the average salary of male workers was Rs 9580, and Rs 9140 only for women.

Under-utilised Potential of Canteens

There are several areas of improvement, of which three need urgent attention. First, ensuring a nutritious menu; second, guarding against petty politicking and third, curtailing surveillance practices in the scheme that undermine its very compelling motivation: ensuring food security for all, with dignity.

Nutritious and Adequate Food

Greater variety and nutrition in the menu is the most urgent requirement to achieve the scheme's full potential. Menus need more nutritious food like eggs and meat, dairy products such as yogurt, buttermilk, fresh vegetables and a greater variety of cereals. At the very least, these items can be provided as an optional 'top-up', for an extra charge at cost price or a subsidised price.

In Rajasthan, a large share of the population is vegetarian. This has meant that the canteen menu is also vegetarian (roti, dal or kadhi, and a vegetable). At some canteens, we noticed some guests were bringing buttermilk or curd to have with the fixed meal.

When canteens began in Karnataka, the state relied on private centralised kitchens for food supplies, presumably because that model was already being used for other government schemes like school meals. centralised kitchens run by contractors (religious or otherwise) are not suitable for government programmes, because they are likely to cut costs in order to maximise profits. The lack of imagination in the menu at Indira Canteen (a rice-based dish at all meal-times) is perhaps a reflection of this. Moreover, when contractors have religious affiliations (as was the case with the organisation responsible for school meals in Karnataka), they have opposed inclusion of nutritious items like eggs on 'cultural' grounds, and for years in Karnataka, they were successful in preventing the introduction of eggs on the menu.

Tamil Nadu has neither resistance to animal-proteins nor the problems arising from centralised kitchens. In other government programmes (school meals and Anganwadis), eggs are regular fare.[55] One plausible reason for the omission in canteens could be that the current political system is in a bind. They don't want to shut down a popular scheme, but neither do they want to invest in a scheme whose identity is tied to that of their main political rival.

By providing a new and expanded menu at canteens (including nutritious top-ups like eggs, curd-buttermilk, and tea and coffee), along with better infrastructure and fairer terms of employment (especially better wages) to canteen workers, state governments can demonstrate political magnanimity, take credit for a very useful scheme at relatively nominal levels of expenditure.

Surveillance Practices

In Karnataka and Rajasthan, some practices in place in the name of curbing corruption were disturbing. Marshals deployed at canteens in Bengaluru were largely redundant. They were tasked with keeping track of food supplied and consumed, something that any other staff could easily do. The survey teams were disturbed by their presence in army overalls and boots, at a place that was meant to provide meals with dignity.

In Rajasthan, upon arrival, guests have to register. That process includes being photographed, submitting personal details (name, mobile number, and father's or husband's name). This was ostensibly to prevent corruption. One worry was that tokens would be issued to 'ghost' guests, with no one being fed. Over a quarter of our respondents had bought more than one token because one token was not enough to satisfy their appetite. In such cases, the number of guests will be lower than tokens issued, without implying any corruption. Thus, the rationale for collecting so much personal information at the time of registration did not have much merit.

In both cases, the practice was being justified in the name of controlling corruption, but it was not clear to what extent it actually helped in doing so. The Canteen Survey was not designed to suss out corrupt practices, however it is worth noting that the daily average guests according to administrative data for the survey districts in Rajasthan for 2023 (241) is close to the daily average reported in the survey (259, Table 9.3). Indeed, corruption can be a serious issue, but it probably needs other remedies than the ones currently in use.

Petty Politicking

Canteen schemes seem to be plagued by political 'one-downmanship' from the time of Maharashtra's Zunka Bhakar centres in the nineties. More recently, the mass closure of Andhra Pradesh's Anna's Canteens was another such example. When Yuvajana Sramika Ryuthu Congress Party (YSRCP) came to power, Anna Canteens associated with its political rival, the Telugu Desam Party (TDP) were closed en masse. With the TDP being voted back to power, they have reopened. In Karnataka, after the Bharatiya Janata Party (BJP) came to power, Indira Canteens were neglected, some staff were removed, and operations were restricted in a few.

In Tamil Nadu, many canteen workers felt that the Dravida Munnetra Kazhagam (DMK) government was 'tolerating' the canteens and were hesitant to speak openly. In Chennai, workers were upset about stagnation of wages since they were first employed. The infrastructure at many canteens was in poor condition, the water filter systems and deep freezers had not been repaired, information boards were dusty or illegible, there had been no improvement in the seating arrangements. The employees blamed the current government (the workers owed their allegiance to the political party that employed them in 2013-2015), though the neglect had probably set in earlier. Afterall, though the party that set up the Amma Canteens, was in power until 2021, yet there had been no change in the menu or increase in wages.

In states where the state government had changed after the canteen scheme was introduced, workers reported that canteens were 'underutilised' in the sense that they could cater to many more guests than they were currently serving (43 per cent in Karnataka and 70 per cent in Tamil Nadu). On the other hand, 80 per cent of workers in Rajasthan felt that the canteen was 'well used'.

Soon after The Canteen Survey, Rajasthan had its state assembly elections and a new government led by the BJP was voted to power. The new government changed the name of the scheme to Annapurna Rasoi and imposed an arbitrary cap on the number of tokens that can be issued in a day. Analysis of administrative data shows that the daily average for the survey districts declines from 241-252 in 2022-2023 to 177 in 2024 after the caps are imposed. Seemingly innocuous caps can cause considerable damage to the scheme because it can lead to a situation where guests have to be turned away because the token limit has been reached. Quite quickly people might lose faith in them, as the canteen will get a reputation for being an unreliable source for a cheap meal. This can lead to a drop in the number of people 'trying their luck' at the canteen, and the government can use this as evidence to justify the cap on tokens.

Where do Canteens Fit in India's Welfare Architecture?

The need for urban food security policies became apparent during India's COVID-19 pandemic lockdowns. Public canteens provide subsidised cooked meals at popular locations in many Indian cities. Canteens are essential for guaranteeing food security for vagrants, the destitute, the elderly and other vulnerable people. Public canteens are especially attractive for single working men, students and others who tend not to have cooking facilities. For those who use them regularly, savings are substantial: around a third of their reported monthly earnings. For women, they provide two further benefits—job opportunities and partial relief from domestic cooking chores. Canteens also serve a social role: as safe social spaces in an otherwise alienating urban environment, where people from varied backgrounds feel welcome.

Surveys in Madhya Pradesh, Chhattisgarh and Jharkhand suggest that while they are valued (Gummadi and Jyotishi 2025), they perform better in the states covered by The Canteen Survey 2023 (Karnataka, Rajasthan and Tamil Nadu). More cleanliness, better hygiene and nutritious menus, fair wages—many of the issues faced by canteens can be remedied with greater political commitment.

In 2023, Karnataka's budget for Indira Canteens was Rs 100 crore, which Tamil Nadu gave for canteens in 2016. Today, Tamil Nadu's state budget for canteens is lower than what it was in 2016. In 2023-24, Rajasthan allocated Rs 700 crore for Indira Rasoi. After the change of government in Rajasthan, the budget was halved. The budgets for canteens need to be secured from political interference so that they become a regular feature of the social security framework in India. The Brazilian experience suggests that some form of public institutionalisation—say, including it in the National Food Security Act 2013—can help (Fagundes et al 2022).[56] Cost-sharing norms between the Central and state governments on the one hand, and ULBs on the other need to be worked out.

The Canteens Survey 2023 suggests that such commitment

is warranted, as canteens help guarantee a dignified meal for millions, provide protection from hunger, enable savings, create meaningful jobs—especially for women—and foster a sense of oneness and wellbeing among many.

10

COVID-19

Neglect of Health and Education Exposed

Publicly provided quality health services and education are key to reducing inequality. A life of dignity rests on two legs: education and health. They are important for our wellbeing. Education and health should have the first claim in the country's budget. Ideally, each of these requires a dedicated book: one chapter in one section of a book does not do justice to these topics. But to ignore them entirely in a book on social policy is unfair too.

The COVID-19 pandemic provided a powerful lens through which to zoom into the failings in health and education policies of the country. There was a widespread outcry about the state of health, possibly because the failings affected the privileged. It gave hope that it will give rise to a consensus that the government needs to do more. The neglect was evident in the low budgetary support. For example, government expenditure on health in developed countries has been 5-10 per cent of GDP (see Table 2.2). It has managed to get to around 1 per cent of GDP only since the UPA (2004-2014) period. In spite of repeated announcements and claims that health is being prioritised, Central government expenditure has stagnated around 1 per cent of GDP. Even in the Economic Survey 2020-21, a chapter on health stated that it aimed to raise health expenditure from 1 per cent to 3 per cent of GDP (Government of India 2021).[57] Contrary to expectations, little has changed since.

While the failures in the health sector were widely acknowledged during COVID, an equally devastating crisis quietly unfolded in basic schooling. The treatment of school education during COVID-19 was a telling example of its neglect in India. UNICEF and UNESCO issued a statement that schools should be the last to close and the first to reopen during a lockdown. In many countries, primary schools either did not close or were opened soon after closure (Mervosh et al. 2024). In contrast, though primary schools should have been considered an 'essential service', Indian schools remained closed from the first lockdown in March 2020, for almost two consecutive years across the country (see Table 10.1). Many surveys showed that the well-off (about 10 per cent) immediately transitioned to online education, but in rural areas and among the poor, the lack of devices, inability to buy data for internet connectivity, lack of a learning environment at home, etc. became a hurdle to continuing their education. This will likely affect future opportunities of this generation.

Healthcare and Health Systems

Economists have deliberated on the question of private vs public provision of health services (Arrow 1963 and Stiglitz 1986). A broad consensus is that a market-based and profit-oriented health system is likely to fail on equity and efficiency. There are many forms and causes of market failures in health.

It is necessary to abide by human rights principles, aim for equity along with economic principles of efficiency in designing a healthcare system.

Table 10.1 Covid-19: A Timeline

Date	*Events*
End of January 2020	First COVID-19 case detected in India. COVID-19 screening of international passengers arriving in Delhi with fever
12 March 2020	First COVID-19 death recorded
19 March 2020	One-day lockdown
March 2020	COVID-19 screening of international passengers arriving with fever
24 March to August 2020	National lockdowns, including closure of Anganwadis, schools and colleges resulting in a humanitarian crisis
January 2021	COVID-19 vaccination begins
April 2021	Government organises Kumbh Mela
March-August 2021	Deadly Delta wave of COVID-19
November-December 2021	Omicron wave of COVID-19
February 2022	Uttar Pradesh's Legislative Assembly elections
July 2022	Schools and colleges reopen

Universal and free health services for all has gradually become the norm across the world. In the nineties, as a student in the UK, my mother had one concern: what if I got sick? Neither of us could imagine that the UK's 'National Health Service' (NHS) provided free healthcare to all. One could visit their neighborhood 'General Practitioner' (GP) or nurse. The costs are met from government revenues. Most doctors in the UK work for the NHS, for which they get government salaries. Italy and Spain have similar health systems.

In Germany, doctors are private, but it is mandatory for everyone to have an insurance policy. German insurance funds are private, but not-for-profit. It is illegal for them to make a profit. The cost of insurance is shared between the individual, the employer and the government. Since the entire population contributes and since the insurance companies cannot make profits, people get good health services at affordable prices. These are just two examples of the many 'models' available for a good health system (Reid 2010).

In India, affordable and quality healthcare is almost unimaginable for most. Some years ago, a well-wisher advised me to buy a hefty health insurance policy because premiums rise with age. I said that if the need arises, I can get free treatment at a government hospital like AIIMS or Safdarjung. My well-wisher looked at me sceptically: quality healthcare and free for all?

The Indian health 'system', if one can call it that, is a mishmash of private and government, insurance-based and direct provisioning. It is woefully under-funded. In countries like the United Kingdom and Germany, the government spends more than 8 per cent of GDP on health. In Brazil, Russia and South Africa, government spending on health is 3-5 per cent of GDP. Closer home in Nepal, it is about 1.5 per cent of GDP. In India, Central government spending is only 1 per cent (see Table 2.2).

Health Services in India

India has relied heavily on health insurance for the last two decades (e.g., Rashtriya Swasthya Bima Yojana, Ayushman Bharat). Table 10.2 shows that the proportion of households covered by total health insurance has increased substantially over the last twenty years (from 5 per cent to 41 per cent). Interestingly, the share of private health insurance in these has decreased (from 28 per cent to 3 per cent) between NFHS-3 and NFHS-5, suggesting a possible shift towards 'social insurance.'

Health insurance policies tend to focus more on curative rather than preventive healthcare. A major flaw in policies like Rashtriya Swasthya Bima Yojana and Ayushman Bharat is that it is helpful in case of major illness and hospitalisation, but not in disease prevention. It is well-recognised that a health model that focuses on curative rather than preventive healthcare costs more and has worse health outcomes (Shroff et al. 2020). Focusing on curative care amounts to saying that for a small injury the government will not spend on primary care, but should the wound become gangrenous needing amputation, the government will bear the cost associated with hospitalisation. There is an urgent need to refocus government health spending towards preventive healthcare.

Experts advocate a pyramid structure of preventive health care. Such a system is broad at the bottom, so that minor ailments can either be treated or referred upward. Thus, the first step towards strengthening preventive health care would be to provide better services at lowest levels of the pyramid. For that we need more free medicines and diagnostic services and trained nurses who can either treat or screen for referrals.[58] This is also important because there has been a perceptible increase in reliance on government health services in the last twenty years. For instance, Table 10.2 shows that

Table 10.2 Sources of Healthcare

	2005-6 NFHS-3	*2015-16 NFHS-4*	*2019-21 NFHS-5*
Share of households covered by health insurance or scheme (per cent)	4.91	28.72	413
Of those who have any insurance, share of private insurance (per cent)	27.51	4.12	3.43
Share of households (per cent) whose members typically use government healthcare when sick	344	455	506

Source: [1]Table 13.11 NFHS-3; [2]Table 11.13 NFHS-4; [3]Table 11.13 NFHS-5; [4]Table 13.13 NFHS-3; [5]Table 11.17 NFHS-4; [6]Table 11.17 NFHS-5.

while one-third of households typically visited government hospitals in 2005-06, the proportion had increased to half by 2019-21.

While it was always higher (around 80 per cent) in states like Himachal Pradesh, there has been a significant improvement in other states (Table 10.3). For example, Chhattisgarh had the same as the country's average in 2005-6 (about a third), but by 2019-21, 70 per cent of households in Chhattisgarh reported that they typically used a government facility. The reliance on government hospitals for deliveries is also considerable and has increased over the last two decades (Table 10.3). It is in the case of non-delivery hospitalisation that the private sector's grip becomes evident, especially in states like Bihar and Jharkhand.

It seems that people tend to resort to the private sector for hospitalisation and use government health facilities for other health needs. One way to understand their health seeking behaviour is that people go where they get affordable and quality health services. Since almost half of the households reported having access to the insurance option for hospital treatments, they are using it. For the rest (including deliveries) they use the government system.

COVID-19: A Case Study of Failures in India's Health Care System

Early on, public health failures impeded the battle against COVID-19. The pandemic required handwashing and distancing to curtail disease spread. Living conditions in India made these precautionary measures difficult. Lockdowns were announced in other countries to allow distancing. Distancing was not possible for many urban Indians because they live in densely populated slums or small homes. Many did not have adequate access to water for handwashing (Johari 2020b).

Table 10.3 Government Health Services in Select States

	Proportion of households (per cent) whose members typically use government healthcare when sick			*Institutional deliveries (per cent), in public sector 2019-21*	*Share of Government hospitals in hospitalisations other than deliveries (per cent) 2017-18*
	2005-6	*2015-16*	*2019-21*		
Bihar	7	22	20	75	38
Jharkhand	22	28	38	75	41
Chhattisgarh	36	50	70	82	54
Rajasthan	70	65	74	81	50
Himachal Pradesh	83	81	83	81	77
India	34	45	50	70	42

Source: Drèze et al. (2024), Table 11.17 NFHS-4 and NFHS-5, Table 13.13 NFHS-3. Deliveries based on IIPS (2022a), Table 8.13 and IIPS (2022), Table 51, NFHS data. Hospitalisation National Statistical Office (2019), Table A.13.

Government-provided Healthcare: Under-supply and Poor Quality

Public healthcare services suffered from under-provisioning and were lacking in quality care. Under-provisioning was evident in many aspects of COVID-19 management: testing, quarantine, isolation, treatment etc. In the initial months of the pandemic, there was a shortage of testing kits and labs; tests were being done only in government labs. From mid-2020 onwards, to expand testing capacity, private labs were allowed to conduct tests. Yet, availability of testing facilities improved very slowly. For example, in 2021, towards the end of the second wave, 40 per cent of the country's districts still did not have labs (Barnagarwala 2021). When people tested positive, they were sent to isolation facilities. Some tried to flee because government hospitals were in a bad condition (Daniyal 2020).[59] In rural areas, matters were worse; when necessary equipment ultimately arrived, there was no staff to operate it (Saikia 2020 and 2021).

Treatment at hospitals was another challenge: basic facilities such as hospital beds, oxygen cylinders, ventilators, etc. were lacking. India had only 2.3 critical beds per one lakh population (Venkataramakrishnan 2020), compared with 12.5 in Italy, a country where the COVID-19 pandemic was also severe. The shortage of resources was so extreme that several rationing mechanisms began to be improvised: for instance, for a brief period during the second wave, in Ahmedabad those arriving by private vehicle were not being hospitalised (Johari 2021).

Another area where there were shortages due to a sluggish health policy was personal protective equipment (Johari 2020d). There were reports of corruption in the supply of basic items such as masks, gloves, protective gear, oxygen, ventilators (Johari 2020a). A black market for medicines and oxygen emerged (Sharma 2021).

Government health facilities were over-burdened and issues related to quality also arose. Non-COVID-19 patients—women in labour, diabetics, heart patients, etc.—began to be neglected (Lalwani 2020 and Johari 2020c). The government failed to formulate an effective plan to deal with the pandemic; instead, it resorted to the ad hoc policies described above.

Private Healthcare: Inefficient and Inequitable

Did private health suppliers make up for insufficient and poor quality public health services? The short answer is no. Indeed, the pandemic can serve as a case study on the failure of heavy reliance on privately provided healthcare.

One, in a private, market-based system only those who have money will be able to get treatment. For instance, the private sector was reportedly demanding arbitrary prices—for testing kits, oxygen cylinders, life-saving medicines, etc. Similarly, if the government had stuck to its vaccine policy of 19 April 2021, vaccine manufacturers would have given it first to those who were willing to pay a higher price. When there is a shortage, a market system rations access through prices; those who have money will be at the top of the line, not those who need it most.[60] Rather than frontline workers and the elderly who need it most urgently, those who could pay more would get the vaccine first. Should price-based queuing system for vaccines be acceptable?

Besides ethical issues, a market-based system can be inefficient also. For example, even for those who were at the top of the queue, they end up paying more (the private sector was proposing Rs 600-1200 for the vaccine), that was being provided cheaply (at Rs 150) to the government.[61]

Two, there are 'externalities': that is, one person's

behaviour affects others as well; my health outcomes depend not only on my behaviour, but also that of others. For example, when someone else smokes cigarettes, I too am affected.

Infectious diseases and vaccinations are a good example of externalities; unless *everyone* is protected, nobody can be protected. Vaccinations for infectious diseases like COVID can be effective when everyone or at least a substantial share of the population is vaccinated. If the poor cannot afford to get vaccinated because of prices, it also hurts the rich because vaccination will be most effective when 50-80 per cent of the country's population is vaccinated. It was in the interest of all to ensure free and universal vaccination. In this context too, the attempt to privatise vaccination was not in public interest.

With externalities, some form of public intervention is needed. Take the example of cleanliness in public places. If I don't throw my garbage on the road but my neighbours do, my pro-social behaviour is of little use. To enjoy clean surroundings, a collective effort to make arrangements for garbage collection is required. More often than not, it has to be made through government intervention, e.g., by the municipality. COVID-19 vaccinations were a good example of this.

Three, health care is characterised by information asymmetry. Information asymmetry refers to a situation where one entity (e.g., the doctor) knows more than the other (the patient). It causes market-based systems to be inefficient (e.g., wasteful prescription of drugs and diagnostics). When we are sick, we may not be able to tell whether the doctor is good, whether we really need the tests or medicines they are prescribing, and so on. Over-medication or testing may benefit them (if there is collusion with the diagnostics or drug vendors). If treament is provided at a government hospital, and the doctor does not expect to make money from the patient, then there is little incentive for the doctor to advice unnecessary tests and medicines.

Four, the combination of information asymmetry and the profit motive of private providers can be life-threatening for patients. For example, if putting the patient on a ventilator or an operation is advised (e.g., hysterectomies for women even if they don't need it), patients will not be able to assess whether they actually need it.[62] Most private providers work for profits, though there may be some not-for-profit health providers (e.g., through charitable trusts). When the service providers work for profit, there is fear of exploitation of the patient. For example, the tendency to prescribe cesarean instead of a normal delivery, unnecessary diagnostics, and so on has been noticed in India.

Five, competition as a feature of market-based systems that can bring efficiency (lower costs or better quality). If a buyer does not like one vendor, they can buy from another. The fear of losing a customer puts pressure on vendors to compete on quality and price. Healthcare, however, is an exception to this norm. In some cases, there is little scope for competition. For instance, during medical emergencies people cannot shop around for the most competitive option (e.g., when oxygen was required for patients during COVID). Similar arguments apply for pregnant women in labour or in rural areas where hospitals are far from each other.

Further, there are situations where competition may not be helpful: with competition among many private hospitals, the burden of decision making on quality and price falls on the patient, who may not be very well placed (in terms of getting reliable information on these parameters as well as in terms of being well-enough) to make informed choices. By contrast, having a uniform government system can make such a decision easier. This became evident at the time of the COVID-19 vaccination: when the government was making all arrangements, we were only responsible for booking a slot to get the shot. During May 2021, when there was a temporary switch in vaccine policy, it created confusion. In these sorts of situations, a single supplier allows us to fix accountability.

Six, COVID-19 revealed several failings in the regulation of India's private health providers. Initially some private hospitals refused to admit COVID patients (Yamunan and Saikia 2020).[63] Prices were being inflated—private labs were overcharging for test kits with the result that people were evading the COVID test, thereby causing further spread of the virus. If tests had been free or at regulated prices, more people might have tested and isolated themselves.

Private Insurance: Limited Reach and Accountability

While private insurance can mitigate some of the problems listed above (e.g., make health care accessible to those who cannot afford it), it has its limits. Insurance can be effective when it is universal—healthy and unhealthy—because it allows for risk-pooling: when I am healthy, the premium I pay will be used to treat those who fall sick and when I fall sick, the premium paid by others pays for my treatment. Otherwise, those who are willing to buy an insurance policy, are those who are more likely to suffer from illness (healthy people may be reluctant to spend on premiums). This is known as 'adverse selection'. Adverse selection can lead to a breakdown of the private insurance market and/or it results in making healthcare expensive (because whoever is insured is likely to utilise it for some treatment or the other). On the other hand, those with insurance, may start taking less care of themselves due to the assurance of free treatment through their insurance policy ('moral hazard'). This also makes illness and treatment costly.

Private for-profit insurance has other problems. According to estimates by Duggal and Hooda (2021), even those who had health insurance in 2017-18 ended up spending out of pocket. Those with government insurance were reimbursed only 15 per cent of their total hospitalisation costs, while those with private, private- or government- employer supported insurance received 48-57 per cent of their expenses. One reason for this was cumbersome paperwork that makes it difficult to get reimbursed.

Vaccine Policy: Learning from Initial Mis-steps

While the vaccine was being developed, there was complacency in India as it seemed that India had two possible vaccine solutions—Astra-Zeneca's Covishield being developed in Oxford was to be manufactured by the Serum Institute of India (SII) and Covaxin being developed by Bharat Biotech.

When the vaccine was ready for rollout, frontline workers (doctors, nurses, police personnel, civil defence etc.) and older people (considered at high risk) were placed on the priority list. A priority list was necessary because it was not possible to supply for all immediately. Fears of vaccine shortages started emerging in the first week of March itself (in fact, some vaccine centres shut down due to the shortages).[64] When the Delta wave spread rapidly, there was a loud clamour to junk the priority list. Demand increased due to the Delta wave and supply could not keep up.

There were two supply bottlenecks: the Serum Institute of India (SII) was committed to supplying to other countries of the world, the Government of India was exporting COVID-19 vaccines. According to one estimate, by mid-March 2021, more doses were exported than given in India (Chaudhary 2021). Production capacity was being artificially restricted because only two companies were allowed to manufacture the vaccine. International law has a provision of 'compulsory licensing' that allows governments to make the vaccine formula patent free so that other companies can make it. Surprisingly, India was fighting for free patents internationally, but would not implement it here (Kang et al. 2021).

The Central government panicked and sought to wash its hands off the situation. On 19 April, the Central government announced that (from 1 May) all those above 18 years of age will be eligible for the vaccination and all states should make their own arrangements to buy the vaccine. The two major vaccine makers were given the freedom to negotiate price and supply of the vaccine directly with states and private hospitals. Suddenly, states were told to arrange the vaccine themselves. They have fewer sources of revenue. As they were procuring vaccines for the people, like the Centre, vaccines ought to have been made available to them at the regulated price.

The SII announced three different prices for Covidshield—Rs 150 to the Central government, Rs 450 to the state and Rs 600 to the private sector and Bharat Biotech set the price between Rs 600-1200. The producers sought to take undue advantage of their monopoly situation as soon as government policy gave them an opening.

The revised vaccine procurement policy came into effect on 1 May. It led to a mad rush among Indian states to get supplies and a good price from private companies. A month later, not a single state managed to secure supplies. On

7 June, the Centre reverted to its earlier policy of central procurement at Rs 150 and made them available to the states (Kulkarni and Neelakantan 2021).

Apart from supply and price, the government created a third hurdle to quickly ramping up vaccination. It began to rely on apps for basic healthcare facilities such as oxygen, hospital beds, vaccination. Mediating access to them through apps where Aadhaar-based registration tended to be mandatory served to ration access, privileging the privileged in the process. Though vaccine hesitancy was low, those who were not taking the vaccine were being threatened.

By late October 2022, approximately 90 crore people had managed to get the first dose and just under 40 crore had the second dose as well. Vaccination rates were lower in rural areas, compared to urban. Some evidence suggests that the focus on the COVID-19 vaccine displaced other immunisation of children. In spite of this, the vaccination effort demonstrates the importance of government presence in the health sector.

Health services in India are a maze of public and private providers. In a fragmented health system, patients are not aware of their rights and end up stumbling between the two.

Basic Education in India

The importance of education in personal, social, economic and political life and the importance of literacy for education is a drum that is worth beating repeatedly.

In India, too often, education is seen only from the point of view of getting a job. Education is certainly a means towards that end, but is equally valuable as an end in itself. A rich person who cannot read and write is sure to feel that something is missing in their life. The association of education with jobs is the most plausible explanation for the fact that during COVID-19 whenever there was talk of reopening schools, the emphasis was on higher classes (classes 9-12), because that is the gateway to college admissions and therefore, to jobs.

However, from the point of view of a child's development, it is childhood years that are invaluable in a child's growth because the foundation of their life is laid in these years (Heckman 2006). When children learn the alphabet or to count, classroom instruction by the teacher has a great significance. In later years, when children have acquired basic skills such as reading and writing, their ability for self-learning and peer-learning increases substantially.

At the end of the 1990s, not all school-age Indian children were enrolled in school. A major achievement in the last twenty years has been that going to school every day has become a universal social norm. During the COVID pandemic, there was a worry that this might be undone. While COVID-19 lockdown norms were eased for many activities over the two years of the pandemic, for schools the lockdown lasted almost two full years.

Table 10.4 reports enrolment rates for children aged 6-17 years from NHFS-5 (2019-21). It is unlikely to capture dropouts during the lockdown.[65] However, it is clear from the table that there was no improvement in the enrolment rate between 2015-16 (NFHS-4) and 2019-21 (NFHS-5) for children aged 6-17 years, nor was there much progress in the median years of schooling (which increased by about half a year for boys and girls).

Banerjee and Wadhwa (2023) found that while in 2018, 2.5 per cent of 6-14 year olds in rural areas were not enrolled in school, it almost doubled to 4.6 per cent in 2021. Boys were affected more—in 2021, 4.7 per cent of boys aged 7-10

Table 10.4 Some Basic Indicators of Education

	NFHS-3, 2005-06	*NFHS-4 2015-16*	*NFHS-5 2019-21*
Enrolment, 6-17 years (children of primary age) [1-3], per cent			
Female	66 (81)	84 (95)	87 (95)
Male	75 (85)	86 (95)	88 (95)
Literacy Rate (15-49 years)[4], per cent			
Female	55.0	68.4	71.5
Male	77.5	84.4	83.2
Median years of schooling [5,6], per cent			
Female	1.9	4.4	4.9
Male	4.9	6.9	7.3
More than 10 years of schooling [7-9], per cent			
Female	14.3	23.3	27
Male	23.8	33	36.1

Sources: [1]Table 2.9, NFHS-3 [2]Table 2.19, NFHS-4 [3]Table 2.26, NFHS-5 [4]Table 3.3.1 and Table 3.3.2 of NFHS-3, NFHS-4 and NFHS-5 India Reports [5]Table 2.17, NFHS-4 India Report, [6]Table 2.24, NFHS-5 India Report [7]Table 2.7, NFHS-3 [8]Table 2.18, NFHS-4 [9]Table 2.25, NFHS-5 India Report years were not enrolled in school (compared to only 1.4 per cent in 2018). Even among slightly older boys (aged 11-14 years), it increased from 2.9 per cent to 4.3 per cent. They note another interesting trend—in rural areas, enrolment in private schools among children aged 6-14 years had been rising since 2006, and reached 32.5 per cent in 2018. But during COVID (and possibly due to loss of incomes during the lockdowns), it dropped by 8 percentage points (to 24.4 per cent) in 2021.

Chart 10.1 plots the increase in literacy rates for selected social groups between 2015-16 and 2019-21. At one extreme, in both NFHS rounds, one sees near universal literacy (Kerala men). At the other end, Dalit women in rural Bihar among whom less than half (40 per cent) were literate even in 2019-21. In several of the other social groups, literacy rates barely rose in these five years.

Chart 10.2 raises the bar slightly: it plots the percentage of children who have studied beyond Class 10 along with the basic literacy rate for 2019-21. The disparities in educational achievements are clearer as soon as the bar is higher. Three-quarters of urban male in Kerala had more than ten years of schooling, whereas less than one-fifth of rural Dalit women in Bihar had attained the same benchmark. The literacy rate among rural Dalit women in Bihar in 2019-21 (40 per cent) was *lower* than the proportion who have completed Class 10 or more at the all-India level (around 46 per cent).

Three main points emerge from these two charts: though schooling has become a social norm (an important achievement given where we started), India has not achieved universal literacy yet (roughly one-fifth of adults are still not literate), progress is very slow, and despite some improvements, there are glaring inequalities in educational achievements by social groups.

Chart 10.1 Inequalities in literacy rates

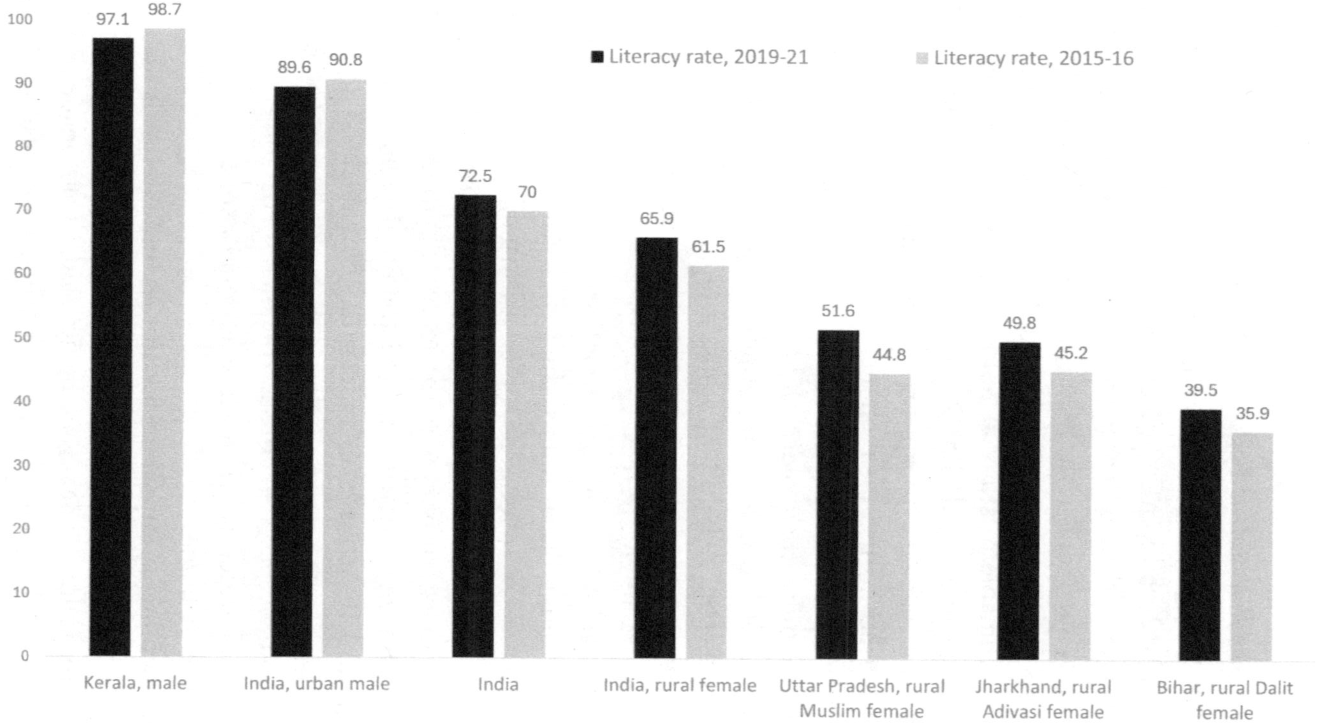

Note: Reference group for level of education is those aged 15-49 years

Sources: Calculated using National Family Health Survey, 2019-21 and 2015-16

The Lockdown and its Fallout on Schooling

In 2021 during the lockdown, I had a casual conversation with 10-12 children in the slums of Munirka (New Delhi). Only one said their father had a phone, but since he drove an auto, she could join classes only in the evening. Another Class 8 student pleaded with us to have her school reopened: she was unable to study at home where she was expected to help with household chores and in running the family shop. She only managed to appear for an exam because a friend allowed her to use their phone.

School closures affected girls more than boys, younger children more than older children and poor children more than the well-off. In many families if girls were home, they were expected to help with household chores. For some boys, there were other pressures: e.g., to help at the shop or with farm work in rural areas.

Education is not just about reading and counting. It is also about other things children learn in school—social skills such as talking to others, learning to sit, eat and drink independently, etc. An important part of a young child's education is eye-and-hand coordination. For this, the classroom environment, the company of other children is helpful. The best age to nurture civic-mindedness (queuing, punctuality, etc.) among individuals is childhood. The school environment plays a crucial role here. For some children, school provides relief from emotional stress and physical violence at home.

Discipline is important for studies and interest is essential for discipline. With online classes, children were not always able to follow what was being said. That made it very difficult to maintain interest and discipline—especially for young children. Children missed the classroom because with online classes they hesitated to ask questions. It was difficult to concentrate on studying due to the noisy atmosphere at home.

Educational challenges during COVID varied by age. For younger children, a learning environment and personal instruction is essential and that was missing during the lockdown. For slightly older children, devices, connectivity, quiet space, etc. were not available when classes moved online. Sometimes even with all the arrangements at home (a device, connectivity, space), education was affected for many. Even among those who have adequate resources, children found it hard to study at home. When in class, whether out of fear or respect for the teacher, children make an attempt to focus. Discipline is not easy in class; at home, it is near impossible.

Although many educational institutions did not insist on live lectures, and provided lecture recordings, students in rural areas were forced to download lectures by visiting e-kiosks or internet cafes located several kilometers away from their village.

At university, students probably learn as much in class as they do outside the classroom. After lectures, assignments and discussion with other students helps them understand things better. Where college education is in English, and students come from Hindi (or regional language) medium schools, the medium of instruction is an additional challenge. Due to the English-speaking environment in college, with other students also using English, those from non-English medium schools pick up English (through friends, listening, etc.). Sometimes help is also available from their college. With online studies from home, these important aspects of campus life were denied to students.

Chart 10.2 Inequalities in educational attainments, 2019-21

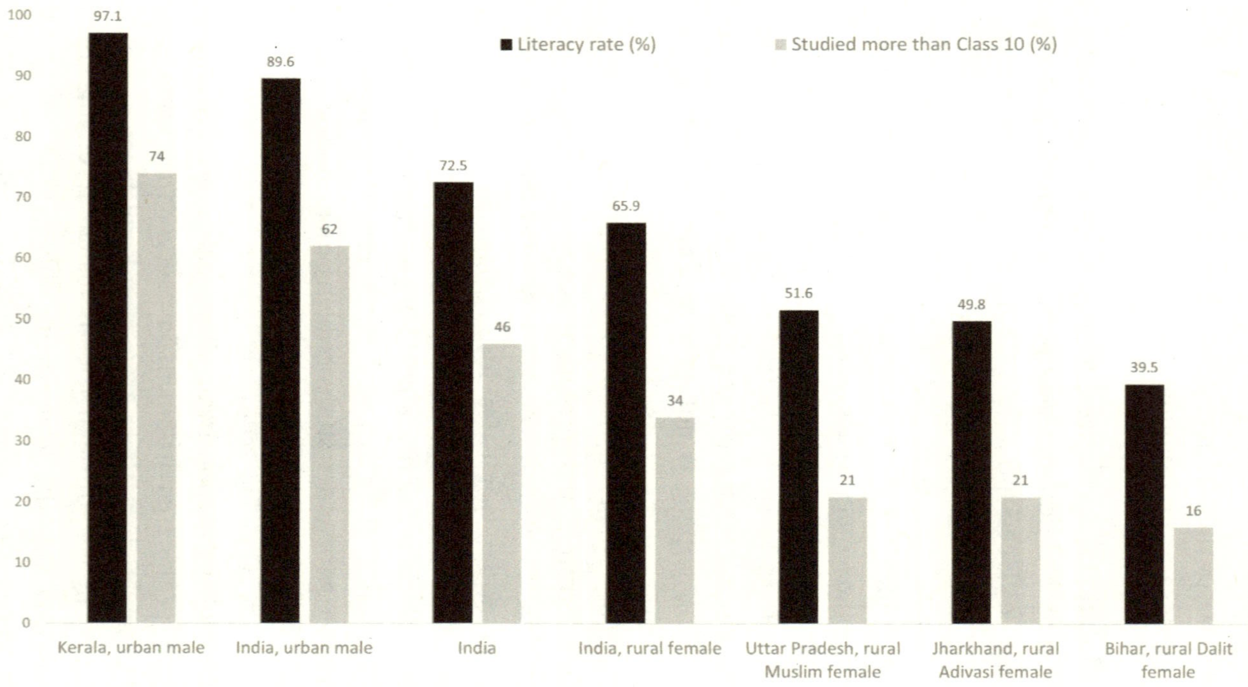

Note: Reference group for level of education is those aged 15-49 years
Source: Calculated from National Family Health Survey, 2019-21

It is worth recalling that the UNICEF and UNESCO had issued a statement that schools should be the last to close and the first to reopen during a lockdown. In India, there was a resistance to reopening schools.[66] Reopening did not necessarily mean that all children go to school every day. There were several ways to regulate the number of children in the school: e.g., some in the morning, some in the afternoon, or half attendance every day and so on. Those who could study at home, could have been directed to stay home while allowing those without a learning environment at home to come to school. Despite these possibilities and needs, the government closed schools and more or less forgot children for almost two full years.

In the Name of Online Education: Locked Out 2021

Soon after schools closed in April 2020, online classes were announced. Many believe that online education was an effective substitute for classroom learning. For some, online classes were a treat: 'attending' a class on 'mute' mode, in bed with the camera off. Yet for students from less privileged classes, online education opened up a new battlefront in their already difficult lives.

Our report 'Locked Out 2021' brought out the reality of online schooling among children from disadvantaged groups (Bakhla, et al. 2021). The report was based on a survey conducted in August 2021 in fifteen states and we interviewed 1362 parents. The findings of Locked Out 2021 were alarming. It made clear that although online education may have been an effective choice for children from well-off homes, it did not offer a real option to disadvantaged children, both rural or urban.[67]

There was a widespread misconception that only children

in villages suffered due to online education. However, our study found that only a quarter of children in urban areas were studying regularly, and in rural areas, the number was less than 10 per cent. More than half of the children had not met their teacher in the past month.

Online education required devices such as laptops, computers or smartphones, but according to NFHS-5 (2019-21), 4.4 per cent of rural households and 19 per cent in urban areas had computers; 65 per cent had internet (41 per cent in rural areas). A 'Save the Children' (2020) report suggested even higher exclusion (76 per cent) on account of lack of internet access. Lack of computers/laptops can be made up to some extent by smartphones. According to a 2019 Lokniti Survey, however, only one-third of households had smartphones.

Half of the respondents in rural areas and one-fourth in urban areas did not have a single smartphone. Out of concern for the child's future, parents in some poor families bought smartphones on credit. Even when a phone was available, sometimes it would be with one of the parent. Ownership does not guarantee that the child would have access to it when required. Sometimes there was more than one school-going child in the house, but only one phone between them. In such cases the older child was prioritised, the younger one was likely to be left out. Despite all these arrangements, many children were completely left out.

While the electricity supply has improved across the country, continuous supply is still not common in rural areas. Power failures meant that children were in danger of losing their homework, losing precious exam time or even failing it.

Reliable internet connectivity is also important for online education. Nearly two-thirds (57 per cent urban and 65 per cent rural) of children studying online reported that network was a big problem. In some places, they had to climb to a hilltop for network, and then after some time they had to come down in order to charge the phone! To avoid such uncertainties, in some cases school going children were sent to live with relatives so that their studies would not be interrupted. Recharging the phone imposed an additional financial burden at a time when the lockdown impacted parents' earnings.

Many children did not have adequate learning environments at home. According to the Census, a quarter of the country's population lives in a single room (Anand and Thampi 2016). If there are two to four people in the same single-room home, with everyone working or studying from home, that thew up its own challenges. With online education, the need for family support at home was high but many children's parents were not particularly well-equipped to do so because of low educational achievements among them. There were many where either the child or the parents experienced difficulty in using smartphones properly. Often even those whose parents were educated, were not able to support their children because they had to go out all day to earn.

Respondents said that in the name of online study material what they got was some pictures or files on a WhatsApp group. Sometimes the handwriting would not be legible. Sometimes, the instruction on WhatApp would be 'read the story of the tortoise and rabbit'. That's it. Many children said that when they were assigned worksheets or homework, they were simply expected to copy the lines sent to them on WhatsApp, in their book. They did not understand what was written. Children enrolled in Class 1 were also assigned homework, though they had not gone to school for a single day, nor had anyone taught them to write. The teacher instructed the mothers to get the older child to do the homework for the younger child and submit it.

Only 8-25 per cent of the children who studied regularly or occasionally were relying on online classes or videos. In rural areas, in households where smartphones are available, 43 per cent respondents said they could not study regularly as they were not being sent any study material from school.

Where phones were available, but study material was lacking, parents expressed concrerns about phone addiction among children. Some children watched cartoons or played games on the phone when they were meant to be studying.

During the lockdown, teachers in some states did voice their concerns about their students' future. In Punjab, when the state government did not release funds for mid-day meals, the teachers tried their best to keep it going for two months. Teachers in states like Tamil Nadu and Maharashtra spoke up in favour of resuming offline education.

At least at the primary and secondary level, even among well-off families, online education pales in comparison to classroom learning. Online education is a myth when the child comes from a disadvantaged background. Despite these widespread challenges, the Union Minister stated in the Lok Sabha that no child was deprived of education due to COVID in India. Such a statement was insensitive, which ignored the struggle of a large section of people.

'Back to School'—Was the System Ready?

After two years of school closures, by the time all schools opened in 2022, a substantial portion of the child's formative years had passed. The long closure posed several challenges when children went back to school.

The first challenge was to ensure that children did not drop out of school. Government data for 2020-21 suggested that the drop-out rate was 14.6 per cent among secondary school students (Government of India 2022).

The second challenge was that when the children returned to school after two years, they might have forgotten the difficulties associated with going to school every day. Waking up early in the morning, getting ready, going to school, sitting still in class—all these habits may have been forgotten among the younger children. Getting them back into this habit needed the support of the family. The government could also have taken some steps to attract children to school. Although schools reopened everywhere, mid-day meals did not resume immediately. Serving mid-day meals can help to lure children back to school, while also ensuring that they are attending classes on a full stomach to improve their ability to concentrate.

When children who could not study during the two years of the lockdown returned to school, they struggled without proper support. Without encouragement from the school teacher and compensatory measures (such as extra time), there was a fear that these students would be easily demoralised, to the extent of wanting to drop out of school. To avoid this, there was an urgent need to create a welcoming and sensitive environment at school.

According to the Annual Survey of Education Report (ASER), before COVID-19, learning achievements among school-going children were abysmally low. With the school closures, there was a situation where a student would be sitting in Class 5 without having gone to school at all since she was in Class 3, because of the automatic promotion policy. If as per ASER findings, in Class 3 she was already lagging behind in her learning achievements (e.g., could not read the text that should have been possible for a Class 1 child to read), now she would be expected to cope with the Class 5 syllabus with skills that were suited for a Class 2 syllabus! Special measures, such as remedial classes were necessary for such students. Absent such support, the child would have to cope with a syllabus that is four years ahead of her abilities. Findings ways of making up for this backlog was a huge challenge for teachers.

Some states recognised these challenges and took proactive steps. The Jharkhand government launched a month-long 'Back to School' campaign, with a 'No Bag' day, to help students deal with anxieties related to returning to school. When higher class schools opened in Tamil Nadu in 2022, they tried to provide counselling for mental support to children. The Delhi government introduced a 'Happiness Curriculum', which included spending two hours a day on basic abilities. Some states created 'bridge courses' based on assessments regarding how much ground children had lost in terms of basic abilities. Much more was required and could have been done with available resources. For instance, additional support for primary school children could have been provided by Anganwadi workers for a small additional honorarium. In most states, however, these issues did not receive enough attention.

The challenges were not limited to India and there were a variety of initiatives around the world to provide sensitive support to children returning to school. The biggest challenge in India was the lack of attention to these issues, which led to the fear of children dropping out of school at the primary stage without even acquiring basic literacy skill.

Decoding Inequality in a Digital World

COVID-19 gave an impetus to greater digitisation of health services. This tends to be a convenience for the well-off who have access to and are comfortable with the use of digital technologies. However, for ordinary people, it is either inaccessible or more difficult than offline, in-person access. Those who have smartphones get ahead in the queue for getting these services.

Virginia Eubanks' widely acclaimed book, *Automating Inequality*, alerted us to the ways that automated decision-making tools exacerbate inequalities, especially by raising the barrier for people to receive services they are entitled to. Aadhaar has de facto become compulsory and widespread for both education and health services. For certain sections, this has also led to a lot of trouble in enrolling children in school, and made access to healthcare a bit harder.

Post COVID-19, schools in Delhi especially announce closures at the drop of a hat: high pollution, heavy rains, heat waves—anything goes.[68] The decision is justified on the grounds that it affects the child's health and welfare. These justifications would have been more plausible if the state governments were taking long-term measures to combat pollution, heat waves, flooding, etc. In fact, even short-term measures such as banning construction (a major cause of air pollution) are not always taken, though a school closure is announced. Unlike the Delhi government, the Tamil Nadu government has managed to keep schools open even when there has been flooding in Chennai. For instance, guides have been deployed to get children to school safely. Moreover, it is said that when schools close, classes can be held online. As during COVID-19, this is true only for privileged children. The pandemic may have contributed to 'normalizing' school closures, switching sporadically to online education which will disrupt learning for students of disadvantaged groups. Greater digitisation of health and education serves the better-off and the challenges faced by disadvantaged groups remain hidden. This creates the impression that digitisation has no downside for anyone and paves the way for more (and sometimes compulsory) digital health and education, surreptitiously exacerbating inequalities.

11

Emerging Issues in Social Policy

So far, I have dwelled on the challenges and achievements in social policies over the past two decades. This chapter turns to four emerging issues that affect social policies but are not very well understood.

The first among them is corporate greed—as laws were enacted making some social policies legal rights, there needed to be a committed budget. This kindled the interest of the private sector, looking to get a share of the pie. The second issue is technocracy. Technology can increase government capacity and bring transparency but technocracy undermines both accountability and public interest. When the two are conflated, there is a danger that democracy ends up being undermined. Third, as cash transfers are becoming an increasing part of the social policy framework, the challenges associated with them—budgets, inflation-indexing, banking infrastructure, etc.—need closer attention. Finally, for too long we have taken availability of a robust statistical system for granted. As it was weakened over the past decade or so, one needs to learn to appreciate its importance for policy making, and more broadly, in a democracy.

Corporate Greed

As spending on social security increased, the private sector has been eyeing this as a potential 'market'. There is a sense that they should also have a share in it. The concern with such private involvement is that government spending could end up subsidising or supporting the private sector, in the name of serving public interest. Three examples can help understand this issue.

In 2008, the Biscuit Manufacturers Association (BMA) appeared to have noticed that the budget for the Mid-Day Meal (MDM) Scheme was Rs 8000 crore. At the time, someone thought, why should BMA not have a share of this spending. (According to an estimate, the market of the biscuit industry in India at the time was only Rs 4800 crore). The BMA tried to lobby for replacing cooked food with fortified biscuits in the government's MDM scheme.

The way BMA went about it was educative. They prepared a brief outlining all the problems with the current operation of the MDM scheme, and presented fortified biscuits as a neat solution to all those problems. This brief was sent to Members of Parliament (MP). Instigated by an enterprising middleman, many MPs forwarded these suggestions to the concerned minister. On the face of it, it would appear that when so many MPs are making such a demand, it should be taken seriously; in fact, it was just a lobbying effort by an industry group.

One might ask, what is wrong with a proposal to replace cooked meals with fortified biscuits? It could be viewed as a win-win for both—food for under-nourished children and profits for companies. The proposal, however, raises several questions: can biscuits replace cooked meals (could you have biscuits instead of rice/rotis with dal or vegetables on a daily basis)? Is micronutrient fortification effective in mitigating under-nutrition? Would it lead to more corruption through diversion of biscuit packets to the open market? Would such an arrangement not hurt accountability? When the food is cooked at schools, they are easier to supervise and monitor. In Delhi, where MDMs are supplied by centralised kitchens and delivered to all schools, teachers said that even they did not know who to complain to when the need arises. Fortunately, in the case of BMA's lobbying, vigilant officers in the ministry got wind of what was happening and the plan failed.

Another example of 'diverting' public funds to the private sector is the Central government's announcement in 2021 that rice provided through the Public Distribution System (PDS) and for mid-day meals and Anganwadi will be fortified with iron. This move was meant to be an important step to reduce widespread anaemia. In February 2026, the government announced a "temporary discontinuation" of fortification (Press Information Bureau 2026).

Can fortification of rice help reduce anaemia? To support its decision, the government resorted to a single study by an organisation called 'PATH'. But according to a Cochrane Review, such micro-nutrient fortification has no significant benefit (Peña-Rosas et al. 2019).[69]

More than half of the country's children and women suffer from anaemia. It is estimated that iron deficiency anaemia accounts for about half of all anaemic cases in India. Iron fortification cannot help those who have anaemia due to other reasons (say, a Vitamin B12 deficiency).[70]

Iron deficiency anaemia can be due to lack of iron in diet, reduced ability of the body to absorb iron, etc. To combat iron-deficiency anaemia, the quantity and the manner of intake of iron supplements are important. Iron supplements are best taken on an empty stomach, as ingesting it with food reduces absorption by the body. The National Health Service recommends roughly a 200 mg of ferrous sulphate (65 mg of elemental iron) a day for iron-deficiency anaemia. The iron supplement proposed to be added to rice is a fraction of this recommended dosage. As per available information, the proposal is to mix 28-42.5 mg of iron in 1 kg of rice. Thus, in the government's proposal the dosage is inadequate and the manner of supplementation is inappropriate.

Sharing information about this policy at a public meeting, the Food Secretary said that the government ran it on a pilot basis in fifteen districts (Jakhar 2021). Implementation of the proposal would require rejigging a large part of the supply chain. Indeed, it was wise to pilot it before implementing such a major policy. The Food Secretary detailed several major challenges they encountered, and by and large, the results of the pilot were disappointing. Only eleven out of fifteen districts could implement it. Supply-side challenges included quality and standardisation of iron pellets, the mechanism for mixing iron pellets with rice, the scientific need for uniform mixing and so on. For example, to enrich rice with iron, folic acid and vitamin B12, rice flour has to be prepared, pre-mixed, and then reconstituted into rice grains. These are to be mixed evenly with the rest of the rice (if not done properly, they can cause health issues). The reconstituted grains must look exactly like rice grains, otherwise they will be discarded as pebbles while 'cleaning' the rice at the cooking stage. There are a variety of private players in this system (pre-mix suppliers, equipment suppliers, etc.), which raises the question of quality control and supervision of private players. Who will ensure that they follow the entire process as instructed?

Surprisingly, despite the challenges (and failures, even) faced during the pilot, the Food Secretary said that the government decided to scale up nationally. Why? The explanation given was that all private players involved in the supply chain needed 'policy certainty' and an assurance about the 'business proposition' for them. This raises the question: was the policy being implemented to maintain guaranteed demand for pre-mix suppliers and blending factories?

If steps are to be taken against anaemia, does it make sense to give it to *everyone* (regardless of whether they need iron or B12) in such small quantities, together with rice, where it is also possible that it will be discarded as pebbles while cooking and there is a possibility of harm (if quality control is not maintained in the production process)?

Wouldn't it be better (and cheaper) to improve the existing iron supplementation programme of the government? Spend more on identification of the type of anaemia, provide iron and/or B12 supplements through the government's health centres and Anganwadis, where blood tests are already being conducted. Simultaneously, increasing nutrition education among people—such as the important role of Vitamin C in increasing iron absorption, foods rich in iron and Vitamin C, etc.—will have long term benefits. These measures have been successfully tried around the world including India. The decision on rice fortification is an example of how corporate involvement and technocratic solutions, can be anti-science, prioritising private sector interests rather than public interest or science.

The third example relates to the proliferation of the use of digital technologies in the progammes discussed in this book. Digital products (smartphones and other devices, software, fingerprint readers, drones, etc.) are being bought by the government under the guise of increasing efficiency and reducing corruption. The Aadhaar project is a good example of this: while the public was being sold Aadhaar as a social intervention, to bring efficiency in welfare spending, industry was calculating the business that would come to it from Aadhaar. CLSA's May 2010 report described Aadhaar as a $20 billion market, with the 'commercial pie' estimated to be worth $10 billion annually including hardware, software, training, etc. The eagerness to integrate Aadhaar with various welfare programmes even though there were few a priori or demonstrated efficiency gains from it, ramping it up and making it compulsory in more and more programmes in spite of the mounting evidence on the problems it has created suggests that the commitment to it is not driven by public interest (see Khera 2018).

There are possibly other examples too: e.g., in healthcare, one needs to know whether a large part of the health expenditure in the government budget is now increasing the business of private health insurance companies.

One way of understanding the hostile attitude of a major section of the power elite towards some of the social policies discussed in this book (e.g., NREGA or MDM) is that the real character of the government is pro-business and it tries to maintain a balance between that and the pressure to undertake redistributive policies. Making space for private entities in social spending is one way of striking this balance.

Conflating Technology with Technocracy

The integration of Aadhaar and its cousins, with the welfare programmes discussed here, illustrate the technocratic takeover of social policy. Technocracy is turning social policies into a testing ground for unreasonable—and often, counter-productive—technologies.

The experience of NREGA demonstrates the fallout of technocratic impulses. From the beginning in 2005, NREGA embraced digital technology for transparency and better administration. NREGASOFT, a Management Information System (MIS), was specially designed, rolled out in 2007 and scaled up by 2010-11. It has/had flaws but it also greatly facilitated implementation by enhancing administrative capacity and brought unprecedented transparency to the programme.

Very quickly though, NREGA went from being technology-savvy to technology-servient. Much of the technocratic experimentation has come in the name of reducing corruption. Before evaluating the impact of the transition to account payments[71], electronic Muster Rolls (e-MRs) were introduced in 2012. When e-MRs failed to solve the problem, Aadhaar-linking with job cards and worker's accounts was imposed on NREGA workers. After that, Aadhaar-Based Payment System (ABPS) was made compulsory, even though it remains vulnerable to corrupt practices, even offering some new methods of siphoning off wages. The rationale for Aadhaar-integration has never been clear, yet it has been imposed on NREGA workers—for job cards, demanding work, receiving their wages and so on. The payment process has been reengineered multiple times to make it Aadhaar-compliant. Other inappropriate technologies include geo-tagged attendance. At each step, NREGA workers have suffered. At each step, the corrupt have found a workaround.

The problems arising due to technocratic interventions like Aadhaar are not restricted to NREGA. The Public Distribution System, social security pensions, school enrolment, maternity benefits—each of these has been hit by Aadhaar-related problems. The justifications for linking Aadhaar provided by the government have been debunked repeatedly (Khera 2017). For instance, in the PDS, the main form of corruption is under-selling something that Aadhaar-linking or Aadhaar-based Biometric Authentication (ABBA) cannot stop. Aadhaar proponents rake up the existence of 'duplicate' and 'ghost' ration cards even though the available evidence suggests that it is a minor issue and in any case, Aadhaar-linking may not help in identifying them (Khera 2017). In the case of the PDS, each month ration card holders have to perform 'Aadhaar-Based Biometric Authentication' (ABBA)—their fingerprint or, if that fails, iris has to be authenticated. This creates multiple points of failure: connectivity issues, server issues, biometric failures among others. At least two studies have shown that the introduction of ABBA was 'pain without gain'—it made no difference to corruption in the PDS, but inflicted more hardship on PDS ration card holders.

In most states, getting their ration card or social security pension (or other social benefits) sanctioned is a hurdle race. The integration of Aadhaar in the process has added three new hurdles between entitled individuals and the finishing line: enrolling for Aadhaar, linking it and in some cases, ABBA. Even the elderly, single and widowed women, and the disabled have not been spared. They have been forced to jump over these hurdles and subjected to the uncertainties associated with Aadhaar—just to keep existing benefits.

In spite of the failures of Aadhaar to reduce corruption in the NREGA, PDS, and NSAP, now programmes for children and pregnant women are being brought under its ambit. Since 2024, a drive to create an Automated Permanent Academic Account Registry 'APAAR' ID for school children began. The same implementation issues as elsewhere (mismatch in spellings of names, wrong date of birth, etc.) are preventing the creation of APAAR that is endangering the child's Right to Education (Gupta 2025). Even supporters of Aadhaar have questioned the creation of APAAR (Assisi 2024).

In mid-2025, Aadhaar-based 'Facial Recognition Technology' was made compulsory for pregnant and lactating women at the time of collecting their 'take-home rations' from their local Anganwadi. If an Anganwadi worker wants to cheat a pregnant woman of her THR, she can easily verify the woman and send her home empty-handed. There has been little documentation of bogus beneficiaries among pregnant and lactating women, so the purpose of FRT remains unclear. It is also very odd that the Ministry of Women and Child Development introduced this around the exact same time that the Ministry of Rural Development admitted that NMMS (uploading photos of workers from NREGA worksites) had been a failure.

In the face of all these failures, Aadhaar remains compulsory across the board. Like NREGA workers, PDS ration card holders, pensioners, pregnant and lactating women, school children face exclusion, denial, queues and delays, uncertainties if they do not have Aadhaar or fail to link it to the relevant database (PDS or pension or UDISE, the schooling database). Keeping Aadhaar updated has proven to be another costly and arduous affair for many (Khera and Moharil 2024). Meanwhile, for the Unique Identification Authority of India (UIDAI) these have become important income-generation activities: according to the Annual Report of the UIDAI, in 2023-24, it earned over Rs 60 crores from its correction and updation services at 'Aadhaar Sewa Kendras' and more than Rs 600 crores from authentication services.

The consequences have been devastating—from denial of entitlements, to loss of life. In 2017-2018, when Aadhaar was made mandatory for the PDS and pensions, more than twenty people died of starvation in Jharkhand (Dutta 2020).

Another overarching damage from Aadhaar is its displacement effect. Privileging Aadhaar over all other technologies, which have a proven record of improving administration, displaces efforts to scale up those technologies. For instance, in Bihar, the uploading of NFSA ration card lists (very important to enhance transparency and reduce the arbitrary power of PDS dealers) was delayed. Under pressure from the central government, the short-staffed food department prioritised Aadhaar seeding over uploading NFSA lists. Abandoning experiments with smart cards, in favour of ABBA, for last-mile authentication is another example. The use of Aadhaar (and other technocratic solutions) is an admission of 'governance' failure. The government has failed to hold to account the minority who indulge in corrupt practices. Instead, by deploying untested and fragile technology, the victims of corruption are paying the price.

Technocracy and some philanthropies are paving the way for more private interests in social policy. A myth is being created: that technocracy is the only cure for the weaknesses of our administrative machinery. What is conveniently ignored is that technocratic solutions, in the hands of the same administration, can be equally damaging.

The Lure of Cash Transfers

Cash transfers are increasingly becoming important in the realm of social policy. Most recently cash transfers to women have gained popularity among political parties. In a way, the cash transfers to women can be traced back to the Congress party's promise of a Nyunatam Aay Yojana (NYAY) in the 2019 General Election. Even though NYAY did not promise a 'nyunatam aay' (minimum income) or universal coverage, it was inspired by the ongoing debate at the time on 'Universal Basic Income' (UBI). One of the reasons that the UBI proposal did not go very far was that providing a basic income to all would not be fiscally possible.

At the time, one proposal was to consolidate and universalise two existing cash transfer programmes—social security pensions (such as those provided by the NSAP) and maternity benefits. These are two vulnerable groups, where universal benefits are necessary, where universalizing and providing a 'basic income' is fiscally feasible and which have a decent track record (see Khera 2016).

Narrowing the target group to women has become a way of making a 'universal' promise affordable. Cash transfers to women are an interesting adaptation of the idea of UBI: there is an element of targeting by focusing on women (so the idea of truly universal has been abandoned) yet maintaining an element of universal by making (virtually) all women eligible. Many Indian women do not enjoy economic independence, so putting some money in their hands can be a meaningful intervention. So far so good.

In state elections that followed, the Congress party included a promise of cash to women in their electoral manifestos in Karnataka and Himachal Pradesh. It has been implemented by BJP state governments (Assam, Delhi, Chhattisgarh, Madhya Pradesh, etc.) and also by some state-level parties (Tamil Nadu, Jharkhand, West Bengal). According to available information, such schemes have been implemented (or preparations are underway) in more than ten states (see Table 11.1). Women have been promised or are being given Rs 1000 to Rs 2500 per month (in Telangana and Delhi). Eligibility for the scheme varies across states—women between the ages of 18 or 21 years to 59 years (when they are meant to transition to pensions); in some states it is restricted to married women (Chhattisgarh) but in others unmarried women are also eligible (Tamil Nadu). In spite of implementing it themselves, political parties accuse their political opponents of distributing 'freebies' when they announce a scheme of cash transfers to women.

Table 11.1 Cash Schemes for Women

State	*Scheme*	*Amount (Rs/month), eligibility and coverage*
Assam	Orunodoi	Rs 1250, 37 lakh women[1]
Chhattisgarh	Mahtari Vandan Scheme	Rs 1000
Delhi	Mukhya Mantri Mahila Samman	Rs 2500, 18 years
Himachal Pradesh	Pyari Bahan Sukh Samman Nidhi Scheme	Rs 1500, 18-59 years
Jharkhand	Maa Beti Swavalambam Scheme/Maiya Samman Yojana	Rs 2500, 21-50 years
Karnataka	Gruha Lakshmi	Rs 2000, 1.33 crore women (2023)
Telangana	Mahalaxmi Scheme	Rs 2500
Madhya Pradesh	Mukhyamantri Ladli Behen Yojana	Rs 1000, 21-60 years
Maharashtra	Majhi Ladki Bahin Yojana	Rs 1500, 21-65 years
Tamil Nadu[2]	Kalaignar Magalir Urimai Thittam	Rs 1000, 21 years and above
West Bengal	Lakshmir Bhandar	Rs 1000-1200

Source: [1]Saikia (2021) [2]*The Indian Express* (2023) and other states, Raghavan (2024)

What are the stated objectives of these schemes and how do these cash transfers fit in with the existing welfare architecture? Madhya Pradesh's scheme lays out three objectives: economic independence for women, better health and nutrition for children, helping women have greater say in decision making.[72] If the idea is to achieve greater economic independence for women, is this the best policy instrument available? Would that objective not be met as effectively by providing work and wages through the NREGA? If the focus is on urban areas, Rajasthan has experimented with an urban employment guarantee scheme like NREGA (Indira Rozgar Guarantee Yojana) to ensure financial independence and money in the hands of women (Choragudi 2025). Would this not be a better instrument for women's empowerment? A comparative assessment of these two interventions would be interesting.

If the objective is to ensure better health and nutrition outcomes for the mother and child, that objective can be met more directly by improving the implementation of PMMVY and providing more nutritious food through the ICDS and better health services.

Such transfers are meant to supplement household expenditures, and are currently, complements to the support provided through the PDS. Yet there is a possibility that it will be used to replace in-kind benefits like PDS grains. Where states are using the list of PDS beneficiaries to identify recipients of cash transfers (several are), there is duplication-by-design; i.e., exclusion errors in the PDS list spillover to these cash schemes, rather than the schemes being an opportunity to remedy existing exclusion errors.

There are other integration issues too: for instance, after having enlisted all women, reports from several states suggest that the list of beneficiaries are being pruned to identify ineligible women. In Karnataka, an Anganwadi helper who had been included initially, found her name struck off because she was deemed to be a government employee, even though she does not enjoy any benefits and her salary is quite low. Similarly, mid-day meal cooks and helpers have been listed as ineligible on account of their jobs, but in some states a helper earns less than the cash transfer that has been promised to other women.

In Tamil Nadu, when cash transfers for women were being discussed, the public debate focused on compensation to women for unpaid domestic work. According to 2019 data, women spent 352 minutes (about six hours) on housework per day, whereas men spent only fifty-two minutes (less than an hour). There are broadly two schools of thought among feminists about such interventions (Kotiswaran 2022). Some believe that as women bear the burden of household chores without any compensation, many are unable to earn their own money outside the home due to their uncompensated domestic responsibilities. However, if women are compensated for household work in this manner, then there is a risk that the patriarchal conditioning that domestic work is the responsibility of women may get more deeply embedded rather than being dislodged. Instead of encouraging behaviour that would reduce the burden of domestic work on them, it may increase the expectation that they do 'their' job; men's participation in household work may decrease further.

Related to the question above, is the issue of budgets. The cash transfers to women are not cheap. According to one report, in 2024, 11 crore women were getting money from such schemes and the total expenditure on these was 0.8 per cent of the domestic product of the states that had the schemes (Raghavan 2024). States are already struggling to find resources to fund their respective cash transfers programmes. For instance, in Maharashtra, one-fifth of the budget for the Ladki Bahin Yojana in 2025-26 has been made available by taking funds from the Tribal and Social Justice and Special Assistance Department (*The Hindu* 2025). In Jharkhand, there are reports of social security pensions becoming irregular after its Maiya Samman Yojana began.

Very little is known about the impact of the women's cash transfer schemes. In Assam, a small survey of 108 women was conducted in 2021 where women were being given Rs 850 per month at the time (Kotiswaran 2022). While it would be unfair to see such a meagre amount as compensation for six hours of domestic work, it was still a big relief for women who were getting it. They appreciated having their own money and contributing to the family pot. According to the survey, two-thirds of the women who received this money had a monthly income of less than Rs 5000. Thus, in Assam (where the cash transfer amount was quite low), the transfers were about 20 per cent of the monthly earnings of the women.[73]

Does money in the hands of women affect their status, access to the labour market and their domestic workload? Do they have an impact on social attitudes towards women? Will they complement the existing welfare architecture outlined in this book or become a substitute?

A Data 'Blackhole'

The issue at stake is availability of credible data, as it plays an important role in guiding policy-making. India is in danger of becoming a data blackhole. If the lives of people are to be improved (health, education, jobs, earnings), assessing the situation accurately is necessary, for which reliable data is required. Where is a school necessary, where are teachers missing, who earns how much in what kind of job, etc.? Data is essential to answering these basic questions.

Visionaries like PC Mahalanobis created a robust statistical system in the country. For decades, the Census of India, the National Sample Survey Organisation (NSS), etc. have been providing valuable information that informed policy debates and decisions. The last decade has witnessed a weakening of our statistical system.

For instance, this is the first time since Independence that India failed to conduct the decennial Census. The 2021 Census was delayed on account of the COVID-19 pandemic, yet during and after the pandemic, the government managed to organise one General and many state elections, political rallies, a Kumbh Mela, etc., but not the Census.

The delay in the Census is not an obscure academic issue. It has a direct impact on people. Today, even basic statistics such as the proportion of urban population or literacy rates are unavailable. Moreover, as per the National Food Security Act, the coverage under the Public Distribution System is determined on the basis of population figures in the last published Census. According to our estimates more than 10 crore people are deprived of PDS today because the government still relies on outdated 2011 population numbers. As coverage is frozen, it sometimes means that children born after the rollout of the NFSA (between 2013-2017) have not been added, even while other family members get their due.

Another example of the 'data blackhole' pertains to the NSS's 'thick rounds' that collect reliable survey data on people's employment and consumption expenditure every five years. After 2011-12, the data collected in 2017 was not released. The allegation is that because the data did not show significant improvement in the economic situation, the government claimed that there was a problem in the conduct of survey. After 2011-12, the next round of NSS data on consumption expenditure was finally released in 2024, based on the 2022-23 round. Thus, no reliable data was available for over a decade. Similarly, during the UPA years, ten years passed between NFHS-3 (2005-6) and NFHS-4 (2015-16) though they should be conducted roughly every five years.

The issue is not limited to non-availability of data. In Table 4.1, we saw that as per NFHS-5, compared to NFHS-4, incidence of anaemia increased by a few percentage points. When people questioned the deterioration, news came that in the next NFHS, the questions on anaemia have been removed (Nagarajan 2023).

Another data-related issue is that in the garb of remedying earlier measurement issues, the estimation methods of certain economic indicators (e.g., GDP, employment, consumption expenditure) are changed, without accounting for the need to maintain some comparability over time. In an economy like India, where many people work in the unorganised sector, it is not easy to define or measure employment. A few years ago, the method of measuring employment changed, as a result of which it is not possible to readily compare the current situation with the earlier, or it requires many adjustments and assumptions to make it comparable (see Jajoria and Jatav 2020).

Creating data blackholes is an easy way to suppress failures and create fanciful narratives. When data are missing, it becomes easy to hide realities and avoid accountability. There are several examples of this. In August 2021, the Central government told the Rajya Sabha that no state reported deaths due to lack of oxygen. In July 2021, a minister said that no manual scavenging deaths had been recorded in the last five years. Another minister told Parliament there was no record of deaths during the farmers' protest. In 2020, the government began Shramik trains for labourers stuck away from home during the COVID-19 lockdown. In September 2020, the Labour Minister told Parliament that information on deaths in Shramik trains was not being collected. In each of these cases, it later emerged that some data were available. For instance, in a written reply in February 2021 in the Lok Sabha, 340 manual scavenging deaths were acknowledged in the previous five months (*The Hindu* 2021). An application under the Right to Information (RTI) Act found that the government had recorded eighty deaths on Shramik trains (*The Wire* 2020).[74] Citing lack of information was a ploy for avoiding accountability.

In some ways, instead of improving, things appear to be getting worse in the past ten years. Under the RTI Act, the government is required to make a lot of information available to the people through its websites (or in other forms) proactively, without anyone asking for it. Instead, a lot of data until 2014 that used to be available earlier, disappeared from the NREGA website. On being asked for it through an RTI application in 2024, the reply stated that the information was not available with the NREGA section, although it could be found in a reply to the Rajya Sabha. (A substantial chunk of the earlier data was reinstated as this book was being translated into English.) Information on the MDM that used to be uploaded on their website has become more restricted since 2022-23. The number of women who got cash under the Pradhan Mantri Matru Vandana Yojana is not made public on the website of the Ministry of Women and Child Development; one has to file an RTI to get this basic information.

Does the availability of data from private surveys and 'big data' make censuses and government surveys redundant? Many are gaga about the potential of Big Data, even though getting the most basic data (employment, poverty, death rates) remains a struggle. So far, one is hard pressed to find good examples of big/real time data serving public interest.

The Economic Survey 2018-19 presents an overly optimistic view of what can be achieved by collecting and compiling real time data. Merely compiling data in 'real time' and on scale, cannot lead to understanding or solving economic, social or political problems. An anecdote reported in a Gujarati daily from Ahmedabad illustrates this point quite well. A person whose scooter was stolen filed a report at a police station. After that, the owner kept getting steady news about his stolen scooter but not the scooter itself. How so? Traffic police were 'capturing' the scooter on its cameras at traffic junctions whenever it jumped a traffic light, and challans were being sent to the owner to pay the fine. This is not to deny that real time data has its uses, especially if it is accompanied by capacity and willingness to use it.

Similarly, the experience with private surveys has been quite sobering. After 2011-12, when NSS data was not available, economists had to rely on phone surveys conducted by a private entity, the Centre for Monitoring the Indian Economy (CMIE) for basic economic data. Unemployment data from the CMIE was at the centre of an important debate (on unemployment in India) in 2021. However, when Drèze and Somanchi (2021) matched the average of respondents' socioeconomic status with the same indicators from other government surveys, they found that something was amiss.

For instance, as per CMIE in 2015, the adult literacy rate was 83 per cent, and it increased to almost 100 per cent by 2019—an implausible result; in the CMIE dataset, 98 per cent of households had electricity in 2015 compared with only 88 per cent in NFHS-4 (2015-16). CMIE's claim that their survey statistically represented the country's population was under question, meanwhile major policy debates were using it without adequately taking these issues into account. Thus, while 'big data' and private surveys have their place, they cannot replace censuses and government surveys.

Data shines the light to guide policy-making and is important for informed public debates. Without facts, it becomes difficult, if not impossible, to assess the economic, social and political situation. In the absence of facts, the truth as perceived by the loudest person is established as 'the' truth.

12

Where Is the Money?

This chapter discusses three related issues: first, is it really true—as some believe—that the Indian state spends 'too much' on 'freebies'? Second, how can we create fiscal space for a more generous and more comprehensive welfare state? Finally, what are the possible barriers to implementing some of the measures outlined in section two?

New Welfare?

The years of the National Development Alliance (NDA) government are often, in mainstream media, lauded as years with a generous welfare agenda. Do budgetary allocations support this assessment? As Chart 12.1 shows, in terms of the combined spending on ten major welfare schemes, as a percentage of GDP, welfare expenditure in 2023–24 was not very different from where it was twenty years ago, in 2004-5 (Khera and Md. Asjad 2024).

Chart 12.1 compares the NDA years (2014-2024) with the previous decade (2004-14), the years of the United Progressive Alliance (UPA) government. It also looks at a break-up of overall welfare spending by the Union

Chart 12.1 Central government expenditure on social policies (% of GDP) 2004-05 to 2023-24

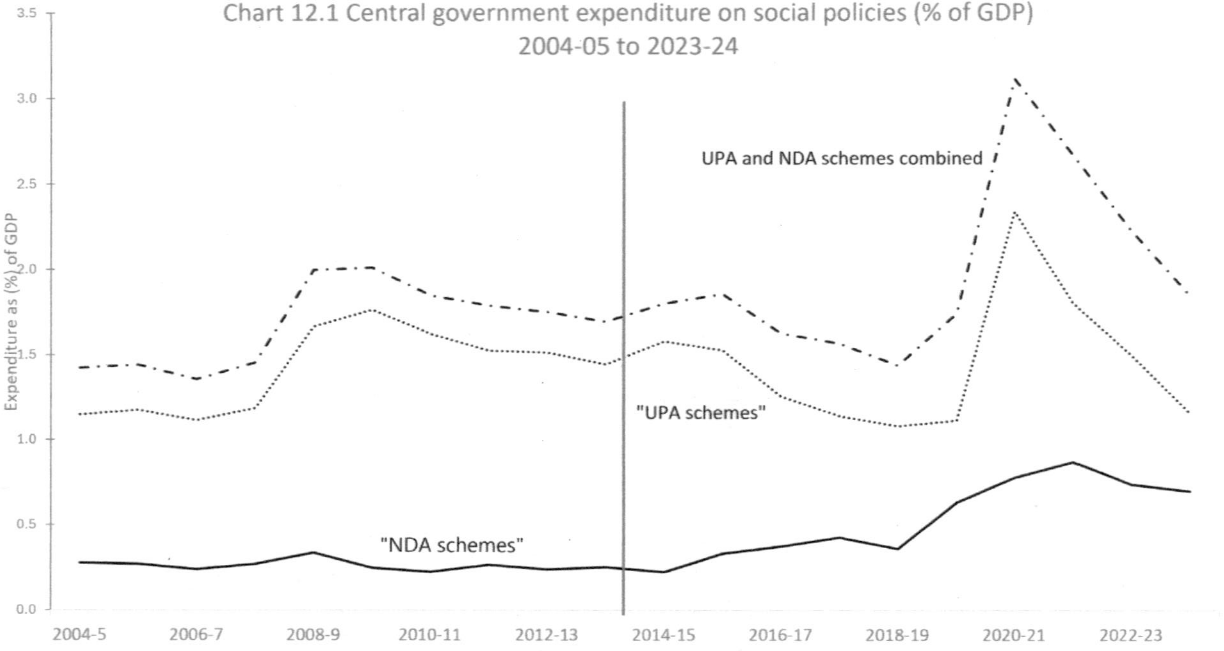

Note: "UPA schemes" include the food subsidy, NREGA, MDMs, ICDS, PMMVY and NSAP. "NDA schemes" include Swachh Bharat Mission, PM-AWAS, PM-Kisan, Jal Jeevan Mission and the LPG subsidy (for Ujjwala Yojana).

Source: Budget documents, various years. When actual expenditure was not available, revised expenditure (RE) has been reported, and when RE was not available, budget estimates have been reported.

government, by classifying the schemes into two broad categories—those associated with the UPA government and the NDA government. When we do so, we find that the schemes associated with the UPA government witnessed a squeeze in funding during the NDA years and that those associated with the NDA absorbed the fiscal space thus created, leaving the total unchanged.

Anand et al. (2020) contrast welfare spending during the UPA period with the NDA period. In their assessment, during the NDA regime, private goods (toilets, housing, LPG cylinders, and water connections), rather than public goods such as health and education have been emphasised by the government. They label this model new welfarism. (New because in the traditional welfare model, facilities like education, health are prioritised.)

Following them, for the NDA period (2014-2024), the Swachh Bharat Abhiyan (SBA) launched in 2014, PM-Awas (urban) in 2015 and PM-Awas (rural) the following year along with the Pradhan Mantri Ujjwala Yojana (PMUY), PM-Kisan Samman Nidhi (PM-Kisan) and Ayushman Bharat in 2018, and Jal Jeevan Mission (JJM) in 2019 are clubbed together as 'NDA schemes'.

Six major programmes associated with the UPA governments (2004-14) are the National Rural Employment Guarantee Act (NREGA) 2005 and four schemes of the National Food Security Act (NFSA) 2013: the Public Distribution System (PDS), Mid-Day Meals (MDM), Integrated Child Development Services (ICDS) and maternity entitlements (provided through the Pradhan Mantri Matru Vandana Yojana that became operational very belatedly in 2017). Lastly, the 'UPA schemes' include National Social Assistance Programme's (NSAP) social security pensions to the elderly, single women and persons with disabilities.

The reason we are able to study the so-called 'NDA schemes' over the earlier UPA period also is because several of them existed in the UPA years, with different names (Swachh Bharat was Nirmal Bharat, PM-Awas was Indira Awaas, and so on) and lower budgets.[75] The NREGA of UPA was modelled on earlier drought relief public employment works and made a legal entitlement. The same is true for the NFSA that converted three pre-existing schemes (PDS, MDM and ICDS) into legal entitlements. The PMMVY was the only new addition in the NFSA. PM-Kisan is a new scheme introduced in the NDA years whereas the others existed in some form even earlier. The classification of schemes as NDA or UPA is therefore somewhat artificial. It is not so much about who introduced each scheme, rather how well they were funded in the past two decades.

There are some differences between these two sets of schemes. The NDA schemes follow a 'saturation' approach that allows an element of 'self-targeting'. Only those who do not have a toilet or pukka room or LPG connection, etc. are eligible, and once they receive it others get a chance, i.e., most benefits are one-time benefits.

In the case of UPA schemes, entitled people get benefits enshrined in these laws year after year (100 days of work for rural families), or month after month (PDS grains) or daily (meals in schools and at Anganwadis). Here too, there is some self-targeting, in the sense that only those who cannot get any other work show up for NREGA work and children in government schools and Angwandis tend to be from poorer families.

If one looks at the break-up of total welfare spending by dividing the schemes into two broad categories (UPA- and NDA-schemes), one can see whether the welfare budgets in the two decades actually differed.[76]

Chart 12.1 plots the welfare budgets over both decades. Comparing the NDA years (2014-2024) with the previous UPA decade (2004-14), there is not much difference in terms of total expenditure. The top line in Chart 12.1 shows the combined welfare expenditure: the level of welfare expenditure is low and stagnating, in spite of good GDP growth that could have facilitated more welfare spending in this period. It exceeds 3 per cent of GDP only for one of the two COVID years. Whatever increase there was over the longer period, occurred during the initial UPA years.

Note, however, that the expenditure depicted in Chart 12.1 is only that of the Union government. State governments also contribute to these schemes and as per the norms laid out in the Fourteeth Finance Commission their share increased. Preliminary estimates suggest that in 2023-2024, out of the total (centre and state combined) expenditure on NREGA, 80% was borne by the Union government; the corresponding figures for PMMVY, MDM and NSAP are 62 per cent, 49 per cent and 7 per cent respectively.

In contrast to NDA schemes, none of which are legal entitlements, the UPA schemes are enshrined in law, so it is not easy to defund them entirely. The former, thus, are much more like 'freebies' or 'revdis' in the sense that they depend on the whims of the government.

In spite of the legal compulsions, UPA schemes (middle line in the chart), especially those for children, suffered budgetary neglect under the NDA. The cuts were drastic in the case of Mid-Day Meals and the ICDS. In real terms, it declined by 40 per cent compared with 2014-15 (Paliath 2023). The share of the UPA schemes in the Union budget declined gradually from around 1.5 per cent of GDP in 2014 to 1.1 per cent of GDP in 2019-20, when COVID forced the government to ramp it up.

Did NDA schemes compensate for the decline in spending on UPA schemes? Just about. Though spending on NDA schemes (bottom most line in the chart) rose steadily in the past decade, it remained well below 1 per cent of GDP. This explains the modest achievements of these schemes: according to the National Family Health Survey, LPG usage increased from 43 per cent in 2015-16 to 58 per cent in 2019-21 (the most recent year for which the data is available). In the same period, the proportion of households practicing open defecation has halved (from 39 per cent to 19 per cent) and those residing in pukka homes has increased from 56 per cent to 60 per cent.

In fact, precisely because the NDA did not create any support mechanism that could compensate for the UPA schemes, during COVID the NDA government relied heavily on two big UPA initiatives, including the NREGA that it had insidiously attacked.

The NDA's fraught relationship with the UPA schemes is more evident in the case of the PDS, that now goes by the name of Pradhan Mantri Garib Kalyan Anna Yojana (PMGKAY). The NFSA 2013 mandated 50 per cent coverage in urban areas and 75 per cent in rural areas (i.e., 80 crore in all based on the 2011 population), with 5 kg per person per month at Rs 2-3/kg (for wheat and rice, respectively) for those covered by the PDS.

During COVID-19 (from April 2020 to December 2022), the NDA government doubled people's basic PDS entitlements (from 5 kg each month to 10 kg, providing the extra 5 kg free). When the COVID top-up was discontinued in December 2023, to blunt the blow, the original NFSA entitlement (5kg for a total of Rs 10-15) was made free. This repackaged NFSA-PDS entitlement, that saves each person an additional Rs 15/month at most, was grandly announced as the PMGKAY.

The NFSA-PDS (or, PMGKAY) is now associated much more with BJP/Narendra Modi than UPA/Congress because it made PDS grain free. This is astounding because while the NDA claims benefit for the coverage of 80 crore people under NFSA-PDS that has little to do with them, the reality is that its inaction is keeping over 10 crore entitled persons out of the NFSA-PDS. The passage of the NFSA 2013 expanded PDS coverage, so that we have the current coverage of 80 crore through PDS (Khera 2024). Before the NFSA was passed, it was around 50 crores. Meanwhile, the NDA's failure to conduct the 2021 Census has resulted in the exclusion of millions from the PDS. Applying NFSA mandated coverage ratios (50 per cent in urban and 75 per cent in rural areas) to the projected population in 2021 would add more than 10 crore people to the PDS.

Some point out that as GDP grows, even 1-2 per cent of GDP is a much larger amount today than it was twenty years ago. They argue that there is nothing wrong if welfare spending stagnates as a percentage of GDP, when GDP itself is growing fast.

This is wrong on at least three counts. One, implicit in this line of thinking is the belief that GDP growth translates into increase in per capita GDP for everyone, i.e., it assumes that when GDP grows, everyone gets an equal share of the larger pie. We know that this is not true in the Indian case where inequality has been rising (see Bharti et. al 2024). Two, the past decade has seen major economic crises: demonetisation, haphazard implementation of GST and the humanitarian crisis arising from the COVID-19 lockdowns. All three necessitated greater social support, but barring one year of the lockdown such support was not available. Finally, as an economy grows, one expects more—not less—generous welfare spending. Economic growth makes more resources available to the state. This is certainly true—historically speaking—for most developed countries.

The NDA government has managed to build a reputation as a big welfare spender by renaming existing welfare programmes and then claiming credit for them (as if they are new schemes). At the same time, it has been starving the pre-existing welfare architecture of funds without compensating for it with something of its own.

Creating Fiscal Space: Mobilizing Resources

Can the stagnation in social spending be explained by the lack of resources? Redistributive welfare programmes that could reduce inequality require governments to mobilise revenues. The discussion on redistributive government expenditure is often stifled by limiting the discussion to the need to contain fiscal deficit by lowering expenditure. In the public discussion around the budget, 'fiscal deficit' is a key concern. This is fair enough, given that the budget is about balancing our expenses with revenues. What is troubling, however, is that fiscal deficit has become a code word for, almost synonymous with, reducing expenditure. The budget and fiscal deficit are often reduced to a cost-cutting exercise. There is much less discussion, if any, of the revenue side.

India's tax-GDP ratio is on the lower side, and has been stagnating somewhere around 12 per cent (comparable to the levels in the US). BRICS countries tend to have higher tax revenues. A major reason for this is that in 2019 the government gave big corporate tax exemptions, although direct taxes are regarded as better than other forms of taxation (Rajkumar and Shetty 2020). Incidentally, this corporate giveaway was not labelled a freebie by mainstream media.

What pinches tax payers the most, however, are income taxes. The fact is that India has a small income tax base and relatively low tax rates at the entry-level compared to international norms. According to Piketty and Qian (2009), between 1986 and 2008, the income tax paying population in China grew from 0.1 per cent of the population to about 20 per cent of the population. The corresponding number was 6 per cent in Brazil and nearly 10 per cent in South Africa. After tax breaks were provided in China in 2011, it brought down the income tax paying population to about 8 per cent. The move was accompanied by raising top income tax rates. Meanwhile, throughout this twenty-two-year period in India the corresponding proportion remained around 2-3 per cent.

Even though the 2000s have been a period of high rate of growth of the GDP, the top income tax rates have stagnated around 33 per cent since the late nineties and the income tax base remains low (81 million in 2018-19, i.e., roughly 5 per cent of the Indian population). In 2018-19, the Indian government cut the entry level income tax rate from 10 per cent to 5 per cent (Central Board of Direct Taxes 2019). In some countries, the entry level income tax rate is 40 per cent, whereas in India 40 per cent is not levied even in the highest tax bracket. The key reason for the income-tax paying population being stuck in India was that the government raised the tax exemption limit year after year. As people's income reached the threshold for income tax, the threshold was raised, and that contributed to the smallness of the income tax base in India.

There are several other options to increase government

revenues. In 2025, 205 Indians were on the world's richest lists; it was the third largest contributor to the number of the world's billionaries (Peterson-Withorn et al. 2025). The NDA government, however, abolished the estate duty and wealth tax in 2015-16. According to one estimate, a wealth tax of 4 per cent on the richest 953 people (whose net worth is on average Rs 5000 crore, i.e., about a quarter of the country's GDP overall), can yield one percent of GDP (Subramanian 2020 and Bharti et al. 2024). Estate and inheritance taxes apply only to the super-rich, but there is scope to increase revenue from it. In the United Kingdom, such taxes apply to less than 3-5 per cent of all deaths, yielding a revenue of 0.2 per cent of GDP (Advani et al. 2024).

Property taxes are another under-utilised taxation instrument in India, whose neglect has long been highlighted. Earlier estimates suggest that India raised only 0.2 per cent of GDP through property taxes, when the developing country average was 0.6 per cent and 2 per cent in OECD countries (Rao 2013). An updated estimate in 2017-18 shows a reduction in these collections to 0.1 per cent of GDP. Contrast this with NSS data for 2018, which estimates that 63 per cent of the urban population owned freehold property and nearly half (47 per cent) of urban homes had more than one floor (Government of India 2019). This suggests that a broad-based, yet low rate of property tax could be used to mobilise substantial revenues. Simple technology (e.g., computerised records) for assessing and collecting property taxes can help expand the base, reduce default rates and thus improve collections without raising property tax rates (Srivastava 2020).

Some countries (e.g., Israel) have experimented with additional taxes when a company's pay ratio exceeds a certain threshold (*The Guardian* 2016). A similar proposal was made by Bernie Sanders in 2019 (Stevens 2019): impose higher taxes on companies where the pay ratio for CEOs to median workers exceeded 50x. His proposal was to increase the tax rate by 0.5 per cent for companies where the ratio was between 50-100, and progressively higher if it exceeded that. In 2019-20, we had found that among the 42 NIFTY-50 companies for which data was available, the pay ratio of the highest paid employee to the median remuneration ranged from 39 (Maruti) to 752 (Hero Motorcorp).

Instead of cutting expenditure on social policies in the name of containing fiscal deficit, the government could target 'non-merit' subsidies. Subsidies on merit goods are those that increase public welfare (health, education, sanitation, etc.). On the other hand, non-merit include concessions on electricity, fuel, etc. According to estimates by Mundle and Sikdar (2019), non-merit subsidies were about 6 per cent of GDP in 2015-16.

Reducing revenue loss from foregone taxes ('tax revenue foregone') is another unexplored channel. In 2021-22, tax revenue foregone caused a loss of about Rs 7-8 lakh crore, of which a large part was exemptions on customs duty. These foregone revenues are roughly 30 per cent of government revenues.[77] Austerity measures should also be a greater part of the cost-cutting efforts of the government. Instead, taking a cue from the Centre, poorer states have also been spending lavishly on meaningless ads. The Centre could set an example by reducing such wasteful expenditures. Vanity projects (statues, central vista, bullet trains, etc.) also need to be questioned. The estimated cost of the bullet train is Rs 88,000 crore (NDTV 2017); the Central Vista reportedly cost Rs 20,000 crore (*The Telegraph* 2020) and according to a news report the estimated cost of statues built in the five years before 2020 was over Rs 11,000 crore (Bhalla 2020).

Can't or Won't?: The Missing Consensus

Is it an unwillingness to mobilise resources or an inability to do so?

Take the case of income tax. The small income tax base can mean two things: one, only 6 per cent have an income greater than the income tax threshold or two, there are actually more people whose income is higher, but they have remained out of the reach of the government's tax net. If the latter is true, it implies that they are out of the income tax net because of the government's inability to ensure tax compliance. To prevent tax evasion and tax avoidance, the government needs staff and political will.

Some time ago, the Finance Minister sympathised with the 'middle class', saying being middle class herself she could feel everyone's pain. In response, someone retrieved information on her assets from her election affidavit, where she declared total assets at Rs 1.8 crore. Going by the data given in the 'World Inequality Database' this would put her in the top 1 per cent in India.

Such misperceptions about class position are not limited to the Finance Minister alone. Many English speakers, owning one or more cars, investing in stocks, relying on domestic help, with flights as the default mode of travel, often holidaying abroad refer to themselves as 'middle class'. Their children study in private schools where the annual fee exceeds the annual per capita income in India. Data, however, suggests that around a tenth of Indians are English speakers or own four-wheeled vehicles; e-wallet use was confined to 14 per cent of urban Indians and 2.4 per cent of rural residents (Government of India 2021). Investment in shares was recorded by less than 2 per cent of Indians (see Table 12.1).

During an interaction with a rural resident of Alwar, not the poorest corner of Rajasthan, one got another conception of 'middle class'. He combined farm income with a salary as a private teacher—a man of modest means. Talking about the COVID-19 lockdown he remarked that the middle class had suffered a lot. When asked to define the middle class, his definition was far more modest than the Minister or the aforementioned middle-class person (English-speaking, car-owning, air-traveller, etc.): 'A middle class person is someone who, if he gets work today, can afford vegetables for his evening meal. Otherwise, he will have plain roti.'

These contrasting conceptions of the middle class—from paying a lakh or more per year as school fees for one child to earning enough in a day to buy fresh vegetables for your evening meal—capture something important about our society today. Many of the well-heeled urbanites who consider themselves as part of the middle class are, in fact, among the top 10 per cent of Indians, if not the top 1 per cent.

Intrigued by this, a few years ago, I asked students in class: Do you consider yourself middle-, lower- or upper-class. Nearly 90 per cent of the students classified themselves as middle class; most had motorised vehicles (77 per cent) and toilets connected to a sewer line (93 per cent). When this information is compared with the all-India urban averages in Table 12.1, it becomes revealing. According to the National Family Health Survey (NFHS-5), 2019-21, among urban households, only 14 per cent owned cars and just under a quarter of urban households (23 per cent) had sewer-connected toilets. How does one reconcile facilities that only 14-24 per cent of urban households enjoy, as 'middle class'? Indeed, these are 'middle class' comforts, but they are enjoyed by roughly the top 20 per cent in the country.

Table 12.1 Middle Class or Well Off?

Proportion of urban households that	*Per cent of households*
Have an AC or cooler in the house, 2019-21[1]	39.5
Have a car, 2019-21[1]	13.8
Have a toilet connected to sewer line, 2019-21[1]	22.8
Speak English[2]	6-10
Buy shares, 2018[3]	1.9
Have an e-Wallet, 2018[3]	14.3

Source: [1]Table 2.2 and 2.11 NFHS-5, 2019-21, [2]Srinivasan (2019) [3]Government of India (2021) Statement 4 (page s13) and Table A14U (page A625)

Similar findings emerge in the International Social Survey Programme (ISSP) data from India.[78] According to ISSP data, median monthly household income was Rs 8000. It was Rs 15,000 at the 75th percentile. Among respondents who were at or above the 95th percentile in terms of income (Rs 75,000), three-quarters believe that they were in the 60th percentile or below that. Respondents were also asked to classify themselves into 'lower', 'working', 'lower middle', 'middle', 'upper middle' and 'upper' class. The mean income reported by those who identify as 'lower' or working' class is greater than Rs 8000, the sample mean.

The resistance to use the tax instruments listed in the previous section can be partly explained by the fact that some of them (e.g., property taxes and inheritance taxes) would affect the super-rich and 'middle class'. These are the classes whom India's power elite would like to touch, if at all, only with a velvet glove.

Several of India's democratic institutions (making up India's power elite) have been captured by these classes. The Association of Democratic Rights compiles data from the affidavits filed by contestants of various elections in India. These affidavits contain information on asset ownership of Lok Sabha (the lower house of Parliament) contestants. Combining that with NSS data on asset ownership, one finds that the average wealth of those who contested elections in 2019 was 21 times the all-India average (see Table 12.2). Of this, those who won the elections declared wealth more than 100 times the all-India average. Similar remarks are likely to apply to Indian media, academia, bureaucracy and so on. When one sees that India's power elite are not representative (in terms of caste, class, gender, etc.), the muted public discussion on taxation, redistribution and inequality is easier to make sense of.

Another reason why the misconception of class position might matter is that this class feels beleaguered, oppressed by the belief that while the entire burden of taxation falls on them (not true) they get nothing in return (also not true). Such statements from government employees are especially surprising because their job/salary itself comes from taxes paid to the government. They forget that their tax money provides modern sewage systems to them so that sewage is magically taken away from their homes, roads with traffic lights that they can drive their cars on, street lighting, parks, museums, and much more. Such misconceptions are one probable reason for 'tax hesitancy', a reluctance to comply with tax laws.

Table 12.2 Class and India's Power Elite

	Assets/Wealth (Rs Crores)	*Ratio of wealth to Indian average*
Average value of assets per *household*, physical and financial as of 30.6.2018[1]	0.197[2]	1.0
Average value of assets in the highest (wealth) decile, 2018[1]	1.04[2]	5.3
Wealth		
Average, those contesting Lok Sabha elections, 2019[3]	4.1	21
Average, elected Lok Sabha MPs, 2019[3]	20.9	106
Richest MP (Nakul Nath), 2019[3]	660.2	3349
Richest candidate, 2019 (Ramesh Sharma)[3]	1107.6	5619
Richest person, 2021 (Mukesh Ambani)	7,18,000	3,64,467

Source: NSS Report No. 587 and 588 (p. 18 and p. 22), Economic Survey 2020-21, Association of Democratic Rights (ADR) reports, Hurun Rich List.

Notes: [1]Includes land, building, livestock, poultry, agricultural machinery and equipment, non-farm business equipment, transport equipment, deposits and shares. [2]Weighted average of Rs 1592 (rural) and Rs 2717 (urban), and Rs ('000) 8117 and 15035 for richest decile weighted by estimated rural (1724297) and urban (876260) households. [3]Includes assets, movable and immovable.

In 2016, I had the opportunity to study the rise of welfare states in other parts of the world, especially England. An important thread that emerged was the development of broad (even if tenuous) consensus among otherwise conflicting sections of society. Fragile and fractured though it might have been, it can happen, as it did after the Second World War. At the time, the Conservative, Liberal and Labour parties acknowledged the need for broad-based social interventions (Timmins 2001).

One factor, among many, that led to the creation of the welfare state in many parts of the world was the Second World War. In the case of England, it brought home the fact that when the bombs fell, they would not distinguish between the rich and the poor and that they were all in it together. At that time, on 1 September 1939, days before England declared war, 3.5 million children were evacuated from their homes to safer places (Wicks 2013). This led to poor children from London going to live with rich families in rural England. Children unaccustomed to using toilets urinated on the carpet of posh women. Some refused to drink milk because when they saw cows being milked they thought they were being given cow urine. The rich encountered the conditions of the poor for the first time, and perhaps helped them empathise with their condition.

India had one such moment in recent history: the humanitarian crisis during COVID-19 arising from the lockdowns. It was a moment of reckoning when the privileged began to see just how fragile people's lives were. However, it was the big corporations that capitalised on the opportunity. Out of the total COVID-19 relief package that the government announced, less than 2 per cent of GDP was for the most disadvantaged. The rest (roughly 6-8 per cent of GDP) went to other sectors.

In discussions on inequality in India, there is agreement that something must be done. Indeed, the ISSP data suggests that the high levels of inequality are widely acknowledged. More than four-fifths of the respondents believe that inequality was high or too high. Not only that, there is widespread support for government action to remedy this. Nearly 80 per cent of respondents believe that it is the government's responsibility to reduce inequality.

Yet, when specific policy options (including the policies mentioned here) are floated, we hit a roadblock. In the ISSP survey, when respondents were asked about progressive taxation, just over half (55 per cent) said that they believed that those with higher incomes should pay a much larger share of their incomes as taxes. Support for progressive taxation rises with education; it is lowest among those at the top (i.e., who self-identify as 'upper' or 'upper middle' class).

The hostile environment in which redistributive policies are debated in India is striking. Labelling socio-economic rights as 'freebies' is one indication of this. In 2020, officers of the Indian Revenue Service Association (IRSA) prepared a report titled 'Fiscal Options and Response to COVID-19 Epidemic' (FORCE) that advocated higher income tax (40 per cent) for income above Rs 1 crore or a re-introduction of the wealth tax for those with wealth of more than Rs 5 crores. A few months later, the Central Board of Direct Taxes charge-sheeted three of the IRSA officials. The Finance Ministry said it created 'panic and tax policy uncertainty'. A more recent example of the resistance to redistributive taxes arose during the campaign for the 2024 General Election in India, when the ruling party (BJP) 'accused' the Congress party of wanting to introduce an inheritance tax, the Congress went out of its way to deny any such promise in its manifesto (Drèze 2024).

One reason for the lack of empathy seems to be that the better-off are shielded from the brutal realities of the daily lives of a large part of the population. We live in our bubbles preoccupied with our own struggles. The media, caught in the race for better ratings, advertising revenues, and with corporate control breathing angrily down their necks, cannot perform the role of information sharing that might bring about a better understanding as the Second World War did in Britain. Social media, which can potentially be more democratic is increasingly in the grip of large companies.

Moreover, redistributive measures are seen as a zero-sum game—the poor will gain at the cost of the 'middle' class, so such measures are resisted. Ultimately, consensus and support for social security among elites is weak. Reprioritizing wellbeing requires, among other things, a broader understanding and consensus.

13

The Way Ahead

One often hears the refrain 'Nothing has changed in the last seventy years'. This statement has little basis in facts: around Independence, life expectancy in 1951 was 32 years; by 2022, it increased to 68. The infant mortality rate was 180 per 1000 births, in 2020 it was down to 28 per 1000. In 1951, only 9 per cent girls were literate, and by 2011, two-thirds were literate (Drèze and Sen 2015). Meanwhile, though the numbers remain disputed, poverty has also declined. Thus, the real problem is not things have not changed, but that they have improved too slowly. In the past decade some things continued to improve (e.g., literacy is higher, infant mortality rates are lower), but there are some worrying developments too. On some fronts we may have slowed down (e.g., stunting, real wages) or some things may have worsened (e.g., anaemia has increased). This is true of the performance of the social policies discussed in this book as well—the 2004-14 period was better than the following decade. The previous chapter shows that overall welfare expenditure has stagnated, and within that the budget for these social policies has been squeezed further.

In the nineties, the low rates of GDP growth were likely to be cited for the low allocation for social spending. This was followed by a period of greater commitment to health, education and other social policies. In the past decade, the vision seems to have narrowed rather than widening, reverting to a single-minded focus on GDP growth rate rather than overall human development. For instance, India's rank on total GDP has been making the headlines; not even per capita GDP, let alone focusing on inequality or other indicators of wellbeing such as health and education.

The silver lining is that though the central government is losing interest in social policy, increasingly state governments, especially those ruled by non-BJP parties, are beginning to take a proactive interest.

The Question of Models

Some readers might wonder if there is a 'model' state for development economists or for social policy. For many years, Kerala was considered a 'model' by those interested in development economics. The main reason was that it did well on all three indicators—income, health and education—included in the Human Development Index (HDI).

In the run up to the 2014 General Election, however, there was a lot of buzz about a so-called 'Gujarat model'. Gujarat has done well on the growth rate of per capita GDP—it is ranked number one throughout (see Table 13.1). Indeed, this was a key message of those who pushed it as a model: focus on growth of GDP. The slogan 'Minimum Government, Maximum Governance' emerged from this thinking. Yet on other indicators of wellbeing, Gujarat pales very quickly: it was ranked ninth (out of 20 major states) on infant mortality and eleventh on female education around 2020.

Table 13.1 Gujarat's Falling Rank on Key Indicators

	1990s		*2000s*		*2019-21*	
	Gujarat (India)	*Rank*[a]	*Gujarat (India)*	*Rank*[a]	*Gujarat (India)*	*Rank*[a]
Per capita state domestic product, real growth rate	6.2 (4.0)[1]	1	8.2 (6.0)[1]	1	3.0 (0.7)[3]	1
Infant Mortality Rate	63 (71)[1]	4	41 (44)[1]	9	21 (27)[5]	9
Girls aged 15-19 years (per cent) who passed Class VIII	43 (36)[1]	7	53 (56)[1]	11	84 (84)[6]	15
Human Development Index (HDI)	0.43 (0.38)[2]	7	0.53 (0.55)[2]	7	0.64 (0.63)	11
Population purchasing food grains from PDS (per cent)7	38 (27)	7	23 (45)	18	47 (70)	19

Note: [a]Rank among twenty major states for which data is available throughout.

Sources: [1]Drèze and Sen (Table A.3, 2002 and Table A.3, 2013); [2]Drèze and Sen (2013), Table 1.2 Appendix I; Government of India (2002) Table 1.2 (page 141) and Government of India (2012), Table 13.10; [3]Reserve Bank of India, (2023, Table 26); [4]Global Data Lab (2021); [5]Government of India (2025), Table 1; [6]National Family Health Survey—5 (2019-21); [7]Himanshu and Sen (2013) and Khera (2024)

Table 13.1 hints at the limits of focusing on GDP alone: the foundation of Gujarat's rapid economic growth was laid several decades ago. In the nineties, when it was ranked number one on per capita GDP growth rate, Gujarat was ranked from 2-7 on selected indicators reported in Table 13.1 (Khera 2014a). By the 2000s, barring per capita GDP growth its rank had slipped from 9-19 (last column).[79]

In the realm of social policy it would be hard to make a case for Gujarat as a model (see Drèze 2014a and 2021). Over the past twenty years, what is encouraging is that several states have successfully experimented with various social policies. Some examples have already been mentioned. Among them, three—Tamil Nadu, Himachal Pradesh and Odisha—are worth a few more words.

Odisha was often in the news more for poverty, poor human development indicators and corruption. Earlier the Kalahandi-Bolangir-Koraput (KBK) region of Odisha was known outside the state because it was plagued with starvation deaths (Drèze, Khera and Mishra 2014). But in the last two decades (coinciding with the twenty-year Biju Janata Dal government), there has been impressive social policy action. Twenty years ago, Anganwadis, Mid-Day Meals, the Public Distribution System (PDS), and pensions were not particularly visible, but today people treat them as reliable sources of social support. The practice of giving eggs to child feeding programmes originated in Tamil Nadu, but Odisha went a step further. In Odisha, eggs began to be given to children under the age of three as take-home rations and to pregnant and lactating women as well. Secondly, in the PDS the state has achieved considerable success in reducing theft of food grains. Third, Odisha is perhaps the only state in India where social security pensions to the elderly widows and the disabled are given every month (almost always) on time. These pensions used to be given as cash in hand at the panchayat office on the 15th of every month. Besides, more than half of all pensioners are supported exclusively by the state pension scheme, the Madhu Babu Pension Yojana (see Map 8.3) and it tops up the measly Central pension from state resources.[80] Fourth, before the National Food Security Act recognised maternity benefits as a universal right, Odisha had launched its Mamata scheme for maternity benefits in 2011. The scheme is reasonably widely implemented there: two-thirds of women who gave birth in 2021-22 got these benefits.

Nestled in the Himalayas, the achievements of Himachal Pradesh, though a small hilly state, may not yet be a model, yet its achievements in this field are definitely commendable (Khera 2014c). The two PROBE Reports on primary education, conducted at a ten-year interval (in 1996 and 2006), showed heartening results for the state (De et al. 2011). In a survey in 2004-05, children studying in government schools were tested on reading, writing and subtraction. Children from Himachal stood first in reading, fourth in writing and second in subtraction (Drèze and Sen 2015). More recently, in the National Achievement Survey 2025, Himachal was among the top five states (Panwar 2025). In a 2007 survey on NREGA, women were participating in large numbers, panchayats were playing a key role in its implementation, and corruption was also relatively low. The Public Distribution System in Himachal was the best performing in a survey among nine states in 2011 (Khera 2011). The PDS in HP stood out on three counts: one, PDS was universal (though not uniform), two, it provided not only cheap wheat and rice, but also nutritious pulses and edible oil and three cardholders reported getting almost their full entitlement of ration in the three months before the survey. This does not mean that there aren't any challenges in Himachal. The increasing reach of private schools at the primary level seems to be weakening the public education system, on the basis of which the state has been able to become among the top states on HDI. Among the major causes of concern in social policies are reports of caste-based discrimination. The fallout of environmental degradation have become apparent too.

A third 'model' state—the OG (Original Gangster)—is Tamil Nadu (Khera 2018). Before they were adopted as central schemes, Tamil Nadu pioneered several programmes at the state level. The Mid-Day Meal is one such scheme. Tamil Nadu also took the lead in maternity benefits for women in the unorganised sector (the state's Dr Muthulakshmi Reddy Scheme was implemented in 1987). Cheap food through public canteens (Amma Unagavams) in urban areas, baby care kits for new mothers, the breakfast scheme in school—Tamil Nadu has always had a creative approach to social policy (see Srinivasan 2014, Sinha 2019, among others). There is a lot to learn from Tamil Nadu on public heathcare services.

Tailenders Can Also Hit Sixes

In the early 2000s, the Public Distribution System was defunct in most north Indian states. Tamil Nadu was the only state where PDS was delivering more or less in accordance with its mandate—universal access providing subsidised grain, pulses and edible oil with low leakage rates. Around 2010, we tried to convince Swami Anklesaria Iyer (a columnist for *The Times of India*) that north Indian states could deliver like the PDS in Tamil Nadu. Our assertion was based on laggard states (like Chhattisgarh, Odisha, etc.) that were witnessing a revival. In Chhattisgarh, the state government gives more food grains than mandated by the NFSA (5 kg per person per month) through the PDS, and has introduced protein-rich black gram at Rs 5 per kg. In Tamil Nadu, Andhra Pradesh, Telangana and Himachal Pradesh, the state governments provide pulses and edible oil. The template for the reforms in states like Chhattisgarh, Odisha, Jharkhand, etc. was provided by Tamil Nadu.

Unconvinced, Iyer said, 'The entire Indian cricket team cannot bat like Tendulkar.' We responded to him by saying that the tailenders had begun hitting the sixes. Despite the social, political and economic challenges, there is much to learn from many states. For almost every scheme discussed in this book, there have been interesting experiments at the state level that have sometimes inspired other states to 'replicate' them.

Similar remarks apply to social security pensions. According to a CAG report, between 2017-2021, only 24 per cent of the total expenditure on the National Social Assistance Programme (NSAP) came from the Central government (Comptroller and Auditor General of India 2023) though it is meant to be funded fully by the Centre. There are two reasons behind this: one, the central contribution to social security pensions is very low (Rs 200-500 per month), so most states 'top-up' the pension amount, going up to Rs 4000 in Andhra Pradesh. This is true in poorer states as well: in Jharkhand, the state government contributes Rs 800 so that pensioners get Rs 1000 per month. Two, many states have added a substantial number of pensioners through state pension schemes to increase coverage. For example, in Rajasthan, 85 per cent of all social security pensioners are supported by the state scheme.

In Rajasthan, pensions have been integrated with a modest top-up of NREGA entitlements (150 days of work, instead of just 100) through a state Minimum Guaranteed Income Act, 2023. The Act makes the top-up a legal entitlement and integrates work with pensions. Two major innovations of the Act are worth highlighting: one, annual indexation of the pension amount and two, the launch of an 'urban NREGA'—i.e., an employment guarantee programme in urban areas. Such urban employment guarantee schemes are being experimented with in a bunch of states.[81] Like Rajasthan, several other states have topped up NREGA days.

The case of maternity benefits for women in the unorganised sector is one of several where the Centre was possibly inspired by the states when it was included in the NFSA. Tamil Nadu's Dr Muthulakshmi Reddy Maternity Benefit Scheme began in 1987 and provides Rs 18,000; Odisha followed in 2011 with the Mamata Yojana that provides Rs 10,000 per pregnancy. Before the NFSA, maternity benefits were shunted around: it was part of the NSAP under the Ministry of Rural Development; it was transferred to the Ministry of Women and Child Development in 2001, then renamed as the Indira Gandhi Matru Sahayog Yojana but only ran on pilot basis in fifty-odd districts. Sadly, the central scheme following the passage of NFSA (PMMVY), provides only Rs 5000-6000.

In the ICDS and Mid-Day-Meal Scheme, while the Central government has barely increased the cooking cost per child for hot cooked food, states have made efforts to provide better food with their own budgets. Even poorer states like Odisha, Bihar and Jharkhand have added eggs to the menu in MDM and ICDS. Some states (Odisha and Tamil Nadu) have also introduced breakfast for primary school children and pre-schoolers (aged 3-6 years) at Anganwadis.

***

Overall, India's welfare architecture has been outlined through this book. It examines achievements and shortcomings, interstate variations and the ups and downs over time. The hope is that more people will be able to appreciate why it is important to revive and build on the framework that is in place. During demonetisation and the COVID-19 pandemic, it was this very welfare architecture that the government fell back on. The support it provides is modest, but often a lifeline for the poor.

Before closing, it is worth reiterating that out of seven schemes discussed here barring social security pensions (NSAP) and public canteens, the rest are protected by law. This remains true—at least on paper—even after the replacement of NREGA by VB-GRAM-GA. Besides this, the biggest gap in India's welfare architecture is that it has not yet recognised healthcare as a Constitutional right.

The importance of legal guarantees is evident in the longstanding neglect of the NSAP as well as the dipping budgets of the NDA's own pet schemes that are not legal entitlements. The legal protection helps schemes weather political ups and downs in political support. As political adversaries, parties may threaten to limit them (as happened with NREGA in 2014-15 and late 2025) or rename them (as they did the NFSA's PDS entitlements to Pradhan Mantri Garib Kalyan Anna Yojana, PMGKAY), or squeeze their budgets, or surreptitiously strangle them (e.g., through increasing techocratisation)—but outright winding up is not easy. While the current NDA government has replaced NREGA with VB-GRAM-GA, it was forced to keep a pretence of bringing a 'better' law than NREGA. Once the foundations of a welfare state have been laid, it can be built up on over time. Each of the state- and scheme-wise examples above give hope that the welfare architecture can be strengthened, and to the extent that has been diminished in the past decade, it can be resurrected.

The Preamble of the Constitution of India includes a resolve:

> '*To secure to all its citizens*
> *Justice, social, economic and political,*
> *Liberty of thought, expression, belief,* faith *and worship,*
> *Equality of status and opportunity and to promote among them all*
> *Fraternity assuring the dignity of the individual...*'
> (italics added)

The welfare architecture outlined here contributes to achieving these constitutional aspirations.

Economic and fiscal concerns aside, the Indian Constitution makes social policies the responsibility of the government, and economic and social justice the right of the people. Social policies are an integral part of the government's role. To oppose them as 'freebies' is against the spirit of the Constitution.

Acknowledgements

This book brings together collaborative research with—literally—hundreds of public-spirited people. Notable among them is Jean Drèze. We have worked and written together on many of the issues covered in this book; we plotted together on almost all the field studies that the book draws on. In some ways, this book carries forward issues in his earlier books *Sense and Solidarity:* Jholwala *Economics For Everyone* and *Social Policy: Essays from Economic and Political Weekly.*

Apart from Jean, the motivation to work on these issues came from many 'roadscholarz'. Some—Ankita Aggarwal, Vyom Anil, Nirali Bakhla, Saloni Chopra, Sweta Das, Siraj Dutta, Naman Garg, Aashish Gupta, Prankur Gupta, Aarushi Kalra, Nazar Khalid, Sandesh Lokhande, Rishabh Malhotra, Karuna Muthiah, Sudha Narayanan, Nandini Nayak, Navjyoti, Vipul Paikra, Aditi Priya, Jessica Pudussery, Raghav Puri, Kanika Sharma, Ria Singh Sawhney, Anmol Somanchi, Meghna Yadav—have played a key role in making the field studies possible.

Roadscholarz' surveys have involved hundreds of students over the past twenty years, who have spoken to thousands of respondents across the country. Many rural residents fed and sheltered us in their homes, their insights and experiences have helped us understand the issues better. Without this all-round generosity—of students and respondents—this research would not have been possible.

For me, the journey around Rajasthan in 2001 is where I first understood the importance of learning from outside usual academic sources. The magnetic energy of Paras Banjara, Nikhil Dey, Khemu, Bhanwar Meghvanshi, Aruna Roy, Shankar Singh and others associated with the Mazdoor Kisan Shakti Sangathan and Kavita Srivastava (in Jaipur) made it impossible to not work in Rajasthan. Norati Bai, Ram Karanji, Norat Mal, Ram Niwasji and Bunker Roy in Tilonia, Bhanwarji, Shyamji, R. D. Vyas at Aastha Sanstha in Udaipur; Pavitra Mohan and Sanjana Mohan from Basic Health Services, Richa Singh in Sirohi, Chetan Ram Godara and Rawat Ram in Bikaner, Akbar Ali, Tulsaram Meghwal, Khetubai Meghwal and Partaparam Meghwal in Barmer were instrumental in making the demanding nature of data collection a rewarding exercise.

Our field studies would not have been imaginable without the support of public-spirited collaborators who enthusiastically teamed up with us: in Palamu-Latehar (Jharkhand), Niyamat Ansari, James Herenj, Jawahar Mehta, Lalit Mehta, Bhukhan Singh, Shyama Singh, Pachati Singh; Sugiya Devi, Balbir Munda and Rajender in Khunti, Siraj Dutta in Chaibasa and in Ranchi Balram, Gurjeet Singh, Stan Swamy. Gangabhai Paikra, Narendra Das and Yogesh Jain in Chhattisgarh. Rajkishore Mishra, Bidyut Mohanty, Sameet Panda, Shambhu Sahu in Odisha, Sachin Jain, Madhuri Krishnaswamy and Raghavendra-ji in Madhya Pradesh, Arundhati Dhuru, Richa Singh and Roma in Uttar Pradesh; Ashish Ranjan and Kamayani Swami from Jan Jagran Shakti Sangathan (Bihar) and Sanjay Sahni in Muzaffarpur; Kuldeep

Verma in Himachal Pradesh. Their support and encouragement made it possible to undertake extensive fieldwork and develop an understanding of these issues. This book was originally written in Hindi (*Revdi Ya Haq: Samajik Suraksha par ek Nazariya*, published by Rajkamal Prakashan) because many of them read only Hindi.

The generosity of friends from the South has been equally valuable because they helped me learn in spite of not knowing the local language. Dipa Sinha, Karuna Muthiah and Sudha Narayanan in Tamil Nadu, Babu in Puducherry, Soundarya Iyer and Kruthi in Karnataka, Chakradhar Buddha in Andhra Pradesh, Jasmin Naur Hafiz in Kerala have all happily come along for the journey over the years.

Ishan Anand, Arindam Das, Clément Imbert, Maalav Mehta, Kavita Ranganathan and Swati Tirkey shared feedback, and data used in the book. Many bureaucrats, Block Development Officers, Child Development Program Officers (CDPOs), Junior Engineers, Gram Sevaks, etc. shared their perspectives and followed up on our findings and suggestions with administrative or policy action.

The book was written during a short sabbatical from the Indian Institute of Technology Delhi (IIT Delhi) where I have worked since 2011. IIT Delhi provided institutional space for our work, as well as financial support—including through the Narendra and Chandra Singhi Chair—for several surveys. My PhD scholars—Neha Arya, Krishna Priya Choragudi, G. Lavanya, Shabnam and Madhurambal Sundaresan—stepped in at several points. Safia Siddiqui helped vet the initial translation into English. Mohd. Asjad provided invaluable research assistance that made this book possible.

Writing a book, especially in Hindi, was a big deal for me. I thank Satyanand Nirupam of Rajkamal Prakashan for giving me the opportunity. Ravi Singh readily agreed to publish the English translation. Dyuti Roy for her encouraging feedback during the production process. Translating into English was not part of the original plan—for that I owe my friends and family who grumbled about an English version not being available.

Notes

1. Freebies or Rights?: A Sympathetic View on Social Policies

1. Tillin (2025) is among the first attempts to trace, historically, the trajectory of the Indian welfare state.
2. See Muralidharan (2024), Rahman and Pingali (2024), Drèze (2017), Drèze and Sen (2015) for more on these issues.
3. Given the timing of the advent of Aadhaar (post the 2008 financial crisis), it made one wonder if it was something like an 'employment guarantee' programme for India's IT sector. With the constant need for enrolment of people, updation and correction of their demographic and biometric details, it certainly has spawned a whole micro-industry of such services.
4. Fiscal deficit concerns cannot explain the neglect of NREGA and NFSA. For instance, when the NREGA budget was only 0.5 per cent of GDP, the 'tax revenue foregone' which benefit rich companies, was 3 per cent of GDP.
5. Data sources are provided so that readers compare with other countries of their choice. More detailed data related to most schemes is in the Appendix I.

2. Key Debates in Social Policy

6. Amartya Sen himself admitted that the attempt to reduce the richness of human life to merely three outcomes was 'vulgar'. They went ahead, nevertheless, because the HDI is better than the single-minded focus on GDP.
7. Commodities included in GDP could be things that are beneficial to us (such as food, education and health) or those that do not

benefit ordinary people (such as war goods, 'financial services', etc.). When harmful material is produced (e.g. polluting industries), it also increases GDP. See Diane Coyle 2014.

8. In the bottom 20 per cent, 46 per cent were stunted, 20 per cent were underweight and 72 per cent were anaemic. See also Muralidharan (2024), chapter 10.
9. The US is considered a 'model' in some people's imagination because of its prosperity: but during COVID-19, the US had the highest COVID-19 deaths in the world, and was second in terms of COVID death rates (per 100,000 people) (BBC News, 2022).
10. In recent times, gun violence and crime among the youth has increased in Sweden. Some of those involved in the violence, end up in gangs because they want to avoid the indignity associated with relying on social benefits.
11. From Ambedkar to the present day, its importance and impact have been documented by researchers. Some examples of research on this are, Attewel and Thorat 2007, Agarwal, Drèze and Gupta 2015, Deshpande 2017, Drèze 2020, Thorat 2010, Thorat and Joshi, 2020.

3. Maternity Benefits: Some Women Are More Equal

12. The Act also states that for all pregnant women and up to six months after the child is born, food will be provided at the Anganwadi. Though NFSA 4(a) mentions 'food', Schedule 2 of the Act only mentions 'Take Home Rations' (National Food Security Act, 2013).
13. Even if we reduce the duration of the leave to 18 weeks (as per the ILO recommendation), at this rate women should get Rs 50,400.
14. In 2022, the central government issued an order extending the benefit if the second child is a girl. If the second child is a girl, they get Rs 6000 in a single instalment. For the first child, PMMVY money was given in three instalments; it has now been reduced to two instalments.
15. When the law for women in the formal sector was amended in 2017, some pointed out that the costs associated with providing maternity benefits would discourage the private sector from hiring women.

16. This section draws on an earlier paper Drèze et al., 2021 based on the JABS Survey 2019.
17. There were reports of hot cooked food for pregnant and lactating women in some states in 2024, but systematic monitoring or reports are not available.
18. At the time of the state elections in 2021, the Dravida Munnetra Kazhagam (DMK) promised in its manifesto that it would be increased to Rs 24,000, but this had not happened until the 2026-27 budget.
19. In the denominator, one could use either the total number of first-born or all births. In the maps, all births are in the denominator. Using first-born only will raise the proportion covered by PMMVY benefits.

4. Anganwadis: The Foundations of a Child's Future

20. Between NFHS-4 and NFHS-5, the Multidimensional Poverty Index (MPI) declined by 10 percentage points to 15% in NFHS-5. The MPI is a composite index with health, education and standard of living indicators, and most of the improvement was driven by the standard of living indicators (Government of India 2023). https://ophi.org.uk/sites/default/files/2024-03/India_National_MPI_2023.pdf
21. There was a provision of 'mini Anganwadi' in villages with a population of less than 300. In addition, in the Right to Food case in the Supreme Court, it directed that in habitations with 40 children there should be one Anganwadi Centre.
22. Some might argue that the AWW, AWH and MDM cooks are not in a 'full time' job. This argument does not hold much weight especially for AWWs who, de facto, end up putting in a full day's work; for the AWH and cook, not being available for a full day's work renders them more or less unemployable elsewhere. Even if we count these salaries as wages for half a day of work, it would remain below agricultural wages in most cases.
23. Similarly, the Central government's contribution to the MDM cook's salary has not increased from Rs 1000, set in 2009, 15 years ago (Government of India 2022).

24. Though NREGA wages are indexed, the rate of indexation has yielded increases that have been abysmally low.

5. Mid-Day Meal: Much More Than Food

25. As an aside: the contrast between the palpable fear of violating the Supreme Court's orders among district officials then, and the past few years where its orders and final judgment that children cannot be denied any benefits because of Aadhaar have been gleefully disregarded is quite telling. The violations of the Aadhaar orders for children are not even newsworthy now.
26. The Supreme Court ordered on April 20, 2004, that 'Dalits and Adivasis shall be given priority in the appointment of cooks and helpers.' (Right to Food Campaign, undated).
27. Even accounting for the change in Centre-State sharing norms based on the recommendations of the Fourteenth Finance Commission, the MDM scheme suffered a funding squeeze from the Central government.
28. When these draconian rules were questioned, the government issued a press release within a week. The headlines that followed (e.g., 'Government Relaxes Aadhaar Norm, Makes Other IDs Acceptable for Subsidy Schemes.' (Press Trust of India, 2017)) gave the impression that enrolment of children in the Aadhaar database had been made 'voluntary'. In fact, the rules remained more or less the same.
29. Interested readers may read Kritika Bhardwaj (2016) article 'India is Enrolling Infants and Children in Aadhaar—But What About Their Consent?'.
30. The same situation had arisen with NREGA and PDS where programme functionaries were finding it difficult to carry out their routine tasks due to Aadhaar-related work. The application of Aadhaar in pensions, PDS and NREGA had shown high failure rates of this technology (Khera, 2019c). As it happens, biometric authentication was not scaled up for school children, but since 2025 teachers have been busy with generating APAAR (Automated Permanent Academic Account Registry) IDs for school children.

6. Public Distribution System: Beyond Foodgrains

31. Others define inclusion errors as 'leakage' instead of 'mistargeting'. Thus, in those estimates, grain bought by those who are not BPL (as defined by the authors) but in fact purchasing PDS grain, is counted as a leakage.
32. This was an earlier avatar of the Monitoring and Information System (MIS) and a lesson from the Right to Information Act's clause for proactive disclosures. For example, the names and employment details of all job card holders in the village would be painted on the walls of the Gram Panchayat office, which helped identify and eliminate fake job cards and fake muster rolls. In subsequent years, the MIS replaced these transparency walls.
33. In most states NREGA wages, pensions and scholarships are transferred directly into bank accounts because the modern banking system is considered secure. It has never been clear why bank accounts needed to be linked to Aadhaar. 'Bogus' beneficiaries are a problem, but evidence suggests that they are a smaller problem than they are made out to be. For instance, a government report in 2015 found that when Aadhaar was linked to LPG, only 2% connections were 'bogus'.
34. Until the COVID-19 lockdowns, some states provided PDS grains at NFSA prices (e.g., Rs 2 per kg of wheat and Rs 3 per kg of rice), but others subsidised it further (e.g., rice was free in Tamil Nadu) using state resources. During COVID-19, the NFSA PDS was repackaged as Pradhan Mantri Gramin Kalyan Anna Yojana (PMGKAY). Under PMGKAY, PDS grain is free until the end of 2025.
35. Another logistics issue relates to accommodating regional diversity in staples. In Rajasthan, wheat is the main staple and for Jharkhand and Odisha it is primarily rice. Under ONOR, can ration card holders from Jharkhand get rice in a Rajasthan PDS outlet? Relatedly, how will the supply logistics (of reaching rice to wheat-eating states) be managed given the fluidity in migration patterns?
36. In a small survey conducted by IIT Delhi students in eight cities across four states in October 2021, some PDS dealers reported authentication and server failures.

7. NREGA: Challenges to Realising its Vision

37. Another possibility is that due to lack of awareness about the right to demand employment and/or the procedure, actual demand has been supressed.
38. In the initial year (2006-07), NREGA was implemented in 200 districts only. In the following year, 130 more districts were added and by 2008 it was extended to all districts. This explains the jump in the NREGA budget in 2008-9.
39. When the proposal to restrict NREGA to 200 districts was formulated, this aspect was emphasised. In a government note, it was said that NREGA has been used politically. The pattern is possibly a reflection of the better administrative capacity of Andhra Pradesh and Tamil Nadu.
40. The previous year's budget estimate was Rs 38,500 crore, and was revised to Rs 48,215 crores (the 'largest' until then). Arun Jaitley, the then finance minister, had to budget even more more later. Ultimately, in 2017-18, Rs 55,167 crore was spent on NREGA.
41. There have been cases of fraudulent withdrawal of money from people's accounts using Aadhaar and mobile phone numbers.
42. Apart from political sycophancy, one possible explanation for this proposal was that it would provide a backdoor to corruption: since wage corruption was becoming difficult, higher material expenditure under NREGA would open new avenues for siphoning funds.
43. Around that time 38,000 payments were delayed due to PMFS in Karnataka alone.

8. Social Security Pensions: Contingency Care

44. Under NPS, the government employee contributes 10% of their salary and DA, and the government deposits 14% of the salary and DA in the employee's Tier-1 account (Government of India, 2023, p-254).
45. The NSAP also includes a National Family Benefit Scheme that provides a compensation of Rs 10,000 upon the death of the primary breadwinner of a family and Annapurna that provides

10kg of free grain to some elderly pensioners. Both are implemented patchily.

46. For several years, a group of economists have written letters to the Finance Minister to increase the pension amount, but successive Finance Ministers have ignored them. As pointed out in the CAG report, various Parliamentary Standing Committees have also made this demand, only to be ignored.
47. For this, we have used the number of old-age pensioners from the Central or state portals, and divided that by the projected population aged 60 years and above. In a state like Jharkhand this method overestimates coverage because the state has relaxed the eligibility age.
48. The state has its own slew of social security pensions, but it is not clear if those can make up for the thin coverage of the elderly.
49. This section is based on the findings of a 2013 survey presented in Chopra and Pudussery (2014). Other important studies on NSAP include Dutta et al. (2010), Gupta (2013) and Kaushal (2014).

9. Public Canteens: An Idea Whose Time Has Come

50. This chapter draws on Khera (forthcoming), Khera (2024) and Khera (2016).
51. In Bihar, Didi ki Rasoi were set up but food is not cheap (Rs 50 per plate). Its main aim was to provide employment to women (Jeevika, 2021). Gujarat has a few canteens in 10 districts that are open to workers registered under the Board of Construction Workers (Gummadi and Jyotishi, 2025).
52. In Rajasthan, for a brief period in 2016, 80 Annapurna kitchens were run in 11 cities by Vasundhara Raje's government.
53. In other cities, they began with a daily wage of Rs 250 that was increased to Rs 300 at the time of the survey.
54. The workers are paid by the corporation. In some cases, we heard that wages are paid into the accounts of just one or two members of the team, and they paid other workers. If true, this would mean that the remaining workers are not even being recognised in this hypothetical way for the services rendered.
55. The canteen staff had many ideas for small changes (for example,

serving chutney with idli instead of sambar; adding tea and coffee to increase footfall throughout the day, provision of eggs as top up). No innovations are officially allowed in the menu. In any case, some of these changes require more budgetary support.

56. Canteens and social security pensions were dropped from the National Food Security Act though they were part of early discussions on the framework of the law.

10. COVID-19: Neglect of Health and Education Exposed

57. Though the 2021 Budget showed a huge increase in the health budget (about Rs 2 lakh crore), half of it was the budget of the Department of Drinking Water and Sanitation, something that is not usually counted in the health budget. The bulk of the increase was on account of the COVID-19 vaccine (Rs 35,000 crore). The budget of Ayushman Bharat did not increase.
58. During COVID, there were several reports of doctors, nurses, other hospital workers (for whom the Prime Minister made people 'bang' on plates) being on strike because they were not paid salaries for several months.
59. At one point it was proposed to convert spare railway carriages into an isolation 'facility' to deal with the shortage of isolation facilities.
60. Some people argued that the company has a right to profit because of its vaccine research. But research on the vaccine was done by Oxford University. Astra-Zeneca also promised to sell the vaccine at no profit as long as it was considered a 'pandemic'. In addition, Rs 100 crore was also provided from the PM CARES fund to make the vaccine.
61. At that time, in most states, NREGA daily wages were less than Rs 450.
62. On the other hand, the not-for-profit (or even in government sector) costs are likely to be high—if healthcare is free or affordable, the fear is that people will overvisit, when not even needed, to try to get tested.
63. To ease the shortage of beds and prevent them from charging exorbitant rates, Rajasthan, Chhattisgarh and Madhya Pradesh

(as in some other countries) tried to bring private hospitals under government control (Chakravarty 2020). In Madhya Pradesh, private hospitals were promised compensation for treatment as per the Ayushman Bharat norms.

64. With a Central budget of Rs 35,000 crores and a population of more than 130 crores, only 11 crore vaccines were ordered by the Centre till April 2021.
65. The NFHS-5 survey took place between 2019-21 and coincided with the period of the COVID lockdown.
66. According to researchers, COVID-19 was less likely to infect children, and if they did get it, the chances of it becoming severe were lower. People were afraid that children who do get COVID-19, might infect the elderly at home. To prevent this, a sound strategy would have been to convince the elders that it is necessary to wear masks and their negligence can harm the next generation. Children could be taught the importance of washing hands, wearing masks at school so that they could explain to others at home as well.
67. Similar results were also reported by Save the Children (2020) and Oxfam India (2020).
68. The problem is not only in Delhi. Even as thousands of people gathered at the cricket stadium in Ranchi, primary schools were closed.

11. Emerging Issues in Social Policy

69. In the Cochrane Reviews, the findings of different studies are presented systematically on a single issue. The expectation is that the findings should be collected without bias.
70. Doctors believe that in some instances excess iron can also be harmful though the aforementioned Cochrane Review found no harmful effects either.
71. When NREGA wages began to be paid through bank and post office accounts from 2008-09 onwards, wage corruption decreased significantly—from 44-58% to 22-32% between 2007-08 and 2011-12. Estimates based on the second India Human Development Survey suggest an even sharper decline (Drèze 2014).

72. Political parties claim that these schemes will empower women by putting money in their hands, something they can treat as their own. In fact, it is as much a way for political parties to garner votes (Saikia, 2021).
73. Initially Rs 830 was given, now increased to Rs 1250 (Government of Assam, 2020 and Business Standard 2024).
74. According to Priya et al. (2021) between 6 April and 21 July 2021, 682 deaths were due to lack of oxygen. According to the Punjab Chief Minister, more than 400 people had lost their lives during the farmer's protests. Based on information gathered from the newspaper, Aman et al (2021) counted 989 lockdown related deaths in 2020 (ambulance was not available, due to hunger and thirst, etc.), of which 96 died on a Shramik train.

12. Where Is the Money?

75. After 2014, UPA schemes continue with new names: MDM is now PM-POSHAN, the PDS is Pradhan Mantri Garib Kalyan Anna Yojana (PMGKAY). Renaming of schemes was an important feature of the NDA decade.
76. Verma and Suhel (2023) track these expenses on 'UPA schemes' over the NDA decade (2014-2023). We ignore health and education because they did not change significantly in the period under consideration.
77. In 2015, tax breaks to industry were nearly 3 per cent of GDP. Gold and diamond companies alone received almost twice the NREGA budget (Rs 65,000 crore) as tax exemption. According to the website of the Ministry of Commerce and Industry, the industry employed 30 lakh people, while NREGA employed 4.5 crore people.
78. In July-August, 2022 ISSP's India team surveyed 1578 adults and asked respondents questions about their incomes, self-perceived class position, support for taxation, etc. (Deshmukh 2023).

13. The Way Ahead

79. On some indicators, it has become difficult to distinguish between Gujarat and Bihar (Table 4.2).

80. The state issued an order to all the pensioners to take pension from the bank due to pressure from the center, but when the problems of the elderly came to the fore, the pensioners of the Madhu Babu Pension Scheme started getting it again in the panchayat.
81. Little is known about the implementation of these schemes that are supposed to be in operation in Kerala and Himachal Pradesh and announced in a few other states such as Jharkhand, Odisha, Tamil Nadu (Choragudi, 2022).

References

1. Freebies or Rights?: A Sympathetic View on Social Policies

'COVID Map: Coronavirus Cases, Deaths, Vaccinations by Country.' *BBC News*, 5 July 2022. https://www.bbc.com/news/world-51235105.

'Does Anyone Know What Modinomics Means?' *India Today Conclave*. YouTube video, 8 March 2014. https://www.youtube.com/watch?v=K_HPSshwDsc.

Drèze, Jean, ed. *Social Policy*. EPW Reader. New Delhi: Orient BlackSwan and *Economic and Political Weekly*, 2017.

Drèze, Jean, and Reetika Khera. 'Recent Social Security Initiatives in India.' *World Development* 98 (2017): 555–572.

Drèze, Jean, and Amartya Sen. *An Uncertain Glory: India and Its Contradictions*. Princeton: Princeton University Press, 2015.

Esping-Andersen, Gøsta. *The Three Worlds of Welfare Capitalism*. Princeton: Princeton University Press, 1992.

Khera, Reetika. 'A Phased Approach Will Make a "Basic Income" Affordable for India.' *The Wire*, 20 December 2016. https://thewire.in/88350/basic-income-phased-approach/.

———. 'Impact of Aadhaar on Welfare Programmes.' *Economic and Political Weekly* 52, no. 50 (16 December 2017).

———. 'Kya Bharat Ek Data Blackhole Banane Ke Raste Par Badh Raha Hai.' *The Wire Hindi*, 14 September 2021. https://thewirehindi.com/184807/is-india-turning-into-a-data-blackhole/.

Marmor, Theodore, Jerry L. Mashaw, and Philip L. Harvey. *America's Misunderstood Welfare State: Persistent Myths, Enduring Realities*. New York: Basic Books, 1990.

Pierson, Christopher, and Francis Castles, eds. *The Social Policy Reader*. London: Polity Press, 2006.

Qazi, Aabshar. 'New Ration Cards in Hand, but No Free PDS Food Packets for Sahariya Tribals.' *Hindustan Times*, 30 January 2018. https://www.hindustantimes.com/jaipur/sahariya-tribals-issued-new-ration-cards-in-rajasthan-s-baran-not-getting-free-pds-food-packets/story-VD1q9AMDqk3eEULfMNNW7H.html.

Rahman, Andaleeb, and Prabhu Pingali. *The Future of India's Social Safety Nets: Focus, Form and Scope*. Palgrave Studies in Agricultural Economics and Food Policy. London: Macmillan, 2024.

'Rajasthan BJP Government in Dock over Alleged Malnutrition Deaths.' *Business Standard*, 27 September 2014. https://www.business-standard.com/article/news-ians/rajasthan-s-bjp-government-in-dock-over-alleged-malnutrition-deaths-114092700232_1.html.

Rawls, John. *A Theory of Justice*. Cambridge, MA: Harvard University Press, 1971.

'The World Bank Calls NREGA a Shining Example of Rural Poverty.' *The Economic Times*, 10 October 2013. https://economictimes.indiatimes.com/news/economy/policy/world-bank-calls-nrega-a-stellar-example-of-rural-development/articleshow/23850985.cms?from=mdr

United Nations Development Programme. *Human Development Report 2023/2024: Reimagining Cooperation in a Polarised World*. New York: United Nations Development Programme, 2024. https://hdr.undp.org/system/files/documents/global-report-document/hdr2023-24reporten.pdf.

Vashisht, Swati. 'Rajasthan: Raje Plans to Downsize Gehlot's Free Medicine Scheme.' *CNN-IBN*, 6 August 2014. https://www.news18.com/videos/politics/raje-govt-pkg-706308.html.

2. Key Debates in Social Policy

Aggarwal, Ankita, Jean Drèze, and Aashish Gupta. 'Caste and the Power Elite in Allahabad.' *Economic and Political Weekly* 50, no. 6 (7 February 2015). https://www.epw.in/journal/2015/6/special-articles/caste-and-power-elite-allahabad.html.

Ambedkar, B. R. 'Caste, Class and Democracy.' In *Selected Writings of B.R. Ambedkar*, edited by Valerian Rodrigues. New Delhi: Oxford University Press, 2004.

Attewell, Paul, and Sukhadeo Thorat. 'The Legacy of Social Exclusions.' *Economic and Political Weekly* 42, no. 41 (13 October 2007): 1–14. https://www.epw.in/journal/2007/41/caste-and-economic-discrimination-special-issues/legacy-social-exclusion.html.

Bharti, Nitin Kumar, Lucas Chancel, Thomas Piketty, and Anmol Somanchi. 'Towards Tax Justice and Wealth Redistribution in India.' *The India Forum*, 21 May 2024. https://www.theindiaforum.in/economy/towards-tax-justice-and-wealth-redistribution-india.

Coyle, Diane. *A Brief but Affectionate History of the GDP*. Princeton: Princeton University Press, 2014.

Deshpande, Ashwini. *Grammar of Caste*. New Delhi: Oxford University Press, 2017.

Drèze, Jean, ed. *Social Policy: Essays from Economic and Political Weekly*. New Delhi: Orient BlackSwan, 2016.

———. *Sense and Solidarity: Jholawala Economics for Everyone*. New Delhi: Permanent Black, 2017.

———. 'The Revolt of the Upper Castes.' *The India Forum*, 18 February 2020. https://www.theindiaforum.in/article/revolt-upper-castes.

Drèze, Jean, and Reetika Khera. 'The BPL Census and a Possible Alternative.' *Economic and Political Weekly* 45, no. 9 (27 February 2010).

Drèze, Jean, Prankur Gupta, Reetika Khera, and Isabel Pimenta. 'Casting the Net: India's Public Distribution System after the Food Security Act.' *Economic and Political Weekly* 54, no. 6 (9 February 2019).

Gadenne, Lucie, Sam Norris, Monica Singhal, and Sandeep Sukhtankar. 'In-Kind Transfers as Insurance.' *American Economic Review* 114, no. 9 (2024): 2861–2897.

International Labour Organisation. *World Social Protection Report 2017–19*. Geneva: International Labour Organisation, 2019. https://www.ilo.org/sites/default/files/wcmsp5/groups/public/@dgreports/@dcomm/@publ/documents/publication/wcms_604882.pdf.

———. *World Social Protection Report 2020–22*. Geneva: International Labour Organisation, 2022. https://www.social-protection.org/gimi/Media.action?id=7368.

Khera, Reetika. 'Access to the Targeted Public Distribution System: A Case Study in Rajasthan.' *Economic and Political Weekly* 43, no. 44 (1 November 2008). https://www.epw.in/journal/2008/44/special-articles/access-targeted-public-distribution-system-case-study-rajasthan.

Marshall, T. H. 'Citizenship and Social Class.' In *The Social Policy Reader*, edited by Christopher Pierson and Francis Castles. London: Polity Press, 2006.

Muralidharan, Karthik. *Accelerating India's Development: A State-Led Roadmap for Effective Governance*. New York: Viking Penguin, 2024.

Ortiz-Ospina, Esteban, and Max Roser. 'Government Spending.' *Our World in Data*. Global Change Data Lab, 2023. https://ourworldindata.org/government-spending.

Thorat, Amit. 'Ethnicity, Caste, and Religion: Implications for Poverty Outcomes.' *Economic and Political Weekly* 45, no. 51 (18 December 2010). https://www.epw.in/journal/2010/51/special-articles/ethnicity-caste-and-religion-implications-poverty-outcomes.html.

Thorat, Amit, and Omkar Joshi. 'The Continuing Practice of Untouchability in India: Patterns and Mitigating Influences.' *Economic and Political Weekly* 55, no. 2 (11 January 2020). https://www.epw.in/journal/2020/2/special-articles/continuing-practice-untouchability-india.html.

Titmuss, Richard. 'Universalism vs. Selection.' In *The Social Policy Reader*, edited by Christopher Pierson and Francis Castles, 128–137. London: Allen & Unwin, 1968.

World Bank Group. *World Development Indicators: Domestic General Government Health Expenditure*. Washington, DC: World Bank Group.

———. *World Development Indicators: Government Expenditure on Education, Total (% of GDP)*. Washington, DC: World Bank Group, 24 April 2024. https://databank.worldbank.org/source/world-development-indicators/Series/SE.XPD.TOTL.GD.ZS.

——. *World Development Indicators: Gross Domestic Product 2022*. Washington, DC: World Bank Group, n.d. https://databankfiles.worldbank.org/public/ddpext_download/GDP.pdf.

——. *World Development Indicators: Per Capita GDP*. Washington, DC: World Bank Group. https://data.worldbank.org/indicator/NY.GDP.PCAP.CD.

——. *World Development Indicators: School Enrolment, Primary, Private (% of Total Primary)*. Washington, DC: World Bank Group, 24 April 2024. https://data.worldbank.org/indicator/SE.PRM.PRIV.ZS.

3. Maternity Benefits: Some Women Are More Equal

Amin, Mohammed, and M. Asif Islam. 'The Impact of Paid Maternity Leave on Women's Employment: Evidence Using Firm Level Data from Developing Countries.' Global Indicators Group and the Middle East and North Africa Region. World Bank Group, 2022. https://documents1.worldbank.org/curated/en/099624009192215952/pdf/IDU0613dc8520b06604bc709b9604eb61253bea6.pdf.

Balasubramanian, P., and T. K. Sundari Ravindran. 'Pro-Poor Maternity Benefits and Rural Women.' *Economic and Political Weekly* 47, no. 25 (23 June 2012). https://www.epw.in/journal/2012/25/commentary/pro-poor-maternity-benefit-schemes-and-rural-women.html.

Drèze, Jean, Reetika Khera, and Anmol Somanchi. 'Maternity Entitlements: Women's Rights Derailed.' *Economic and Political Weekly* 56, no. 47 (20 November 2021).

Fallon, Kathleen, Alissa Mazar, and Liam Swiss. 'The Development Benefits of Maternity Leave.' *World Development* 96 (2017): 102–118. http://dx.doi.org/10.1016/j.worlddev.2017.03.001.

Gopal, M. Sai. 'KCR Kits Scheme Stalled in All Govt MCH Facilities in Hyderabad.' *Telangana Today*, 14 August 2024. https://telanganatoday.com/kcr-kits-scheme-stalled-in-all-govt-mch-facilities-in-hyderabad.

Government of India. *National Food Security Act*. New Delhi: Ministry of Law and Justice, 2013. https://nfsa.gov.in/portal/NFSA-Act.

International Institute for Population Sciences. *National Family Health Survey (NFHS-4): National Report*. Mumbai: International Institute for Population Sciences, 2017. https://dhsprogram.com/pubs/pdf/FR339/FR339.pdf.

——. *National Family Health Survey (NFHS-5): National Report*. Mumbai: International Institute for Population Sciences, 2022. https://dhsprogram.com/pubs/pdf/FR375/FR375.pdf.

Janayala, Srinivas. 'K. C. R. Kits: How Institutional Deliveries Rose by 22 Percent.' *The Indian Express*, 16 March 2020. https://indianexpress.com/article/governance/telangana-healthcare-reform-kcr-kits-how-institutional-deliveries-rose-by-22-per-cent-6316122/.

Jarvis, Alice-Azania. 'The Timeline: Maternity Leave.' *The Independent*, 22 October 2010. https://www.independent.co.uk/life-style/health-and-families/features/the-timeline-maternity-leave-2113236.html.

'KCR Kits Scheme: Over 13.29 Lakh People Benefited in Telangana.' *Telangana Today*, 19 September 2022. https://telanganatoday.com/kcr-kits-scheme-over-13-29-lakh-people-benefited-in-telangana

Khera, Reetika. 'Children's Development: Baby Steps in Odisha.' *Economic and Political Weekly* 50, no. 40 (3 October 2015).

Navarro-Rosenblatt, Deborah, and Maria-Luisa Garmendia. 'Maternity Leave and Its Impact on Breastfeeding: A Review of the Literature.' *Breastfeeding Medicine* 13, no. 9 (2018). https://www.liebertpub.com/doi/abs/10.1089/bfm.2018.0132.

Paikra, Vipul. 'Correction Queues Trip Up Maternity Benefit Applicants in Chhattisgarh.' *IndiaSpend*, 14 February 2020. https://www.indiaspend.com/correction-queues-trip-up-maternity-benefit-applicants-in-chhattisgarh.

Press Trust of India. 'Jharkhand Cabinet Approves Financial Assistance Scheme for 45 Lakh Women.' *Deccan Chronicle*, 28 June 2024. https://www.deccanchronicle.com/nation/politics/jharkhand-cabinet-approves-financial-assistance-scheme-for-45-lakh-women-1308553.

Sharma, Kanika. 'Domestic Work, Pregnancy and Women's Health in Rural India.' *The India Forum*, 16 September 2024. https://www.

theindiaforum.in/public-policy/pregnant-women-rural-india-are-overworked-home-thats-breaking-them.

Siegel, Mona. 'The Forgotten Origins of Paid Family Leave.' *The New York Times*, 29 November 2019. https://www.nytimes.com/2019/11/29/opinion/mothers-paid-family-leave.html.

Sinha, Dipa, Shikha Nehra, Sonal Matharu, Jasmeet Khanuja, and Vanita Leah Falcao. 'Realising Universal Maternity Entitlements: Lessons from Indira Gandhi Matritva Sahyog Yojana.' *Economic and Political Weekly* 51, no. 34 (20 August 2016). https://www.epw.in/system/files/pdf/2016_51/34/sali34200816dipasinha.pdf.

Taneja, Bhawna, and Indranil Roy Chowdhury. 'From Cash to Care: Impact of Conditional Cash Transfers on Continuum of Care for Maternal and Child Health in India.' *The Journal of Development Studies* (2025): 1–26. https://doi.org/10.1080/00220388.2025.2590453.

Tillin, Louise. *Making India Work*. New Delhi: Cambridge University Press, 2025.

4. Anganwadis: The Foundations of a Child's Future

Accountability Initiative. *Poshan Abhiyan, GOI 2020–21*. Budget Briefs 12, no. 3. 2021.

Centre for Equity Studies. *Progress of Children Under Six: Revisiting ICDS in the FOCUS Districts*. New Delhi: Centre for Equity Studies, 2016.

Drèze, Jean. 'New Evidence on Child Nutrition Calls for Radical Expansion of Child Development Services.' *The Indian Express*, 17 December 2020. https://indianexpress.com/article/opinion/columns/new-evidence-on-child-nutrition-calls-for-radical-expansion-of-child-development-services-7107810/.

——. 'Universalisation with Quality.' *Economic and Political Weekly* 41, no. 34 (26 August 2006).

Drèze, Jean, and Reetika Khera. 'Recent Social Security Initiatives in India.' *World Development* 98 (2017): 555–572. https://doi.org/10.1016/j.worlddev.2017.05.035.

Drèze, Jean, and Amartya Sen. *An Uncertain Glory: India and Its Contradictions*. Princeton: Princeton University Press, 2015.

Government of Bangladesh. *Bangladesh Demographic and Health Survey 2014*. National Institute of Population Research and Training. Dhaka: Ministry of Health and Family Welfare, 2016. https://dhsprogram.com/pubs/pdf/fr311/fr311.pdf.

Government of India. 'Increases in Wages of Anganwadi Workers.' *Rajya Sabha Unstarred Question No. 633*, 7 February 2024. https://sansad.in/getFile/annex/263/AU633.pdf?source=pqars.

_____. *India, National Multidimensional Poverty Index: A Progress Review 2023*, NITI Aayog. https://ophi.org.uk/sites/default/files/2024-03/India_National_MPI_2023.pdf.

_____. *POSHAN Abhiyan*. Web Archives. New Delhi: NITI Aayog, n.d. https://web.archive.org/web/20220121045457/https:/niti.gov.in/poshan-abhiyaan.

_____. 'Revision of Material Cost During 2022–23 under PM Poshan Scheme.' Department of School Education and Literacy. New Delhi: Ministry of Education, 7 October 2022. https://pmposhan.education.gov.in/Files/Cooking_Cost_Revision/Revision%20of%20Material%20Cost_letter%20dt.%2007.10.2022.pdf.

_____. 'Specially Designed Software to Help in Strengthening Service Delivery and Improving Nutrition Outcomes through Effective Monitoring and Timely Interventions in Poshan Abhiyan.' Press Information Bureau. New Delhi: Ministry of Women and Child Development, 25 June 2018. https://pib.gov.in/Pressreleaseshare.aspx?PRID=1536456.

Heckman, James. 'Skill Formation and the Economics of Investing in Disadvantaged Children.' *Science* 312 (2006).

Hossain, Naomi. *The Aid Lab: Understanding Bangladesh's Unexpected Success*. New Delhi: Oxford University Press, 2017.

Impact4Nutrition. 'Supporting Private Sector to Promote Importance of Health and Nutrition.' *Impact4Nutrition*, n.d. https://www.i4n.in/.

International Institute for Population Sciences. *National Family Health Survey (NFHS-2) 1998–99: National Report*. Mumbai: International Institute for Population Sciences, 2000. https://www.dhsprogram.com/pubs/pdf/FRIND2/FRIND2.pdf.

_____. *National Family Health Survey (NFHS-3) 2005–06: National Report*. Mumbai: International Institute for Population Sciences,

2007. https://www.dhsprogram.com/pubs/pdf/frind3/frind3-vol1andvol2.pdf.

———. *National Family Health Survey (NFHS-4) 2015–16: National Report.* Mumbai: International Institute for Population Sciences, 2017. https://dhsprogram.com/pubs/pdf/FR339/FR339.pdf.

———. *National Family Health Survey (NFHS-5) 2019–21: National Report.* Mumbai: International Institute for Population Sciences, 2022. https://dhsprogram.com/pubs/pdf/FR375/FR375.pdf.

Jain, Monika. 'India's Struggle Against Malnutrition—Is the ICDS Programme the Answer?' *World Development* 67 (2015): 72–89. https://doi.org/10.1016/j.worlddev.2014.10.006.

Khanam, Mariam, and Nahid Akhtar Jahan. 'Determinants of Vaccination Coverage Among Children Aged 12–23 Months in Bangladesh: A Comparison Between High and Lower Performing Divisions.' *International Journal of Paediatrics* 2024 (15 May 2024). https://doi.org/10.1155/2024/7787593.

Kabeer, Naila. *Renotiating Patriarchy, Gender, Agency and the Bangladesh Paradox.* 2024. LSE Press.

Khera, Reetika. 'Children's Development: Baby Steps in Odisha.' *Economic and Political Weekly* 50, no. 40 (3 October 2015). https://www.epw.in/journal/2015/40/special-articles/childrens-development.html.

———. 'Hunger Index May Have Limitations—But There's More Than Enough Proof That India Has a Problem.' *The Wire*, 26 October 2021. https://thewire.in/rights/global-hunger-index-india-limitations-evidence.

Nandi, Arindam, Jere Behrman, and Ramanan Laxminarayan. 'The Impact of a National Early Childhood Development Program on Future Schooling Attainment: Evidence from Integrated Child Development Services in India.' *Economic Development and Cultural Change* 69, no. 1 (2020).

Press Trust of India. 'PM Modi Announces Hike in Incentives for ASHA and Anganwadi Workers.' *NDTV*, 11 September 2018. https://www.ndtv.com/india-news/pm-modi-announces-hike-in-incentives-of-asha-Anganwadi-workers-1914874.

Sinha, Dipa, Mohini Gupta, and Diksha Shriyan. 'High Risk Without

Recognition: Challenges Faced by Female Frontline Workers.' *Economic and Political Weekly* 56, no. 19 (8 May 2021).
'State to Start ICDS—Common Application Software from December.' *The Hindu*, 26 October 2019. https://www.thehindu.com/news/national/karnataka/state-to-start-icds-common-application-software-from-december/article29802377.ece.
United Nations International Children's Emergency Fund. 'Private Sector Participation.' *UNICEF India*, n.d. https://www.unicef.org/india/our-partners/private-sector-partnerships.
'World of Anganwadis, Jacha-Bacha Survey 2019.' YouTube video, *Hard Work No Pay*, 11 September 2019. https://youtu.be/RsRd2k4cARE?si=lKbFERrQL1Yh6InO.
World Bank. *World Development Indicators*. World Bank, n.d. https://databank.worldbank.org/reports.aspx?source=2&country=ARE#.

5. Mid-Day Meal: Much More Than Food

Afridi, Farzana. 'Child Welfare Programs and Child Nutrition: Evidence from a Mandated School Meal Program in India.' *Journal of Development Economics* 92 (2010).
———. 'The Impact of School Meals on Student Participation in Rural India.' *Journal of Development Studies* 47 (2011).
Afridi, Farzana, Bidisha Barooah, and Rohini Somanathan. 'School Meals and Classroom Effort: Evidence from India.' Working Paper. International Growth Centre, London School of Economics, 2013.
Akshaya Patra Foundation. *Tapestry: Annual Report 2024–25*. 2025. https://www.akshayapatra.org/includefiles/financialreports/Annual_Report_24-25_Tapestry_web.pdf.
'Akshaya Patra Reconstitutes Board of Trustees.' *The Hindu*, 17 November 2020. https://www.thehindu.com/news/national/karnataka/akshaya-patra-reconstitutes-board-of-trustees/article33109644.ece.
Bhardwaj, Kritika. 'India Is Enrolling Infants and Children in Aadhaar—But What About Their Consent?' *Scroll.in*, 19 September 2016. https://scroll.in/article/816815/india-is-enrolling-infants-and-children-in-aadhaar-but-what-about-their-consent.

CAfCu Media. 'School Lunches in Japan—It's Not Just About Eating.' YouTube video, 19 April 2015. https://www.youtube.com/watch?v=hL5mKE4e4uU.

Chakraborty, Tanika, and Rajshri Jayaraman. 'School Feeding and Learning Achievement: Evidence from India's Midday Meal Program.' *Journal of Development Economics* 139 (2019): 249–265. https://doi.org/10.1016/j.jdeveco.2018.10.011.

Chawla, Prabhu. 'MGR's Midday Nutritious Meal Scheme: A Shrewd Political Move?' *India Today*, 10 November 1982. https://www.indiatoday.in/magazine/special-report/story/19821115-mgr-midday-nutritious-meal-scheme-a-shrewd-political-move-772378-2013-08-01.

Government of India. 'Discontinuation of Reimbursement of Additional Expenditure Incurred for Purchase of Unsubsidised LPG Cylinders w.e.f. 1 April 2015 under the Mid-Day Meal Scheme.' Department of School Education and Literacy, Ministry of Human Resource Development, 7 August 2015. https://pmposhan.education.gov.in/Files/OrderCirculars/2015/Discontinuation_Reimbursement_for%20LPG-cylinders.pdf.

———. 'Gazette of India—Notification School Education and Literacy Section.' New Delhi: Ministry of Human Resource Development, 28 February 2017. https://pmposhan.education.gov.in/Files/Aadhar/Aadhar_mdm.pdf.

———. *Performance Audit of the Mid-Day Meal Scheme (2009–10 to 2013–14)*. Report No. 36 of 2015. New Delhi: Comptroller and Auditor General of India, 2015.

———. *PM POSHAN Guidelines*. Department of School Education and Literacy, 2022.

Jayaraman, Rajshri, and David Simroth. 'The Impact of School Lunches on Primary School Enrolment: Evidence from India's Midday Meal Scheme.' *Scandinavian Journal of Economics* 117, no. 4 (2015): 1176–1203.

Khera, Reetika. *Aadhaar Se Kiska Uddhar*. New Delhi: Rajkamal Prakashan, 2019.

———. 'Demand for Eggs in Mid-Day Meal (MDM), Chhattisgarh.' YouTube video, 11 July 2019. https://www.youtube.com/

watch?v=wpb9-XB08pI&list=PLHq_Bg14X9JKD740BPPlY3hL6g9nWo8iB&index=4.

———. 'Eggs in Mid-Day Meal (MDM), Chhattisgarh.' YouTube video, 11 July 2019. https://www.youtube.com/watch?v=Iic2LNgggcQ&list=PLHq_Bg14X9JKD740BPPlY3hL 6g9nWo8iB&index=6.

'Nine Activists Demand Enquiry into Akshaya Patra.' *The Hindu*, 24 November 2020. https://www.thehindu.com/news/national/karnataka/nine-activists-demand-enquiry-into-akshaya-patra/article33172138.ece.

Press Trust of India. 'Government Relaxes Aadhaar Norm, Makes Other IDs Acceptable for Subsidy Schemes.' *News18*, 7 March 2017. https://www.news18.com/news/india/govt-relaxes-aadhaar-norm-makes-other-ids-acceptable-for-subsidy-schemes-1357380.html.

Right to Food Campaign. 'Order of the Supreme Court, 20 April 2004.' *Right to Food Campaign*, n.d. https://www.righttofoodcampaign.in/legal-action/supreme-court-orders.

———. *Supreme Court Orders on the Right to Food: A Tool for Action.* Supreme Court of India, October 2005.

Samson, Meera, Claire Noronha, and Anuradha De. *Towards More Benefits from Delhi's Midday Meal Scheme*. New Delhi: CORD—Collaborative Research and Dissemination, 2007. https://cordindia.com/wp-content/uploads/2020/04/Midday.pdf.

Singh, Abhijeet, Albert Park, and Stefan Dercon. 'School Meals as a Safety Net: An Evaluation of the Midday Meal Scheme in India.' *Economic Development and Cultural Change* 62 (2014).

'Should Every Schoolchild Eat Free?' *The Economist*, 1 September 2022. https://www.economist.com/international/2022/09/01/should-every-schoolchild-eat-free.

Thorat, Sukhadeo, and Joel Lee. 'Caste Discrimination and Food Security Programmes.' *Economic and Political Weekly* 40, no. 39 (24 September 2005). https://www.epw.in/journal/2005/39/commentary/caste-discrimination-and-food-security-programmes.html.

Whittaker, Lana. 'Are Akshaya Patra Kitchens What They Are Made Out to Be?' *The Wire*, 1 August 2015. https://thewire.in/education/are-akshaya-patra-kitchens-what-they-are-made-out-to-be.

World Population Review. 'School Lunches in Other Countries 2024.' 2024. https://worldpopulationreview.com/country-rankings/school-lunches-in-other-countries.

Yadav, Monika. 'Mid-Day Meal Scheme: Are Corruption Claims Exaggerated?' *Ideas for India*, 31 July 2017. https://www.ideasforindia.in/topics/governance/midday-meals-scheme-are-corruption-claims-exaggerated.html.

6. Public Distribution System: Beyond Foodgrains

Agarwal, Sarthak, and Archana Agnihotri. 'Food Security for Interstate Migrants: An Empirical Analysis of the ONORC.' *Economic and Political Weekly* 57, no. 51 (17 December 2022). https://www.epw.in/journal/2022/51/commentary/food-security-interstate-migrants.html.

Drèze, Jean. *Sense and Solidarity: Jholawala Economics for Everyone.* New Delhi: Permanent Black, 2017.

Drèze, Jean, and Reetika Khera. 'Chhattisgarh Shows the Way.' *The Hindu*, 28 November 2010. https://www.thehindu.com/features/magazine/Chhattisgarh-shows-the-way/article15685530.ece.

———. 'Khady Suraksha: Sudhar Sakte Hain Phisaddi Rajyon Ke Bhi Halaat.' *Outlook Hindi*, 21 August 2015. https://outlookhindi.com/view/thought-for-food-by-jean-Drèze-and-reetika-khera-3818.

———. 'Rural Poverty and the PDS.' *Economic and Political Weekly* 48, no. 45–46 (16 November 2013).

Drèze, Jean, Nazar Khalid, Reetika Khera, and Anmol Somanchi. 'Aadhaar and Food Security in Jharkhand—Pain without Gain?' *Economic and Political Weekly* 52, no. 50 (16 December 2017). https://www.epw.in/journal/2017/50/special-articles/aadhaar-and-food-security-jharkhand.html.

Drèze, Jean, and Vipul Paikra. 'How Loopholes in the Aadhaar-Enabled System Are Putting Poor People at Risk of Being Swindled.' *The Indian Express*, 5 October 2021. https://indianexpress.com/article/opinion/columns/aadhaar-enabled-payment-system-7552163/.

George, Siddharth, and Arvind Subramanian. 'Transforming Sight against Poverty in India.' *The New York Times*, 22 July 2015.

Government of India. *Report of the High Level Committee on Reorienting the Role and Restructuring of Food Corporation of India*. New Delhi: Ministry of Consumer Affairs, Food and Public Distribution, January 2015.

Gupta, Rhythm, Yasoob Haider, and Payoj Jain. 'Chhattisgarh's Food ATMs: Portable Benefits Minus Biometrics.' *India Together*, 15 September 2014. https://indiatogether.org/core-pds-smart-system-in-raipur-chhattisgarh-food-security-portability-government.

Jha, Shikha, and Stephen Howes. 'Urban Bias in the Indian Public Distribution System.' *Economic and Political Weekly* 27, no. 19 (9 May 1992).

Khera, Reetika. 'Cash vs. In-Kind Transfers: Indian Data Meets Theory.' *Food Policy* 46 (2014): 116–128. https://doi.org/10.1016/j.foodpol.2014.03.009.

———. 'Doorstep Delivery of Ration Sounds Like a Good Idea—But It Actually Raises Many Hard Questions.' *Scroll.in*, 12 June 2021. https://scroll.in/article/997300/doorstep-delivery-of-rations-sounds-like-a-good-idea-but-it-actually-raises-many-hard-questions.

———. 'Impact of Aadhaar on Welfare Programmes.' *Economic and Political Weekly* 52, no. 50 (16 December 2017). https://www.epw.in/journal/2017/50/special-articles/impact-aadhaar-welfare-programmes.html.

———. 'Impact of the Food Security Act on Public Distribution System Leakages.' *Ideas for India*, 3 October 2024. https://www.ideasforindia.in/topics/poverty-inequality/impact-of-the-food-security-act-on-public-distribution-system.html.

———. 'Modi Government's One Nation One Ration Is an Attempt to Deflect Attention from Actual Solutions.' *Scroll.in*, 17 June 2020. https://scroll.in/article/964761/modi-governments-one-nation-one-ration-is-an-attempt-to-deflect-attention-from-actual-solutions.

———. 'Nakad Hastantran Se Kya Ho Paayegi Khady Suraksha?' *Amar Ujala*, 26 April 2015. https://www.amarujala.com/columns/opinion/will-cash-transfer-would-give-food-security-hindi.

———. 'Revival of the Public Distribution System: Evidence and Explanations.' *Economic and Political Weekly* 46, no. 44–45

(5 November 2011). https://www.epw.in/journal/2011/44-45/special-articles/revival-public-distribution-system-evidence-and-explanations.

Khera, Reetika, and Anmol Somanchi. 'A Review of the Coverage of PDS.' *Ideas for India*, 19 August 2020. https://www.ideasforindia.in/topics/poverty-inequality/a-review-of-the-coverage-of-pds.html.

LibTech. *Length of the Last Mile: Delays and Hurdles in NREGA Payments*. 2020. https://libtech.in/wp-content/uploads/2020/11/LastMile_ReportLayout_vfinal.pdf.

Parthasarathy, Anognya. 'Jharkhand Pokes Holes in Modi's Claims on Digital Service Delivery.' *The Wire*, 1 February 2019. https://thewire.in/government/jharkhand-survey-pokes-holes-in-modis-claims-on-digital-service-delivery.

Priya, Aditi, and Shagun. 'Even in Delhi, Basing PDS on Aadhaar Is Denying Many the Right to Food.' *The Wire*, 25 October 2016. https://thewire.in/rights/right-to-food-how-aadhaar-in-pds-is-denying-rights.

Ranjan, Akash. '(Not) Direct, (No) Benefits (Cost) Transfer in Jharkhand.' *The Wire*, 23 January 2018. https://thewire.in/banking/not-direct-no-benefits-cost-transfer-jharkhand.

Swaminathan, Madhura. *Weakening Welfare: The Public Distribution of Food in India*. New Delhi: LeftWord Books, 2000.

Tumbe, Chinmay, and Rahul Jha. 'One Nation, One Ration, Limited Interstate Traction: Migration and PDS Portability in India.' *Urbanisation* 9, no. 1 (7 April 2024). https://journals.sagepub.com/doi/10.1177/24557471241237098.

7. NREGA: Challenges to Realising its Vision

Adhikari, Anindita, and Kartika Bhatia. 'NREGA Wage Payments: Can We Bank on the Banks?' *Economic and Political Weekly* 45, no. 1 (2 January 2010). https://www.epw.in/journal/2010/01/insight/nrega-wage-payments-can-we-bank-banks.html.

Barrett, Christopher, and Yanyan Liu. 'Heterogeneous Pro-Poor Targeting in the National Rural Employment Guarantee Scheme.' *Economic and Political Weekly* 48, no. 10 (9 March 2013). https://www.epw.in/journal/2013/10/special-articles/heterogeneous-pro-poor-targeting-national-rural-employment.

Berg, Erlend, Sambit Bhattacharya, D. Rajasekhar, and R. Manjula. 'Can Public Works Increase Equilibrium Wages? Evidence from India's National Rural Employment Guarantee.' *World Development* 103 (2018): 239–254. https://doi.org/10.1016/j.worlddev.2017.10.027.

Bhaskar, Anjor, Sunil Gupta, and Pankaj Yadav. 'Well Worth the Effort: Value of MGNREGA Wells in Jharkhand.' *Economic and Political Weekly* 51, no. 19 (7 May 2016). https://www.epw.in/journal/2016/19/special-articles/well-worth-effort.html.

Buddha, Chakradhar, and Lavanya Tamang. 'MGNREGA's Attendance App: A Tool for Transparency or Exclusion?' *Economic and Political Weekly* 59, no. 48 (30 November 2024).

Cooper, Emilia, Jean Drèze, and Pavlina Tcherneva. *MGNREGA Bibliography*. 2024. www.jobguarantee.org/resources/mgnrega-bibliography/.

Dhorajiwala, Sakina, Niklas Wagner, and Jean Drèze. 'A Bridge to Nowhere.' *The Hindu*, 27 March 2019. https://www.thehindu.com/opinion/lead/a-bridge-to-nowhere/article62110043.ece.

Drèze, Jean, and Reetika Khera. 'Employment Guarantee: Repeal in Lieu of Repair.' *Economic and Political Weekly* 56, no. 15 (11 April 2021): 23–26.

Drèze, Jean, and Nikhila Nair. 'Mango Plantation: A Reminder of How NREGA Can Tremendously Contribute to Rural Development.' *The Economic Times*, 13 March 2023. https://economictimes.indiatimes.com/opinion/et-commentary/mango-plantation-a-reminder-of-how-nrega-can-tremendously-contribute-to-rural-development/articleshow/98613894.cms.

Gupta, Aashish, Ankit Kumar, and Ankita Aggarwal. 'Evaluation of NREGA Wells in Jharkhand.' *Economic and Political Weekly* 47, no. 35 (1 September 2012). https://www.epw.in/journal/2012/35/commentary/evaluation-nrega-wells-jharkhand.html.

Imbert, Clément, and John Papp. 'Labour Market Effects of Social Programs: Evidence from India's Employment Guarantee.' *American Economic Journal: Applied Economics* 7, no. 2 (2 April 2015). https://www.aeaweb.org/articles?id=10.1257/app.20130401.

Khera, Reetika, ed. *Battle for Employment Guarantee*. New Delhi: Oxford University Press, 2011.

———. 'For NREGA, Tamil Nadu Is the Only Hope.' *NDTV*, 2 February 2016. https://www.ndtv.com/opinion/for-nrega-tamil-nadu-is-the-only-hope-1272338.

———. 'Nice to See NREGA Trending, but Urgent Fixes Are Required.' *NDTV*, 3 February 2017. https://www.ndtv.com/opinion/nice-to-see-nrega-trending-but-urgent-fixes-needed-1655627.

———. 'Surveillance Apps: Snake Oil for Accountability.' *The Hindu*, 8 December 2025. https://www.thehindu.com/opinion/lead/surveillance-apps-in-welfare-snake-oil-for-accountability/article70369384.ece.

———. 'The Whys and Whats of NREGA.' *IndiaSpend*, 4 November 2014. https://www.indiaspend.com/the-whys-and-whats-of-indias-rural-jobs-scheme-99284.

Khera, Reetika, and Nandini Nayak. 'Women Workers and Perceptions of the National Rural Employment Guarantee Act.' *Economic and Political Weekly* 44, no. 43 (24 October 2009). https://www.epw.in/journal/2009/43/special-articles/women-workers-and-perceptions-national-rural-employment-guarantee.

LibTech. *Length of the Last Mile: Delays and Hurdles in NREGA Payments*. 2020. https://libtech.in/wp-content/uploads/2020/11/LastMile_ReportLayout_vfinal.pdf.

Muralidharan, Karthik, Paul Niehaus, and Sandip Sukhtankar. 'General Equilibrium Effects of Improving Public Employment Programs: Experimental Evidence from India.' *Econometrica* (2023). https://doi.org/10.3982/ECTA18181.

Narayanan, Rajendran, and Chakradhar Buddha. 'The Right to Work Deleted.' *The Hindu*, 28 November 2024. https://www.thehindu.com/news/national/the-right-to-work-deleted/article68920153.ece.

Narayanan, Sudha. 'The Continuing Relevance of NREGA.' *The India Forum*, 17 March 2020. https://www.theindiaforum.in/article/continuing-relevance-mgnrega.

'Payment Denied for NREGA Workers without UIDAI Cards in Jharkhand.' *The Hindu*, 4 September 2021. https://www.

thehindu.com/news/national/payment-denied-for-nrega-workers-without-uidai-cards-in-jharkhand/article5674969.ece.
Ranaware, Krushna, Ashwini Kulkarni, Sudha Narayanan, and Upasak Das. 'MGNREGA Works and Their Impacts: A Study of Maharashtra.' *Economic and Political Weekly* 51, no. 13 (28 March 2015). https://www.epw.in/journal/2015/13/special-articles/mgnrega-works-and-their-impacts.html.

8. Social Security Pensions: Contingency Care

Arora, Santlal, and Amitabh Kundu. 'Atal Pension Yojana: A Critical Appraisal.' *Economic and Political Weekly* 53, no. 19 (12 May 2018). https://www.epw.in/journal/2018/19/notes/atal-pension-yojana.html.
Chopra, Saloni, and Jessica Pudusserry. 'Social Security Pensions in India: An Assessment.' *Economic and Political Weekly* 49, no. 19 (10 May 2014). https://www.epw.in/journal/2014/19/notes/social-security-pensions-india.html.
Comptroller and Auditor General of India. *Performance Audit of National Social Assistance Programme*. Report No. 10. New Delhi, 2023. https://cag.gov.in/uploads/download_audit_report/2023/Report-No.-10-of-2023_NSAP_English_PDF-A-064d229f832dad7.55068084.pdf.
Drèze, Jean, and Esther Duflo. 'The Future of Old Times in India.' *The Hindu*, 15 September 2022. https://www.thehindu.com/opinion/lead/the-future-of-old-times-in-india/article65891365.ece.
Dutta, Pooja, Rinku Murgai, and Stephen Howes. 'Small But Effective: India's Targeted Unconditional Cash Transfers.' *Economic and Political Weekly* 45, no. 52 (25 September 2010). https://www.epw.in/journal/2010/52/special-articles/small-effective-indias-targeted-unconditional-cash-transfers.html.
Employees' Provident Fund Organisation. 'Pensioner Dashboard.' Accessed 10 May 2026. https://www.mis.epfindia.gov.in/ChartDashboard/pensioner.
Gairola, Hemant. 'Banks Have Been Charging Customers for Government Insurance They Never Wanted.' *The Wire*, 12 September 2022. https://thewire.in/banking/banks-have-been-charging-customers-for-government-insurance-they-never-wanted.

Government of India. *Annual Report 2022–23*. Department of Financial Services. New Delhi: Ministry of Finance, 2023.

———. *Budget at a Glance 2016–17*. New Delhi: Ministry of Finance, 2016. https://www.indiabudget.gov.in/budget2016-2017/ub2016-17/bag/bag10.pdf.

———. *Proposal for Comprehensive National Social Assistance Programme: Report of the Task Force*. New Delhi: Ministry of Rural Development, 2013. https://nsap.nic.in/nsap/Report_Task_Force_Comprehensive_NSAP.pdf.

———. *Pradhan Mantri Maandhan Pension Yojana Dashboard*. New Delhi: Ministry of Labour and Employment, 2024. https://maandhan.in/maandhan/summary.

Gupta, Aashish. 'Old-Age Pension Scheme in Jharkhand and Chhattisgarh.' *Economic and Political Weekly* 48, no. 34 (24 August 2013). https://www.epw.in/journal/2013/34/special-articles/old-age-pension-scheme-jharkhand-and-chhattisgarh.html.

Kaushal, Neeraj. 'How Pensions Affect Elderly Labour Supply and Wellbeing: Evidence from India.' *World Development* 56 (2014): 214–225. https://www.sciencedirect.com/science/article/pii/S0305750X13002416.

Khera, Reetika. 'Lifeline for Crores of Elderly, but Ignored by the Centre: The NSAP Is a Pension Scheme of Delays.' *The Wire*, 12 May 2024. https://thewire.in/government/national-social-assistance-programme-nsap-central-scheme.

Lalwani, Vijeta. 'Budget 2019: New Pension Scheme a "Repackaged Version" of Atal Pension Yojana.' *Scroll.in*, 1 February 2019. https://scroll.in/article/911708/budget-2019-new-pension-scheme-a-repackaged-version-of-atal-pension-yojana.

Malhotra, Rishabh, and Anmol Somanchi. 'Pension Tension: Aadhaar and Social Assistance in Jharkhand.' *Economic and Political Weekly* 53, no. 36 (8 September 2018). https://www.epw.in/journal/2018/36/insight/pension-tension.html.

Press Information Bureau. 'Centralised Pension Payments System Fully Rolled Out in All Regional Offices of EPFO across India.' 3 January 2025. https://www.pib.gov.in/PressReleseDetailm.aspx?PRID=2089875&reg=3&lang=2.

Rajan, S. Irudaya, and U. S. Mishra. 'An Ageing India: The Magnitude and the Multitude.' *The Hindu*, 18 June 2024. https://www.thehindu.com/opinion/op-ed/an-ageing-india-the-magnitude-and-the-multitude/article68299826.ece.

Wani, Samreen. 'India Spends More Than 3% of GDP on Government Pensions; States' Burden Growing.' *Business Standard*, 30 August 2024. https://www.business-standard.com/economy/news/india-spends-more-than-3-of-gdp-on-govt-pensions-states-burden-growing-124083000405_1.html.

9. Public Canteens: An Idea Whose Time Has Come

Finco, Marcus, Fernanda Abadio Finco, and A. F. S. Coelho. 'An Assessment of the Brazilian Popular Restaurant Program as an Integrated Action for Food Security and Health Promotion.' 2012. https://www.researchgate.net/publication/289761154_An_assessment_of_the_Brazilian_popular_restaurant_program_as_an_integrated_action_for_food_security_and_health_promotion.

Government of Odisha. 'After Empowering Lakhs of Women, Odisha Government Has Handed over the Management of All 157 Aahar Kendras to Mission Shakti SHGs as They Resume Operations.' Bhubaneswar: Housing and Urban Affairs Department, 2021. https://odisha.gov.in/news/after-empowering-lakhs-women-odisha-govt-has-handed-over-management-all-157-aahaar-kendras.

Government of West Bengal. *Maa Canteen*. State Urban Development Agency. Kolkata: Urban Development and Municipal Affairs Department, n.d. https://sudawb.org/Program-Details/21.

Gummadi, Sridevi, and Amalendu Jyotishi. *Food for All: The Role of Urban Canteens in Nourishing Communities*. Bangalore: Foundation to Aid Industrial Recovery, 2025.

'Not Happy with Centre's Affidavit, Supreme Court Gives It Three More Weeks to Frame Community Kitchens Policy.' *The Indian Express*, 16 November 2021. https://indianexpress.com/article/india/supreme-court-gives-it-3-more-weeks-to-frame-community-kitchen-policy-7625781/.

Jeevika. *Jeevika's Newsletter*. Issue 52. September 2021. https://www.brlps.in/UplodFiles/Files/Sep%20181121.pdf.

Khera, Reetika. 'Community Kitchens: An Idea Whose Time Has Come.' *Scroll.in*, 22 November 2016. https://scroll.in/article/801742/community-kitchens-an-idea-whose-time-has-come.

——. 'Why Are Government Canteens Important When 80 Crore People Get Free Grains?' *The India Forum*, 1 July 2024. https://www.theindiaforum.in/public-policy/why-are-government-canteens-important-when-80-crore-people-get-free-grains.

Rajendran, S. 'Amma Unavagam of Tamil Nadu: Panacea for Urban Food Security?' *Economic and Political Weekly* 48, no. 50 (14 December 2013). https://www.epw.in/journal/2013/50/commentary/amma-unavagams-tamil-nadu.html.

Sarkar, Arpita, and Anjor Bhaskar. 'Jharkhand's Community Kitchens: Making a Mockery of Food Security?' *Down to Earth*, 26 September 2019. https://www.downtoearth.org.in/food/jharkhand-s-community-kitchens-making-a-mockery-of-food-security-66962.

'State Women SHGs Running Aahar Centres with Success.' *Orissa Post*, 12 April 2021. https://www.orissapost.com/state-women-shgs-running-aahar-centres-with-success/.

10. COVID-19: Neglect of Health and Education Exposed

Adhikari, Anindita, Rajendran Narayanan, Sakina Dhorajiwala, and Seema Mundoli. '21 Days and Counting: Covid-19 Lockdown, Migrant Workers and Beneficiaries of Welfare Measures in India.' Technical Report. Stranded Workers Action Network, 2020. https://publications.azimpremjiuniversity.edu.in/2272/1/lockdown_and_distress_report_by_stranded_workers_action_network-2.pdf.

Adhikari, Anindita, Navmee Goregaonkar, Rajendran Narayanan, Nishant Panicker, Nithya Ramamoorthy. 'Manufactured Maladies: Lives and Livelihoods of Migrant Workers During Covid-19 Lockdown in India.' *Indian Journal of Labour Economics* 63 (21 October 2020). https://link.springer.com/content/pdf/10.1007/s41027-020-00282-x.pdf.

Anand, Ishan, and Anjana Thampi. 'Recent Trends in Wealth Inequality in India.' *Economic and Political Weekly* 51, no.

50 (10 December 2016). https://www.epw.in/journal/2016/50/special-articles/recent-trends-wealth-inequality-india.html.

Arrow, Kenneth. 'Uncertainty and the Welfare Economics of Medical Care.' *American Economic Review* 53, no. 5 (1963). https://assets.aeaweb.org/asset-server/files/9442.pdf.

Banerjee, Rukmini, and Wilima Wadhwa. 'Covid-19 and Global Education: Evidence from India.' In *Covid-19 and Global Education*, chap. 3.2. World Scientific Publishing Company, 2023. https://asercentre.org/wp-content/uploads/2022/12/covid-19-and-global-education_RB_WW.pdf.

Barnagarwala, Tabassum. 'In India, over 40% Districts Still Don't Have a Single RT-PCR Lab for Covid-19 Testing.' *Scroll.in*, 10 August 2021. https://scroll.in/article/1002314/in-india-over-40-districts-still-dont-have-a-single-rt-pcr-lab-for-covid-19-testing.

Chakravarty, Ipsita. 'Three States Take over Private Hospitals: What Does the Fine Print Say?' *Scroll.in*, 30 March 2020. https://scroll.in/article/957556/coronavirus-three-states-take-over-private-hospitals-what-does-the-fine-print-say.

Chaudhary, Angshuman. 'Modi Government Exported Vaccines to Boost Its Global Image Amid Covid-19—But at What Cost?' *Scroll.in*, 1 May 2021. https://scroll.in/article/993293/modi-government-exported-vaccines-to-boost-its-global-image-amidst-covid-19-but-at-what-cost.

'Coronavirus Fears Are Making Indians Boycott, Evict and Threaten Their Neighbours.' *Scroll.in*, 25 March 2020. https://scroll.in/article/957149/as-people-around-india-are-shamed-for-exposure-to-virus-experts-warn-this-will-hurt-war-on-covid-19.

Daniyal, Shoaib. 'Why Are Indians Running Away from Isolation Wards?' *Scroll.in*, 12 March 2020. https://scroll.in/pulse/956280/is-indians-lack-of-trust-in-public-healthcare-hurting-efforts-to-battle-coronavirus.

Drèze, Jean, Nirali Bakhla, Reetika Khera, and Vipul Paikra. *Taalim Par Tala: Schooli Shiksha Par Aapaat Report.* 6 September 2021. https://roadscholarz.net/wp-content/uploads/2021/09/Hindi.pdf.

Drèze, Jean, Reetika Khera and Rishabh Malhotra. 'Health Checkup: The Changing State of Health Centres in North India', *Economic and Political Weekly* 59, no. 8 (24 February 2024).

Duggal, Ravi, and Shailendra Kumar Hooda. 'Covid-19, Health Insurance and Access to Healthcare.' *Economic and Political Weekly* 56, no. 31 (31 July 2021). https://www.epw.in/journal/2021/31/commentary/covid-19-health-insurance-and-access-healthcare.html.

Government of India. *Economic Survey 2020–21*. Department of Economic Affairs. New Delhi: Ministry of Finance, 2021.

———. *Key Indicators of Social Consumption in India: Health, NSS 75th Round (July 2017–June 2018)*. New Delhi: Ministry of Statistics and Programme Implementation.

———. *Rajya Sabha Unstarred Question No. 621*. Department of Health and Family Welfare. New Delhi: Ministry of Health and Family Welfare, 2023. https://sansad.in/getFile/annex/260/AU621.pdf?source=pqars.

———. *Unified District Information System for Education (UDISE+) 2021–22*. Department of School Education and Literacy. New Delhi: Ministry of Education, 2022. https://www.education.gov.in/sites/upload_files/mhrd/files/statistics-new/udise_21_22.pdf.

Heckman, James. 'Skill Formation and the Economics of Investing in Disadvantaged Children.' *Science* 312 (2006).

International Institute for Population Sciences. *National Family Health Survey (NFHS-3): National Report*. Mumbai: International Institute for Population Sciences, 2007. https://www.dhsprogram.com/pubs/pdf/frind3/frind3-vol1andvol2.pdf.

———. *National Family Health Survey (NFHS-4): National Report*. Mumbai: International Institute for Population Sciences, 2017. https://dhsprogram.com/pubs/pdf/FR339/FR339.pdf.

———. *National Family Health Survey (NFHS-5): National Report*. Mumbai: International Institute for Population Sciences, 2022. https://dhsprogram.com/pubs/pdf/FR375/FR375.pdf.

Jain, Yogesh, and Sarah Nabiya (ed.). *Covid-19: A View from the Margins*. New Delhi: Manohar, 2022.

Johari, Aarefa. 'Coronavirus Delays: Why India's Health Workers Are Still Facing Shortages of Safety Gear.' *Scroll.in*, 21 April 2020. https://scroll.in/article/959764/coronavirus-delays-why-indias-health-workers-are-still-facing-shortages-of-safety-gear.

———. 'India's Focus on Coronavirus Leaves TB and HIV Patients Adrift.' *Scroll.in*, 7 April 2020. https://scroll.in/article/958400/invisible-crisis-tb-and-hiv-patients-left-adrift-in-indias-focus-on-coronavirus.

———. 'Investigation: Crucial Coronavirus Gear Supply Clouded by Allegations of Government "Malintention".' *Scroll.in*, 2 March 2020. https://scroll.in/article/956866/investigation-crucial-coronavirus-gear-supply-clouded-by-allegations-of-government-malintention.

———. '"Not Much We Can Do to Keep Ourselves Safe": Fear Grips Mumbai's Slums as Covid-19 Cases Rise.' *Scroll.in*, 1 April 2020. https://scroll.in/article/957843/not-much-we-can-do-to-keep-ourselves-safe-fear-grips-mumbais-slums-as-covid-19-cases-rise.

———. 'Why Is Gujarat Forcing Hospitals to Only Accept Covid-19 Patients Coming through 108 Ambulances?' *Scroll.in*, 26 April 2021. https://scroll.in/article/993285/why-is-gujarat-forcing-hospitals-to-only-accept-covid-19-patients-coming-through-108-ambulances.

Kang, Gagandeep, Shahid Jameel, T. Sundararaman, Satyajit Rath, Vineeta Bal, T. R. Govindarajan, et al. 'Expanding Vaccine Production.' *Economic and Political Weekly* 56, no. 23 (5 June 2021). https://www.epw.in/journal/2021/23/letters/expanding-vaccine-production.html.

Kulkarni, Ashish, and Murali Neelakantan. 'India's New Vaccine Policy Makes Welcome Improvements—But Big Questions Still Remain.' *Scroll.in*, 11 June 2021. https://scroll.in/article/997231/indias-new-vaccine-policy-makes-welcome-improvements-but-big-questions-still-remain.

Lalwani, Vijeta. 'Coronavirus: How Do I Reach a Hospital? Cancer and Kidney Patients Worry about 21-Day Lockdown.' *Scroll.in*, 25 March 2020. https://scroll.in/article/957108/how-do-i-reach-a-hospital-cancer-patients-ask-as-21-day-lockdown-looms-ahead.

Mervosh, Sarah, Claire Cain Miller, and Francesca Paris. 'What the Data Says about Pandemic School Closures, Four Years Later.' *The New York Times*, 18 March 2024. https://www.nytimes.com/2024/03/18/upshot/pandemic-school-closures-data.html.

Nair, Smita. 'Pandemic, Distress, a Broken Phone: How a Family in Goa Lost Their 16-Year-Old Son.' *The Indian Express*, 23 October 2020. https://indianexpress.com/article/india/pandemic-distress-a-broken-phone-how-a-family-in-goa-lost-their-16-year-old-son-6847026/.

Oxfam India. *Status Report on Education During the Pandemic: Government and Private Schools*. 2020. https://www.oxfamindia.org/knowledgehub/oxfaminaction/status-report-education-during-pandemic-government-and-private-schools.

'PM CARES Fund Allocated Rs 3,100 Crore for Fight against Covid-19.' 13 May 2020. https://www.pmindia.gov.in/en/news_updates/pm-cares-fund-trust-allocates-rs-3100-crore-for-fight-against-covid-19/?comment=disable.

Reid, T. R. *The Healing of America: A Global Quest for Better, Cheaper and Fairer Healthcare*. New York: Penguin, 2010.

Saikia, Arunabh. 'As Coronavirus Reaches Rural India, Three Cases Reflect the Steep Challenge Ahead.' *Scroll.in*, 5 April 2020. https://scroll.in/article/958151/as-coronavirus-reaches-rural-india-three-cases-reflect-the-steep-challenge-ahead.

———. 'Investigation: In Bihar, Hospitals Have Ventilators, but No Staff to Operate Them.' *Scroll.in*, 1 May 2021. https://scroll.in/article/993772/investigation-in-bihar-district-hospitals-have-ventilators-but-no-staff-to-operate-them.

Save the Children. *Save Our Education*. 2020. https://image.savethechildren.org/save-our-education-report.pdf-ch11042004.pdf/jftkcd027jjb15d22cfgndkog4j7t1ni.pdf.

Shah, Farrukh, and Deepika Luthra. *A Generation at Stake: Protecting India's Children from the Impact of Covid-19*. 2020. https://resourcecentre.savethechildren.net/pdf/a_generation_at_stake_report_final_3.pdf/.

Sharma, Niharika. 'Covid-19: In Their Desperate Search for Oxygen and Medicines, Indians Are Falling for Online Scams.' *Scroll.in*, 1 May 2021. https://scroll.in/article/993727/covid-19-indians-desperate-for-oxygen-and-medicines-are-falling-for-online-scams.

Shroff, Zubin, Robert Marten, Abdul Ghaffar, Kabir Sheikh, Hendrik Bekedam, Manoj Jhalani, and Soumya Swaminathan. 'On the

Path to Universal Health Coverage: Aligning Ongoing Health Systems Reforms in India.' *BMJ Global Health* (25 August 2020).

Stiglitz, Joseph. *The Economics of the Public Sector*. New York: W. W. Norton & Company, 1986.

Venkataramakrishnan, Rohan. 'Coronavirus: Why It Is Better for India (and You) to Overreact Now than Regret It Later.' *Scroll.in*, 13 March 2020. https://scroll.in/article/956059/coronavirus-why-it-is-better-for-india-and-you-to-overreact-now-than-regret-it-later.

———. 'Covid-19: Imagine the Headlines if Any Other Religion Had Been Responsible for Kumbh-Like Gathering.' *Scroll.in*, 12 April 2021. https://scroll.in/article/992067/covid-19-imagine-the-headlines-if-any-other-religion-had-been-responsible-for-kumbh-like-gathering.

Vyas, Ankit, and Anjela Taneja. *Status Report—Government and Private Schools during Covid-19*. Oxfam India, 2020. https://d1ns4ht6ytuzzo.cloudfront.net/oxfamdata/oxfamdatapublic/2022-03/Status%20of%20education%20report_1.pdf?DUJL26fAPq5Pr2kwIjZ8Hnh4H7F9wWyW.

Yamunan, Sruthisagar, and Arunabh Saikia. 'Admit Coronavirus Patients, Says Centre, Sparking Concerns among Private Hospitals They're Unprepared.' *Scroll.in*, 21 March 2020. https://scroll.in/article/956773/admit-coronavirus-patients-says-centre-sparking-concern-among-private-hospitals-that-are-unprepare.

11. Emerging Issues in Social Policy

'340 Sewer Cleaning Deaths in Past 5 Years: Government.' *The Hindu*, 2 February 2021. https://www.thehindu.com/news/national/340-sewer-cleaning-deaths-in-past-5-year-government/article33732992.ece.

'2289 Government Staff Taken off Beneficiary List of Ladki Bahin Yojana.' *The Hindu*, 4 July 2025.

Aggarwal, Ankita. 'The Slow Destruction of NREGA: Evidence from Jharkhand.' *India Together*, 16 March 2015. https://indiatogether.org/destruction-of-nrega-with-evidence-from-jharkhand-government.

Aman, Thejesh G. N., Krushna Ranaware, and Kanika Sharma. 'Of Denial and Data: Deaths Due to India's Covid-19 National Lockdown.' *Economic and Political Weekly* 56, no. 23 (5 June 2021). https://www.epw.in/journal/2021/23/insight/denial-and-data.html.

Assisi, Charles. 'Too Many Digital IDs Spoil the Broth.' *Hindustan Times*, 9 November 2024. https://www.hindustantimes.com/cities/mumbai-news/too-many-digital-ids-spoil-the-broth-101731092771671.html.

Bharti Kumar, Nitin, Lucas Chancel, Thomas Piketty, and Anmol Somanchi. *Towards Tax Justice and Wealth Redistribution in India: Proposals Based on the Latest Inequality Estimates*. Paris: World Inequality Lab, 2024. http://wid.world/document/towards-tax-justice-and-wealth-redistribution-in-india-proposals-based-on-latest-inequality-estimates-world-inequality-lab-issue-brief-2024-01/.

Chancel, Lucas, and Thomas Piketty. 'Indian Income Inequality, 1922–2015: From British Raj to Billionaire Raj?' *Review of Income and Wealth* (2019). https://doi.org/10.1111/roiw.12439.

Choragudi, Krishna Priya. 'Evaluating Rajasthan's urban employment guarantee program: some key insights and concerns'. *Development in Practice* 35, no. 3, 2025, 398-409.

Chowdhury, K. Ujjwal. 'Demonetization: Millions of Man Hours in Queues, 100+ Deaths. Why Punish 96% of People for Crimes Done by 4%?' *Counterview*, 14 December 2016. https://www.counterview.net/2016/12/demonetization-millions-of-man-hours-on.html.

'Delhi Mahila Samman Yojana: Who Is Eligible to Get Rs 1,000 per Month? Here Is How to Get the Aid and Other Details.' *The Economic Times*, 5 March 2024. https://economictimes.indiatimes.com/news/india/delhi-mahila-samman-yojana-who-is-eligible-to-get-rs-1000-per-month-here-is-how-to-get-the-aid-and-other-details/articleshow/108198749.cms.

Drèze, Jean. 'Learning from NREGA.' *The Hindu*, 4 December 2014. https://www.thehindu.com/opinion/op-ed/Learning-from-NREGA/article62117988.ece.

Drèze, Jean, and Anmol Somanchi. 'View: New Barometer of India's Economy Fails to Reflect Deprivations of Poor Households.' *The Economic Times*, 21 June 2021. https://economictimes.indiatimes.com/opinion/et-commentary/view-the-new-barometer-of-indias-economy-fails-to-reflect-the-deprivations-of-poor-households/articleshow/83696115.cms.

Dutta, Siraj. 'Starvation Deaths and Denial of Welfare Entitlements—Insights from Jharkhand.' Unpublished manuscript, 2020. https://papers.ssrn.com/sol3/papers.cfm?abstract_id=3870242.

Government of Assam. 'Order by the Governor of Assam on the Implementation of Orunodoi.' Guwahati: Finance Division, 14 August 2020. https://socialjustice.assam.gov.in/sites/default/files/public_utility/Orunodoi%20Scheme.pdf.

Government of India. 'Increasing Pension under National Social Assistance Programme.' Press Information Bureau. New Delhi: Ministry of Rural Development, 6 February 2024. https://pib.gov.in/PressReleaseIframePage.aspx?PRID=2003175.

Government of Tamil Nadu. *Dr. Muthulakshmi Reddy Maternity Benefit Scheme—Government Notification*. Chennai: Health and Family Welfare Department, 2019. https://picme.tn.gov.in/picme_public/mrmbs.pdf.

Gupta, Apar. 'Digital Database or Coercive Report Card? APAAR ID.' *Deccan Herald*, 30 March 2025. https://www.deccanherald.com/specials/digital-database-or-coercive-report-card-apaar-id-3469158.

International Labour Organisation, and Institute for Human Development. *India Employment Report 2024: Youth Employment, Education and Skills*. Geneva: International Labour Organisation and Institute for Human Development, 2024. https://www.ilo.org/sites/default/files/2024-08/India%20Employment%20-%20web_8%20April.pdf.

Jajoria, Deepika, and Manoj Jatav. 'Is the Periodic Labour Force Survey 2017–18 Comparable with Employment-Unemployment Survey 2011–12?' *Economic and Political Weekly* 55, no. 3 (18 January 2020). https://www.epw.in/journal/2020/3/commentary/periodic-labour-force-survey-2017%E2%80%9318-comparable.html.

Jakhar, Ajay Vir. 'Mandatory Fortification of Food, Part 1.' YouTube video, 2021. https://www.youtube.com/watch?v=LIz1zMxL8Vg.

Kalra, Aarushi, and Aditi Priya. 'Birth Pangs: Universal Maternity Entitlements in India.' *Economic and Political Weekly* 55, no. 35 (29 August 2020). https://www.epw.in/journal/2020/35/special-articles/birth-pangs.html.

Khera, Reetika, ed. *Dissent on Aadhaar: Big Data Meets Big Brother*. Hyderabad: Orient BlackSwan, 2018.

———. 'Impact of Aadhaar on Welfare Programmes.' *Economic and Political Weekly* 52, no. 50 (16 December 2017). https://www.epw.in/journal/2017/50/special-articles/impact-aadhaar-welfare-programmes.html.

———. 'A Phased Approach Will Make a "Basic Income" Affordable for India, *The Wire*, 20 December 2016.

Khera, Reetika, and Amod Moharil. 'Aadhaar: Costs of Digital Red Tape.' *Economic and Political Weekly* 59, no. 19 (11 May 2024).

Kotiswaran, Prabha. 'Revaluing Unpaid Work: The Case of Orunodoi Scheme in Assam.' *Economic and Political Weekly* 57, no. 26–27 (20 January 2022). https://www.epw.in/journal/2022/26-27/commentary/revaluing-unpaid-work.html.

Nagarajan, Rema. 'NFHS-6 Not to Measure Anaemia as Experts Point Out Method Is Faulty.' *The Times of India*, 27 May 2023. https://timesofindia.indiatimes.com/india/nfhs-6-not-to-measure-anaemia-as-experts-point-out-method-is-faulty/articleshow/100538418.cms.

National Health Service. 'Vitamin B12 or Folate Deficiency Anaemia.' *National Health Service*, United Kingdom, n.d. https://www.nhs.uk/conditions/vitamin-b12-or-folate-deficiency-anaemia/symptoms/.

Pena-Rosas, Juan Pablo, Prasanna Mithra, Bhaskaran Unnikrishnan, Nithin Kumar, Luz Maria De-Regil, Sreekumaran Nair, Maria N. Garcia-Casal, and Juan Antonio Solon. 'Fortification of Rice with Vitamins and Minerals for Addressing Micronutrient Malnutrition.' *PubMed*, 25 October 2019. https://pubmed.ncbi.nlm.nih.gov/31684687/.

People's Research on India's Consumer Economy. *The Rise of India's*

Middle Class: Household Survey on Indian Citizens' Environment and Consumer Economy (Wave 3.0). 2021. https://price360.in/project/ice-360-survey-2021-household-survey-on-indias-citizens-environment-and-consumer-economy-wave-30/.

Press Information Bureau. 'Recalibration of Nutrition Intervention: Temporary Discontinuation of Rice Fortification.' 27 February 2026. https://www.pib.gov.in/PressReleasePage.aspx?PRID=2233779&reg=3&lang=2.

Press Trust of India. 'Assam's 3rd Poverty Alleviation Scheme Launched for 372K Beneficiaries.' *Business Standard*, 19 September 2024. https://www.business-standard.com/india-news/assam-s-3rd-poverty-alleviation-scheme-launched-for-372k-beneficiaries-124091900414_1.html.

Priya, Aditi, Sweta Das, and Krushna Ranaware. 'The Truth about Oxygen Deaths during Covid Second Wave.' *The Indian Express*, 7 July 2021. https://indianexpress.com/article/opinion/columns/covid-second-wave-oxygen-death-coronavirus-cases-7392219/.

Raghavan, T. C. A. Sharad. 'State Govts Are Increasingly Prioritising Women, with 16% of Indian Women Now Getting Income Support.' *The Print*, 12 July 2024. https://theprint.in/economy/state-govts-are-increasingly-prioritising-women-with-16-of-indian-women-now-getting-income-support/2170040/.

Saikia, Arunabh. 'Months Before Polls, Assam Launched a Cash Scheme for Women. Now It Is Paying BJP Dividends.' *Scroll.in*, 23 March 2021. https://scroll.in/article/989868/months-before-polls-assam-launched-a-cash-scheme-for-women-now-it-is-paying-bjp-dividends.

The Wire Staff. 'Almost 80 Persons Have Died on Board Shramik Special Trains.' *The Wire*, 30 May 2020. https://thewire.in/government/almost-80-persons-have-died-on-board-shramik-special-trains.

'Who Is Eligible for Tamil Nadu's Rs 1,000 Monthly Allowance for Women?' *The Indian Express*, 10 July 2023. https://indianexpress.com/article/cities/chennai/tamil-nadu-government-monthly-allowance-who-is-eligible-8823646/.

12. Where Is the Money?

Advani, Arun, and David Sturrock. 'IFS Green Budget: Reforming Inheritance Tax.' Chapter 7. Institute for Fiscal Studies, 2024. https://ifs.org.uk/sites/default/files/2023-09/Reforming-inheritance-tax-1.pdf.

Anand, Abhishek, Vikas Dimble, and Arvind Subramanian. 'New Welfareism of Modi Government Represents Distinctive Approach to Redistribution and Inclusion.' *The Indian Express*, 22 December 2020. https://indianexpress.com/article/opinion/columns/national-family-health-survey-new-welfarism-of-indias-right-7114104/.

Bhalla, Gursharan. 'As PM Unveils Statue of Peace, Here's a List of Statues Built in the Last 5 Years and How Much They Cost.' *Indiatimes.com*, 18 November 2020. https://www.indiatimes.com/news/india/as-pm-unveils-statue-of-peace-heres-list-of-statues-built-in-last-5-yrs-how-much-it-cost/articleshow/127650260.html.

Bharti Kumar, Nitin, Lucas Chancel, Thomas Piketty, and Anmol Somanchi. 'Towards Tax Justice and Wealth Redistribution in India.' *The India Forum*, 21 May 2024. https://www.theindiaforum.in/economy/towards-tax-justice-and-wealth-redistribution-india.

———. *Towards Tax Justice and Wealth Redistribution in India: Proposals Based on the Latest Inequality Estimates*. Paris: World Inequality Lab, 2024. https://wid.world/www-site/uploads/2024/05/WorldInequalityLab_2024_Towards-Tax-Justice-Wealth-Redistribution-in-India_Issue-Brief.pdf.

Central Board of Direct Taxes. *Income Tax Department Time Series Data, Financial Year 2000–01 to 2018–19*. New Delhi: Ministry of Finance, 2019. https://incometaxindia.gov.in/Documents/Direct%20Tax%20Data/IT-Department-Time-Series-Data-FY-2000-01-to-2018-19.pdf.

Chancel, Lucas, and Thomas Piketty. 'Indian Income Inequality, 1922–2015: From British Raj to Billionaire Raj?' *Review of Income and Wealth* (2019). https://doi.org/10.1111/roiw.12439.

Deshmukh, Yashwant. *International Social Survey Programme: Social Inequality V-ISSP 2019 (India)*. GESIS, Cologne. 2023. https://doi.org/10.4232/1.14207.

Drèze, Jean. 'Who Is Afraid of Redistribution?' *Economic and Political Weekly* 59, no. 18 (4 May 2024). https://www.epw.in/journal/comment/who-afraid-redistribution.html.

Government of India. *All India Debt and Investment Survey, National Sample Survey 2019*. Report No. 588. National Statistical Office. New Delhi: Ministry of Statistics and Programme Implementation, 2021. https://mospi.gov.in/sites/default/files/publication_reports/Report_no588-AIDIS-77R-SeptFinal_0.pdf.

———. *Drinking Water, Sanitation, Hygiene and Housing Condition in India, NSS 76th Round, July 2018–December 2018*. National Statistical Office. New Delhi: Ministry of Statistics and Programme Implementation, 2019. https://www.mospi.gov.in/sites/default/files/publication_reports/KI_Health_75th_Final.pdf.

———. *Economic Survey 2011–12*. New Delhi: Ministry of Finance, 2012. https://www.indiabudget.gov.in/budget2012-2013/es2011-12/echapter.zip.

———. 'Increase in Pensions under National Assistance Programme.' Press Information Bureau. New Delhi, 6 February 2024. https://pib.gov.in/PressReleaseIframePage.aspx?PRID=2003175.

———. *SRS Bulletin 2020*. Office of the Registrar General of India 55, no. 1. New Delhi: Ministry of Home Affairs, 2022. https://censusindia.gov.in/nada/index.php/catalog/42687/download/46357/SRS_Bulletin_2020_Vol_55_No_1.pdf.

———. *Statement of Revenue Impact of Tax Incentives under Central Tax System: Fiscal Years 2021–22 and 2022–23*. Budget 2023. Budget Division. New Delhi: Ministry of Finance, 2023. https://www.indiabudget.gov.in/doc/rec/annex7.pdf.

Khera, Reetika, and Md. Asjad. 'Guarantee Is Precarity, Welfare Is Self-Care.' *The Hindu*, 16 April 2024. https://www.thehindu.com/opinion/lead/guarantee-is-precarity-welfare-is-self-care/article68069056.ece.

Khera, Reetika. 'Impact of the Food Security Act on the Public Distribution System.' *Ideas for India*, 3 October 2024. https://

www.ideasforindia.in/topics/poverty-inequality/impact-of-the-food-security-act-on-public-distribution-system.html.

Mundle, Sudipto, and Satadru Sikdar. *Subsidies, Merit Goods and the Fiscal Space for Reviving Growth: An Aspect of Public Expenditure in India*. Working Paper No. 282. New Delhi: National Council of Applied Economic Research, 2019. https://www.nipfp.org.in/media/medialibrary/2019/11/WP_282_2019.pdf.

NDTV. 'Bullet Train Project an "Exercise in Vanity": Manmohan Singh.' *NDTV.com*, 7 November 2017. https://www.ndtv.com/india-news/bullet-train-project-an-exercise-in-vanity-manmohan-singh-1772298.

Paliath, Shreehari. 'The Main Purpose of Central Welfare Schemes Today Is to Promote Modi.' *Scroll.in*, 11 February 2023. https://scroll.in/article/1043549/jean-Drèze-interview-the-main-purpose-of-central-welfare-schemes-today-is-to-promote-modi.

Peterson-Withorn, Chase, Grace Chung, and Matt Durot. 'World's Billionaires List.' *Forbes*, 2025. https://www.forbes.com/billionaires/.

Piketty, Thomas, and Nancy Qian. 'Income Inequality and Progressive Income Taxation in China and India, 1986–2015.' *American Economic Journal: Applied Economics* (2009).

Rao, M. Govinda. *Property Tax System in India: Problems and Prospects of Reform*. Working Paper No. 2013-114. New Delhi: National Institute of Public Finance and Policy, 2013. https://www.nipfp.org.in/media/medialibrary/2013/04/WP_2013_114.pdf.

Rajkumar, J. Dennis, and S. L. Shetty. 'Corporate Tax Reduction: Weak Analytical Foundations.' *Economic and Political Weekly* 55, no. 10 (7 March 2020). https://www.epw.in/journal/2020/10/economic-notes/corporate-tax-reductions.html.

Reserve Bank of India. *Handbook of Statistics on Indian States*. Mumbai: Reserve Bank of India, 2023. https://rbi.org.in/SCRIPTS/AnnualPublications.aspx?head=Handbook%20of%20Statistics%20on%20Indian%20States.

Shrinivas, Rukmini. 'In India, Who Speaks in English, and Where?'

LiveMint, 14 May 2019. https://www.livemint.com/news/india/in-india-who-speaks-in-english-and-where-1557814101428.html.

Srivastava, Pranchal. 'Defaulting on Your Property Tax? Lucknow Municipal Corporation May Seize Bank Accounts.' *The Times of India*, 20 August 2020. https://timesofindia.indiatimes.com/city/lucknow/defaulting-on-your-property-tax-lucknow-municipal-corporation-may-seize-bank-accounts/articleshow/77645582.cms.

Stevens, Matt. 'Sanders Proposes Corporate Tax to Address Pay Gap at Big Companies.' *The New York Times*, 30 September 2019. https://www.nytimes.com/2019/09/30/us/politics/bernie-sanders-tax-proposal.html.

Stiglitz, Joseph E. and Jay K. Rosengard. *The Economics of the Public Sector*, Fourth Edition. New York: W. W. Norton & Company, 2015.

Subramanian, S. 'Doing the Maths: Why India Should Introduce a Covid Wealth Tax on the Ultra Rich.' *Scroll.in*, 16 April 2020. https://scroll.in/article/959314/doing-the-maths-why-india-should-introduce-a-covid-wealth-tax-on-the-ultra-rich.

'Drop Central Vista, Restore Funds.' *The Telegraph*, 16 September 2020. https://www.telegraphindia.com/india/drop-central-vista-restore-fund-mps/cid/1792111.

'Israel Passes Law to Cap Bankers' Salaries.' *The Guardian*, 29 March 2016. https://www.theguardian.com/business/2016/mar/29/israel-passes-law-to-cap-bankers-salaries-pay-gap.

Timmins, Nicholas. *Five Giants: A Biography of the Welfare State*. London: HarperCollins, 2001.

Verma, Mohit, and Fizza Suhel. 'Welfare Spending Has Been Getting a Regular Pruning.' *The Hindu*, 13 May 2023. https://www.thehindu.com/opinion/lead/welfare-spending-has-been-getting-a-regular-pruning/article66843674.ece.

Wicks, Ben. *No Time to Wave Goodbye*. London: Bloomsbury, 2013.

13. The Way Ahead

Comptroller and Auditor General of India. *Performance Audit of National Social Assistance Programme*. Report No. 10. New Delhi, 2023. https://cag.gov.in/uploads/download_audit_report/2023/

Report-No.-10-of-2023_NSAP_English_PDF-A-064d229f832dad7.55068084.pdf.

Choragudi, Krishna Priya. 'Examining Himachal's Urban Employment Guarantee.' *Ideas for India*, 21 March 2022. https://www.ideasforindia.in/topics/poverty-inequality/examining-himachal-s-urban-employment-guarantee.html.

——. 'Evaluating Rajasthan's Urban Employment Guarantee Program: Some Key Insights and Concerns.' *Development in Practice* 35, no. 3 (2025): 398–409.

De, Anuradha, Reetika Khera, Meera Samson, and A. K. Shiva Kumar. *PROBE Revisited: A Report on Elementary Education in India*. New Delhi: Oxford University Press, 2011.

Drèze, Jean. 'The Gujarat Muddle.' *The Hindu*, 11 April 2014. https://www.thehindu.com/opinion/op-ed/the-gujarat-muddle/article5896998.ece.

——. 'The Gujarat Model.' *The Hindu*, 4 December 2021. https://www.thehindu.com/opinion/op-ed/the-gujarat-model/article5993938.ece.

——. 'The Mythology of Social Policy.' *The Hindu*, 8 July 2014. https://www.thehindu.com/opinion/lead/on-the-mythology-of-social-policy/article6186895.ece.

Drèze, Jean, Reetika Khera, and Rajkishor Mishra. 'Vikas Model ke Beech Odisha se Sabak.' *BBC Hindi*, 17 November 2014. https://www.bbc.com/hindi/india/2014/11/141117_odisha_government_model_rns.

Drèze, Jean, and Amartya Sen. *An Uncertain Glory: India and Its Contradictions*. New Delhi: Penguin, 2013.

——. *An Uncertain Glory: India and Its Contradictions*. Princeton: Princeton University Press, 2015.

——. *Development and Participation*. Oxford: Oxford University Press, 2002.

Global Data Lab. *National HDI: Custom Set of Indicators 2021*. Global Data Lab, 2021. https://globaldatalab.org/shdi/table/2021/shdi+healthindex+incinde+lifexp+lifexpf+lifexpm+esch+eschf+eschm+msch+mschf+mschm+lgnic+lgnicf+lgnicm+pop/IND/?levels=1+4&interpolation=0&extrapolation=0.

Government of India. *National Human Development Report.* Planning Commission. New Delhi, 2002. http://www.igidr.ac.in/conf/ysp/nhd2001.pdf.

Government of Tamil Nadu. *Dr. Muthulakshmi Reddy Maternity Benefit Scheme—Government Notification.* Chennai: Health and Family Welfare Department, 2019. https://picme.tn.gov.in/picme_public/mrmbs.pdf.

Himanshu, and Abhijit Sen. 'In-Kind Food Transfers-I: Impact on Poverty.' *Economic and Political Weekly* 48, nos. 45–46 (13 November 2013). https://www.jstor.org/stable/pdf/23528608.pdf.

International Institute for Population Sciences. *National Family Health Survey (NFHS-5), 2019–21.* Mumbai: International Institute for Population Sciences, 2022. https://dhsprogram.com/pubs/pdf/FR375/FR375.pdf.

Khera, Reetika. 'Gujarat's Development Pre-Dates Modi Considerably.' *NDTV.com*, 8 April 2014. https://www.ndtv.com/elections-news/blog-gujarats-development-pre-dates-modi-considerably-556553.

———. 'Himachal ko bhi Dekhiye.' *Amar Ujala*, 16 July 2014. https://www.amarujala.com/columns/opinion/himachal-model-growth.

———. 'Revival of the Public Distribution System: Evidence and Explanations.' *Economic and Political Weekly* 46, nos. 44–45 (5 November 2011). https://www.epw.in/journal/2011/44-45/special-articles/revival-public-distribution-system-evidence-and-explanations.

———. 'Tamil Nadu se Kyun Nahi Seekhte.' *Amar Ujala*, 18 March 2018. https://www.amarujala.com/columns/opinion/why-not-learn-from-tamil-nadu.

Nair, K. Sobhana. 'Now, Drones to Monitor MGNREGA Worksites.' *The Hindu*, 18 August 2023. https://www.thehindu.com/news/national/drones-to-monitor-mgnrega-worksites/article67205578.ece.

Panwar, Tikender Singh. 'How Did Himachal Achieve a High Rank on the NAS?' *The Hindu*, 10 July 2025. https://www.thehindu.com/education/how-did-himachal-achieve-a-high-rank-on-the-nas-explained/article69793282.ece.

Sinha, Dipa. *Women, Health and Public Services in India: Why Are States Different?* New Delhi: Routledge, 2019.

Srinivasan, Vivek. *Delivering Public Services Effectively: Tamil Nadu and Beyond.* New Delhi: Oxford University Press, 2014.

Appendix I
Statistical Appendix

Table A1. List of Surveys Since 2002

Issue/Year	*States in which the survey was conducted*	*Sample size*
Antyodaya Anna Yojana 2002	Chhattisgarh, Rajasthan	
Mid-Day Meal Scheme 2003	Chhattisgarh, Rajasthan, Karnataka	246 households and 81 schools.
National Food for Work Scheme 2005	Rajasthan, Madhya Pradesh, Chhattisgarh, Jharkhand and Uttar Pradesh	
ICDS, FOCUS Survey 2006	Chhattisgarh, Himachal Pradesh, Maharashtra, Rajasthan, Tamil Nadu, Uttar Pradesh	203 Anganwadi Workers and Helpers, 500 Women whose children go to Anganwadis
NREGA Social Audits 2007	Odisha, Tamil Nadu, Jharkhand, Himachal Pradesh	30 villages (Bolangir, Boudh, Kalahandi), 28 (Ranchi), 12 (Kangra and Sirmaur)
NREGA Survey 2008	Bihar, Rajasthan, Madhya Pradesh, Chhattisgarh, Jharkhand and Uttar Pradesh	1000 NREGA workers

NREGA Sahayata Kendra 2009-2010	Jharkhand and Chhattisgarh	
Public Distribution System Survey 2011	Andhra Pradesh, Bihar, Chhattisgarh, Himachal Pradesh, Jharkhand, Madhya Pradesh, Odisha, Rajasthan, Tamil Nadu	1227 households
Public Evaluation of Entitlement Programmes (PEEP) Survey 2013	Andhra Pradesh, Bihar, Chhattisgarh, Himachal Pradesh, Jharkhand, Madhya Pradesh, Maharashtra, Odisha, Rajasthan, Tamil Nadu	1926 households and 898 Pensioners
Public Health Facilities Survey 2013	Rajasthan, Bihar, Himachal Pradesh, Jharkhand	150 Government Health Centres
ICDS and Mamata Scheme 2014	Odisha	49 Anganwadis, 293 mothers of children, 233 Mamata beneficiaries
Public Distribution System 2015	Bihar	997 Rural households
Public Distribution System 2015	Madhya Pradesh	Revisiting PEEP sample in MP
National Food Security Act, Public Distribution System 2016	Bihar, Chhattisgarh, Jharkhand, Madhya Pradesh, Odisha, West Bengal	3800 households
Aadhaar Based Biometric Authentication (ABBA) Survey 2017	Jharkhand	890 households (5000 members)

Jachha-Baccha Survey (JABS) Survey 2019	Uttar Pradesh, Madhya Pradesh, Chhattisgarh, Jharkhand, Himachal Pradesh, Odisha	706 Pregnant and lactating women
School Survey 2021	Assam, Bihar, Chandigarh, Delhi, Gujarat, Haryana, Jharkhand, Maharashtra, Karnataka, Madhya Pradesh, Odisha, Punjab, Rajasthan, Tamil Nadu, Uttar Pradesh, West Bengal	1362 households
Public Health Facilities Survey 2022	Rajasthan, Bihar, Jharkhand, Chhattisgarh, Himachal Pradesh	241 Government Health Centres

Table A2. PMMVY: Maternity Benefits in the Unorganised Sector

	Of all births, (%) who received all instalments of PMMVY				
	2019-20[1]	*2020-21*[1]	*2021-22*[1]	*2022-23*[1]	*2023-24*[1,a]
Andhra Pradesh	38.9	20.2	3.3	42.7	17.6
Assam	41.6	19.3	28.9	23.9	21.8
Bihar	16.0	31.7	10.2	19.3	3.1

Chhattisgarh	21.4	15.9	14.0	19.3	12.6
Gujarat	21.5	7.6	1.5	9.4	11.6
Haryana	22.7	11.2	21.3	25.7	1.7
Himachal Pradesh	42.5	33.4	35.2	41.2	7.5
Jharkhand	19.1	11.7	12.2	9.5	7.5
Karnataka	30.1	25.0	22.9	48.5	13.5
Kerala	32.5	25.8	35.8	31.0	16.2
Madhya Pradesh	28.6	28.6	23.7	25.8	20.1
Maharashtra	35.5	27.3	22.9	32.6	4.4
Odisha[2]	90	-	64	-	-
Punjab	20.4	18.7	5.6	31.3	17.5
Rajasthan	15.1	12.6	13.3	16.3	9.7
Tamil Nadu[3,b]	14-68	18-81	10-79	11-78	12-84
Telangana[4,b]	-	33.6/55	/37.0	/64	-
Uttarakhand	26.2	26.7	23.6	23.5	24.1
Uttar Pradesh	17.1	14.1	10.1	20.2	4.7

West Bengal	25.7	0.3	0.1	49.1	00
North-eastern states	32.4		14.4	19.7	
India	21.5	18.5	15.7	23.0	8.2

Source: [1]Upto 2021-22, Drèze and Khera (2023); 2022-23 and 2023-24, author's unpublished estimates. [2]Odisha (various years) [3]Tamil Nadu government (various years) [4]Telangana government (various years).

Notes: Estimates obtained by dividing the total number of births to the total beneficiaries. The number of beneficiaries of the Pradhan Mantri Matru Vandana Yojana was obtained through an the Right to Information application and the estimate of total births is based on the birth rate of 2020 (Government of India, 2022) [a]In the early years of the Pradhan Mantri Matru Vandana Yojana, benefits were given in three instalments reduced to two instalments now. 'All instalments' for 2023-24 were not shared, so only 'any instalment' are reported. [b]Lower Limit (from Central Government); Upper Limit (from State Government).

Table A3. Rank of Major Indian States on Children's ABC index

	2005-06	*2015-16*	*2019-21*
Himachal Pradesh	3	3	1
Tamil Nadu	2	5	2
Kerala	1	1	3
Jammu and Kashmir	7	4	4
Punjab	4	2	5
West Bengal	8	6	6
Odisha	12	8	7
Karnataka	9	10	8
Uttarakhand	11	13	9
Andhra Pradesh	10	7	10
Chhattisgarh	13	9	11
Maharashtra	5	12	12
Haryana	6	11	13
India	15	14	14
Gujarat	14	16	15
Rajasthan	17	17	16
Assam	16	15	17
Madhya Pradesh	18	20	18
Uttar Pradesh	19	19	19
Jharkhand	20	18	20
Bihar	21	21	21

Note: The table reports rank of the state on the ABC index. The ABC index includes four indicators—children fully vaccinated, literacy rate at 15-24 years, children who are not underweight and the percentage of children whose mothers receive at least ANC during pregnancy. The position of the state has been assessed on each indicator relative to the achievement of other states. The ABC index is calculated as the average of the four. See Drèze and Khera (2012) for details.

Table A4. MDM Scheme: Cooks' Social Background and Cooking Arrangements

State	*Female cook (%)*[1]	*Dalits and Adivasis (%)*			*Children eating from centralised kitchens (%)*[2]		*LPG in the kitchen (%)*[3]	
		% in population 2011	*Cook*[1]					
	2023-24		*2013-14*	*2023-24*	*2013-14*	*2023-24*	*2013-14*	*2023-24*
Andhra Pradesh	100	23.4	33	29	4.7	10.3	30.3	79.3
Assam	95.4	19.1	29	32	1.0	1.5	1.0	30.3
Bihar	63	16.8	30	30.6	4.3	9.1	0.4	100
Chhattisgarh	82.2	42.5	58	55.2	3.0	4.0	7.8	13.7
Gujarat	68.6	21.3	35	39.2	7.2	13.0	84.4	90
Haryana	99.7	20.1	41	45.1	14.5	17.3	99.0	87
Himchal Pradesh	83.3	30.8	25	27.8	0.0	0.0	83.9	99.8
Jharkhand	100	37.8	52	50.5	0.0	2.7	5.2	99.8
Karnataka	100	23.9	37	35.6	19.4	17.1	79.4	90
Kerala	93.8	11.3	18	18.7	0.0	0.0	2.0	100

Madhya Pradesh	98.3	36.1	54	47	0.7	4.3	13.7	96.4
Maharashtra	89	21.1	25	31.6	3.0	0.7	15.0	82
Odisha	97.4	39.5	40	44	3.4	0.8	0.0	93.2
Punjab	97.3	31.9	23	75.5	13.1	0.0	0.0	100
Rajasthan	86.8	31.2	25	30	0.0	7.6	37.1	94.4
Tamil Nadu	95	20.4	19	27.2	0.0	0.0	15.7	94.5
Telangana	88.5	23.4	-	44	-	5.4	-	14.8
Uttarakhand	99.6	20.6	17	18.5	0.0	5.6	27.3	74.5
Uttar Pradesh	94.2	21.1	30	29	5.0	6.2	57.2	93
West Bengal	96.8	29	39	55.3	0.7	1.4	7.9	92.6

Source: Government of India (various years), [1]Table AT- 2, [2]Table AT- 4C and AT- 20, and [3]Table AT-13. (See Appendix II for details).

Table A5. PDS: Access and 'Diversion' of PDS Grains

State	*Estimated diversion (%)*[a]			*Households receiving ration from PDS (% of total households)*[b]		
	2004-5	2011-12	2022-23	2004-5	2011-12	2022-23
Andhra Pradesh	23.2	22.0	1-13[1]	56.8	35	85
Assam	88.7	50.7	28	8.5	30	75
Bihar	91.0	24.4	26	1.9	14	72
Chhattisgarh	51.7	9.3	22[2]	23	61	90
Gujarat	51.7	67.6	40	25	28	47
Haryana	82.7	49.0	19	4.4	17	38
Himachal Pradesh	27.0	27.1	33	47.7	86	74
Jharkhand	85.2	44.4	22	5.6	23	77
Karnataka	28.7	34.7	14-29[1]	49	77	70
Kerala	25.6	37.1	36	27.9	93	80
Madhya Pradesh	50.1	51.5	26	21	42	64
Maharashtra	49.3	48.2	37	21.8	36	54

Odisha	76.3	25.0	9-16	19.8	55	80
Punjab	93.2	58.8	[-1.8][3]	0.4	19	40
Rajasthan	93.9	60.9	6	10.2	18	57
Tamil Nadu	7.3	11.9	28	71.4	62	86
Telangana	-		18.3[1]	-	82	69
Uttarakhand	59.4	34.9	41	20.6	35	56
Uttar Pradesh	58.0	57.6	24	5.7	23	74
West Bengal	80.6	65.3	17-23[1]	12.9	34	89
North-eastern states			27			
India	**54**	**41.7**	**18.2-22.1**	**24**	**39**	**70**

Sources: [a]For 2004-5, Khera (2011), for 2011-12, author's unpublished estimates and for 2022-23 Khera (2024) [b]Author's unpublished estimates from NSS data.

Note: [1]These states have distributed extra ration cards from their budget; the lower estimate is obtained by including the extra grains distributed by them. For number of additional cardholders, Khera and Somanchi (2020). [2]The offtake data of Chhattisgarh is from Government of Chhattisgarh (2024). [3]Punjab distributes food grains every six months (distribution is monthly in rest of the states); people may have reported six months' purchase.

Table A6. NREGA: Days of Employment and Wages

	Average day, per job card[1]			*Wage Rate (Rs/day)*	
	UPA (2009-10 to 2013-14)	*NDA (2014-15 to 2019-20)*	*COVID-19 (2020-22)*	*NREGA, 2023-24*[2]	*Agricultural wages, 2021-22*[3]
Andhra Pradesh	27	23	26	272	412
Assam	11	10	16	238	329
Bihar	9	6	10	228	323
Chhattisgarh	28	28	43	221	224
Gujarat	10	8	12	256	261
Haryana	15	9	14	357	476
Himachal Pradesh	24	18	25	224-280	378
Jharkhand	17	14	19	228	264
Karnataka	18	14	21	316	322
Kerala	25	22	26	333	708
Madhya Pradesh	16	20	39	221	277

Maharashtra	8	9	8	273	329
Odisha	11	13	27	237	327
Punjab	9	12	18	303	432
Rajasthan	28	25	38	255	359
Tamil Nadu	38	35	38	294	470
Telangana	27[a]	19	27	272	377
Uttarakhand	19	19	23	230	401
Uttar Pradesh	18	11	17	230	298
West Bengal	16	21	27	237	309
North-eastern states	51	45	59	237	-
India	20	18	24	236	334

Source: [1]NREGA www.nrega.nic.in website of the Government of India, Government of India (2013) and Government of India (2017), [2]Government of India (2023a) [3]Government of India (2023b), Table 1.1.

Note: [a]Telangana was carved out of Andhra Pradesh in 2014; this average is for Andhra Pradesh.

Table A7. National Social Security Pension: Amount and Coverage of Elderly Pensioners[1]

State	*Coverage (%)*		*Pension (Rs per month)*[b]		*Pension (Rs per month), weighted (by coverage) pension*[2]	
	Total[a]	*State share*[a]	*80+ years*	*60-79 years*	*Maximum*	*Minimum*
Haryana	62	86	3000	3000	1893	1893
Punjab	60	96	2000	2000	1209	1028
Rajasthan	83	85	1300	1150	1082	957
Himachal Pradesh	54	82	1700	1000	922	922
Kerala	55	86	1600	1600	875	875
Telangana	40	71	2016	2016	825	825
Andhra Pradesh	20	51	4000	4000	819	819
Jharkhand	72	61	1000	1000	722	722
Bihar	75	55	1100	800	900	655
Uttarakhand	41	59	1500	1500	612	612
Odisha	57	53	1200	1000	686	572

Jammu and Kashmir	53	81	1000	1000	519	519
North-eastern states	43	39	1504	1289	561	462
Delhi	21	74	2500	2000	531	425
Karnataka	61	85	1200	600	765	382
Uttar Pradesh	31	19	1000	1000	309	309
West Bengal	26	58	1000	1000	264	264
Maharashtra	26	71	1000	1000	259	259
Chhattisgarh	50	50	650	500	326	251
Madhya Pradesh	34	35	600	600	202	202
Tamil Nadu	15	17	1200	1200	171	171
Assam	66	67	550	250	361	164
Gujarat	11	19	1250	1000	135	108
India	**41**	**62**	**500[3]**	**200[3]**	-	-

Source: [a]Rajya Sabha Questions 2212 and 2222, 9.8.2024. (See Appendix II for details) [b]Rajya Sabha Question No. 1475, 9.12.2025 and State Government website.

Note: [1]Arranged in descending order of last column (weighted average of pension to 60-79 year olds). [2]Obtained by multiplying the pension amount (Column c plus Central contribution) by coverage (a), divded by 100. [3]Central government contributions.

Appendix II
Data Sources and Notes

DATA SOURCES FOR MAPS

Map 3.1 and 3.2: Maternity benefits to women in the unorganised sector (any instalment and all instalments)

Government of Odisha. *Odisha Economic Survey*. Directorate of Economics and Statistics. Bhubaneswar: Planning and Convergence Department, various years. https://pc.odisha.gov.in/sites/default/files/2020-03/Economic_Survey_2017-18.pdf.

Government of Telangana. *Telangana Socio-Economic Outlook*. Hyderabad: Planning Department, various years. https://ecostat.telangana.gov.in/PDF/PUBLICATIONS/Socio_Economic_2018.pdf.

Government of Tamil Nadu. *Policy Notes*. Chennai: Department of Health and Family Welfare, various years. https://cms.tn.gov.in/sites/default/files/documents/hfw_e_pn_2021_22.pdf.

Government of India. *Population Projections for India and States 2011–2036*. National Commission on Population. New Delhi: Ministry of Health and Family Welfare, 2019. https://nhm.gov.in/New_Updates_2018/Report_Population_Projection_2019.pdf.

Information received through RTI from Government of India for other states.

Map 4.1: Proportion of children (%) who reported receiving any services from ICDS, 2005-06

International Institute for Population Sciences (2007), National Family Health Survey (NFHS 3), National Reports, (Table 9.24, pages

261-262), (Mumbai: International Institute for Population Sciences). https://www.dhsprogram.com/pubs/pdf/frind3/frind3-vol1andvol2.pdf

Map 4.2: Proportion of children (%) who reported receiving any services from ICDS, 2015-16

International Institute for Population Sciences. *National Family Health Survey (NFHS-4): National Report.* Mumbai: International Institute for Population Sciences, 2017. Table 9.19, p. 288. https://dhsprogram.com/pubs/pdf/FR339/FR339.pdf.

Map 4.3: Proportion of children (%) who reported receiving any services from ICDS, 2019-21

Government of India. *Mid-Day Meal Scheme: Programme Approval Board (PAB) Meeting and State Government of Assam under PM POSHAN, Pradhan Mantri Poshan Shakti Nirman for 2024–25.* Department of School Education and Literacy. New Delhi: Ministry of Education, 19 April 2024. https://pmposhan.education.gov.in/Files/PAB/PAB-2024-25/Minutes-PAB-2024-25/ASSAM-MINUTES.pdf.

——. *Mid-Day Meal Scheme: Programme Approval Board (PAB) Meeting and State Government of Goa under PM POSHAN, Pradhan Mantri Poshan Shakti Nirman for 2024–25.* Department of School Education and Literacy. New Delhi: Ministry of Education, 24 May 2024. https://pmposhan.education.gov.in/Files/PAB/PAB-2022-23/Minutes/Minute_Goa.pdf.

——. *Mid-Day Meal Scheme: Programme Approval Board (PAB) Meeting and State Government of Karnataka under PM POSHAN, Pradhan Mantri Poshan Shakti Nirman for 2024–25.* Department of School Education and Literacy. New Delhi: Ministry of Education, 20 April 2024. https://pmposhan.education.gov.in/Files/PAB/PAB-2024-25/Minutes-PAB-2024-25/Karnataka-PAB%20Minutes.pdf.

——. *Mid-Day Meal Scheme: Programme Approval Board (PAB) Meetings—State-wise PAB Minutes.* Pradhan Mantri Poshan

Shakti Nirman. New Delhi: Ministry of Education, 2022. https://pmposhan.education.gov.in/.

International Institute for Population Sciences. *National Family Health Survey (NFHS-5): National Report*. Mumbai: International Institute for Population Sciences, 2022. Table 9.19, pp. 369–370. https://dhsprogram.com/pubs/pdf/FR375/FR375.pdf.

Map 5.1: States giving eggs in the MDM scheme.

Compiled from Government of India, *Programme Approval Board (PAB) Minutes*, PM POSHAN website. https://pmposhan.education.gov.in/.

Map 5.2: Proportion of children given eggs in the previous day or night (year 2019—2021),

International Institute for Population Sciences. *National Family Health Survey (NFHS-5): National Report*. Mumbai: International Institute for Population Sciences, 2022. https://dhsprogram.com/pubs/pdf/FR375/FR375.pdf.

Map 7.1: Per Job Card NREGA Working Days, 2023-24

Government of India. *Report No. R.5.1.1: Employment Generated During the Year—Mahatma Gandhi National Rural Employment Guarantee Act*. New Delhi: Ministry of Rural Development, various years. https://nreganarep.nic.in/netnrega/citizen_html/demregister.aspx?lflag=eng&fin_year=2023-2024&source=national&labels=labels&Digest=MZ7EPgZ8ZwgnIaImm+t7hA.

Map 7.2: Participation of Dalit and Adivasi labourers in NREGA, 2023-24

Government of India. *Report No. R.5.1.5: Social Category Wise Employment Generated 2023–24—Mahatma Gandhi National Rural Employment Guarantee Act*. Ministry of Rural Development, 2024. https://nreganarep.nic.in/netnrega/state_html/empstatusnewall_scst.aspx?lflag=eng&fin_year=2023-2024&source=national&labels=labels&Digest=MZ7EPgZ8ZwgnIaImm+t7hA.

Map 7.3: Women's participation in NREGA, 2023-24

Government of India. *Report No. R.5.1.5: Social Category Wise Employment Generated 2023–24—Mahatma Gandhi National Rural Employment Guarantee Act.* Ministry of Rural Development, 2024. https://nreganarep.nic.in/netnrega/state_html/empstatusnewall_scst.aspx?lflag=eng&fin_year=2023-2024&source=national&labels=labels&Digest=MZ7EPgZ8ZwgnIaImm+t7hA.

Map 8.1: Old Age Pension (Rs/month), 2023-24

Government of India (2025), Lok Sabha Question No. 1475, answered on 9 December 2025. Department of Rural Development, Ministry of Rural Development.

Government of Odisha. *Schemes and Services for the Elderly.* Bhubaneswar: Department of Social Security and Empowerment of Persons with Disabilities, n.d. https://ssepd.odisha.gov.in/sites/default/files/2024-05/Scheme%20and%20services%20for%20the%20elderly.pdf

Government of Rajasthan. *Social Security Pension.* Jaipur: Department of Social Justice and Empowerment, n.d. https://ssp.rajasthan.gov.in/HtmlPages/Schemes/DisablityDetail.aspx.

Map 8.2: Share of Old Age Pensioners among the elderly (%), 2021-24

Government of India (2024a), Unstarred Questions No. 2222, Rajya Sabha, answered on 9 August, 2024, Department of Rural Development, Ministry of Rural Development.

Government of India (2024b), Unstarred Questions No. 2212, Rajya Sabha, answered on 9 August, 2024, Department of Rural Development, Ministry of Rural Development.

Map 8.3: State-supported Old Age Pensioners, 2021-24

Government of India (2024a), Unstarred Questions No. 2222, Rajya Sabha, answered on 9 August, 2024, Department of Rural Development, Ministry of Rural Development.

Government of India (2024b), Unstarred Questions No. 2212, Rajya Sabha, answered on 9 August, 2024, Department of Rural Development, Ministry of Rural Development.

Map 9.1: Canteen schemes in the country

Chhattisgarh Government. *Schemes—Annapurna Dal Bhaat Yojana.* Raipur: Department of Food Supplies and Consumer Protection, n.d. https://khadya.cg.nic.in/PlanScheme_En.aspx.

Deccan Herald. 'Two Indira Canteens Opened at Bengaluru Airport.' *Deccan Herald*, 12 March 2024. https://www.deccanherald.com/india/karnataka/bengaluru/two-indira-canteens-opened-at-bengaluru-airport-2932191.

Government of India. *Population Projections for India and States 2011–2036.* National Commission on Population. New Delhi: Ministry of Health and Family Welfare, 2019. https://nhm.gov.in/New_Updates_2018/Report_Population_Projection_2019.pdf.

Government of Odisha. *Diet Citizen.* Bhubaneswar: Urban Development Department, n.d. https://urban.odisha.gov.in/sites/default/files/2023-09/AAHAR.pdf.

Government Planning Team. 'Jharkhand Guruji Kitchen Scheme 2024 to Replace Mukhyamantri Dal Bhaat Yojana.' *Government Planning Team*, 10 December 2022. https://sarkariyojana.com/guruji-kitchen-scheme-jharkhand/.

Kaumudi Online. '200 Kudumbashree Janakiya Hotels Closed Down in Kerala, Scheme Successful in All Other States Including UP & Tamil Nadu.' *Kaumudi Online*, 7 March 2023. https://keralakaumudi.com/en/news/news.php?id=1021728.

Rajasthan Government. *Schemes—Annapurna Rasoi Yojana.* Public Information Portal, n.d. https://jansoochna.rajasthan.gov.in/Services?q=l7aag+q8+mx7+U42u/cCR6xBa71R64lDSN5/rB8wR4dyKbepmB1Ltxr7zlhYEh99ZAB4nHG626FMiqoHDjc1cg==.

The Commune. 'Amma Unavagam: Dying a Slow Death under the DMK Government.' *The Commune*, 22 February 2022. https://thecommunemag.com/amma-unavagam-dying-a-slow-death-under-the-dmk-govt/.

The Hans India. 'Refurbished Annapurna Canteens Soon in Telangana.' *The Hans India*, 25 July 2022. https://www.thehansindia.com/telangana/refurbished-annapurna-canteens-soon-in-telangana-754957?infinitescroll=1.

DATA SOURCES FOR CHARTS

Chart 2.1: Government expenditure, percentage of GDP (%)

Ortiz-Ospina, Esteban, and Max Roser. 'Government Spending.' *Our World in Data*. Global Change Data Lab, 2023. https://ourworldindata.org/government-spending.

Chart 3.1: Duration of 100% wage compensation received during maternity leave (in weeks), 2023

Organisation for Economic Co-operation and Development (OECD). *OECD Family Database: Parental Leave Systems*. Paris: OECD Publishing, 2024. Originally obtained from Willem Adema, Chris Clarke, and Valerie Frey, 'Paid Parental Leave: Lessons from OECD Countries and Selected U.S. States.' *OECD Social, Employment and Migration Working Papers*, no. 172. https://www.oecd-ilibrary.org/social-issues-migration-health/paid-parental-leave_5jrqgvqqb4vb-en.

Organisation for Economic Co-operation and Development (OECD). PF2.1: *Parental Leave Systems*. OECD Family Database. Paris: OECD, n.d. Accessed May 11, 2026. https://www.oecd.org/content/dam/oecd/en/data/datasets/family-database/pf2_1_parental_leave_ systems.pdf. (webfs.oecd.org)

Chart 3.2: Difference between requirement and actual in the budget of maternity benefit

Drèze, Jean, Reetika Khera, and Anmol Somanchi. 'Maternity Entitlements: Women's Rights Derailed.' *Economic and Political Weekly* 56, no. 47 (20 November 2021). https://www.epw.in/journal/2021/47/special-articles/maternity-entitlements.html.

Chart 3.3: Percentage of births benefited under Pradhan Mantri Matru Vandana Yojana

Drèze, Jean, and Reetika Khera. 'Maternity Entitlements in Freefall.' *The India Forum*, 14 June 2023. https://www.theindiaforum.in/public-policy/ maternity-entitlements-freefall#:~:text=For%20a%20full%20four%20years,Rs%205%2C000%20in%20three%20instalments.

Government of India. *Population Projections for India and States 2011–2036*. National Commission on Population. New Delhi: Ministry of Health and Family Welfare, 2019. https://nhm.gov.in/New_Updates_2018/Report_Population_Projection_2019.pdf.

Chart 4.1: Children in the Budget Speech of India and Bangladesh ('Child', 'Children' and 'Childhood' Mentioned in the Budget Speech)

Government of Bangladesh. *Budget Speech of the Minister of Finance*. Dhaka: Ministry of Finance, various years. https://mof.gov.bd/site/page/9ea7529b-c8ef-49b5-8b8e-87ef72a2b3ec.

Government of India. *Finance Minister's Budget Speech*. Budget Division, Department of Economic Affairs. New Delhi: Ministry of Finance, various years. https://www.indiabudget.gov.in/previous_union_budget.php.

Chart 6.1: Estimated diversion of PDS grains, 1999–2000 to 2022–23

Drèze, Jean, and Reetika Khera. 'Understanding Leakages in the Public Distribution System.' *Economic and Political Weekly* 50, no. 7 (14 February 2015). https://www.epw.in/journal/2015/7/insight/understanding-leakages-public-distribution-system.html.

Khera, Reetika. 'Impact of the Food Security Act on the Public Distribution System.' *Ideas for India*, 3 October 2024. https://www.ideasforindia.in/topics/ poverty-inequality/impact-of-the-food-security-act-on-public-distribution-system.html.

_____. 'Trends in Diversion of Grain from the Public Distribution System.' *Economic and Political Weekly* 46, no. 21 (21 May

2011). https://www.epw.in/journal/2011/21/special-articles/trends-diversion-grain-public-distribution-system.html.

Chart 7.1: Expenditure on NREGA as percentage of GDP, 2008–09 to 2023–24

Government of India. *Expenditure Budget.* Budget Division. New Delhi: Ministry of Finance, various years. https://www.indiabudget.gov.in/doc/eb/allsbe.pdf.

Chart 7.2: Spending on NREGA and employment created

Government of India. *Expenditure Budget.* Budget Division. New Delhi: Ministry of Finance, various years. https://www.indiabudget.gov.in/doc/eb/allsbe.pdf.

——. *Report No. R.5.1.1: Employment Generated During the Year—Mahatma Gandhi National Rural Employment Guarantee Act.* New Delhi: Ministry of Rural Development, various years. https://nreganarep.nic.in/netnrega/citizen_html/demregister.aspx?lflag=eng&fin_year=2022-2023&source=national&labels=labels&Digest=kODLAkQv8M9FT6WbXb7zhA.

Chart 7.3: Participation of disadvantaged groups in NREGA, 2008–09 to 2023–24

Government of India. *Report No. R.5.1.5: Social Category Wise Employment Generated—Mahatma Gandhi National Rural Employment Guarantee Act.* New Delhi: Ministry of Rural Development, various years. https://nreganarep.nic.in/netnrega/state_html/ empstatusnewall_scst.aspx?lflag=eng&fin_year=2022-2023&source=national&labels=labels&Digest=kODLAkQv8M9FT6WbXb7zhA.

Chart 7.4: Monthly average working days in NREGA Pre-Covid and average of Covid years

Government of India. *Report No. R.2.2.2: Projected Persons and Persons Generated—Mahatma Gandhi National Rural Employment Guarantee Act.* New Delhi: Ministry of Rural

Development, various years. https://nreganarep.nic.in/netnrega/LB_VS_MIS.aspx?fin_year=2021-2022&source=national&Digest=9W1xBQ WtfJS+lGqDnrVHsA.

Chart 7.5: NREGA, Cultivators and non-agricultural wages (Real Terms, 2006–07 = 100)

Government of India. *Average Wages as per Measurement Pattern during the Financial Year—Mahatma Gandhi National Rural Employment Guarantee Act*. Report No. 7.2.1. New Delhi: Ministry of Rural Development, various years. https://mnregaweb4.nic.in/netnrega/avg_wage_paid. aspx?fin_year=2023-2024&source=national&Digest=akdjO9VfTrWA9tZ+TJ0C7A.

——. *Rural Wages*. Labour Bureau. New Delhi: Ministry of Labour and Employment, n.d. https://labourbureau.gov.in/rural-wages.

Reserve Bank of India. *Handbook of Statistics on the Indian Economy*. Consumer Price Index—Annual Average, various years. Mumbai: Reserve Bank of India, 15 September 2023. https://rbi.org.in/Scripts/PublicationsView.aspx?id=21844.

Chart 8.1: Composition of government expenditure on various types of pensions

Government of India. *Expenditure Budget*. Budget Division. New Delhi: Ministry of Finance, various years. https://www.indiabudget.gov.in/budget2021-22/doc/eb/allsbe.pdf.

——. *Outlay on Major Schemes*. Budget Division. New Delhi: Ministry of Finance, various years. https://www.indiabudget.gov.in/budget2021-22/doc/Budget_at_Glance/bag7.pdf.

Chart 10.1: Disparities in literacy rates

International Institute for Population Sciences. *National Family Health Survey (NFHS-4)*. Mumbai: International Institute for Population Sciences, 2017. https://dhsprogram.com/pubs/pdf/FR339/FR339.pdf.

——. *National Family Health Survey (NFHS-5): National Report*. Mumbai: International Institute for Population Sciences, 2022. https://dhsprogram.com/pubs/pdf/FR375/FR375.pdf.

Chart 10.2: Inequalities in education level, 2019–21

International Institute for Population Sciences. *National Family Health Survey (NFHS-5): National Report*. Mumbai: International Institute for Population Sciences, 2022. https://dhsprogram.com/pubs/pdf/FR375/FR375.pdf.

Chart 11.1: Salaries of frontline workers compared with agricultural wages

Government of India. *Honorarium of School Cooking Staff*. Rajya Sabha Unstarred Question No. 1152, 13 December 2023. https://sansad.in/getFile/annex/262/AU1152.pdf?source=pqars#:~:text=They%20are%20honorary%20workers%20who,year%2C%20with%20effect%20from%2001.12.

——. *Increases in the Wages of Anganwadi Workers*. Rajya Sabha Unstarred Question No. 633, 7 February 2024. https://sansad.in/getFile/annex/263/AU633.pdf?source=pqars.

——. *Rural Wages*. Labour Bureau. New Delhi: Ministry of Labour and Employment, various years. https://labourbureau.gov.in/rural-wages.

Chart 12.1: Welfare expenditure as a proportion of GDP

Government of India. *Expenditure Budget*. Budget Division. New Delhi: Ministry of Finance, various years. https://www.indiabudget.gov.in/doc/eb/allsbe.pdf.

DATA SOURCES FOR APPENDIX I

Table A2: Access to maternity benefit in the unorganised sector

Drèze, Jean, and Reetika Khera. 'Maternity Entitlements in Freefall.' *The India Forum*, 14 June 2023. https://www.theindiaforum.in/public-policy/maternity-entitlements-freefall.

Government of India. *SRS Bulletin 2020*. Office of the Registrar General of India. Vol. 55, no. 1. New Delhi: Ministry of Home Affairs, 2022.

Government of Odisha. *Odisha Economic Survey*. Directorate of

Economics and Statistics. Bhubaneswar: Planning and Convergence Department, various years. https://pc.odisha.gov.in/sites/default/files/2020-03/Economic_Survey_2017-18.pdf.

Government of Tamil Nadu. *Policy Note.* Chennai: Department of Health and Family Welfare, various years. https://cms.tn.gov.in/sites/default/files/documents/hfw_e_pn_2021_22.pdf.

Government of Telangana. *Telangaṇa Socio-Economic Outlook.* Hyderabad: Planning Department, various years. https://ecostat.telangana.gov.in/PDF/PUBLICATIONS/Socio_Economic_2018.pdf.

Table A3: ABC Index of children in major Indian states

Drèze, Jean, and Reetika Khera. 'Regional Patterns of Human and Child Deprivation in India.' *Economic and Political Weekly* 47, no. 39 (2012).

Table A4: Social environment and kitchen arrangement of cooks in the Mid-Day Meal scheme

Government of India. *Annual Work Plan and Budget.* MDM Division. New Delhi: Ministry of Education, various years. PM POSHAN website. Various state reports, Table AT-1 (Women Cooks and Tribal/Dalit Cooks), Table AT-13 (LPG in Kitchen), and Table AT-22 (Children Eating from Centralised Kitchens). https://pmposhan.education.gov.in/Files/PAB/PAB-2021-22/States_UTs/Andhra%20Pradesh/2_Final%20AWP&B%20Tables%2021.06.2021.xls.

Table A5: PDS—Access and 'Diversion' of PDS Grains

Government of Chhattisgarh. *Chhattisgarh Economic Survey 2023–24.* Raipur: Directorate of Economics and Statistics, 2024. https://descg.gov.in/pdf/publications/latest/ES2023-24/EconomicSurvey2023-24.pdf.

Khera, Reetika. 'Impact of the Food Security Act on the Public Distribution System.' *Ideas for India*, 3 October 2024. https://www.ideasforindia.in/topics/poverty-inequality/impact-of-the-food-security-act-on-public-distribution-system.html.

——. 'Revival of the Public Distribution System: Evidence and Explanations.' *Economic and Political Weekly* 46, nos. 44–45 (5 November 2011). https://www.epw.in/journal/2011/44-45/special-articles/revival-public-distribution-system-evidence-and-explanations.

Khera, Reetika, and Anmol Somanchi. 'A Review of the Coverage of PDS.' *Ideas for India*, 19 August 2020. https://www.ideasforindia.in/topics/poverty-inequality/a-review-of-the-coverage-of-pds.html.

Table A6: Employment days and wages in NREGA

Government of India. *Agricultural Wages in India*. New Delhi: Ministry of Agriculture and Farmers Welfare, 2023. https://desagri.gov.in/wp-content/uploads/2023/10/Final-Copy-2021-22.PDF.

——. *Gazette of India: Notification*. Ministry of Rural Development, 24 March 2023. https://nregaplus.nic.in/netnrega/writereaddata/Circulars/Wage_Rate_NotificationFY_2023-24.PDF.

——. *Lok Sabha Unstarred Question No. 1196: Job Card Holders under MGNREGA*. New Delhi: Ministry of Rural Development, 9 February 2017.

——. *Rajya Sabha Unstarred Question No. 1522*. New Delhi: Ministry of Rural Development, 11 March 2013.

——. *Report No. R.5.1.1: Employment Generated during the Year—Mahatma Gandhi National Rural Employment Guarantee Act*. New Delhi: Ministry of Rural Development, various years. https://nreganarep.nic.in/netnrega/citizen_html/demregister.aspx?lflag=eng&fin_year=2022-2023&source=national&labels=labels&Digest=kODLAk Qv8M9FT6WbXb7zhA.

NOTES ON DATA SOURCES

Table A7: Note on social security pensioners

State Pension Scheme beneficiaries

In every sub-scheme of the NSAP, the States also include pensioners in their State Pension Schemes *at their own expense*. For the elderly, many states have relaxed the eligibility age (for the Union government scheme, it is for to those above 60 years). For example, in states like

Jharkhand it has been reduced for tribal people. When we estimate the percentage of the elderly covered, we include all pensioners (including those below 60 years of age) whereas in the denominator we use the population only above 60 years. As a result, states that have relaxed the eligibility age will see a higher percentage of coverage. The sub-scheme called widow pension actually includes single, abandoned, divorced, etc. We have included all as 'widow pensions'. Many states have given relaxation in the percentage of disability in disability pension (Government of India gives only if there is more than 80% disability).

Note on data sources for expenditure in the Union Budget on social security schemes

For 2020-21, ICDS data was not available from the budget documents. It has been given as Rs 20,105 in the budget brief of Centre for Policy Research and as per the reply of the Rajya Sabha, it is Rs 15,798 in the PIB press release. We use the latter.

Chart 12.1: For the PDS, we use the food subsidy entirely even though it is the sum of the consumers, producers (i.e., the share of farmers when they sell wheat and rice to the government at the minimum support price) and administrative costs. Splitting food subsidy into these three components is not straightforward. However, the inclusion of only half of the food subsidies (as an estimate of consumer subsidies) does not make much difference to the results. Similarly, for the Ujjwala Yojana, we use the LPG subsidy, though only a small part of it is spent on the Ujjwala Yojana.

Another caveat with regard to food subsidies is that the change in the manner reported first coincided with the Covid-19 year (2020-21). Thus, the increase in welfare spending that year is due to the actual increase in food subsidies as well as the change in registering it.

We exclude Ayushman Bharat in our analysis for two reasons: First, the total expenditure on Ayushman Bharat during 2019-2024 was quite low—Rs 32,000 crore, i.e. half of the annual expenditure on PM-housing, on average over the same period. (Even if we add this as the NDA scheme, there will be a slight change.) Secondly, Ayushman Bharat is part of health expenditure, and if we include it, for the sake of comparability, we should have included the budget allocated for the National Rural Health Mission (NRHM) during the UPA years.

Finally, the cost-sharing norms for some schemes changed after the Fourteenth Finance Commission increased the share of revenue to be transferred to states. The Centre reduced its liabilities from 75-90% to 60% in some cases. While the focus here is on the Union Budget, what happens if we increase the total (Centre plus State) budget on MDM, ICDS and PMMVY assuming that states contribute their stipulated share. Doing this, the picture does not change substantially.

Index

Name Index

Subject Index